Ministry of Crime

Ministry of Crime

An Underworld Explored

Mandy Wiener

MACMILLAN

First published in 2018
by Pan Macmillan South Africa
Private Bag X19
Northlands
2116
Johannesburg
South Africa

www.panmacmillan.co.za

ISBN 978-1-77010-575-1
E-ISBN 978-1-77010-576-8

*Every attempt has been made to ensure the accuracy of the details, facts, names, places
and events mentioned in these pages, but the publisher and author welcome any feedback,
comments and/or corrections on the content, which is based on numerous interviews, court
documents, newspaper reports, author experiences and other sources.*

Editing by Sean Fraser
Proofreading by Russell Martin
Design and typesetting by Triple M Design, Johannesburg
Cover design by Fire and Lion
Author photograph by Lisa Skinner/SKINNDERELLA

Printed by *paarlmedia*, a division of Novus Holdings
1684687

We know that there are rogue police officers who work with criminals, in the payroll of criminals. Gangsters are owning police officers in this Republic. You give an order and then police officers put a blind eye to that particular order because they are in the payroll of criminals. Report them. It might take time but the wheels of the law are grinding. We will find them. Don't worry.

– Fikile Mbalula, former South African minister of police, May 2017

DESPONDENCY IS THE OVERWHELMING EMOTION I ENCOUNTER each time I sit across from a suspended, fired or retired police officer, general, SARS investigator or senior prosecutor, regardless of their race or rank. I meet with many of them over 2016, 2017 and 2018. Good people who have intentionally been worked out of the system. They have tried to fight back, but that's proved an impossible task. They spend thousands on legal fees; they live vicariously through newspaper reports and strategise over disciplinary hearings. They dwell, they obsess, they develop a neurosis about the state of affairs of the country and in their own lives. And they all say the same thing: the police are rotten. The NPA is rotten. It's all become political.

The high-ranking cop sitting opposite me in early 2017, as I embark on the journey of writing this book, is no different. A career police officer who spent years chasing organised crime, cash heist kingpins and mobsters.

'It's the proximity between police, organised crime and politics in this country. In South Africa it's just another day in paradise. It's not as blatant in other countries. Nobody seems to give a damn. It's as old as time. People corrupt politicians and they corrupt cops. The mafia has done it for how many years. But it's never been this blatant. CI [Crime Intelligence] has gone to the dogs. The appointments that have been made. There was a helluva lot, people off the street, they just got appointed into CI and given rank. Family members were appointed with no qualifications. There were a lot of safe houses that were looted, a lot of things that were done that were wrong. It was allowed to happen because of politics. It became a political mechanism. There was no longer fighting to get criminal intelligence. It was all politics and protecting politicians.'

The cop despairs. 'How would I describe the current state of Police?

Captured!' There is a sense of loss in the officer's eyes. It's depressing.

'The country is fucked. It is bad. It leaves the man on the street – and that includes me – with very little hope. Krejcir made the policemen turn on the innocent victims out there. Your head of detectives nationally! Isn't that supposed to be somebody who you know will go to the ends of the earth to protect you? And yet that is the man who is captured by Krejcir to such an extent that he will plant you to get you out the way.'

For nearly two decades now, I have tracked the dynamic between the people whose job it is to uphold the law and those who make a living breaking it. I sat through the corruption trial of the world's most senior policeman, Interpol head Jackie Selebi, heard about how envelopes stuffed with cash were slid across boardroom tables by a drug trafficker and how Selebi pocketed the cash. There was evidence of lavish shopping sprees at upmarket clothing stores. In *Killing Kebble: An Underworld Exposed*, the book I wrote about the Selebi trial, the murder of Brett Kebble and the relationship between organised crime, business and the police, the proximity of those different worlds to one another was laid bare. Selebi was convicted of corruption and Glenn Agliotti was acquitted of the Kebble murder in 2010. The three self-confessed hit men had since kept a relatively low profile, out of the media glare. But what had happened in the 'underworld' and in the world of policing in subsequent years?

The country's law enforcement agencies and the criminal justice system, from SARS to SAPS to the NPA, had been ravaged. A high-stakes political battle centred around President Jacob Zuma had been raging, and part of the project to protect him was the intentional, malicious hollowing out of the institutions that were meant to uphold the law. The collateral damage was the careers of all those good men and women, like the officer sitting across from me in the restaurant, who were banished. Crucially, the cost to you and me and our democracy was the damage done to the rule of law and the capacity to combat crime.

In this fertile landscape, organised criminal networks were able to flourish. Enterprising individuals, such as Radovan Krejcir and others like him, were able to grow empires. State officials were ripe for corrupting, very little proper intelligence was being collected and there was barely any political will to bring the kingpins to book.

What we witnessed was the conflation of politics, organised crime and the police. Dubious characters put in positions of power and influence at the behest of politicians, corrupt and complicit in criminal behaviour, with organised syndicates on the rampage across the country.

This is the story of the rise and reign of the Ministry of Crime.

STANDING ON THE DECK OF THE ENCLOSED PATIO, THE ASSEMBLED group of men and women seem impressed by the vista that stretches out before them. The landscape sets the narrative of a decade of crime, from murders to bomb blasts and James Bond-esque assassination attempts. On the far left is the Wedgewood Green townhouse complex where Serb side-kick Veselin Laganin was shot dead in front of his wife and son by armed intruders one night. Slightly off to the right is the Bedford Centre shop-ping complex and the Harbour Fish Market with its bulletproof glass, a de facto mafiosi headquarters. The group can also see the intersection where Lebanese drug dealer Sam Issa was gunned down early one Saturday morn-ing in a gangland-style hit. Directly down and in front of them is the house once owned by the 'King of Sleaze', Lolly Jackson. There's the Nicol Hotel near the highway where associates would be put up for indefinite periods, often in hiding. There was even a bulletproof room in case things went belly up. Further off to the right, there's Eastgate shopping centre and the Money Point shop where deals were struck, fraud was committed, plans hatched and bombs exploded. There was also that bizarre Hollywood-style incident in the parking lot when, on a regular weekday morning, remote-controlled barrels popped out of the number plate of a car and opened fire.

All these landmarks are blanketed in greenery, a characteristic of Johannesburg. In the distance, set against a grey haze, is the silhouette of the city centre, punctuated by the iconic Ponte and Hillbrow towers. It is a portrait of beauty, yet of destruction. The mansion on the mountain in Bedfordview is like a beacon of all that Radovan Krejcir managed to amass and destroy in his relatively short time in this country. Built on 2285 square metres of prime Kloof Road estate, the angular modern house is perched on a cliff, with four levels of faux rock piled on top of one another, each floor with a view more spectacular than the previous.

It's 2pm on a hot, dry Saturday afternoon in early December 2016. The sense of irony in the location of this end-of-year function is not lost on forensic consultant Paul O'Sullivan. He had reportedly bought Krejcir's mansion a year previously for R12.8 million, through an intricate company shareholding. One of only three bidders, he was rumoured to have been smuggled into the auction under a blanket on the back seat of a car so that the media would not know he was a potential buyer. He has also consistently denied having bought the property, despite several sources confirming otherwise.

The gathering on the patio is an eclectic mix of characters. The suspended head of police watchdog Independent Police Investigative Directorate (IPID), Robert McBride, a man with a chequered history and a veteran of law enforcement who was suspended from his job for 18 months, from March 2015 until October 2016. Major General Shadrack Sibiya, fired as the head of the Hawks in Gauteng and the man who once oversaw the police investigation into Krejcir and arrested him on three separate occasions. Candice Coetzee, a captain in the police's Crime Intelligence department who had infiltrated Krejcir's inner circle with her reputation as 'Beeka's cop'. Also suspended. O'Sullivan's assistant Sarah-Jane Trent, who would later be arrested alongside the Irishman for impersonating an IPID officer while investigating the acting national police commissioner. The identity of the man standing at the braai is not as obvious as the others. Jacob Nare, a state witness who had agreed to testify against Krejcir about his eyewitness accounts of kidnap, assault and murder, is responsible for braaiing the meat. He is being kept under guard by O'Sullivan because the state's witness protection programme is so compromised that Nare's safety cannot be guaranteed.

They sit at the table outside where Krejcir conducted numerous TV interviews, the jacuzzi and pool alongside them. There's a statue of Buddha and, incongruously, a figurine of a naked female torso. The group mills about the house, which is a shell of the gangster headquarters it had once served as.

Radovan Krejcir bought this home in 2008 for R13 million, one year after arriving in South Africa and being arrested on an Interpol red notice. Legend has it that he stepped onto the property with a briefcase full of cash and announced it would be his. But, of course, that could just be wild rumour, embellished to further enhance the myth of the man who came to run Joburg's underworld.

At the top of the zigzag driveway are three garages, which now all stand empty. A couple of years ago, they housed Krejcir's fleet of high-performance cars, motorbikes, boats and jet skis, including a Mercedes-Benz CL 63 AMG and a Lamborghini Murciélago. All with personalised DKR number plates, of course. An empty dog kennel stands alongside the main entrance but there is no sign of the pets now that their owners have moved out.

The en-suite bedroom on the first floor is where one-time bodyguard and fellow Czech Miloslav 'Milosh' Potiska lived. The former associate claimed to have worked for Krejcir between 2010 and 2012 and alleges he left the country because he could see Krejcir was sinking deeper into criminal activity. He is now a potential state witness against his ex-boss and has made explosive revelations in a tell-all book, *The Godfather African*. With his dubious credibility, the book had a mixed reception.

The second floor is the heart of the home, dominated by a TV room furnished with cream leather couches and a fully kitted kitchen replete with top-of-the-range Miele appliances. It was here that the Hawks handcuffed Potiska and Krejcir's teenage son Denis during a high-profile raid in 2011 while his father was apparently on the run from authorities. Sensationally, the police used an armoured vehicle to gain entry to the property but, in a comedy of errors, they rammed down the neighbour's gate, causing hundreds of thousands of rand in damage. It was during this raid that the cops allegedly found a hit list in a safe with the scribbled names of those Krejcir wanted dead.

What the cops did not know at the time – and what many still don't know today – is that Krejcir was inside the house the entire time, hiding out in a secret bunker while task-team members swarmed the property. Straight out of a John le Carré novel, there is a hidden room behind a wall of the living room, accessible only by deftly pushing a wine rack in a certain direction. It's where Krejcir kept his arsenal of firearms too, I'm told.

It isn't difficult to visualise former security operative Cyril Beeka in his leather jacket seated at the bar stool at the counter. You can practically hear Clemenza telling Rocco: 'Leave the gun. Take the cannoli.' There's an ominous-looking meat slicer and an orange squeezer left behind by the previous owner.

Outside the kitchen door, a metal walkway elevated over a ten-foot drop stretches out to a building site where a granny flat is being built. There was a raw shell there when O'Sullivan reportedly bought the house and he has been renovating the place. State witness Jacob Nare has been the resident caretaker.

Only on the top floor is it possible to appreciate any sense of warmth in the clinical house. The home feels cold. When Krejcir's family moved out, they left a painting hanging above a gas fireplace in the main bed-room, one depicting a ship run aground during a violent thunderstorm and a bolt of lightning striking down from a heavy grey sky. In the second adjacent bedroom, a black-and-white framed print of a fingerprint used to hang on the wall, almost teasing the viewer into a CSI reference. Now it hangs in O'Sullivan's Sandton office, an appropriate symbol for the forensic investigator.

Much has changed for Radovan Krejcir since he first bought this house in Bedfordview 10 years ago. During that period, some would argue he has broken the police service by corrupting rank-and-file cops and keeping generals on his payroll. He has been arrested and charged with a variety of crimes and has been convicted of attempted murder, kidnapping and drug dealing. He insists he is the victim of a conspiracy and is not the gang-ster boss everyone makes him out to be. He also faces at least three other criminal trials with many more still on the horizon. His name has been associated with over a dozen underworld hits, but authorities have only charged him for one of these. They are keeping him pinned down with peripheral cases as they work to build evidence on the really dirty crimes.

It is because of Krejcir's tax problems that this house went under the hammer. The South African Revenue Service (SARS) secured a preserva-tion order against him and several other respondents, placing his assets under curatorship. SARS alleges he under-disclosed his taxable income to the amount of R114 million and that he used the corporate identities of companies, including Groep Twee Beleggings, to hide the income accrued to him, as well as his assets, with the intention of evading the payment of tax.

With a slew of lawsuits and ballooning legal costs, Krejcir is also struggling to gain access to his vast financial resources. He has been forced to fire an army of lawyers and has had to go to court to try to access money sent to him by his mother in the Czech Republic. In the past she has been known to fly into the country with briefcases stuffed with cash, but things are not quite as simple these days.

It seems as though Krejcir has been caught up in a morass of criminal charges, court cases and tax woes. His future in South Africa certainly looks bleak, much like the ship in the painting that once hung on the wall in his master bedroom, run aground in a thunderous storm. The only prospect of light breaking through the clouds is an escape, and already authorities have foiled an elaborate plot to flee to South America. They are watching his every move.

Over drinks on the patio, O'Sullivan hands out copies of his document entitled 'Joining the Dots', which lays out systemic corruption within the police service and the proximity of high-level politicians to gangsters. The retired general, police investigator and IPID head discuss their ongoing investigations and the threatening text messages they have received. O'Sullivan has to rush off as he is flying overseas, so the others drain their wine glasses and set off home, making their way down the steep driveway and into Kloof Road.

A week later, General Prince Mokotedi – Sibiya's successor at the Hawks – opens a case at the nearby Bedfordview police station and levels claims of espionage, high treason and conspiracy to commit murder against the group that had gathered for the braai. Mokotedi claims the group had conspired to dig up dirt and smear the acting national police commissioner, the current head of the Hawks, the head of the National Prosecuting Authority and the head of the State Security Agency. The motive for targeting these individuals is apparently because they were close to, or in support of, President Jacob Zuma. He speaks of plans to mobilise an Arab Spring-type revolt and attempts to destabilise the security forces. Mokotedi goes as far as claiming that Zimbabwean Intelligence agents and Serbian hit men have been colluding with the group to carry out assassinations. It is spy-era stuff.

This entire incident, from the Saturday afternoon braai at Krejcir's house to the far-fetched allegations of treason and treachery, is the perfect illustration of what has become of the country's crime-fighting capacities and the crippled criminal justice system. It clearly sets out how agencies have been eroded by personal vendettas and private agendas and how corruption and politics have won out over justice.

How did it come to be that this motley group of law enforcement officials, some of whom were themselves accused of corruption, came to lunch with the country's premier dirty-cop catcher, and a self-confessed criminal, at the house that was once the headquarters of the country's most high-profile gangster? And how did that apparently innocuous meeting become the subject of top-level allegations of treason and espionage? It is a story that winds its way through the depths of the underworld, via multiple mysterious unsolved murders, to the very top of the police force.

I T WAS A SCENE THAT WOULD BE REPLICATED AGAIN, MANY TIMES, during his life. A swarm of police officers with automatic rifles occupied his palatial villa on the outskirts of Prague as the flashy billionaire crime boss was placed under arrest. Investigators had got wind that there were plans for a custom official to be taken out – he was a key witness in a fraud case against Radovan Krejcir. For six hours from midnight until the morning, Krejcir was held under police guard while officers turned his house upside down. They found counterfeit cash, classified police documents and forged passports, firearms and piles of evidence of criminal conduct. But at dawn, the flashy mafioso who had earned a reputation in the Czech Republic as one of the top organised crime kingpins, pulled off a stunt that reinforced that reputation. He walked out of his mansion, under the watch of a team of police officers, and vanished.

Some say he escaped through a window in a bathroom. Others that he paid off the cops and they let him walk free. According to his own version, Krejcir says the officers asked him for a bribe, and when he went to look for money to pay them, he disappeared. Czech TV journalist Jiří Hynek has spent most of his career tracking the eventful life of one of his country's most notorious characters.

'I had the opportunity to see the recording of the cameras and I can say that there was one picture when Radovan's wife came out and put something on the floor and, maybe 10 minutes after, Radovan pick up something, maybe passport, and escaped out of the house. There was a little gate from the garden to the forest and through this gate he escaped according to the security cameras he had at the house and I could see,' Hynek tells me. He says there were rumours that policemen had been corrupted but there was never any proof. 'He became the most famous when he escaped from the

Czech Republic. It was really big scandal because our chief of police had to step down and Radovan, for maybe around two years, was number one in this crime business in the Czech Republic.'

Media reports claimed that that morning he made his way to a friend's house, ate breakfast and was then seen at a petrol station in Slovakia filling up his Lamborghini a few days later. Krejcir has given his own account of events in a book that he wrote about his life, as well as in multiple court affidavits.

He says that he spent 14 days in the mountains around Prague while friends arranged a false passport for him in order to escape the country undetected. He assumed the false identity of 'Tomiga'. He rode a bicycle into Poland, travelled by train to the Ukraine and then went on to Istanbul and then Dubai. There he met up with his wife Katerina and son Denis. From Dubai, his family flew to the Seychelles where he already had both citizenship and a home. Back in the Czech Republic, he topped the list of the country's most wanted men.

Radovan Krejcir was born an only child in the town of Český Těšín in the region of Moravia in 1968. His father was active in the Communist movement at the time. 'He grew up in a very poor region in the Czech Republic. Northern Moravia is a very industrial area. Radovan was part of the family when the father before the Velvet Revolution was a very high-profile Communist local leader. I'm sure he was influenced by his father,' explains Hynek. Krejcir completed a four-year degree in Economics in Ostrava before going into business, although some believe he studied Engineering. It was after the fall of communism in Czechoslovakia in 1989 that he made his fortune.

In the 1990s, when the borders were opened, he was smuggling watches from Austria to the Czech Republic. 'We had a shortage of goods like that after the Velvet Revolution,' Hynek tells me. 'It was a good opportunity for Krejcir to make his first money. After that he started to do the bigger business. When he was in the Southern and Northern Moravia in this poorer region, he opened the company for leasing; people could buy cars and they didn't need to have whole amount of the money, and it was a really good and successful business for him.'

Krejcir says he entered the entrepreneurial world by establishing himself in real estate and then acquiring a printing company that grew to be one of the largest in Europe. With his newly amassed wealth, he moved to Prague, built a mansion and began to flash his money around, driving luxury cars and living the good life. 'Until the nineties, he was invisible but when he moved to Prague he became part of the group of high-profile mafia bosses in the Czech Republic. He was in high society in Prague and I would say media called him mafia celebrity,' says Hynek.

Along with this high profile came the attention of the law enforcement authorities, and Krejcir was accused of tax evasion, fraud and counterfeiting. He was arrested for the first time in 2002 on what he called 'trumped-up charges' and spent seven months in jail. A company he owned, which imported oil into the country, was accused of avoiding taxes.

Krejcir became politically active around the same time and began to ingratiate himself with powerful politicians and state officers. In 2002, he allegedly funded the election campaign of Stanislav Gross, the presidential candidate for an opposition party known as the CSSD. This relationship was negotiated by a middleman, businessman Jakub Konečný. The agreement was that he would lend Gross the money, two million euros, to fund his campaign and, in return, Gross would hand him control of a state-owned petroleum company known as CEPRO should he become prime minister.

If Gross did not succeed, the money would be repaid with interest. Part of the deal was that Konečný, the intermediary, would obtain a promissory note from Gross confirming the debt. Similarly, Krejcir received a promissory note.

Gross won the election and became prime minister, but Krejcir never got his petroleum company. Krejcir was furious and threatened to go to the media. He believes this was why he was arrested and tortured, to try to reveal the whereabouts of the promissory note confirming the loan. While he was behind bars, Krejcir's father disappeared. His body was never found and there are varying theories about what may have happened to him. It's believed he was kidnapped because Krejcir had failed to pay business debts. Krejcir believes the government was behind it and that his father was dissolved in a vat of acid.

I've even heard claims that Krejcir himself had his father stuffed into the vat of acid, but this has never been confirmed. A prominent football club owner in the Czech Republic was arrested for the murder but denied being behind it.

Krejcir also earned a reputation for bribery and corruption.

'We heard the stories that he bribed a lot of police officers, judges and officers in the government. We heard the stories that he had some link to the former prime minister and he gave him some money, but I didn't see the proofs and in fact Radovan was said to be in connection with the people from the government and from the police,' explains Hynek.

Krejcir was arrested again in 2003 but was not convicted of any crime. Despite not having a criminal record, Krejcir's name began to be linked to a number of murders. A key state witness, Petr Sebesta, who had testified against Krejcir in a massive tax fraud case, was murdered in 2003.

Konečný, the middleman in the Gross deal, disappeared in much the same way Krejcir's father had. Krejcir believed the businessman was eliminated because he had witnessed the deal between him and Gross. When the Don of the Czech Republic, František Mrázek, was taken out in a hit in 2006, it was assumed that Krejcir was the man behind it because he blamed the crime boss for his father's murder.

Krejcir denied this. He maintained that he was linked to these crimes by government officials who had orchestrated a smear campaign against him. Gross was ultimately removed as prime minister following allegations of fraud, and any hope Krejcir had of owning CEPRO fizzled out. The new regime was not interested in honouring the agreement and again Krejcir felt that his life was under threat. It was against this backdrop that his house was raided in 2005.

In 2006, Krejcir was convicted in absentia on a charge of fraud and given a jail sentence of 15 years. An Interpol red notice was issued for his arrest. Meanwhile he made a home for himself in the Seychelles, along with his wife and son. He started a car-rental company, Quick Cars, penned his memoirs and elevated himself into the island country's high society, associating himself with former President France-Albert René. He became a regular feature at government offices and at the homes of top officials.

Hynek tracked Krejcir down in the Seychelles and went to see him. 'He was connected to the government and he started some business with the people in government. The government started to blackmail him; they say, give us the money for election and we won't extradite you back to the Czech Republic. If not, we are going to make a treaty with the Czech Republic. So for Radovan it was a problem to stay in the Seychelles. South Africa for him was a bigger market so that's why he moved to South Africa,' says Hynek. The journalist got the sense that Krejcir was bored; in the Seychelles, he was like a prisoner trapped in a gilded cage in paradise.

A Johannesburg businesswoman, originally from the Czech Republic, worked for Krejcir in the Seychelles during his years on the island. At the time, she was in the tourism industry and one of the few people fluent in Czech and English who could help him.

'He arrived in the country and didn't speak a word of English. He really taught himself the language so well, surprisingly well,' she tells me. 'What was quite remarkable about him, he was a highly intelligent guy; he spotted opportunities that people can only dream about. He is an incredible entrepreneur. He was always surrounding himself with top people. He wanted to know who is the best in anything in town, the best lawyer, the best tax consultant. He connected himself with top people, holding conversations on the same level as them. He understood very quickly the legal system.

'You know how entrepreneurs get excited about something, like Elon Musk gets excited about rockets? He was interested in finding loopholes in the system. Interested in connecting the dots. He would say, "Guys, don't you see there's an opportunity?" If anything, he was a true entrepreneur; he got excited in that area.'

She says Krejcir never struck her as violent or having criminal intent, and she was shocked when she found out about his past. 'He was always very self-controlled, very well spoken. He was very funny, but he was never a criminal. I remember when I found out what had happened, I was thinking that's impossible, that's not the guy!'

The businesswoman agrees that she thought Krejcir felt trapped and wanted to scale up. 'He was looking for a bigger playground. Seychelles can be very limiting as an entrepreneur. He underestimated the South African legislative system. You think you're going to Africa and it's going to be the Wild Wild West, and meanwhile it's one of the best institutions in the world and you only learn that over time when you're actually here.'

Krejcir says that while in the Seychelles, his friends in the Czech Secret Service alerted him to an operation to have him eliminated. Operation 'Lomikar' was set in motion to have him killed – it would appear to be an accident or from natural causes. He says that until that point he had lived a reasonably protected life in the Seychelles and the local police force was aware of his position and protected him 'accordingly'. But then, under pressure from the Czech government, the Seychelles government demanded four million dollars from him to ensure his safety. The situation became untenable and so, he says, he applied for a passport under a new identity so that he could leave the country and seek political asylum elsewhere.

Krejcir was issued a passport in the name of Julius Egbert Savey, whilst his wife and son also received new identities, Sandra and Greg Savey. It is believed that this was done with the assistance of the former president, but Krejcir claims it was done entirely through official channels. Regardless of who was responsible, the government was left shame-faced, with the public clamouring for an explanation as to how the fraudulent passports were issued. Much as he did in the Czech Republic, Krejcir left a scandal in his wake when he departed from the Seychelles.

He says his intentions of travelling to South Africa were twofold. He wanted to apply for political asylum, but he also required an MRI scan because of his medical condition. Krejcir left the Seychelles by boat in April 2007 and headed to Madagascar before flying to South Africa and launching a new life for himself.

The pattern he followed in the Czech Republic and again in the

Seychelles, of elevating himself into the criminal elite, ingratiating himself with the politically powerful, corrupting senior government officials, claiming a conspiracy theory against him and allegations of assassination attempts, was set to repeat itself once again.

THREE TIMES THE MAGISTRATE WAS TO DROP HIS PEN ON THE floor. Three times he would bend down to retrieve it. By doing so, he apparently gave the signal that he was 'on board' with the terms of the agreement. Arrangements would be made for the delivery of an upfront payment to him, ensuring the release of the Czech accused on bail in the Kempton Park magistrate's court. Allegedly, it cost R1 million to secure Radovan Krejcir his freedom, paid over in a bag drop on the side of a highway near the airport in Johannesburg.

This is the version of events presented by George Louca about Krejcir's early days on South African soil – replete with claims that, from the outset, Krejcir began to corrupt his way into the country.

The cops were waiting for Krejcir as he stepped off the plane. An Interpol red notice had been issued and there had been a tip-off that the Czech fugitive would be arriving in South Africa from the Seychelles via Madagascar on a Madagascar Airlines commercial flight on 21 April 2007. Czech authorities had put out feelers to their South African counterparts requesting them to arrest the man they had spent years hunting. Farcically, in the hope that he would be able to slip through the net, Krejcir wore a disguise of glasses and a fake beard. He also had his fake passport issued in the Seychelles under the name of Julius Egbert Savey.

'Mr Savey' disembarked from the airplane, passed through an immigration cubicle, and an entry stamp was punched into his passport. He stepped into the queue to make his way through customs and, just metres from the airport exit, he was pulled aside by two men who asked him to accompany them to their office. They introduced themselves as police officers and began to question him about his identity and why he was visiting South Africa. Krejcir did not disclose that he was planning on applying for political asylum and, after interrogating him for several hours, they confirmed that they knew his true identity and explained that Interpol was seeking his arrest.

Savey, aka Krejcir, was subsequently detained at the airport's holding cells and later transported to the Kempton Park police cells a few kilometres away, where he was kept for several weeks while applying for bail.

It was in the holding cells at Kempton Park that Krejcir met a man who became a conduit to the criminal underworld in Johannesburg, a fixer who led him to people of influence and power. The meeting might have been fortuitous. It also might have been strategically manipulated. Sharing the holding cell with Krejcir was a petty thief and known criminal, George Louca, a Cypriot who also went by the name of George Smith. Short, fat and dishevelled, Louca had established himself as a go-to guy on Johannesburg's East Rand but also had a reputation for being a drug addict. There are some who believe that Louca and Krejcir's meeting was orchestrated and that they were placed together in a cell intentionally.

Some sources, who do not want to be named, claim that Krejcir's arrival in April 2007 was not his first visit to South Africa. They allege he came to the country in secret a year previously to meet with the National Intelligence Agency and pave his way. A law enforcement officer who tracked Krejcir's business dealings during his time here explains.

'Here's the fascinating thing. We were told that he met with people from the then National Intelligence Agency. He apparently came into South Africa, met with people from the NIA for one reason or another, we don't know what, and then left South Africa again, back to the Seychelles. We confirmed it. My thinking is that he had already in Seychelles decided to come to South Africa permanently, but he needed to find a way or means to ensconce himself here and ensure that the law enforcement agencies wouldn't extradite him. So he would have cooked up a scheme to present himself as an asset to Intelligence of some sorts, perhaps in Europe or, you know, organised crime in general, and that would have given him a protection factor to come to South Africa and live here and then operate as a so-called spy or informant for the Intelligence Agency. That's my theory.'

This is a theory that has not been officially confirmed by any law enforcement authority and has in fact been denied by those close to Krejcir.

Louca struck up a friendship with his new Czech buddy and played a central role in his being released. The story goes that Krejcir and Louca were locked in their cell at night, but for most of the day they were free to walk about as they pleased and had access to the fenced yard at the courthouse.

Louca recalls that one day a young girl aged about 15 or 16 appeared at the gate of the yard and signalled to get his attention. He walked over to her and through the fence she asked in English whether he knew a 'Mr Radovan'. The girl passed a letter through the gate and asked him to hand it to Krejcir. Louca did so and his new friend told him that, while it was written in Czech, it appeared that it had been done so using a free language application off the Internet.

'Krejcir said it had been sent to him by someone connected to the magistrate dealing with his bail application and that he had been offered an opportunity to guarantee his release on bail in consideration for payment of a bribe.' Louca remembers that Krejcir was interested in exploring the opportunity but was cautious, unsure whether he could trust the person making the approach.

The next step was for Krejcir to make telephone contact with a person whose number was supplied in the letter. Krejcir asked his fixer Louca to source a mobile phone. He then also asked Louca to make the call on his behalf.

'I called the number provided in the letter and spoke to a woman who identified herself as a "girlfriend" of the magistrate dealing with Krejcir's bail application.' The magistrate was Steven Holzen, a presiding officer well known in Kempton Park. Louca continues:

'I learned that the magistrate, a certain Mr Holzen, would grant bail to Krejcir subject to the following conditions:

(1) Krejcir would have to make an "upfront" payment to the magistrate, in the nature of a "guarantee", upon receipt of which the magistrate would ensure that Krejcir was released on bail; and

(2) Upon Krejcir's release on bail, [he] would make a further payment to the magistrate.

'After several discussions with the "girlfriend" it was allegedly agreed that the "upfront payment" should be in the amount of R1 million and that Krejcir, following his release on bail, was required to pay a further amount of R3 million.'

According to Louca, it was at this point that Krejcir insisted on a procedure to be implemented at his next court appearance that would require Holzen, by way of a prearranged signal, to show he had agreed to the terms and conditions of the deal. They agreed that Holzen would drop his pen three times and then pick it up. Once this had been done, Krejcir would ask Louca to make contact with a woman known as Ronelle. She featured prominently in Krejcir's early days in South Africa and was pivotal in establishing a business framework within which Krejcir could operate.

Today Ronelle Engelbrecht is a beauty therapist at an 'upmarket, family-owned beauty spa' in Pretoria called MatiSpa. She's blonde, with short heavily highlighted hair, middle-aged and carefully put together. It's understood that her dealings with Krejcir were set in motion well before he arrived in Johannesburg. Some suggest she met him when on holiday in the Seychelles while another version is that they were introduced by her sister, a government employee who worked in the Seychelles. Either way, Ronelle Engelbrecht set up Krejcir's primary financial vehicle, the company Groep Twee Beleggings, months before he arrived. She was also a director of a number of other Krejcir-associated business entities. During his first court appearances she was in the public gallery benches, doing unofficial PR for Krejcir, telling journalists about the charity work he had been doing when out for a short stint on a technicality. She related how he had bought hundreds of blankets for an old-age home and for various Pretoria townships, as well as about a thousand soccer balls for children in Soweto.

Engelbrecht initially agreed to speak to me about her relationship with Krejcir but then supplied a variety of excuses for not being able to make appointments, excuses that ranged from a broken hand to a broken car.

As Louca explains in his version, Engelbrecht was the only person Krejcir knew in South Africa and she was someone he believed could be trusted to secure and deliver the upfront payment to Holzen. Louca and

Engelbrecht allegedly handed over the R1 million cash in a bag drop-off on the side of the R21 highway one dark night.

Krejcir was granted bail.

The magistrate found that Krejcir was legitimately issued a Seychelles passport, even if it was under a different name, and that he had made considerable investment in South Africa, buying a business and property and expressing a wish to move his wife and son to the country permanently. Krejcir had also applied for asylum in South Africa, claiming that he would be persecuted in his homeland and that the former government had ordered his father's murder. Outside the court, Krejcir hugged and kissed his son Denis. The words he uttered then were filled with foreboding. 'This is a country under constitutional law, which will allow me to appeal, and I am convinced that I have done the right thing,' he said. 'It's nice, very nice. Next step? Now I will pay bail and I have to take some rest,' he said.

As part of the alleged agreement, Krejcir was then expected to pay a further R3 million to the magistrate. In August 2007, Louca claims Holzen approached him at the courthouse and asked him to follow him to his office.

'Your friend has let me down; he hasn't made the other payment. You can tell him from me I'm going to lock him up,' the magistrate allegedly told him.

A few days later, Krejcir asked Louca to drive to Pretoria to meet the magistrate at a restaurant. He watched as the two men spoke and apparently came to the agreement that there would be a reduced payment of R500 000.

In 2010 the South Gauteng High Court overturned the decision by Holzen to refuse to extradite Krejcir to the Czech Republic. The Court found that Holzen should have recused himself from the extradition hearing, as the magistrate appeared to have prejudged the matter during a 2007 bail hearing, when he called the state's case 'certainly questionable'. The High Court ordered that the extradition application be reheard.

In February 2018, I went to see Holzen at his office at the Kempton Park magistrate's court. I wanted to hear from him why he had never publicly rebutted this allegation. His lawyer had sent letters to newspapers that had written about Louca's affidavit, but Holzen had never given an interview or spoken out about the claim. He has long held a reputation as a strong presiding officer, a straight arrow, who isn't shy to apply the law. There was never any disciplinary action taken against him and no internal investigation.

I found a man who had been deeply affected by this scandal and who was faced with a predicament. I got the distinct impression that he was desperately frustrated by the fact that he was not allowed to speak publicly about this matter because he is restricted by policies imposed by the Magistrates Commission. Also, how could anything he say make him look innocent?

I can't say for certain whether I believe Holzen that he didn't take money, but it is the word of a known criminal and liar who is now dead against that of an officer of the law. There is no hard evidence to back up Louca's allegation.

Holzen, who subscribes to a Buddhist belief system, has relegated himself to the Traffic Court where he doesn't have to deal with people, only with paper. Any prospects of a career promotion have been extinguished by the niggling doubts that trail Louca's affidavit. From a man who was once assigned the area's biggest cases, he now chooses not to be bothered. He just wants to be left alone.

In 2007 when Krejcir washed up on South African shores, the country was an appetising option for many shadowy characters who sought opportunities to establish a foothold in clandestine markets. The criminal justice system was in flux, the intelligence services were distracted by a bruising battle for control of the heart of the African National Congress, and the police service was being abused as part of a fight for political survival.

It was a tumultuous time. The elite crime-fighting unit known as the Scorpions, situated within the National Prosecuting Authority, was conducting an intensive investigation into the country's most senior police officer and the head of Interpol, Jackie Selebi.

As a result of the Selebi investigation the country's most senior prosecutor, the head of the National Prosecuting Authority, Vusi Pikoli, was placed on suspension by then President Thabo Mbeki. This was ostensibly to ensure Mbeki's friend would be protected from a corruption trial. Mbeki, however, argued that it was because Pikoli had authorised controversial deals with self-confessed hit men Mikey Schultz, Nigel McGurk and Faizal 'Kappie' Smith in the sensational assisted suicide of businessman Brett Kebble in 2005.

The entire web of corruption and illicit criminal conduct around Kebble and Selebi was unravelling, which also saw a massive drug bust involving an international syndicate in Germiston. None of those responsible for trafficking the drugs was given a particularly lengthy sentence, but the bust was used by the Scorpions to leverage complicity in the pursuit of Selebi, the police chief. Krejcir and other eager underworld entrepreneurs would have known that law enforcement was in disarray and that it was possible to corrupt and be sufficiently connected to avoid conviction if the right palms were greased.

The Scorpions were also fighting for their own survival, with critics in the ruling ANC insisting that the unit should be disbanded because it had outgrown its mandate and was picking and choosing politically sensitive cases to serve its own agenda.

This resulted in a full-blown turf war between the Scorpions and the South African Police Service (SAPS), as Selebi unleashed his intelligence operatives to dig up dirt on Scorpions members in order to dismantle the case against him. This battle saw individual agencies being manipulated, clandestine recordings being made in hotel rooms and conversations of top-level politicians and prosecutors being recorded, to be kept as ammunition for another day.

The head of Crime Intelligence at the time, Mulangi Mphego, was even charged with defeating the ends of justice by meddling in the case against Selebi. He appeared in court for trying to get the Scorpions' main witness against the police chief, Glenn Agliotti, to contradict previous statements he had made detailing the corruption of the top cop.

As clear battle lines were drawn and factions established, the events of the period between 2007 and 2009 had a domino effect on the leadership of the criminal justice system for years to come. As a result of this series of events, favours had to be paid back and there was ammunition to be used as blackmail for some time.

On 10 September 2007, Gauteng Scorpions head Gerrie Nel had an arrest warrant issued for Selebi. Days later, Vusi Pikoli was suspended and the arrest warrant was cancelled by acting NPA head Mokotedi Mpshe.

In November 2007, it emerged that Nel was the subject of a police probe, headed by Gauteng Deputy Police Commissioner Richard Mdluli. Later that month, Scorpions prosecutor advocate Nomgcobo Jiba was suspended from the NPA after evidence appeared that she helped police secure an arrest warrant for Nel, who was her colleague. The alliance formed between Jiba and Mdluli held for years. Added to this union was the NPA's former head of its Integrity Unit, Prince Mokotedi, and then head of the NPA's Commercial Crimes Unit, advocate Lawrence Mrwebi, who both testified for Selebi in his corruption case, against their own organisation (the NPA).

Early on the morning of 8 January 2008, at the instigation of Richard Mdluli, Gerrie Nel was arrested by dozens of armed officers at his home on charges of corruption and defeating the ends of justice. It was quickly apparent that the charges were trumped up and Nel was released from custody. It was clear that Jiba, Mdluli and Mrwebi had colluded to obtain the warrant of arrest for Nel.

In January 2009, it came to light that Richard Mdluli had signed an affidavit in support of a Labour Court challenge brought by Jiba, the suspended prosecutor. It was in this statement that Mdluli revealed that police bugged the phone of Scorpions boss Leonard McCarthy during the police investigation into Nel. It is these recordings, along with others made by the National Intelligence Agency, that would become known as the 'Spy Tapes', which would be used by Jacob Zuma to get rid of corruption charges against him. Mdluli also supplied Jiba with transcripts of a tape recording and an excerpt from Nel's diary to assist her in her Labour Court application. She successfully returned to her post at the NPA but years later was again suspended, along with Mrwebi, after they were struck from the roll of advocates.

These events were all part of a proxy war among factions in the ANC set against the backdrop of a bruising leadership battle within the ruling party. This was ahead of the Polokwane elective conference in December 2007, which saw Thabo Mbeki and Jacob Zuma contesting the position of party president.

Ultimately, Zuma won the leadership race and, just months later, the NPA withdrew corruption charges against him relating to the hugely controversial arms deal. The decision was based on the 'Spy Tapes'. The tapes purported to prove that the prosecution of Zuma was politically motivated and that there had been improper interference in the investigation.

One law enforcement insider, who doesn't want to be named, sets out how turbulent the landscape was at the time, with various agencies pulling in different directions, working against each other rather than together in the fight against crime.

'At a macro level, that was an extremely tumultuous period in the world of law enforcement agencies in the country for various reasons.

So, if you go back in time when democracy happened in this country, what the new government inherited was a criminal justice system that was, by design, a simple criminal justice system. We had the police, we had the prosecuting authority, that was it, that was the sum total of the criminal justice system.

'Then the criminal justice system started modernising and looking towards how the rest of the world was functioning and dealing with crime, and so out of that you started seeing different aspects of modernisation, such as the birth of the Scorpions, the Asset Forfeiture Unit, the Special Investigations Unit, the Revenue Service, starting to move towards developing an enforcement capacity. Home Affairs, Public Works, multiple state agencies began to develop their own in-house investigative capacities. There was this spirit of pulling together.'

It was during this heyday of cooperation in the late 1990s and early 2000s that several high-profile breakthroughs were made in the fight against organised crime. At the time, the state had the capacity to take on big syndicates. But in the mid-2000s, the law enforcement insider says, things began to go 'horribly wrong'.

'And they go horribly wrong for a variety of reasons, but the primary one, I believe, is first of all that the Scorpions outgrew their statutory mandate and became a tool to achieve certain ends at a political level. We certainly recognised it in those days already, because you could almost see it in the way in which the relationship was very good up to a point and then all of a sudden it changed. In my view, politically that caused a big crack in this criminal justice system.'

It was chaotic. Smokescreens were being thrown up all around the criminal justice system. Battle lines were drawn and fairly clearly defined factions were distinguishable. Law enforcement was distracted and this proved to be an ideal breeding ground for someone like Radovan Krejcir.

'He would have seen great opportunities,' says Gareth Newham, head of the Governance, Crime and Justice Division at the Institute for Security Studies.

'He would have noticed that the corruption in the state was causing weaknesses in the criminal justice system. When your political elite are involved in corruption and criminality, your people who are the [commissioners] of police, the president who appoints the person or the people, are corrupt or they are not concerned with corruption.

'So Krejcir would have been seeing all this; he would have seen that the Scorpions were being shut down, that there was a lot of war between the Scorpions and the police, and the cells were at war with each other. He would have seen that this provides plenty of opportunity because when you kind of have that situation when the institutions are at war with each other, then they become more loyal to the institution, the person that heads the institution than the overall system, the overall Constitution. The law and Constitution go out the window when you're fighting another organisation. So, he would have just thought, you know, there's cops here I can do work with ... I can do business with. It would have been a very clear indicator that there was destabilisation in the criminal justice system. That destabilisation would have opened up opportunities for people to take money because they're not sure what's going on. They're willing to abuse their powers to fight with each other. That would just be signals for him.'

Not only was the criminal justice system in disarray over that period, so too was the 'underworld'.

When Radovan Krejcir walked out of the cells in the Kempton Park magistrate's court in 2007, he was stepping into an underworld that had imploded. It was fractured and without any discernible leadership. For the better part of a decade, the town had been run by the security-company-cum-enforcement-racket Elite, led by the gritty fighter Mikey Schultz from the South, with ice-blue eyes and a body wrapped in tattoos. But Schultz, along with Nigel McGurk and Faizal 'Kappie' Smith, had strayed from his usual business and had taken money to carry out a corporate hit. Kebble's murder, and its proximity to politics and the country's top policeman, meant that the activities of Schultz became very public. 'The eyes were on him,' as he was wont to say. Schultz, McGurk and Smith entered into a deal with the state in terms of section 204 of the Criminal Procedure Act, which meant they would receive immunity from prosecution in exchange for their evidence in court. It also meant that the trio obtained a get-out-of-jail-free card for any crimes they had committed. As a result, they chose to lie low, avoid the spotlight and at least try to live clean. This left a void for someone to step in and seize the city.

NEWS OF THE NEW CZECH BILLIONAIRE IN TOWN SPREAD QUICKLY. It was difficult to ignore. With the help of Louca, Radovan Krejcir began to set up shop in the largely affluent suburb of Bedfordview northeast of Johannesburg. It was like moths to a flame.

With its village-like atmosphere and Mediterranean feel, Bedfordview felt comfortable to both Louca the Cypriot and Krejcir the Czech. Populated largely by Greeks, Lebanese and Portuguese immigrants, the suburb is defined by its café culture and close-knit society. Built on an elevated ridge on the seam of the city's major highways, with views of the CBD and northern suburbs, Bedfordview is as central as Krejcir could get. Perched in his multi-storey home, he also had a bird's-eye view over the areas he and his associates frequented, much like a sentinel in a tower monitoring a potential assault in medieval times. Krejcir selected a restaurant at the Bedford Centre shopping mall, the Harbour restaurant, regularly frequented by other European immigrants, and it quickly became his regular haunt – in effect, his headquarters. With a view over a parking lot, the restaurant provided easy access to the outside deck area where Krejcir always sat at the same table behind a sheet of armoured glass. From this location he could carry out transactions that were both legitimate in the business environment and criminal in the illicit trade.

Forensic investigator Chad Thomas is a veritable encyclopaedia of Joburg's underworld. With his thick gold chain and carefully manicured goatee, Thomas is a boet, a boytjie, who knows every player in town. The names of characters, such as The Duke, spill off his tongue. He talks about 'laaities' and 'dolly birds', and employs a lexicon that only true Joburgers can comprehend. He has a history in the police and in state intelligence and isn't shy to talk about his own gun battles and feuds and friendships with major players. Thomas monitored Krejcir as he began to stretch out his tentacles and take control of the city. So how did he do it? I ask over a Strawberry Lips shooter in the middle of a weekday afternoon at a random bowling club in eastern Joburg.

'Café society to a large extent, spending money, making sure people saw him spending money. He set up by ensuring you've got the props first. You brought in those Porsches; he looked for a nice property to buy. He got involved in café society; he then got his own place with the Harbour. He just found the right guys. Bedfordview is very small. Bedfordview is an area where people are looking to make money. They came from nothing, they made a few rand, they've established themselves. Money doesn't last forever so they're looking for the next best thing. It's not like old money in Saxonwold, it's not old money in Sandhurst, it's not old money in Westcliff. Bedfordview is new money and the guys around Bedfordview that came from Kensington, Bertrams, Bez Valley, Malvern, always aspired to more. They didn't want to be too far from home and that's why Bedfordview is such new money and those guys are different to the guys you see sitting in Sandhurst, different to the guys you see sitting in Rosebank that come from Houghton. You'll see the chains, you'll see the sports cars; the guys want to show that they've made it because they came from nothing and they're rough. You look at Mikey. They grew up and they only had their fists and that's what made them money. Mikey thought that was gonna make him money. So, these guys were not shy to use their hands and it's not far removed from using your hands to start using a pistol to make your mark.'

(As a side note, the controversial Gupta family also first set up shop in Bedfordview when they arrived in the country in the 1990s from India. The first offices of Sahara computers were in the suburb.)

With Louca as his guide, Krejcir became a regular feature on the local circuit and introductions were made to all the right people. Thomas says having someone like Louca to pave the way for him was invaluable.

'Remember, he already had somebody great there to guide him. He had George Louca. George Louca, George Smith, he was never regarded as one of the main guys, but he wasn't somebody you would mess with, [and] he wasn't somebody you would trust either because he would turn you in. He was always an informer and this is one thing people need to understand. All your players are informers; they have protection from some or other section of law enforcement, whether it's defence intelligence, whether it's police intelligence, whether it's police detectives, somewhere along the line they've got protection and they've got a relationship with a cop; that is, it's not a good relationship, and these guys are normally sociopaths; they're normally very social, they're exceptionally charming and George was one of them. However, people knew when George turned to the rocks he wasn't trustworthy, but he'd been an informer for a long time and he obviously had moved up the ranks. He was very valuable at a stage but then the crack really fucked him because when you're on that crack and you're on a downer, you'll sell your own mother. He became very unreli-able because of that, so the guys started distancing themselves from him and you must remember he only started hitting the crack once Radovan was here, once he'd established his relationship, because he had a lot more disposable income.

'To this day, I do not believe it was fortuitous or coincidental that George Louca was in the same cell as him. I will never believe that for as long as I live. I honestly believe he was planted there. Because they knew this guy was coming. Just think about it. What are the chances that an international gangster is in the same cell as a local gangster? The one guy is caught at Kempton; the other guy, he wasn't caught for much. It just doesn't gel with me how perfect that scenario was. Every bit of me says that something's not kosher with that story. George was a plant from day one. They knew this oke was coming and they knew this oke had money.'

Krejcir also began extending his network to other local players of influ-ence. He reached out to Mikey Schultz, although that relationship did not last very long. He befriended Glenn Agliotti too.

'I can't even remember how I met him, but it was like an arb … I can't even remember,' Agliotti tells me vaguely about how he first met Krejcir. 'It was a "Hi, how are you? What do you do?" It was a very arb chitchat thing and nothing more. We never ever did a business deal together. Nothing, nothing, nothing. He was this high-flyer, ran from the Seychelles, ran from the Czech Republic. He was a very dynamic, charismatic guy. We just spoke shit. We'd sit, have a coffee. He helped me once when I was under house arrest with my legal fees, which I paid him back with interest. It was R200 000.

'He is an opportunist. He tried to do gold deals, and crime deals, and so many business deals. If you've got half a brain you sit there and look at him and you know you're going to get fucked, so why even entertain doing a deal with him? I think he'd done it before. I can't even remember when he came into the country. Remember, I met him under house arrest. I was arrested in 2007 so he was already here. It's always been his nature, when he was in the Seychelles he befriended – what I heard – the president, you know; that's how he operates. Thank God I never had anything to do with him other than that loan that I've repaid him. He invited me to his son's twenty-first and I went to that. When I was in the area he'd say I have to come for a drink or coffee. I lived in Pecanwood so I never liked to leave late. I would pop in and have a coffee and go. Funny enough, whenever I walked into his office and there were people there, he would dismiss them. We would chat, have a coffee and I would leave. I never sat in on any of his business deals or discussions,' insists Agliotti.

Through Louca, Krejcir was introduced to strip club king Lolly Jackson, who had established the Teazers chain of entertainment venues. Like Krejcir, Jackson owned a mansion on Kloof Road and the two men shared a passion for fast cars, women and money. It was an instant friendship fraught with competitive friction. While their relationship developed, so too did the potential for suspect business deals.

According to Thomas, Krejcir also forged relationships with other local players who weren't as well known in the public eye, but who had earned reputations on the streets. One of these individuals was Kevin Trytsman, also a private eye and debt collector, who often boasted about his influence in state intelligence circles. He claimed to have connections to the Civil Cooperation Bureau, an apartheid-era state-sponsored hit squad. He also said he befriended apartheid killer Ferdi Barnard, and bragged that Barnard had confessed to him that he had shot and killed activist David

Webster. He even testified at the Truth and Reconciliation Commission and was granted amnesty in connection with charges of illegal possession of firearms and ammunition, vehicle theft and perjury, having confessed to holding weapons for the ANC's military arm MK.

Thomas continues: 'Kevin Trytsman was a big feature at the time in the scene, but Trytsman was strange. He drove a Merc Vito and his registration was NIA, you know, National Intelligence Agency. Krejcir saw these guys and he saw where he could use them, but no one was sure of Trytsman. Trytsman was seriously connected but no one knew whether he was open about his connections because he didn't want you to find out another way. So he'd make you think, yes, I am connected but go away, it's for my own benefit, but whereas it could've been he was actually spying for the establishment.'

Krejcir struck up a strategic relationship with another powerful and influential figure who traversed the 'upper' and 'under' worlds, a man who was as well known and at home in the gangster traps on the Cape Flats as he was in the boardrooms of Sandton or in the corridors of the country's intelligence agencies. Cyril Beeka was known as a Don in Cape Town's criminal circles, a man who once ran extortionist protection rackets in the Mother City's clubs through his security companies. He had also brokered a peace deal of sorts between the city's opposing gangs and had earned a reputation as a major player. Beeka was an informer for various state agencies, a position he invariably used to provide himself with immunity for his criminal activities. Officially, he was the head of security for a major transportation company, RAM Hand-to-Hand Couriers, and spent the bulk of his time in Johannesburg.

The Czech also sought out other immigrants with shady backgrounds involved in nefarious activities. It is widely believed that these individuals had sought refuge in South Africa because they were running from one secret or another abroad. There was the Cypriot Michael Arsiotis, the Serb Veselin Laganin, the accountant Ivan Savov, the Bulgarian Boris 'Mike' Grigorov and the Lebanese Sam Issa.

Issa was a fascinating character, referred to as 'Cripple Sam' or 'Black Sam'. He walked with a limp and with a crutch, was known for throwing frenzied Champagne-fuelled parties and for being trigger-happy, firing off his weapon in the air.

'He claimed to be Maronite Catholic; he wasn't,' says Thomas. 'He was Palestinian, who had grown up in the south of Lebanon in the refugee camps. He had been arrested for terrorism in Paris. They found him with plans to bomb a synagogue. I think he spent six years in prison there before he was released and came to South Africa, and he had been injured somewhere along the line. He used to drive a black Q7 and he used to park in the cripple parking right outside the Harbour. He was a nice guy, but there was a dark side to him, which is why we call him Black Sam. Cripple Sam was for people who didn't know him. We called him Black Sam because of his heart. He could be very charming, very engaging, but he could switch like this,' Thomas clicks his fingers. 'There was always talk that he was involved in drugs.'

Krejcir staffed his circle with lieutenants, men who buttressed his criminal organisation, and men he could do business with – whether lawful or illicit. Before long, he had established a formidable network.

'I don't think he wanted to get involved with crime, to be quite honest with you; I honestly don't think he came with the intention of becoming "*Capo di tutti capi*",' suggests Thomas. 'I think it just followed him and it was a natural progression for him here and because he saw there was a vacuum and a void and it needed somebody to take the helm. It was his position that he'd have to fill and he took it.'

Krejcir began to flourish.

GENERAL JOEY MABASA IS A GHOST. HE IS THE KIND OF GUY WHO can wear a different hat and change his identity in an instant. Not one authentic photograph of Mabasa exists in the public domain. And he is difficult to describe. He is thick-set, of average height and has a clean-shaven head. The only vaguely notable identifying feature is his slight buck teeth and even those aren't that obvious. He practically wrote the hand-book on surveillance and knows every trick in the book about operating in the shadows. He is a career cop who never wanted to be a cop.

Mabasa was born in Tshiawelo in Soweto in 1964. He went to school there and his life was relatively unremarkable until the student riots of 1976 rocked the township. His mother never worked, but his father had a job in a factory. Despite the single income, the Mabasa family lived in a four-bedroomed house. Although his father was aligned to the ANC, the family was not particularly politically active. Mabasa vividly recalls raids in the township in the middle of the night, his first experiences of the police force of which he would one day be a part.

As a young boy, Mabasa wanted to be a doctor. He wanted to help people. 'I saw people dying in the community I grew up in because the health system wasn't like it is now. My father couldn't afford it,' he explains. As a teenager, he fell into activism and his life was taken down a path he had never predicted. Around the age of 15, he became part of a small cell, not aligned to any organisation. It seems as though he became politically active more because of peer pressure than out of any overwhelming sense of outrage against the apartheid regime.

'We were involved because if you stay in the location you cannot stay behind. They will ask you why you are not joining the other boys. After finishing my matric we couldn't sleep at home. If you sleep here tonight you have to move to another place tomorrow. One of our boys sold us out when we went to town and they caught us. When they caught us they said we can either go to prison or join the police. I didn't want to go to prison so I thought I would rather join the police.'

It was an act of self-preservation. He doesn't believe he sold out to the oppressors in any way, or that he mutinied. 'I never sold anyone out; it was just to be safe. My father was very angry with me for joining the police. I never wanted to join the police. But after that I just opened myself up to the idea that I will be a policeman. I went to Hammanskraal for training for six months. I was 20 or 21.'

His commanders wanted him to join the notorious Security Branch, but Mabasa was not interested. 'I didn't want to do it because I saw what they were doing in the location. They then posted me in Midrand, at the charge office. Midrand wasn't like it is today. It was a small house and there was one shop owned by Greeks. When I arrived there I wasn't happy. There were only old people; I was the only young guy. When I asked a question, I was in trouble. They sat on my head; I just had to agree with them. They approached me and said they wanted me at this side. At John Vorster. So I went to John Vorster and the old black policemen said I am a comrade and they don't trust me.'

Mabasa was appointed to the surveillance unit, the only black man on the team, and found himself working on all high-priority political cases. Indirectly, he was doing the work he did not want to be doing. 'We went for training. I became a team leader and my members were only white. I'm not stupid, I can operate, so they trusted me.'

'I was in surveillance until I became a colonel. I started training people in surveillance. I'd go to Cape Town and Durban to train people. I trained with the FBI. I know surveillance like the palm of my hand.'

Mabasa has a clearly defined stance on the politicisation of the police. It is a position he has cemented within himself over time and internalised. 'I told myself that if you are a cop you cannot serve a political party, you have to serve the people of South Africa.'

Ultimately, he believes, it would be this principle that would undo him. He refused to meddle in politics and 'pick a side' in what would become a heavily politicised police service. Although he was briefly a UDM member, he never joined the ANC and now is not a member of any political party.

'I told myself I am an officer and I must serve the people of South Africa. I don't want to align myself with any political party. That was my downfall. We were working opposite Luthuli House. My members would go to Luthuli House to get instructions. When they came back I told them they must go to the minister and the minister must talk to the national commissioner. We cannot take instructions from a political party.'

After 1994, Mabasa remained at the surveillance unit within Crime Intelligence and continued to climb the ranks of the organisation. He became the provincial commander of surveillance, interception and monitoring, which was also responsible for cyber-crimes and the bugging of offices, and was then appointed Gauteng head of Crime Intelligence.

'Whatever I achieved wasn't because I had somebody aligned to me. It was through hard work. All the people knew about me; when I follow something I get it. I believed in getting dirty to get what I want, but getting dirty within the framework of the law.'

During his time in charge of intelligence in the province, a powerful position, he says he took a strong stance on corruption. It was during this period that he watched as National Police Commissioner Jackie Selebi was accused, stood trial and was then convicted of corruption. Mabasa insists corruption is 'bad' and even worse when it is the top boss that is responsible.

'You are the head and all the members are under you. If the head is rotten, what will happen to the people on the ground? It's like cancer.'

From his experience, it is alarmingly straightforward for criminals and organised crime networks to corrupt police officers. This is particularly true in the intelligence environment where situations are murky and lines can be blurred.

'A criminal will bring you information. He won't give you information from his own group, so he needs to be clever. He needs to lie low because he is also a criminal. To get intelligence is not easy; that is why there's no intelligence now because they are scared to get dirty. You need to infiltrate somebody to get intelligence. They make friends and they bring you into the organisation. They will start with bringing information; then you become friends. You go with them and they introduce you to all the operators, so you as the police need to protect those people – that's how they operate. Most of the time it's favours. Most of the cops are corrupt, but they are not rich; if it was money, their lives would be different. Sometimes they will buy cellphones for the cops. You can give a cop R2 and he will be happy. Their minds aren't working.'

What makes police officers so vulnerable to corruption in the South African environment? Is it a culture, systemic within the organisation, or is it pure greed and poor salaries?

'It is because of the pay. If I cannot afford this phone and somebody gives me this phone, I will close one eye to that person,' he hypothesises. 'I think the recruitment of police nowadays is wrong. Previously, if you wanted to be a policeman, the security officers will check everything secretly. They will give that information to the recruiting officer to say it's a good guy or a bad guy. They will go around your neighbourhood and ask people about you without you knowing. Nowadays they don't do that, they just hire anyone. Sometimes they've hired somebody and they are actually looking for him [because he's a criminal]. He went to training and they don't see him until he is finished. I think the recruitment is bad.'

Corruption, he offers, is rife within the intelligence environment. He says he has even acted against his own members. 'I've arrested them. If you don't know how they operate, you won't be able to find it. There are secret funds and open funds in Intelligence. So the corrupt ones will take money from the secret funds. They will say, "Mandy is an informer," they will open a file about you being an informer. The commander must approve this because every month the impimpis are being paid, but that money won't come to you; they will eat it. The cops claim the money to your name, but the money is not coming to you. The handler has to meet the source and write a report about the information received from the source.'

The difficulty comes in drawing the line between being corrupt and having to 'get dirty' in order to get information from criminal syndicates. Mabasa says that during his career he infiltrated various criminal organisations, from drug-dealing syndicates to car-theft gangs.

'If there is a syndicate, we will identify the groupings of the syndicate. We look for the weakest link in that group and then target that person with our own member. If it's cars, you also have to produce a car, so we'll buy a car from the syndicate and we want to get to the group through this one; we know this one maybe likes money. He is the one who will introduce you to the rest of the organisation. I've done it many times.'

He says it is this crucial information gleaned by the police's Crime Intelligence unit that helps to catch bad guys and crack big cases. 'It is very important because without intelligence, how are you going to solve your crime? Intelligence must be the eyes and ears of the police. If you are blind, the whole body would be blind. If Intelligence is blind there is nothing that is going to happen.'

During all his years as a ghost, surveying, spying and bugging, Mabasa got dirty many, many times, delving deep into the grime and grease of organised crime. But never, ever, did he cross the line and become a criminal.

At least, that is his version.

GEORGE THE GREEK, AKA FAT GEORGE AKA GEORGE SMITH AKA George Louca, was a police informant. He peddled information he gleaned about criminal networks, taking cash for news. It was his prized commodity.

'George Louca was a source for one of my officers,' explains General Joey Mabasa. 'He was giving information; he had a lot of cases at the airport. They were bringing in goods through the airport, drugs and everything. So I think one of my officers recruited him. You know, what some of these officers will do, if they know you have a case, they will say they are going to arrest you or you work for me and give me information. So he's obliged to give information, otherwise he will go to prison.'

Louca was known to be a habitual drug user and, according to many accounts, often appeared to be bewildered and high. Mabasa says this was his memory of Louca's visits to the Gauteng Crime Intelligence headquarters in the Johannesburg CBD.

'When he came to my office it was like he was drugged or drunk; he was not normal. His behaviour wasn't normal.'

But Mabasa says Louca's information was solid, tip-offs about OR Tambo International Airport and activities there, as well as about a criminal syndicate operating around Bedfordview. With his relationship as an informant established, Louca then offered up another potential source, the friend he had made in the Kempton Park police cells. It was around 2009, just as Krejcir was establishing his network.

'He said there is someone who came from Czech who has lots of information. We didn't know who this was. So he came there with him; he came to the office. He came with George and another guy; I don't know who it was. They were three people. He was telling us how the drugs were coming from overseas to South Africa, so we were interested in that.'

For the intelligence officers, Krejcir was potential gold. He seemed to know a great deal about drug-trafficking operations and he was willing to work with them. To Mabasa, Krejcir did not appear to be a gangster, mob boss or bad guy.

'I didn't think he was a criminal because if you don't know him you wouldn't suspect anything. We interviewed him. I never interviewed him alone. He told us that they had lawyers. We said we just want him to help us because we are interested.'

Mabasa insists that he immediately wrote a letter to the SAPS head office to inform his superiors that he had met Krejcir. That letter was sent to the national head of Crime Intelligence at the time, General Mulangi Mphego, as well as to the head of the Hawks, General Anwa Dramat.

'I even went to Dramat's office. I said to him there is an individual here whom we don't know, but I don't know if other people are investigating him. I gave him the report of what we got from him and that we want a big bust because he agreed that he will give us a big bust.'

Curiously, according to Mabasa, Krejcir did not want to be paid as an informant. He says he did not know what Krejcir's motive was and it never occurred to him that Krejcir was interested in corrupting cops. The Czech's information was 'good', but the cops had to be patient before moving on their targets. 'His information was very good but you need to lie low like a snake. We wanted to get the big bust.'

The second meeting took place at the offices of Krejcir's lawyer, who at the time was Ian Small-Smith. Mabasa knew Small-Smith from various criminal cases. Small-Smith is well known for representing several high-profile accused, most famously the three self-confessed hit men who killed Brett Kebble. Small-Smith has told me he first met General Mabasa at The Grand in Rivonia when the police were raiding Andrew Phillips's property. Some reports have suggested that it was, in fact, Small-Smith who introduced Krejcir to Mabasa. Both Small-Smith and Mabasa emphatically deny this.

The third meeting was back at Mabasa's office. Again, he says he was not alone. 'He brought a lot of information. It was handwritten. I didn't keep

43

that information. I sent it to the Hawks,' Mabasa assures me.

According to Mabasa, he only ever met Radovan Krejcir three times. There was always someone else present at the meetings and the Czech was a source, providing information in anticipation of a major bust of an international drug-smuggling syndicate operating through OR Tambo International. That big bust never came because before anything could happen, explosive allegations burst into the open about Mabasa's relationship with Krejcir.

ALEKOS PANAYI IS A REGULAR JOBURG GUY IN HIS LATE THIRTIES. He was born and bred in the city and went to Jeppe High School and Wits. His parents are Greek Cypriot, but he considers himself a South African who identifies strongly with his heritage. After graduating, he took up a position at Laiki Bank, a private bank registered in Greece and Cyprus with a representative office in Johannesburg.

He had been in the job of general assistant at Laiki for just over a year when Lolly Jackson walked through the doors. It was early 2007 and the Teazers boss wanted to buy a Pagani Zonda, a jaw-dropping luxury sports car. The vehicle was owned by a businessman in Singapore and Jackson needed Panayi to transfer money from the Bank of Cyprus to Laiki Bank in Cyprus.

Panayi wasn't entirely au fait with all the details, but he did know that the Zonda was being purchased from an investment company in Singapore. Jackson had to pay €380 000 to the sellers and the car would be released. Top-end car dealer Justin Divaris, well known for his now defunct friendship with disgraced Paralympic superstar Oscar Pistorius, acted as something of a middleman in the sale.

Jackson had to make the payment in euros so Panayi's task was to source foreign currency for his client. Although this transaction was not above board, it was not an entirely novel request for the general assistant at the bank either. Panayi went off to the network of people he knew who were trying to bring funds into the country. He then partnered Jackson with someone who had euros offshore and they did a deal.

Jackson paid over the cash in two tranches. Panayi picked up the money from the strip club boss's mansion at 40 Kloof Road in Bedfordview where it was hidden in an inconspicuous safe under the stairs in his garage, tucked behind a picture. Panayi held onto the cash, stashing it in a bag at the homes of friends, relatives and acquaintances.

In the second half of 2007, this arrangement became trickier for Panayi. The bank was set to shut its doors in South Africa in January 2008. In addition, another character had been introduced into the mix. Panayi met Radovan Krejcir through an acquaintance – George Louca – because his offshore company had an account with Laiki Bank in Cyprus. He told Panayi that he was relocating to South Africa and needed to start bringing in funds, both legally and illegally. At first, Panayi refused but he was put under pressure by Louca and other members of the Greek community in Bedfordview. He relented.

So it was that Panayi paired Krejcir with his existing client, Jackson. It was a perfect match. Jackson needed money offshore to pay for his Zonda and Krejcir needed money in South Africa to support his lavish lifestyle. On the face of it, the arrangement seemed to work, but then a transaction in January 2008 got very sticky.

Emotions ran high and Panayi found his life on the line.

Jackson was to swap R1 million with Krejcir for euros. The funds were being transferred from an account in the name of George Smith (Louca) in Cyprus. Smith was the front for the account, but Krejcir held signing powers. Suddenly, the bank threw a spanner in the works, refusing to process the transfer because it appeared to be an act of money laundering and because Krejcir was involved. The sale of the euros was thus put on hold until Krejcir could make alternative arrangements to transfer the funds from an account in Poland operated by his mother.

All of this coincided with the closure of the bank's office in South Africa and Panayi's gut told him he should keep some evidence of what was going on. He made a copy of the closing statement of the account and kept it.

With Krejcir's euro payment hanging in the balance, Panayi's relationship with Jackson was under strain: the strip club boss was putting pressure on the bank manager. So when Krejcir handed Panayi a Swift confirmation of the apparent deposit, he handed the cash over to the Czech. Panayi drove to his house and gave him a canvas tog bag stuffed full of notes.

As far as Panayi was concerned, the deal was done. Krejcir had deposited the cash offshore and he had transferred the cash from Jackson to Krejcir. For his trouble, he received R10 000, which he deducted from the cash in the tog bag.

Only, things were not quite so straightforward.

A few months later, in May 2008, Panayi received a call from Jackson. He was raging and full of colourful profanities. He accused Panayi of taking his money. Panayi says Jackson 'said he would send someone to fuck me up, and fuck up my family and make my life a living hell'. He was petrified.

In a sworn statement signed as part of an indemnity deal with the state, Panayi explained that he set up a meeting between Krejcir and Jackson 'as they had never met each other before this'. This is odd, as several individuals have explained to me that Louca had introduced the two men to one another shortly after Krejcir arrived in the country.

On the banker's version, Krejcir was surrounded by at least 10 armed guards at the meeting, all either ex- or current police officers. Panayi says that at this meeting Krejcir admitted that he hadn't paid the full amount to Jackson and withheld funds because he was unhappy with the rates on prior transactions. It was classic Krejcir – on the face of it, he had agreed to a deal in good faith and then attempted to swindle the other party out of their share. The good old 'knocking' trick so common in underworld circles. But Lolly Jackson had been around this block a few times.

Panayi was so terrified that he called up an uncle in Cyprus and asked for US$12 000. He was willing to pay Jackson what he could himself, even though he had acted in good faith.

But Jackson wasn't giving up so easily. Panayi claims that Jackson sent two debt collectors, 'to start threatening me and visiting me at my new employment and threatening me personally'. By this stage, Panayi had quit the banking game and had taken a new job at the Fruit and Veg City in Greenstone.

Almost a year later, in November 2009, Jackson arrived at Fruit and Veg City again, looking for Panayi. He had got wind that the former banker turned greengrocer had turned state witness against him. Panayi assured him this was not the case.

'He then phoned a cop, whose name is not known to me, and said he was sitting with me and that I had told him I was not a state witness and could he check for Jackson. The other guy, I assume to be a cop, then said something and the call ended. I subsequently received a letter from his lawyer demanding R650 000.'

Clearly it wasn't only Krejcir who had cops on the payroll just a phone call away. With all his run-ins with the law, Jackson also had a list of contacts on his phone, with numbers for officers who owed him a favour or two.

Panayi never heard from Jackson again. But somebody else soon came knocking on his door, asking him for the inside track on the wheeling and dealing he had been involved in. Paul O'Sullivan would take his statement, cracking open the money-laundering scheme.

LOLLY JACKSON LIVED LIFE AT FULL THROTTLE. AS THE FOUNDER of the Teazers chain, he achieved near-iconic status in South Africa as the patriarch of the strip industry, lauded by men from Primrose to Bellville and beyond.

Brash, cocksure and abrasive, Jackson was known for his many flirtations with the law, his penchant for flashy, expensive cars and an insatiable appetite for publicity. He spoke with a thick Joburg South accent and had a tongue as rough as sandpaper. He was unrefined, crude and a misogynist.

Jackson was a self-made man. His parents were middle-class Greek immigrants who crashed through the border from war-ravaged Congo and down into South Africa in the 1960s in a specially reinforced Oldsmobile. As a high-school dropout, Jackson worked as a second-hand car salesman, a paver, a part-time DJ and a diamond cutter. His father warned him, 'If it has tits or wheels, it will give you trouble.' Jackson chose both.

From a brothel called the Gold Card Club, Jackson built up his empire until he was able to buy his Kloof Road home and a fleet of luxury racing cars as well as satiate his appetite for poker. With his explosive temper and disregard for authority, Jackson was regularly hauled before magistrates following brushes with the law.

I have vivid memories of sitting on the pavement outside the Sandton police station off Rivonia Road, watching Jackson walk in and out of the building with his lawyers to be ferried away in a supercar. He always wore a Teazers shirt and stopped for an interview. It was always about the brand and he never missed an opportunity to be in front of the cameras.

In 2005, Jackson was arrested for driving his Lamborghini Gallardo at 249km/h on the N3 highway. At the time, he said he was running late for church. In 2008, he was arrested on charges of contravening the

Immigration Act in connection with the falsification of visas for European strippers and released on R7000 bail. Jackson believed the charges were trumped up and part of a conspiracy against him. In February 2010 he was again arrested for speeding. This time he claimed he was rushing to hospital after trying to save the severed leg of a motorbike crash victim.

In February 2010, the 53-year-old pleaded guilty to a charge of intent to cause grievous bodily harm for shooting a staff member with a paintball gun. He was fined R20 000 as part of a plea-bargain agreement. He was also convicted of instructing someone to 'moer' another black employee in 2007, in an apparent racist attack. I was investigating several of these claims at the time and recall being shown photographs of employees with welts on their skin from the paintball bullets. To Jackson, it was all hilarious and simply his way of handling his uppity staff.

The strip club tycoon was also arrested in February 2010 on charges of crimen injuria, kidnapping and extortion. The charges were related to his feud with Kensington pawn dealer Michael Kalymnios, who had fallen in love with a Ukrainian dancer, Yuliana Moshorovs'ka. Kalymnios claimed that Jackson wanted him to pay R50 000 to date the 23-year-old dancer. The money was to cover the visa, accommodation and flights, and when Kalymnios didn't pay up, Jackson acted.

Despite all this, Jackson described himself as 'a good oke'. He knew how to play the game and how to play the media.

Despite his abrasive nature, some who knew him best still described Jackson as something of a softy. So when Sean Newman found himself down and out, desperately looking for a job, Jackson threw him a lifeline and became a father figure. Newman would become the spokesperson for Teazers.

We're sitting at a table at Tashas restaurant in Bedfordview, the beating heart of the neighbourhood. It's midweek and Newman is in tracksuit pants and a T-shirt, a luxury of being his own boss now. He ran a massage parlour around the corner from Krejcir's Money Point shop for a few years and organised the Sexpo exhibition in South Africa. Now the massage parlour has been transformed into a popular children's restaurant and playground.

'So I sent in my CV and I walked in and my first encounter with Lolly Jackson was him screaming and shouting in his office, throwing things around and the managers just sitting there wide-eyed watching him,' Newman laughs.

He took a job in the office alongside Jackson's financial manager Ricardo Fabre and PA Robyn Teixeira. One of Newman's first jobs was dealing with the media fallout from a billboard Jackson had erected that read 'No need for gender testing' at a time when athlete Caster Semenya was in the headlines.

Newman is quick to regale me with stories about working for Lolly. He even wrote a book about his former boss's murder and evidently has an emotional connection to the man. A portion of his life was defined by the events surrounding Jackson and, in a way, Newman has been vicariously living through those experiences.

'He was either in an incredibly good mood or incredibly bad. You could trigger his bad mood by saying "SARS". Literally, four letters could send him off the cliff. You could just talk about the dreaded SARS virus and he would just hear that word and that would trigger him. Or he could be incredibly fun.'

Of course, Newman was under no illusion that his employer was an angel. He realised quickly that laws were being bent, if not outright broken.

'It was all money laundering. You can't hide it when he's asking Ricardo to find out the US$ rate. Eventually, when he's happy with the rate, he's gonna phone Ricardo and say, "Okay, there's a million dollars coming into the account," and Ricardo would be like, "Okay, fine." Instantly after that transfer had been made, you'd see a whole bunch of cheques being written, go out and then people would start arriving at the office. Michael Arsiotis would pitch up and we all know now that he was Radovan's 2IC at that stage. He would arrive and there'd be Globe Flight bags of R200 notes. He would take those bags and stuff them so that they were a solid brick of cash.'

Newman also suspected that some of the nefarious and unsavoury characters his boss was interacting with weren't entirely in step with the law. 'Lolly never closed the door to his office. He was brash, he was loud, he was

51

open; he didn't care who knew what, but if Radovan Krejcir walked into that office, that door closed. It was the only time that door closed.'

He distinctly recalls the first occasion he met Krejcir.

'So this guy arrived. Now I'd met him with Michael Arsiotis before, I just didn't know who he was. He walked in and he asked for a lighter. I handed him one. He was in a white shirt, jeans. What struck me straight off the bat was that he was the first visitor who greeted Ricardo and greeted Robyn. We would have attorneys walk in and they would be so rude to Robyn and be like, "Go get me a toothpick. I need to pull the pubes out of my mouth after lunch!" They had just gone downstairs and were crude because they were in a strip club. They thought they didn't have to act professionally. Radovan was the very first person to walk in, greet Ricardo like an old friend, give Robyn a kiss on each cheek and walk up to me and say, "You're new. Who you? My name's Radovan Krejcir. How you? Nice to meet you,"' Newman mimics in a bad imitation of a Czech accent.

'It shocked me because it was such a disparity between the local guys like bank managers and lawyers. The only other person who I met who was friendly was Ian Jordaan [Jackson's lawyer]. Everyone else seemed to think the moment you walk into a strip club you can be a pig.'

It was only once Krejcir had introduced himself that Newman's colleague pointed out who the visitor was.

According to Newman, the celebrity gangster would occasionally pop into Teazers, but relatively rarely. 'He went to poker quite often with Lolly at Midrand on a Tuesday night. Him and Lolly would go for lunch quite often. On Sundays they'd literally go race each other. Radovan recounts how they'd go towards Hartbeespoort neck and neck, and he said that that old man had the biggest balls he'd ever come across in life because Lolly would drive on the wrong side of the road and would not back off for anyone or anything, until he got in front of Radovan and he beat him.'

It wasn't long, Newman says, before he and his colleagues in the Teazers office began to feel uneasy about the relationship. They got the sense that Jackson was being led astray. Krejcir was masterfully using Jackson's own weaknesses against him.

'Lolly was a big fish in a small pond in South Africa. He had so much money he could beat everyone financially and here this dollar billionaire walked in because that's how he was sold, as a dollar billionaire. I think it became competitive because there was somebody with more money, more clout,' Newman surmises.

Newman seems deflated and expels a deep breath. He recalls how Ricardo predicted how things would play out.

'Ricardo would start telling me things, you know, like, "He's doing things that he shouldn't be doing. That Radovan connection is going to be the death of Lolly because he's becoming something he's not; he's trying too hard to live up to him."'

Fabre's words did indeed turn out to be frighteningly prophetic.

Some say he's a white knight vigilante, a public hero, self-appointed defender of justice. Others are less complimentary, describing him as an anarchist, a foreign spy, a lunatic or just plain mad. Paul O'Sullivan prefers to be referred to as a forensic consultant rather than as a private investigator. I like to call him The Cop Hunter because that is what he is renowned for doing – ensnaring top police officers who have indulged their venality, who have displayed a nauseating level of greed and hubris.

O'Sullivan is credited with bringing down the world's top policeman, Jackie Selebi, by meticulously building a case of corruption against him, tracking down witnesses and interviewing them personally, and bombarding Selebi and his allies with a deluge of abusive emails in CAPITAL LETTERS. For this, O'Sullivan has achieved public notoriety.

He is seen as a keeper of the law that society must turn to when the state fails to act against its own, a balding superhero in a baggy black suit, his Big Five animal-print tie flapping in the wind and his spectacles resting on his forehead like a mask.

However, most of the public who praise him for his successes are not entirely aware of O'Sullivan's methodology and approach to his cases. He stretches the boundaries of the law, careful never to break them. He is in your face, aggressive, rude and combative. Essentially, a bully. But, importantly, he gets the job done.

This methodology came under the spotlight in court with several cases of extortion being levelled against the PI. His accusers, mainly role players in previous cases he has investigated, have claimed that O'Sullivan effectively extorted them by using their own accounts against them and taking on their opponents as clients.

In one specific case, he was accused of threatening, intimidating and kidnapping Cora van der Merwe from her office at law firm Ronald Bobroff & Partners in October 2016. He was found not guilty of kidnapping, extortion and intimidation.

O'Sullivan maintains that these allegations are no more than an attempt to prevent him from carrying out his work: exposing corruption amongst the top echelons of the police.

While some have questions about where exactly his funding comes from and the motives that drive his selective investigations, O'Sullivan has always insisted that he is entirely self-funded and that he pursues corrupt officials out of a sense of duty to the country.

Born in Ireland as the son of a policeman, he was always told by his father that if a country was worth living in, then it was worth fighting for. It is this dogma that has always driven the Roman Catholic Irishman. He qualified as an engineer, but O'Sullivan has spent the bulk of his life working in law enforcement. While he has been labelled a foreign spy working for MI6 or the Czech intelligence authorities, that is not quite the truth.

O'Sullivan has admitted spending time in law enforcement agencies in the UK, the US, Cyprus and South Africa. He has also said that he worked for the British government in the field of counter-terrorism and espionage for six years but he cannot discuss the work he did for them because he is bound by a contract.

He moved to Johannesburg in 1989 and bought a house, ironically, in Bedfordview. O'Sullivan began to develop properties locally but he also took on a series of corporate jobs. At one point he was the MD of the Randburg Waterfront.

On the side, the Irishman sought out a way to use his law enforcement experience to the benefit of his new home country. He enlisted as a police reservist at Halfway House, now Midrand, and got to work cracking big fraud cases, amongst others. He had a prolific career as a reservist, training recruits at the Police Reserve College and making high-profile arrests. He also made sure he hit the road working the beat, and one night while patrolling on the East Rand, he was shot three times by hijackers. He still walks with a limp and suffers from chronic back pain as a result of his wounds.

O'Sullivan's life was altered by an experience he had at OR Tambo International Airport one morning in March 2000 when returning from an exhibition in Berlin. A thief tried to make off with O'Sullivan's suitcase but he had targeted the wrong guy outside the airport that morning. True to form, the Irishman chased him down, arrested him and frogmarched him to the charge office inside the terminal. As a result of this encounter, O'Sullivan requested a transfer to the SAPS office at the airport. He recruited dozens of other reservists to join him and began to make a sizeable dent in crime at the national keypoint. Ultimately, he landed up being employed by the Airports Company South Africa (ACSA) as its head of security.

It was in this role that O'Sullivan's path first crossed that of then National Police Commissioner Jackie Selebi. When Selebi attempted to prevent O'Sullivan from cancelling a R130-million contract with ACSA's ineffective security providers, the head of security smelt a rat and set his sights on the top cop. The result, after years and years, was that O'Sullivan uncovered a deeply corrupt relationship between Selebi and a network of organised criminals.

A decade later, Selebi went on trial in the High Court in Johannesburg, charged with corruption and taking bribes from his friend, 'finished and klaar' Glenn Agliotti.

I sat on the hard benches of courtroom 4B watching aghast as a parade of witnesses testified about envelopes stuffed with cash being handed over in boardrooms, lavish shopping sprees to fancy stores in Sandton City and dinners with controversial captains of industry the Kebbles. For a journalist, hearing this kind of testimony first-hand about the country's most senior policeman left me cold. How rotten was the SAPS, if the very head could be compromised to this extent? What kind of culture was there in the organisation?

What my colleagues and I didn't realise at the time was that what we were hearing about was the early onset of state capture. The Kebbles, through their consigliere Glenn Agliotti, had captured the country's police service, specifically the police commissioner. Selebi was beholden to the Kebbles, making himself available to the family at their homes in Illovo and Inanda for dinners with influential business people. He was also at their beck and call when they needed problems with the police or SARS sorted out.

This is precisely what the Gupta family would do a decade later on a far grander scale. The Kebble and Selebi relationship should have served as a forewarning of what would come from the Guptas and the concept of 'state capture' that would delegitimise Jacob Zuma and his government. It should also have served as a canary in the mineshaft for how compromised the country's police service could become and how it could be abused for partisan political gains.

What the Selebi trial did show us was the potential strength of the prosecution services and the criminal justice system. It spoke volumes that a trial of this nature was actually being conducted and that witnesses were able to give evidence in open court without intimidation. It showed that if a prominent ANC member with political influence could be charged and convicted, then no one was above the law.

While Jackie Selebi was facing the fight of his life in the courtroom, Tim Williams had taken the fight to the criminals on the streets. Williams was appointed acting commissioner after Selebi was placed on extended leave amidst the corruption allegations.

Williams, a loyal ANC man who spent time in exile, was known to be a steady captain who would be able to right the listing SAPS ship. Calm, measured and level-headed, he had been the head of Crime Intelligence for a period under Selebi. He also had the credentials. When he returned from exile in Botswana, he had been hand-selected to build a democratic police force. Debonair and cultured, Williams was well respected within the organisation, even though there was a belief at the time that he would merely be a stand-in without any real authority as Selebi would continue to hold the reins.

With Williams elevated to the position of acting national commissioner and Mulangi Mphego facing criminal charges, a new head of Crime Intelligence had to be found. So it was that on 1 July 2009, Richard Mdluli was appointed head of the police's Crime Intelligence unit, a significant development in the battle for control of the intelligence forces.

Mdluli was a career policeman. He joined the force in 1979, at the age of 21. During apartheid, he was part of the notorious Special Branch, the unit responsible for a litany of politically driven cases. Mdluli could have been involved in arresting, torturing and interrogating anti-apartheid activists. Rising through the ranks, he was appointed to command the detective branch in Vosloorus, near Boksburg on the East Rand, between 1979 and 1999. He then became deputy head of the Gauteng police, preceding Joey Mabasa as Gauteng's head of Crime Intelligence.

Mabasa, who lives and breathes surveillance, doesn't believe Mdluli knew anything about the intelligence field.

'I think he is not an intelligence person, he is a detective. So that faction in the ANC brought him to Intelligence. He didn't understand the culture of Crime Intelligence, so when he found out there was a lot of money around in the slush fund, he became tempted.'

Red flags were immediately raised about Mdluli's appointment, suggesting that it was irregular and political in nature. This was because the normal process was not followed. Instead, Mdluli was elevated by a panel of cabinet ministers who allegedly 'hijacked' the appointment process.

In an exclusive interview with *City Press* in April 2011, Williams hit out at Police Minister Nathi Mthethwa and three other ministers who served on a panel that appointed Mdluli. He described the appointment as politically motivated, calling it 'completely unusual' and 'not regular'. The three other ministers on the panel included then Minister of State Security Siyabonga Cwele, then Minister of Public Enterprises Malusi Gigaba and then Deputy Minister of Safety and Security Susan Shabangu.

Williams told the newspaper that it was not normal that this process be carried out in such a manner. 'The normal process would involve the commissioner, deputy national commissioners and the deputy minister.'

Despite this, according to Williams, he was 'instructed' by Mthethwa that a 'special' ministerial panel would interview Mdluli and make a recommendation.

'At the time, there were a lot of arguments about this between myself and the minister [Mthethwa]. I was completely opposed to it,' said Williams. 'They couldn't give me a reason why there was such a special panel to appoint an officer. I asked for reasons why he was appointed differently and they wouldn't give me any reasons.'

Williams was extremely concerned that 'not one public servant was on the panel'. Asked by *City Press* whether Mdluli's appointment had been politically motivated, Williams said: 'I regarded it as such at the time. He was appointed by the minister.'

Senior Institute for Security Studies researcher and former police officer Johan Burger told *City Press* at the time that if Mdluli's appointment had, in fact, been made by a panel of cabinet ministers, it was a clear case of political interference and was tantamount to a political appointment. 'If a panel of ministers was involved it would be an exception to the rule. It is unacceptable. It sends only one message: that politicians want to ensure that a person who is politically acceptable to them is appointed. Then it would seem the head of Crime Intelligence was appointed not for policing purposes, but for other purposes,' said Burger.

The minister's spokesperson confirmed to *City Press* that the panel had made the recommendation, but stated that this was not an unusual process and that the appointment was in no way political. Officials gave an assurance that the process was done 'transparently and above board, and there was no haphazard process of arriving at a decision hastily'.

The reason there was so much concern around whether Mdluli's appointment was political was because of the massive amount of influence wielded by the person who heads the police's intelligence capabilities. The Crime Intelligence unit is responsible for all things clandestine, including the secret gathering of information, the surveillance of criminals, the bugging of phones and spying. By virtue of its very nature, it must operate in the shadows and is often left to its own devices on a need-to-know basis. It employs sources and informants, and frequently their identities have to be kept anonymous. This means that there must be an enormous degree of trust. At the same time, the process can also be open to gross abuse.

In March 2012, in a move that upped the stakes even higher, government decided that the police's VIP Protection Unit would also fall under Crime Intelligence. The VIP section is responsible for protecting and transporting all very important persons, including the president, deputy president and cabinet ministers. By implication, this meant that Crime Intelligence officials would have direct knowledge of who meets who where and what they are talking about. This could be dangerously manipulated by one faction against another in pursuit of political goals.

It is because of these high stakes that there has been so much consternation and concern about the integrity of Richard Mdluli. Occasionally, a character emerges in the media who takes on the form of a bogeyman, a pariah who is the embodiment of fear and evil in the minds of the public. To a degree, General Richard Mdluli came to fill this role in South Africa during his years at the helm of the unit.

In the same month that Mdluli was appointed as head of CI, the Directorate for Priority Crime Investigation, known as the Hawks, was set up to replace the defunct Scorpions. There were immediately concerns about how independent this unit would really be.

The Scorpions, defined by its troika-style investigations that saw prosecutors being coupled with detectives, had been firmly located within the National Prosecuting Authority. It was entirely separate from the police and this proved to underline its independence from any kind of political influence. It was precisely this independence that raised the ire of politicians.

The DPCI, aka the Hawks, was situated within the SAPS, not the NPA, leading to concerns that the unit could and would be manipulated and influenced by the police, throttling any independence. Civilian activist and businessman Hugh 'Bob' Glenister had spearheaded a legal campaign to save the Scorpions from being killed. Having failed in that impassioned bid, he then led the charge to the Constitutional Court to ensure the Hawks would enjoy the same freedom as its predecessor. His application to the Constitutional Court resulted in a ruling that sections of the Act that disbanded the Scorpions and created the Hawks were inconsistent with the Constitution. The Constitutional Court ordered that chapter 6A of the South African Police Service Act of 1995 be sent back to parliament until it had been rectified. The order of constitutional invalidity was suspended for 18 months.

Glenister's court battle involved numerous rounds of legal skirmishes and, in 2014, the Helen Suzman Foundation (HSF) also went to the

Constitutional Court in a further attempt to ensure the independence of the unit. Glenister and the HSF wanted to ensure the Hawks would be separated from the police, who they claimed were corrupt and compromised the investigative unit's independence.

The Court agreed with most of the Foundation's argument and emphasised the need for an independent anti-corruption unit.

'All South Africans across the racial, religious, class and political divide are in broad agreement that corruption is rife in this country, and that stringent measures are required to contain this malady before it graduates into something terminal,' read the majority judgment. 'We are in one accord that South Africa needs an agency dedicated to the containment and eventual eradication of the scourge of corruption. We also agree that that entity must enjoy adequate structural and operational independence to deliver effectively and efficiently on its core mandate. And this in a way is the issue that lies at the heart of this matter.'

Judge Edwin Cameron summed up the risk for anti-corruption institutions located within government departments. 'The more the institution's mandate threatens political office bearers, the greater is the risk of political weight being brought to bear on its appointments. Where the institution's core mandate is to investigate crime committed by political office bearers, the risk may become severe.'

What this all meant was that as long as the Hawks were headed by someone who had impeccable integrity and was profoundly honest, then the unit would be able to pursue all-powerful politicians who were corrupt or business people with far-reaching influence. It also meant that those most at threat also had the most to gain by ensuring that someone pliable became the head of the Hawks.

Both the appointment of Mdluli and the establishment of the Hawks took place in July 2009, a time of turmoil in the SAPS. Just one month later, in August, a gale-force wind of change blew into Wachthuis. The swashbuckling, big-talking KwaZulu-Natal politician Bheki Cele was appointed police commissioner in place of Jackie Selebi. Cops were told to shoot to kill. Morale was through the roof in the SAPS but in Mdluli's Crime Intelligence unit, the looting was in full rampage.

Seeing Jackie Selebi go on trial was a resounding victory for Paul O'Sullivan but he couldn't sit idle as the case unfolded in Judge Meyer Joffe's courtroom. So he took down the spider organograms that had been tacked up on his office walls in Sandton and replaced them with new ones – these had the name 'Radovan Krejcir' marked in the middle.

Just two days after Jackie Selebi went on trial in the High Court on 5 October 2009, Paul O'Sullivan received word from one of his closely guarded sources, whom he had code-named CS7, that there was trouble brewing.

He explained that private-investigator-cum-intelligence-operative Kevin Trytsman had confronted him in the parking lot of a supermarket and threatened him. Trytsman had allegedly told the source that he was working closely with top intelligence officials at the time, Moe Shaik and Gibson Njenje, and they were going to shut down the Selebi trial. Trytsman was known for throwing around names of high-ranking intelligence players and claiming he was working for the NIA, but the veracity of these claims was often in question. O'Sullivan knew this, of course.

'I had certain state witnesses lined up that were going to give evidence against Selebi. I kept the witnesses close to my chest, only myself and Gerrie Nel and Andrew Leask [the prosecuting team] knew of their existence. Then it became apparent that the witnesses were being contacted by Kevin Trytsman,' O'Sullivan recalls.

We're sitting in the boardroom at his headquarters in a boomed-off suburban neighbourhood in Sandton. It's quiet and residential. He once, for a short time, counted EFF commander-in-chief Julius Malema amongst his neighbours. Driving by the house, you would probably do a double take when you saw a large satellite mast reaching out from behind the high walls and a bank of CCTV cameras pointing in every direction. You would wonder, 'Who lives there?'

On the table in the entrance are small plastic containers of nail clippings with handwritten labels scrawled on them, no doubt evidence from some forensic investigation O'Sullivan is currently conducting. On the wall, there's the black-and-white framed image of a large forensic fingerprint that once hung in Radovan Krejcir's Kloof Road mansion. Considering O'Sullivan has always denied having bought the house on auction, I raise my eyebrows when I see so obvious an indicator of the truth holding pride of place in his office. In the boardroom, there are various framed news-paper clippings cataloguing the investigator's career of bringing down corrupt policemen, rhino poachers and other criminals. The articles about Selebi enjoy prominence. The whiteboards flanking the room are covered in keywords and spider diagrams, each one revealing the tentacles of an organised crime network or fraud syndicate. Most, though, feature the names of top police officers and their relationships with bad guys.

O'Sullivan is rushing between meetings and tells me at regular inter-vals how he doesn't have enough time, how he's spent so much of his own money on these investigations and how sore his back is. He is also extremely generous with his information and keeps shooting off emails to me with various affidavits and letters attached. He is clearly very proud of what he has achieved.

He rocks back in his chair and resumes his story about Trytsman. He pronounces 'Trytsman' oddly with an Afrikaans rolling of the 'r' and over-accentuating the first syllable. It's a sound that sticks in my mind as he goes on.

'Kevin Trytsman didn't work for NIA. He told people he was NIA. In fact, the number plate on his car was NIA 001 or something. The whole thing was fake. Kevin Trytsman was nothing more than a criminal. He and I had an exchange in 2009 and he threatened me and I told him I will deal with him. I had a whole exchange of SMSes with him where he threatened me with a guy at NIA who was the godfather of his child or whatever and I told him to get lost. What happened is he approached a particular state witness and told him he was under surveillance and it would be in his best interest not to give evidence against Selebi. Then that state witness was picked up by Richard Mdluli and at that stage Mdluli's offices [were] in Braamfontein. Mdluli was then head of Crime Intelligence for Gauteng. After Mphego left, he became head of Crime Intelligence for the whole country and Mabasa took over in Gauteng.

'I confronted him at the Spar in Bedfordview on the corner of Nicol and Van Buuren. I saw his car go past me and I turned and followed him. He parked and went into the Spar. I waited until he had his hands full of shopping and I just walked up to him. I told him he is getting himself into a whole heap of shit and, the way I have it, he threatened this witness and then this witness had been arrested by Mdluli and taken to Mdluli's offices in Braamfontein and told that it would be in his best interest not to have any further communication with me and definitely not to have anything to do with the Scorpions. They said they will be monitoring him and if he would have any communication with me or with the Scorpions, he would be in trouble. Now that particular person had been involved with prior criminal conduct, not of a violent or serious nature – relating to tax fraud and money laundering. That person made contact with me and met with me to tell me what happened. I shared it with Leask and Nel, but the effect of it was that that witness was of no use any more.'

O'Sullivan's tactics worked and he got Trytsman to agree to leave his witnesses alone. 'He agreed because he realised he was going to be in trouble. I dug up his past and told him I was going to publish all of that against him. Nobody knew of Trytsman. No newspaper would've bothered to publish it because it wasn't of any relevance.'

At the same time, O'Sullivan was busy with a separate investigation into none other than Lolly Jackson, probing the links between Teazers and human trafficking.

'I was involved with an organisation called Spotlight, which is a global organisation where we put focus on people involved in human trafficking and we expose them. So I had taken a decision in 2008 already to expose Lolly Jackson for being involved in human trafficking. I got sworn statements from a Bulgarian guy. He was a human trafficker in Johannesburg, but he is gone now because I scared the crap out of him. He had street men in places like Sofia and Varna in Bulgaria. What he would do, his street men would entice young girls – one of the girls was 18 – this guy would walk around the streets and see a good-looking chick and invite her for coffee and tell her that he might have a job for her, involving being a waitress in a nightclub in South Africa. It was like a nibbling process.'

As O'Sullivan explains, the recruiter would tell the girl she would have to pay over R50 000 to get the job. She would not have that kind of money, so the man would offer to 'lend' her the money and she could repay it once she had started working in South Africa. She would have to pay the money to a proxy in Johannesburg, who would have a photograph of her so he could recognise her when she stepped off the plane from Bulgaria.

'And then Jackson would keep these girls. They'll get three months on their passport and then he would take a whole batch of these passports down to the Swaziland border and they would all leave the country – of course, only the passports – so they would go out at the Swaziland border and then a guy would be paid R50 per passport. The guy will spend the night in Swaziland and come back and get it stamped. This is how corruption and crime works; whether you have cops on your payroll or immigration officers, that's how it works.'

So O'Sullivan started digging deeper into the link between Kevin Trytsman and Lolly Jackson. In fact, it was the source 'CS7' who brought him the most interesting info, tipping O'Sullivan off about a Cypriot banker called Alekos Panayi who knew about a money-laundering scheme involving the Teazers boss. O'Sullivan had similar information from another source.

'I had built some houses in Bedfordview because that is my main business, property development. I built and sold six houses in Bedfordview for a couple of million each. I sold one of them to a Lebanese guy. He advised me that he gets a big bag of money from Lolly Jackson and gets an instruction to hand the bag of money to Radovan Krejcir a few days later. He told me that the middleman involved in the process was Alex Panayi.'

O'Sullivan found the banker, sat him down, and in his expert manner, drew the truth from him. 'I debriefed him for about three days from morning to evening. That culminated in a very detailed sworn statement from him. What was of interest in Panayi's statement is that it makes it crystal clear, all the money laundering with Jackson and Radovan Krejcir.'

Five days later, another incident occurred that jolted O'Sullivan's path towards Krejcir. 'Then what happened, Trytsman was shot and that really pissed me off,' O'Sullivan says, clearly irritated.

I was in the newsroom at EWN when I got the call that Kevin Trytsman had been shot in lawyer George Michaelides's office in Bedford Centre. I had vaguely heard of Trytsman and knew he was on the periphery of the so-called underworld. I raced from Sandton and got onto the N3 towards the east, tore through the Gilloolys interchange and parked on the 'old' side of the shopping centre. Michaelides's office was in the office tower, through a manned security boom, hidden alongside a hardware store. Somehow, despite the police officers milling around, I made it through the boom, up the lift to the eighth floor and into the passage outside the office. That's about as far as the cops would let a nosy journalist go. I couldn't see much besides the police tape and all I knew was that Michaelides was saying that he shot Trytsman in self-defence.

O'Sullivan, convinced that it was murder and not self-defence, began to sniff around Trytsman's death.

'I had several meetings with Michaelides and my meetings were more to find out about the shooting of Trytsman. In August 2011 I was approached by a client who had placed R20 million in Michaelides's trust account and couldn't get Michaelides to give the money back. The client produced a whole lot of documents, including court orders and stuff. When I went to the court with the case numbers, they were false. Michaelides was forging documents; he sent the client bank statements showing how much money [was] in the trust account for that client. What I did was I got one of the staff members in Michaelides's offices and I went to see her at her home where she confessed that Michaelides had forged all the documents. I then phoned Michaelides and told him, because I wanted my client's money back, that he had 48 hours to put the money on the table and if he didn't we were going to open a criminal docket. So he left the next day.'

Michaelides fled to Australia. But O'Sullivan wasn't finished. He managed to establish that until he was shot, Trytsman was being paid R50 000 per month by Michaelides.

It also emerged that George Louca was at Michaelides's office not long after Trytsman was killed. O'Sullivan did not think this was a coincidence, although the office is less than a minute's walk from the centre's Harbour restaurant. Michaelides also told the PI that Louca had walked into the offices and congratulated him and then invited him to lunch with Krejcir because he wanted to 'show his appreciation' for killing Trytsman.

'It was murder; we know it was murder because Trytsman is a con-man and what he had been doing is squeezing Radovan Krejcir,' explains O'Sullivan. 'He got R500 000 out of Radovan Krejcir. Between 2007 and 2009 this guy convinced Radovan Krejcir that he was with National Intelligence, which he wasn't. He convinced Radovan Krejcir that he would look after him and that he wouldn't get into trouble or be deported.'

O'Sullivan quickly realised there was a new gangster in town, one who needed his full attention. 'My focus was on Lolly Jackson, but it became clear to me that what the fuck is this Radovan Krejcir up to, so I started looking into him. I had heard about him. In fact, it's quite interesting because he wanted a meeting with me to hire me. That would've probably been sometime around 2008. When I did my due diligence, I just said no. We don't have clients like that.'

While the PI kept one eye on the Selebi trial in the High Court, he busied himself gathering evidence as part of his new investigation, which he labelled 'Czechmate'. In *To Catch a Cop*, written by Marianne Thamm in 2014, O'Sullivan perfectly describes his thoughts on his new target, stating that Krejcir 'made Glenn Agliotti look like a spoilt poodle and, if the Czech who was out on bail after applying for refugee status, were to remain inside South Africa, he would present a bigger threat to national security than the corrupt Jackie Selebi. Radovan Krejcir was an unwelcome guest, and the sooner he left the country, the better.'

As 2009 rolled towards its close, O'Sullivan was sitting with an explosive affidavit from the banker Alekos Panayi and alarm bells were ringing around Trytsman's death. He thought it was time to begin moving on Krejcir. 'I met with Radovan Krejcir and I told him things were closing in on him and it would be time for him to come clean. I met with him again in February and March 2010,' he explains. Then he stepped up the pressure and brought in the cops. Who did O'Sullivan turn to? The head of Crime Intelligence in the province, General Joey Mabasa.

'I made the mistake of sitting with Joey Mabasa, not knowing that Joey Mabasa was in business with Radovan Krejcir,' O'Sullivan seems to admonish himself, as if he should have known better. 'Joey Mabasa contacted *me*, by the way. I never contacted him. He told me he was very happy with the work I did with Jackie Selebi and he was very happy for the country. Of course, I now realise he was blowing smoke up my backside. He told me that he understood I was investigating other links with Selebi and he would like to help me.'

O'Sullivan took Mabasa into his confidence and told him about the Panayi statement. He had already given the original to the head of the Hawks, Anwa Dramat. He then sent the affidavit to Mabasa.

'I emailed the sworn statement to him because he asked me to supply it to him so I had a trail to prove that I have given it to him. About two weeks later, probably towards the end of March, he asked for a meeting again and we met at Melrose Arch at JB's Corner. During our discussion we said it must be agreed that he won't tell anyone he was meeting with me and I won't tell anyone that I was meeting with him.'

O'Sullivan believes he gave too much away. He made a revelation to the cop that might have set off a series of underworld murders and saw the bodies begin to pile up.

'I supplied him with further information regarding Lolly Jackson and I also told him that I'd met with Lolly earlier in the week and Lolly was indicating that he might come clean and tell us everything about human trafficking and the underworld and money laundering and everything. So now I had just told Radovan Krejcir's partner in crime, who is a general in charge of Crime Intelligence, that Lolly Jackson is probably going to come clean.'

According to O'Sullivan, that may have been Lolly Jackson's death knell. He believes Mabasa went straight to Krejcir with the information and Jackson was taken out before he could flip against the Czech.

CORRUPTION IS WOVEN INTO SOUTH AFRICA'S SOCIAL FABRIC. IT is familiar, ubiquitous and sadly deemed acceptable on many levels of our society.

It is not unusual for a metro police officer pulling over a motorist to request 'cooldrink money' or 'tjo-tjo'. It is also not uncommon for an official at a licensing department to request cash to pass someone attempting to get their driver's licence. It is this kind of endemic, low-level corruption that has resulted in South Africans' perceptions that corruption is on the increase.

So when news broke on the front page of the *Mail & Guardian* in 2010 that Gauteng's head of Crime Intelligence, Joey Mabasa, was allegedly in a cosy and corrupt business relationship with a Czech mobster and fugitive from justice, it should not have come as a surprise to the South African public. Yet, despite the context – and bearing in mind that at this point in time, the country's national police commissioner was on trial for corruption of a remarkably similar nature – the revelations about the Mabasa–Krejcir relationship still caused a scandal.

The investigative reporting unit amaBhungane revealed that Krejcir's wife Katerina and Mabasa's wife Dorcas were directors of a shared company, Radlochron. According to official records, the company was established in October 2009. At the time, Krejcir claimed that the link between the two women was entirely innocent and that the company never traded. The Czech told the *New Age* newspaper that lawyer Ian Small-Smith had introduced him to Mabasa because he was terrified of being killed or kidnapped by Czech secret agents. 'I needed a contact in the police to help me secure my safety in the country. Joey is a good policeman who was always prepared to help me if I felt my life was threatened,' he told journalist De Wet Potgieter.

Mabasa's explanation is that he and Dorcas had separated and he was not even aware that his estranged wife was involved in the business.

But it was as though a scab had been picked. The disclosure of this dubious business relationship triggered a procession of allegations about the nature of the relationship between the two men, as well as claims of corrupt payments.

Milosh Potiska, the Czech who wrote the tell-all book about working for Krejcir, said that as a consequence of his time in South Africa, he had intimate knowledge of some of his criminal dealings. He laid bare the details of the capture of the cops, from low-level station constables to high-ranking commissioners.

> I think Krejcir had a 'secret' number for Mabasa. Every time Krejcir arranged to meet Mabasa, Michael Arsiotis, who was one of Krejcir's associates, would pick Mabasa up from a small Shell garage near Eastgate on his way to the meeting place at Krejcir's house. Mabasa would lie down in the car and the car would be driven up the driveway at 54A Kloof Road and into the garage, with the lights off, before Mabasa would climb out unseen. Mabasa and Krejcir would have their meeting inside the house, on the balcony in the dark and in secret. I have witnessed this personally on two occasions, but I cannot say for sure when this was. The times I was there I would see Krejcir give Mabasa money but I don't know how much, usually R5000 to R10 000 in the case of senior police officers.

Potiska claims that the corruption extended beyond Mabasa and that there were many other police officers on the payroll.

> There were many other Bedfordview policemen that I paid on instruction from Krejcir. If I remember correctly, they were all black police officials. I don't know the names of these policemen. One day I saw Krejcir pay Colonel Sambo, who is a police officer at the Bedfordview station. Krejcir paid Sambo for 'little jobs'. He just wanted Sambo to notify him if anything was going to happen that involved Krejcir in the area.
>
> Krejcir would meet other cops at the Chinese restaurant at Bruma

Market in Johannesburg, and inside this restaurant there are private sections. The owner knew us and I recall rotating serving dishes. These were the cops that were supposed to be investigating Krejcir. Krejcir would meet these men inside this small area in the restaurant, and each time Krejcir would tell me to prepare cash, R5000 and R5000, or just one R5000, depending on if it was two or one cop for the meeting. I carried it and Krejcir would tell me to hand it to him and I would do this and then he would pay the money to the cops. Krejcir would also meet a small guy, with one gold tooth, who worked at the Narcotics Section of the Provincial Office. This guy would wear the same cap every time they met.

Potiska elaborates on the corrupt meetings that allegedly went on in Bedfordview.

Mabasa was really a big boss with the police in Johannesburg. I sometimes drove him from secret appointments he had with Radek [Radovan]. I can remember him well. Mabasa was as black as coal. Just as his conscience. On his big head you could distinguish just the eyes, which only flashed when he was counting bank notes. I imagined him as Uncle Scrooge, from whose eyes pictures of dollars shot out in Duck Tales. From this man's eyes South African rands shot out. I've known dozens of corrupt cops in my life. But this one was not of the garden variety. He took handfuls of dough. And he didn't care who and where the person was going to end up because of him. Mabasa was the first high-ranking policeman who Radek twisted around his little finger. When I was driving him from Radek's residence, he never said a word. He was just quiet, breathing heavily in the back seat.

Mabasa strongly denies Potiska's account and says this incident never occurred.

An intelligence source, who spoke to me on condition of anonymity, paints an alarming picture of the network of cops that Krejcir allegedly managed to build around him. His Money Point offices in Bedfordview served as a cash takeaway spot for cops hungry for money.

'The Bedfordview cops used to pull in there to collect their money in the mornings. They used to just rock up there. Detectives and uniform cops. They would drive into Money Point and walk out with envelopes. There would be a couple of them. There would be four or five on a shift that would pull in there during the day. They would make sure he knew anything that was taking place in Bedfordview.

'It starts off with "Ja, my brother, come have lunch" and you sit and chat for lunch and it's a couple of hundred: "Go buy Nando's for supper tonight." It starts off like that. One of the guys working for him will know one of the cops, asks him to pop around with a problem, someone is bothering him, needs some advice from the police, they'll come in, it starts with lunch, go buy supper, go buy your wife dinner tonight.'

A sworn statement signed in May 2011 by an investigator attached to the Hawks anti-corruption unit, published in part by the *Mail & Guardian*, revealed further details of the mutually beneficial relationship between Krejcir and Mabasa.

According to the investigator, Mabasa 'appeared' to have 'acquired' a R300 000 silver Toyota Hilux Double Cab from Krejcir's company, Groep Twee Beleggings, in August 2009 'without paying any money' for it.

The newspaper reported that allegations included that 'Krejcir could call Mabasa if he ever "needed help" and that the Czech provided Mabasa with "information"'. It is claimed that Krejcir introduced Louca to Mabasa (Mabasa claims that it was Louca who introduced him to the Czech). The Hawks investigator also presented circumstantial evidence that rubbished Mabasa's explanation that he was estranged from his wife Dorcas when she went into business with Katerina Krejcirova.

The *Mail & Guardian* reported that the Hawks officer obtained information from the Department of Transport that revealed that Mabasa resubmitted forms on his wife's behalf after she failed to attach a copy of her driver's licence during the transfer of the Hilux in August 2009.

According to the investigators' statement, Mabasa is alleged to have completed the new forms 'using the wife's details, and … attached his driver's licence for change of ownership from Groep Twee to Mrs Mabasa's name'. It adds that bank statements provided no evidence that any payments or monthly instalments on the car were ever made by Joey or Dorcas Mabasa to Groep Twee or to a bank.

Mabasa was not the only high-profile and influential cop that Krejcir had allegedly caught in his net. Colonel Francois Steyn, who headed up the Organised Crime unit in Germiston, under which Bedfordview falls, found himself indebted to the Czech after taking a loan from him under dubious circumstances.

AmaBhungane reported that in January 2010 Steyn had received a loan of R408 000 from Krejcir-linked company Groep Twee Beleggings. Steyn confirmed to reporter Sally Evans that he had taken the loan, but claimed he had not known at the time of Krejcir's connection with Groep Twee. Speaking to amaBhungane in the presence of his attorney, Gary Mazaham, Steyn said the money was part of a 'financial commitment' he had made to Cyril Beeka.

> Steyn said Beeka approached him 'in mid- to late-2009' with an opportunity to get involved in a security company. Steyn said Beeka said he would 'arrange a loan' for him through Groep Twee Beleggings, which would serve as Steyn's share of the start-up capital.
>
> According to the policeman, Beeka also said that he would service the loan 'up until such time that the proposed company is operational and then you can pay back the loan'.
>
> Beeka took the colonel to see a lawyer acting for Groep Twee Beleggings to sign a loan agreement on December 1, 2009. Groep Twee's lawyer agreed on a loan of R300 000 to Steyn. He claims that he assumed the company was a 'loan/investment company' and he 'had no idea and no reason' to think that it belonged to Krejcir or 'to anything bad'.

The colonel says he never actually took any cash as part of the deal. 'I never took possession of the money. I never saw the money. This money, as far as I could gather, was handed to Cyril Beeka. The loan was meant to have been from 1 December 2009, to be repaid on 28 February 2010,' Steyn said. He was found not guilty in an internal disciplinary hearing.

It was becoming increasingly evident that as Krejcir's profile began to rise and his reputation as a crime boss began to grow in Johannesburg, he needed more and more influential cops on his payroll. Cops who were willing to be bribed. They didn't seem hard to find.

First Avenue in Edenvale is a busy suburban road. It runs past Edenvale and Dowerglen high schools, the Edenvale police station and magistrate's court, crosses over Linksfield Road and then two separate lanes become one as it runs down towards Bedfordview and the R24 highway. As the roads converge and the middle island disappears outside the Holy Rosary Primary School's sports fields in Elma Park, there are vendors on the pavement selling hand-crafted metal and beaded ornaments. Directly across from the blue palisade fencing around the school's fields, at 64 First Avenue, is a nondescript house hidden behind a white wall. It has a grey slate roof and burglar bars on the windows. Today it operates as the residence of a law firm and accounting company. Four towering conifer trees in the garden distinguish it from the neighbouring properties, which include a Thai massage parlour, a dentist's rooms and a Montessori pre-school. It's just three houses away from the security boom to the enclosed suburb of Dunvegan. You might have driven past this innocuous house, just a couple of hundred metres from the police station, dozens of times. I know I have.

It is behind these white walls, in the shadow of the tall fir trees, that internationally renowned 'car tuner' Uwe Gemballa was murdered in February 2010. The 55-year-old was celebrated as the world's leading luxury car converter, upgrading high-end vehicles and turning them into supercars with modifications and new parts. He had worked on cars for footballers, movie stars and musicians.

The 'whack house' was rented by Ivan Savov, Radovan Krejcir's business partner, in the name of his company, Scara Technologies. It was in this house that Gemballa was held for several days, his head covered in grey duct tape. His hands were tied behind his body with tape, his feet were bound together. After three days his kidnappers attempted to secure a ransom from his wife, Christiane, in Germany. They put Gemballa on the phone and, speaking in English, he told her to prepare €1 million and he would let her know where to deposit the cash. But he never called her back.

Inside the house on First Avenue, Gemballa's kidnappers sat on his back, forcing every last breath out of his body. The German was starved of oxygen, and died of suffocation. They then wrapped his body in a black plastic bag and secured it with more duct tape. The men tossed him in the boot of a car and drove all the way to western Pretoria where they buried the body in a shallow grave in an old cemetery in Lotus Gardens, near Atteridgeville. Gemballa lay undiscovered for months as the mystery about his disappearance lingered.

It took a combination of German police, Interpol, private investigator Paul O'Sullivan and SAPS Organised Crime Detective Inspector Ludi Schnelle to crack the case.

On 6 February 2010, Gemballa left Germany and travelled via Dubai to South Africa, where he hoped to open a franchise of his company. Business had been slow and he was searching for opportunities to increase revenue. Gemballa had been communicating with a local businessman, 'Jerome Saphire', who was apparently passionate about his cars and was keen on being an importer of his products. Saphire assured Gemballa that he had financial backing for the project and the German was so excited by the prospect that he booked a flight to South Africa.

Gemballa arrived in Johannesburg just after 9pm on an Emirates flight from Dubai on 8 February 2010. He only intended staying for two days and had booked a flight home. CCTV footage in the international arrivals hall shows Gemballa walking into the passport control area at 9:26pm. Waiting for him on the other side was a man dressed in black pants and a black jacket, with a white brimmed hat with a black band. The man was holding a sign.

White Hat had arrived at the airport an hour earlier in a VW Golf GTI, which he parked in the police section at international arrivals. He then met up with a second man and together they walked into a public bathroom. When they emerged from the toilet, they parted ways and White Hat went off to wait for Gemballa. At 9:47pm Gemballa strolled through pushing a trolley, and walked right up to White Hat, who seemed to be holding a sign bearing the car tuner's name. White Hat pushed the trolley to the car and Gemballa accompanied him, appearing not to be in any kind of distress. He got into the VW with White Hat and disappeared. Most likely, he was ferried directly to the whack house in Elma Park.

What Gemballa did not know is that he had been lured to South Africa – and to his death. There was no 'Jerome Saphire'. The emails had been sent by Jerome Safi, one of Krejcir's associates. It didn't take long for the police to work this out and they pulled Safi in for questioning. Krejcir arranged for his lawyer, Ian Small-Smith, to accompany Safi to the police station where he underwent a voice stress test and was shown articles about Krejcir's criminal activities.

Safi had an epiphany; he realised he had been duped, but he knew he could not come clean to the police. His life would be in danger. It took two years before he revealed, in a 2012 affidavit, what he claimed was the truth about how Gemballa landed up in South Africa, doing an about-turn on his earlier version.

Safi moved in the same circles as Lolly Jackson and Krejcir and spent many evenings drinking with them on the deck at the Harbour restaurant. The parties would turn raucous, Krejcir once firing several shots into the air at a New Year's Eve celebration. Safi had worked as a manager for Jackson at the Midrand Teazers and met Krejcir through George Louca. Over time, Safi built up a mutually beneficial relationship with Krejcir by doing odd jobs for him.

One day at the Harbour restaurant, Jackson pointed out Krejcir's white Porsche parked in his VIP parking spot directly outside the restaurant. It was a 911 with a Gemballa conversion kit. Jackson and Krejcir thought there might be a market for the conversions in South Africa and suggested Safi should get in touch with Gemballa to float the idea. They couldn't do it themselves because Gemballa might not want to do business with a strip club owner and a fugitive from justice. But Krejcir offered to back the deal with R100 million and Safi would get a share of the business if he pulled it off.

Safi says that on the night of 8 February he was having a few drinks at the Harbour with Krejcir and some others. They all had big plans to go to The Grand later in the evening, but Safi was anxious about Gemballa's arrival and didn't want to drink in case he had to talk business with the car dealer. After Gemballa's scheduled arrival time, Safi tried to call him, but the phone just rang. He paced up and down on the deck of the restaurant, just metres from Krejcir. Safi asked his girlfriend Tenielle Dippenaar and his uncle Dave to go to the airport and fetch Gemballa, but they were unable to find him. Police would later pick up the girlfriend and uncle on the CCTV footage walking up and down past the international arrivals area.

The following morning Safi tried again to reach Gemballa on his phone but it was switched off. He was growing increasingly anxious. He even tried to contact Gemballa's office in Germany. The other men had been at The Grand until the early hours of the morning but Safi had chosen not to go. He met with Krejcir and Jackson at the Harbour restaurant that morning, but they appeared indifferent and downplayed Gemballa's non-appearance. Krejcir suggested that perhaps he had changed his mind and Safi should not chase him. Safi thought it was a peculiar reaction for a man who had been pushing him to get the German into the country to set up a business. Two days later the police came looking for answers. After that, everything changed between him and Krejcir.

Meanwhile, all the cops had to go on was the call made to Gemballa's wife. The cops triangulated the call to the Dowerglen-Klopperpark area. A prepaid-SIM card had been used. It had only been used to make that single call and the airtime voucher had been bought from the Gardenview Shell garage in Smith Street, right near Bedford Centre. The cops checked the CCTV footage from the Shell garage and could clearly identify a woman in the uniform of the Harbour restaurant running into the shop and purchasing airtime vouchers. A waitress identified herself on the surveillance footage but would only say that a customer had sent her to buy the airtime. She was terrified to reveal any further details but ultimately cooperated and told police that it had been Krejcir's right-hand man, Michael Arsiotis. Arsiotis was with Krejcir and four other men at the Harbour at the time.

The police and Paul O'Sullivan continued to dig for the truth, but it would take months before there was any real breakthrough and the secrets of the nondescript house at 64 First Avenue in Elma Park, opposite Holy Rosary Primary School, were revealed.

WHEN JUAN MEYER PULLS UP AT TONY'S SPAGHETTI GRILL ON his white Harley-Davidson and removes his 'piss-pot' helmet, he is a caricature of the West Rand biker. Meyer is enormous, with muscles bulging, arms hanging wide at his sides. He takes off his Harley-Davidson leather jacket to reveal another Harley-Davidson shirt, its sleeves cut off to the shoulders and buttoned down to his navel. He has large dark tribal tattoos wrapped around his right arm and chest and has thick black rings in each stretched earlobe. He is wearing cowboy boots with a heel, making him appear even larger than he already is. He is also wearing two watches on his arm, one for fashion and one for workouts. He puts his iPhone on the table and I can't help but notice the gold glitter cover. It's a little incongruous. He has glaring open wounds and scabs on the knuckles of both his hands and he is missing a few teeth.

Meyer was born and raised in Welkom. Instead of going to the army when he finished school, he was conscripted into the police force for his computer skills. He ended up staying in the force for eight years before he resigned.

'Due to the unit I was working in, I did a lot of work for the guys at Vlakplaas and the Black Bag Squad,' Meyer explains. The Black Bag Squad, apparently, was responsible for 'taking care of someone', although no one else I've asked is even aware of its existence.

Meyer says he is 'an accountant by trade'. According to his online CV, he studied a BCom in Information Systems at Unisa but did not complete his final year because the material was 'outdated as to what was going on in the industry in the real world' so he decided to go into business instead of finishing his studies.

He says he began working in the medical industry, importing and exporting equipment into Africa, but when he was made an offer to fund a mining project in 1999, he accepted it and his mining career took off. Meyer's main business has been Pan African Refineries (PAR), which operates out of Krugersdorp. He maintains that it has always been above board, operating within the law. Throughout our meeting, I get the sense that Meyer's version of the truth tends to be somewhat embellished, if not entirely distorted.

A former law enforcement officer who investigated Meyer says the biggest challenge with the man is the fact that he mixes a little fact with lots of fiction.

'It is very difficult to attach value to the bits that may be true, especially when the bulk is just nonsense. People like Meyer tend to embroider in a way that elevates themselves in the minds of people. He therefore tends to embellish and refer to things in a manner that is so sensational, that it is difficult to resist believing aspects, or at least convey the allegations – however they may be couched.'

'Basically, up until Krejcir came into my life, I wasn't on the radar of the police or SARS or any politician. I was operating normally,' Meyer insists.

This isn't entirely true. The law enforcement official says PAR was limping along until Meyer started scamming through the refinery. 'He made a lot of money all of a sudden. Because he was open to the underworld, people would bring him stolen, smuggled jewellery and gold, and gold from zama zamas, and legitimise the gold through PAR.'

Meyer explains that he first met Krejcir through his friend Djordje Mihaljevic, who ran the Sandton Gold and Diamond Exchange on Sandton Drive.

I had been to see Mihaljevic once at the Sandton Gold offices on Sandton Drive for a story I was working on. He was charming and slick. He left the country a few years later after his father was kidnapped, tortured, his pelvis and legs broken with hammers, and subsequently died.

Meyer says it was Mihaljevic who introduced him to Krejcir.

'At the time I only heard the name Radovan, I didn't know who he was. So when Radovan told me that he's looking to invest in a few local businesses, I asked him what figure we're talking about. He wanted to buy the controlling shares in my business. I told him that wasn't an option because at that stage I was doing R120 to R150 million a month turnover. I told him I'm running a successful business without his funding, so if he wanted to come on board I would discuss minority shares with him but he needed to come with serious money to buy shares in my business. He was a likeable guy. We started talking and he found out more about my business. I was told Cyril Beeka is involved with him. I knew Cyril Beeka from my police days.'

'Because of my relationship with Cyril, I felt a lot more at ease because although Radovan had all the money that he claimed he had, you do not cross Cyril. Cyril would take Radovan out if he crossed him. If you've ever met Cyril, he didn't talk a lot. He is one of the guys you don't screw around with. If he said he was going to take you out, he took you out.'

According to his version, Meyer struck a deal with the Czech. Krejcir would invest €300 million in his business. In exchange, he would receive 26 per cent of the company. 'The more I started spending time with Cyril and Radovan about the structure of my business, Radovan started trusting me a lot more and specifically due to my relationship with Cyril.'

Once a relationship of trust had been built up, Meyer says Beeka came clean and explained why Krejcir was really so intent on buying shares in his business. 'The one day we had a meeting where Cyril outlined his plans to me, which was the real reason why they needed to buy shares in my business. The reason was to launder Radovan's money into the country because he had stolen €3.3 billion from the European Union and he had to bring that money into the country. That is how the gold refinery came into the picture.'

Tucking into his seafood risotto, Meyer paints the picture of how the money-laundering operation worked. It is a truly surreal experience: Money Laundering 101. An episode straight out of the TV series *Ozark*. The only problem was that his 'explanation' was low on fact and high on fiction.

In simple terms, Meyer's explanation was that Krejcir had a massive stash of money overseas that he needed to get into South Africa and Meyer's gold refinery was going to be the vehicle to bring it in. Meyer's motive was to make money from the process.

'My commission would have been 10 per cent of everything I moved for him. So if you're looking at €3.3 billion, that would basically have given me over €300 million in commission. I could've moved that money into the country in a year. That is the only reason why I agreed to go ahead with it,' he admits.

Meyer says that for a period of about six months he was given the impression that Krejcir was 'legit'. A legal firm and accountants were employed to do a proper due diligence on his company. But then things turned and Meyer says he realised he was being scammed. 'In hindsight, I think the due-diligence process was only his way of getting to know my business, to see how I used the legal system and banking system to move gold and turn it into money. What I realised, after a while, he didn't intend to go ahead with buying shares in my business. Basically what he was trying to do was get to know my business as far as he could, make me dependent on him and then the moment I was dependent on him, he would kick me out of the business. That's how he took over a lot of businesses in this country. I am one of the few guys that survived. Literally.'

But while Krejcir was studying Meyer's business, the gold refiner says he was also learning plenty about what the Czech was up to. He spent a great deal of time with him and Beeka at the Harbour restaurant and was privy to deals and discussions.

'He was an expert in state capture. He learned his trade in the Czech Republic, which is why he was kicked out of there. A lot of people don't realise how he made his money in the Czech Republic. That is what he wanted to do in this country. Radovan already had a shitload of money before he went to government and he already learned via his set-up in the Czech Republic how to run a government, who to bribe, who to have on your side.'

Meyer says he was present at a number of meetings between Krejcir and General Mabasa and personally witnessed cash being handed over. He later signed an affidavit detailing these transactions.

'I met him several times with Radovan and Mabasa's wife and Lolly's wife,' says the gold refiner. He claims these meetings took place mostly at Teazers and at the Harbour restaurant and he definitely got the sense that Mabasa was on the payroll.

'There were two meetings at the Michelangelo Hotel where I saw Radovan give at least R2.5 to R3 million in cash to Mabasa. In a bag.'

Not only did Meyer claim to see the handover, but he also claimed that he had actually sourced and prepared the cash for the bribe. 'I organised the cash for him – that is why I know about it. Because of my gold business, the majority of my raw material that I bought for my gold refinery, I bought cash from the mining communities. At that stage I ordered R200 million cash each month, so for me to justify ordering an extra R25 million for him wasn't an issue. I used to basically act as the cash banker for him and for Lolly. They moved a lot of cash around and I took the cash from them and put it into the system and made it legal. When they needed cash they asked me to organise it for them.'

Meyer even suggests that Mabasa was going to be part of the company he and Krejcir were going to go into together. 'Mabasa and his wife's name came up several times in the planning sessions for the company structures that had to be put in place. Mabasa would have resigned at that stage, as things would become too hot for him in the police. At that stage there were already question marks about Mabasa.'

Meyer says they were busy with the first transactions in early 2009 when he decided to walk away from the deal with Krejcir. And he believes that is when the trouble started for him. It wasn't long before his bank accounts had been seized, along with his properties. He also believed that his life was in danger so he hired a bevy of bodyguards. 'They came after me five times. If it weren't for the fact that I could afford the best bodyguards in the business, I would have been dead. They shot at me while I was in traffic.'

I ask who exactly came after him and he says 'police guys', but that he has the names in a notebook somewhere, which he never produces. Meyer is clearly bitter about how he believes Krejcir ruined his life. He says he has been arrested a total of 65 times. The first time was when he was picked up by cops in Sandton while driving a grey BMW. When they searched the vehicle they found three bars of gold. The police stated that Meyer was unable to prove the legality of the gold so he was detained. They then came out in the media to defend the arrest, saying it was all above board and warranted, when claims emerged that Meyer had been the target of harassment by Krejcir. Meyer told journalists he believed he had incurred Krejcir's wrath after he had decided not to do business with him. In response, Krejcir told *The Citizen* newspaper that Meyer was lying.

'That man is paranoid. He is on drugs,' Krejcir said when asked if he was in fact pursuing a harassment campaign against Meyer. 'He wanted to do business with me last year, but I learnt he was in financial difficulty and I walked away.'

Meyer launched his own fight-back campaign, which included a media onslaught against Krejcir; he also turned to Paul O'Sullivan. Crucially, he gave O'Sullivan an affidavit in which he detailed evidence that helped in the Uwe Gemballa case and about the allegations of corruption involving Mabasa.

A former SARS investigator who worked on the projects on PAR and Krejcir tells me that much of what Meyer has told me is 'laughable'. 'Simply put, he is exaggerating his prominence in the entire Radovan syndicate in the extreme. He was never really a close associate of Radovan. Radovan's primary interest in Meyer at a point in time was to acquire control of Pan African Refineries. Just that and nothing more. Radovan considered the man a means to do so and nothing more.'

While Meyer struggles to hide his disgust for Krejcir, there is still an element of respect for what the Czech was able to achieve, all of it through money and influence.

'His chequebook, his money – he would buy what he wanted. He would impress people by throwing around money, specifically the guys who worked for him. If he wanted you to work for him he would spend a lot of money on you, showing you the high life. That is how he got most of the guys to work for him, until it came to payment. He grew up with the idea that if you want something, you have to take it by force. If you want something, you have to kill them. That's his mentality. The underworld, that is what made him dangerous; he thought he could walk on water because he could buy what he wanted to and people will fall for his tricks. He wanted to be known as the mafia boss of the country and he also wanted to be in the limelight. If you want to be the mafia boss of the underworld, you need to decide if you want to be the mafia boss or in the limelight, because you can't be both.'

'SHIT,' I EXCLAIMED AS WE PULLED INTO JOAN HUNTER STREET. 'I think we've missed everything.'

It had been raining and my husband and I had been driving around in the dark in the suburbs of Kempton Park chasing a crime scene. We had gone to the wrong address in Sebenza first, so when we arrived at the correct house in Edleen, I assumed we had missed all the action. It was late in the evening of 3 May 2010. Earlier that day I had received a phone call from Mikey Schultz, asking if I had heard that Lolly Jackson had been shot. No one seemed to know anything about it and the newsroom was following up with the police, so I went out for dinner. It was only when I was back home and got another call from a source in the private security industry that I thought the news might be true. The source provided an address and I dragged my husband along as I rushed off to break the story.

Outside the house in Edleen, a marked Sebenza police van was parked in the driveway, alongside a small silver Chevrolet sedan. The bricks on the driveway were shining wet from the persistent drizzle, reflecting the yellow light from the house.

There was no one in sight so I climbed out of our car and walked towards the front door. Standing sentinel at the entrance on either side of the closed security gate were two fierce stone lions with eerie eyes. On the wall was a round plaque bearing a map of Cyprus, the number 25 in white and the words 'Joan Hunter'. Above the address was the word 'Paradisos'. However, this was certainly no paradise. A '25' in fairy lights hung on the wall above the sign, but most of the bulbs had blown. The house belonged to a supermarket owner but he had rented it to George Louca.

I thought how ironic it would be if Lolly Jackson had been rubbed out in such an arbitrary, middle-class face-brick house in suburban Kempton Park after having lived such a flashy, decadent life.

I peered through the security gate and immediately noticed a large smear of blood on the white tiles leading away in an arc, as if someone had been dragged. I couldn't see much beyond that. It was only when the bulky frame of police spokesperson Eugene Opperman appeared at the doorway that I realised I wasn't late on the scene. In fact, I was very, very early.

I had known Opperman for many years and had a good rapport with him. He confirmed that someone had been shot and killed at the house. A colleague had been in touch with Teazers spokesperson Sean Newman to ask whether he could confirm it was Jackson who had been killed. Newman was rushing to the scene in a taxi and arrived a short while later, dressed in chinos and a red-, white- and black-striped Teazers shirt. He was flustered.

'Is it true that my boss has been killed?' he wanted to know from us and we sent him over to speak to Opperman. Within moments, Newman collapsed on the driveway.

Newman's phone had run flat so my husband lent him his and we listened as Newman broke down in tears on the phone to Demi Jackson, Lolly's wife, and to his colleague Ricardo. 'Dem, where are you? Where are you?' he sobbed. 'It's true, it's true, 25 Joan Hunter. Please get here. I don't know … they won't tell me,' I heard him continuing.

Once the news had broken on Eyewitness News, more and more people began to arrive. Jackson's son Manoli appeared, along with a black Teazers-branded minivan. The paramedics came to assist with the grief-stricken and a pastor to help with trauma counselling. Huddled under umbrellas, journalists were corralled on the pavement across the road as we waited for more information.

Meanwhile, Sean Newman was being ushered into the sedan parked in the driveway.

'It was the only car sitting there, other than the police van, and inside was a black cop, in a suit, with a docket in his hands and he was making notes on the front of the docket, you know nothing really written inside. It wasn't thick,' Newman recalls. The cop was Joey Mabasa.

'He said to me, "Who are you?" I said, "I'm Sean." "Do you know the deceased?" I said, "Yes, I work for him." "Who is the deceased?" and I looked at him as if to say, but you guys just told me who he is, and he looked at me and all I could muster was I grabbed the badge on my shirt and I just pointed at it. He launched straight away into, "When you talk to the media, you are not to put us under pressure because any form of pressure you put us under in the media can let criminals get away." Basically I looked at him as if to say, "Hang on, 10 seconds ago you didn't know who I was, you didn't know who Lolly Jackson was, but you know I deal with the media." It perplexed me and the whole line was, I was not to talk about the case in the media, the line that I was to use was, "We have full faith in the police and we are giving them the space to catch Lolly's killer." In hindsight, it almost feels like we gave room for the likes of George to leave the country.'

Suddenly a guttural wail cut through the night along with the sound of quick, heeled footsteps. We swung around to see Demi Jackson, hysterical, running along the street and then collapsing onto the tar. Heaving, she cried, 'Ah, my baby! What was he doing here?' she demanded.

At that stage, all the police were saying was that a man had been shot and his body had been found in a pool of blood. They also stated that someone had called the police and had confessed to the shooting and told the cops where to find the body. Jackson's Jeep Cherokee was missing.

Amongst those to arrive at the crime scene in the drizzle later that evening were Radovan Krejcir and Cyril Beeka. Newman remembers the events as they unfolded.

'So while I was talking to media I saw the white Porsche 911 pull up and I'm finished with you guys, and it's ironic because you didn't know who was standing 10 metres away from you, at the side at the exact tree that I'd stood under that night and there was Radovan. He got out of the car and Cyril Beeka got out with him. They stood there and he was like, "What's going on? I hear Lolly's been shot?" He played dumb.'

At that stage Newman did not know that Krejcir and Beeka had already been on the scene earlier that evening, accompanied by General Mabasa. This would only be revealed years later.

'Cyril stood on the other side, didn't really say a thing. He had the most unnerving fucking stare on the planet. I still maintain that man scared me more than anyone in my entire life, purely based on his stare – it felt like he was staring into your soul. And then Radovan turned around and said, "Okay, I go now … Phone me later, guys, and if there's anything you need I'm there," and he left as quickly as he arrived, but the media didn't realise who was standing there because until the next morning when the cops took him in for alleged questioning or he agreed to cooperate, nobody knew who Radovan Krejcir was. He wasn't a story.'

Just after midnight, Jackson's son Manoli was allowed inside the house to view his father's body and he emerged holding a plastic packet containing his father's crucifix and his watch. It wasn't clear whether these had been fully examined for evidence purposes.

And then, in the early hours of the morning, a Pathology Services van reversed up the driveway and the body of the King of Sleaze was loaded into the back and driven away amid the flash of cameras.

LOLLY JACKSON'S DEATH HAS BEEN SHROUDED IN MYSTERY AND intrigue since that rainy night in May 2010. Bits and pieces of information have emerged, some strategically, in order to create a narrative about the events of that evening. But, as is so often the case with such crimes, there is no one truth. Each person has his or her version of events that has been released into the public domain to serve a particular agenda. Over the past eight years, I have attempted to wade through reams of information and misinformation to piece together what happened.

The most uncompromised piece of evidence is the autopsy report compiled by forensic pathologist Johannes Steenkamp. The autopsy was done at 8am in Germiston the day after the shooting. The official cause of death was 'multiple bullet wounds'. Jackson was shot six times – twice over the left posterior chest wall, which resulted in a fractured rib and a perforated left lung; once through his left lateral chest wall, perforating his diaphragm and his stomach; twice in the parietal region of his head, causing trauma to his brain; and once 3cm in front of his left ear. This shot was fired from close range and there was 'tattooing', dark marks that spread out over the left cheek. Numerous bullet fragments, a 'snow storm' of shards, were found in his facial area.

Jackson's body was found without a shirt and his jeans had been pulled down around his legs – most likely because the corpse had been dragged from the lounge to the garage, his pants bunching up around his legs in the process. He was still wearing the old, scuffed brown Bronx boots he so loved.

Within hours of Jackson's murder, Paul O'Sullivan began to release information about what might have led to the shooting. I soon knew, as did other journalists, that it was George Smith/Louca who was on the run from police and that it was Smith/Louca who had phoned Gauteng Intelligence boss Joey Mabasa to confess to the murder. Smith's ID document was made public and the hunt was on for the missing Cypriot. It was also quickly revealed that on the night of the shooting, Louca had gone to the Harbour restaurant, ostensibly to meet Mabasa. He spoke briefly to Krejcir and Beeka, then bought two packets of cigarettes and disappeared. Jackson's Jeep was found several days later, abandoned on King's Road in Bedfordview, a stone's throw from Krejcir's Kloof Road home.

Cellphone records – leaked to Sean Newman – reveal that Louca contacted Krejcir seven times on the day of the shooting. Jackson's last call was made to Louca and it was 27 seconds long. At 6:22pm, Louca called Mabasa's cellphone and they spoke for 96 seconds. The data shows that Louca was not at the crime scene at the time of that call.

The overwhelming narrative in the public domain in the days following Jackson's death was that Louca had shot Jackson, panicked, phoned Mabasa to confess and then fled.

But what about a motive?

It didn't take long before Alex Panayi's statement detailing the money-laundering scheme appeared in the newspapers and the suggestion was that Louca had killed Jackson because he was going to turn state witness and spill the beans.

It was common knowledge that Jackson had a number of ongoing feuds with numerous individuals and any one of them could have had him whacked. Jackson and Andrew Phillips, who owned The Grand in Rivonia, despised one another. When I called Phillips to get comment from him about Jackson's death, he told me, 'He was a bigot, arrogant and a racist. A proud racist. He was a pig, trash. I detested the man. He was always busy with some mischief.' And yet, Phillips wasn't an obvious suspect.

Another enemy of Jackson was Kalymnios, the Kensington pawnshop owner, who had been embroiled in a legal battle with Jackson over the stripper Moshorovs'ka. But he, too, was not a suspect.

While investigators were trying to wade through the evidence and uncover a motive, Louca was still nowhere to be seen. There were rumours he had slipped into Mozambique, that he had been spirited through the

VIP terminal at the airport. Some even claimed he was at the bottom of a dam somewhere.

In the meantime, Krejcir was busy. His lawyer, Ian Small-Smith, told the media his client was cooperating with police and would be a state witness in the murder trial. In return, the Czech would be granted immunity from prosecution in other criminal cases and the matter of his extradition would be quashed. The deal was unfathomable. Interpol was particularly outraged, as were the Czech authorities who had been working furiously to get their most wanted man back onto their own soil.

Over time, as the main characters began to speak their truths, different versions of events seeped into the public domain. However, one predominant narrative held firm – and that was the one put forward in those first few hours following Jackson's death.

MABASA CALLED ME AND TOLD ME, 'CAN YOU CALL LOLLY ON his phone?' I said why and he said, 'Just call Lolly and tell me if you get hold of him.' I didn't know what was happening so I call Lolly and his phone is off. I call Mabasa and say his phone is off. After one or two hours he called again and said can you call Lolly again. I called and I said no his phone is off. It was strange to switch his phone off. Meantime before Mabasa arrive George, he was parking Lolly car there, where there is this white car, he was parking this Jeep. We didn't know it was Lolly Jeep. He was walking inside. I was sitting here in this table with another six guys. He came and said, 'I killed Lolly Jackson.' You know George, drugs and everything, he looks normal, no marks or fight or whatever. I say, 'What you talking about?' We laugh at him. He said okay no problem, he went to order two packets of Camel Filter soft, the cigarettes, he took them and he left to the car; we were watching him, walking through the whole parking sitting in this white Jeep Cherokee and he left. After I click white Jeep Cherokee – when we find out he was killed – it was Lolly car because they said Lolly car disappear. From this time I do not see George.

Mabasa arrive. Mabasa came and arrived to this place and he said, 'Where is George?' We were sitting with six friends of mine, we said what do you mean, George was here and he left. He said George called me and he wants to see me. I said for what and he said no, George said to him he killed Lolly Jackson. I said he said to us as well, what you talking about? He said no he told me he want to hand himself over. I said what is the story? From all this friends around, Mabasa asked me where he was staying; I said I don't know brother I have never been there. Michael who was working for me knows this Greek guy where he was staying. Mabasa said he wants to go to the place where George is staying. [This] time he came with us; Cyril Beeka, Hein Metrovich, Jason Domingues, Michael, and somebody else, we were all here sitting at this table. Mabasa was following us, we was following Michael. We end up somewhere in Kempton Park. We standing in front of the house, quiet, proper. We ring the bell, nobody opening. Michael give us the number for this guy who is owner of this house; he called him, Michael or Mabasa I don't remember. He said listen we are here in front of your house where are you? He said no I am at Pick n Pay here in Malibongwe or somewhere, they said no he must come to his house, it's the police come and open your house. We were waiting one hour, nothing happening around the house, we didn't see anything. We were joking, just talk shit, we were playing and whatever.

Funny enough, this guy arrive after an hour. It was two main gates in the garage, he press the one fucking button – he didn't go for the main door of the house – and the garage was opening, one of the garage door and exactly opposite this garage door was lying the body cover in the clothes or carpet or something. First of all in my mind how he knows, he open this fucking gate, he could go this way or that way in the house but he open exactly by the body. Mabasa went there, I saw it because I remember Lolly old shoes, always I tell him Lolly you fucking pissing me off you have money you always walking with this old scrap shoes. I like the shoes, you know what I mean. When I see these shoes from a distance I said to myself it's Lolly. They went there tried to open his clothes and whatever. He was naked, not naked, his jeans was pulled out. I went closer there because I saw the shoes for me was finished, I knew. They open his cover I see it was Lolly. For me it was strange that his jeans were on the half, on his knees, like somebody want to rape him or something. I left from his house fucking upset, smoking. Mabasa was calling some cops whatever. I went there again to this place.

After I spoke with Demi to tell me she's going there so I told her I'm coming with you. I didn't tell her I was there already. I met there Robbie and Sean and Manoli and Demi. I never went inside again. George, he contact me after I don't know how many weeks from Cyprus. He didn't want to talk about the case, what happened between him and Lolly, I tried to push him. He said don't get involved it was nothing to do with *you, it was with me and Lolly. He just informed me how he end up in Cyprus.*

I know, it was Mabasa. He told me he went to Mozambique, he get a new passport from Mozambique. From Mozambique he went to Portugal, from Portugal he went to Spain, from Spain he went to Greece and from Greece he went to Cyprus.

I tried to help Joey Mabasa because everybody allege him that he helped George to run away from this country. I ask him did Mabasa help you run away and he said no, I asked did I was involve and he said no nothing, it is nothing to do with you. All this question was on purpose that I give him.

What people are saying [about Mabasa] is nonsense and what they did to him is the biggest mistake in this country. Joey Mabasa is an honest cop, he loves to work as a cop, he work for the government, he will die for the government.

Radovan Krejcir
Interview for When Fantasy Becomes Reality
Harbour restaurant, 2012

IT WAS MISTY AND OMINOUS IN EDLEEN THE MORNING AFTER THE shooting. I returned before dawn, parking near Louca's house. I sat in my car as I did live crossings for Radio 702 and spoke to John Robbie, all the time keeping watch for activity. There was little happening.

A few kilometres away, in Kempton Park, Colonel PW van Heerden checked his phone and noticed he had missed a call from General Norman Taioe. Taioe, the head of detectives in Gauteng, had heard about Lolly Jackson's murder and wanted Van Heerden to check whether it was true and if the scene had been handled correctly.

At the time, in May 2010, Van Heerden was one of two police officers seconded to the Scorpions 'Bad Guys' team to investigate the Brett Kebble murder. When the case fell apart later in 2010, Van Heerden and his colleague Corrie Maritz were blamed and there was consensus that they had botched it. But Van Heerden was an experienced cop. Instead of national service, he had joined the police straight out of school. He spent time working undercover on SAA flights as a sky marshal and then transferred to a firearms unit before being asked to join a special task team investigating a murder in Mabopane. When he received the call about the Lolly Jackson case, he was stationed at Organised Crime North Rand. After speaking to his general, Van Heerden climbed into the car and switched on the radio, listening to my reports as he went looking for the murder scene.

'Staying in Kempton and knowing Kempton, I thought there are only two areas where a person of Lolly's stature – because the reporting was that it happened at his house – would have a house in. The first one is down the road in Edleen. I went there and spoke to the boom guard, asking him if there was a shooting there that night and he said, "Ja." I knew I was in the right place. I was listening to you on the radio and you were sitting around the corner,' Colonel Van Heerden tells me seven years later. He chain-smokes Chesterfields and strokes his ginger-blond moustache as he recalls the events. The Hawks media officer has given him permission to speak about the case and Van Heerden is open and candid.

I was less than complimentary about Van Heerden in my reporting on the Kebble case, but his humility about that period is admirable. 'I've learned some things and some things I would've done differently,' he says hesitantly about his first underworld-related case. As he had worked on that high-profile investigation, it made sense for him to take over the Lolly docket. There were many similarities in the murders and, in fact, some of the characters even overlapped. Mikey Schultz had, after all, been the best man at Jackson's wedding.

Van Heerden made his way to Joan Hunter Street and contacted the local detectives at Sebenza station who had processed the scene the night before. Then he and his colleagues took over the docket.

I want to know whether he was happy with the way the scene had been processed. Crime-scene handling is notoriously poor in South Africa and the quality of the work often undermines the credibility of evidence in court. His answer doesn't surprise me, but his honesty does.

'They had allowed the owner of the house to clean up the scene. After they completed their work, they said to him they had finished so he cleaned up the blood etcetera. When we got into the house it was completely clean and that was a problem. I think it was treated like an everyday murder and they didn't realise who the victim was. There was nothing at the scene to tell you except all that was still visible was blood on the carpet going towards George's room. That was it; the tile floors were clean. The garage where Jackson's body had been found had also been scrubbed of evidence. It was impossible to make a determination about what had happened.'

The first obvious suspect was George Louca, mostly because news reports claimed that he had phoned General Joey Mabasa to confess. 'The news was reporting George had phoned Joey Mabasa and admitted. That was the first report I read on News24. According to the news reports, George was the suspect. We then established that George was, in fact, staying there and on that same day George was supposed to appear in Kempton on charges of stolen property. He then became a suspect in the matter because the blood was leading to his room and there was blood in front of his cupboard where he had taken out clean clothes or a clean shirt. George was definitely a person to speak to.'

Despite the alleged confession call to Mabasa, Van Heerden says that in the initial stages of the investigation the head of Crime Intelligence in Gauteng was not directly involved in the probe. 'We spoke telephonically just to arrange to meet to get a statement from him.'

Van Heerden says they followed all the correct procedures to try to find Louca, who was believed to be on the run.

'Well, we checked if he had left the country, which he hadn't, according to movement control records. The lead officer who was investigating him for stolen property was at our office so we immediately used that warrant of non-appearance to circulate him as a wanted person,' he explains, confirming that the borders had been alerted.

'That was done the same day. At that stage there wouldn't have been an Interpol alert. Lolly was murdered on the third. That next day, after I got the call, we circulated at the borders at the latest 1 o'clock that afternoon. By that time, he had already left the country.'

There have been many conflicting stories about how Louca escaped from the country, but Van Heerden believes the narrative is supported by the facts. 'What I can confirm, from looking at control records, he met up with a pal of his, Yannis Louca [George's cousin]. They met up in Bedfordview close to the Nicol Hotel and they immediately travelled to Mozambique that night. According to movement control records, Yannis left the country at about 2am in the morning and returned at about 5am or 6am that morning. So before I got to the scene or even heard about it, George had already left the country.

'When George came back he gave me a version that he left that same night. It is confirmed with Yannis's movement that he left at 2am and came back at about 6am. George apparently went out without a passport; he bribed a guy. From Maputo he arranged with somebody there to apply for a new passport and he had a passport couriered to him; he left with that passport via Lisbon to Cyprus.'

With Louca out of his reach, Van Heerden focused on Krejcir, who had claimed to have seen Louca at the Harbour restaurant on the night of the shooting. I want to know from him whether Krejcir was officially cooperating with the cops. 'O'Sullivan gave me a hiding about that in the media,' Van Heerden says dismissively.

'[Krejcir] provided a witness affidavit and everything. What happened was, we got information via one of our other officers that George was hiding at Krejcir's house so we met that night, the same night that we had taken over. Because the scene had been cleaned up, the forensics guys said they had to wait for it to get dark in order to spray the house to see where the blood had been. At that same time we got information that George had apparently been hiding at Krejcir's house. We got guys together and they said tackling that house at night will be problematic without us knowing the layout of the house.

'We kept an observation of the house and we would do it the following day. It was a task force that was mobilised. I returned there early the next morning and the whole operation was being organised by a colleague of mine. By about 9 o'clock when they haven't pitched, they were still busy with planning; I saw a vehicle leave, which was driven by Michael Arsiotis. I stopped him and he wouldn't allow us into the premises. We had a discussion and he got on the phone with Ian Small-Smith. I said to Ian, we want to get into the house. Ian spoke to the chap and we went into the house; checked the house. Wherever we could check, we checked and there was nothing.'

Small-Smith, Krejcir's lawyer, arranged for Van Heerden to meet with Krejcir at the Harbour restaurant for an interview with the investigators.

'Krejcir was his typical self. Until this day I cannot say, but if he played a role beforehand or if he played a role just afterwards; that is the question. Somewhere he played a role in the thing. He had Cyril there, Arsiotis and then a guy by the name of Hein Metrovich. I obtained their statements and they all said George had rocked up there – they were there the whole afternoon in a drinking session. I took Cyril's statement and Cyril said he noticed blood on George's jeans. They all said George said he made shit and killed Lolly. They said they thought he was joking because they thought he was high and talking bullshit. Later Joey arrived but George had already left.

'I didn't know Cyril from a bar of soap at that stage. Neither did I know Radovan or his background. He was just a normal person to me at that stage. Something was off: why would you laugh off someone's statement that he killed somebody and not take it seriously?'

Van Heerden confirms that Krejcir did cooperate with the cops and even provided phone numbers for Louca in Cyprus. He also told them that he had been in touch with Louca and had spoken to him on the phone.

After securing statements from Krejcir and his associates that Louca had apparently confessed to the murder, Van Heerden felt he had enough to apply for a warrant of arrest.

'We had the confession to Joey and prima facie enough to get a warrant of arrest for murder. I sent the red notice application to Interpol.'

However, in what appeared to be a case of Keystone cops, the Interpol red notice was never issued. This meant that Louca could have travelled around the world and vanished into thin air, without ever being picked up as a wanted suspect. It was thought that Van Heerden had just not bothered to do his job, but he clarifies this, stating that the fault was not on his part.

'It was a year later at a meeting with Interpol which my boss convened, Brigadier Ebrahim Kadwa. He was acting head of Organised Crime at that stage. Only at that meeting did I learn from a guy from Interpol that he didn't submit the red notice application. Because – and this is something I still want clarity on because it differed from what happened to John Stratton [in the Kebble case] – his version was that we first had to submit an application for Mutual Legal Assistance for George's extradition before we could issue a red notice. To this day, that doesn't make sense to me.'

Several months after the shooting, with Louca living it up in Limassol, he apparently reached out to South African officials, offering to speak to them about what had happened and claiming innocence. Louca phoned McIntosh Polela, spokesperson for the Hawks at the time, so Van Heerden called him back.

'It was 2011. I had a couple of chats with George. He didn't want to go into detail on the phone. He was very reluctant to speak on a phone. He was willing to meet with us and with the investigating officer that had his case of the suspected stolen property; he said to me if I bring this guy along he is willing to have a chat to us because he knows and trusts the guy.'

Van Heerden put in an official application to go see Louca, but it was unsuccessful. 'There were people who were saying it wasn't necessary to go – we had to get him here and press him once he is here. I had a different viewpoint, my viewpoint was go and have a chat to the guy in his own environment and see what he has to say.

'I couldn't be sure that he was the guy who pulled the trigger, but what I could be sure of with the blood leading back and it was later determined at that time already, it was Lolly's blood in front of George's cupboard and on George's shirt that we found lying in the room. It was Lolly's blood and there was some of George's blood on it too. It could be a nose bleed or something like that. Majority of the samples were Lolly's but one or two indicated it was George's. Somehow George was involved and he was on the scene.'

The cop also had to decide what to do with the claim made by his colleague Joey Mabasa that Louca had confessed to the murder. Van Heerden says he wasn't suspicious of Mabasa at the time and he's diplomatic about the allegations surrounding the intelligence officer.

Van Heerden also rubbishes a report that claimed that it was Mabasa's gun that had been used to kill Jackson. 'That was a load of BS!' exclaims the cop. 'Remember, prior to that Joey's 9mm was stolen here at the Rosebank Mall. The firearm that was used was a .22 Beretta. The serial number was erased. The firearm was hidden in the garage under a blanket on top of boxes. Close to where the body was found. The owner had stuffed boxes there. Ballistically – there were five cartridges found on the scene and there was one spent cartridge found still in the chamber – three of those were positively linked to the firearm that was used. The bullets that were used disintegrated so they couldn't confirm above reasonable doubt that that was the firearm, but the girl at ballistics said it's 80 per cent sure.'

The docket lay idle on Van Heerden's desk for several years as the extradition process wound its way through the Cypriot courts. It seemed unlikely that South African officials would be successful. Van Heerden wasn't updated all that often and would find out about court developments via the media. Every few months I called him and his standard response was, 'I am a mushroom. I know nothing ...'

It took almost four years for Louca to return to South Africa and officially reveal his version of events about what happened the night Lolly Jackson died.

GEORGE LOUCA RESURFACED IN LIMASSOL IN CYPRUS. HE SETTLED there with his four children and went on with his life. For well over a year, there was no attempt to send South African investigators to speak to him or to have him expatriated to stand trial for Lolly Jackson's murder. Yet the narrative that he was the shooter was perpetuated in the media. Louca gave a handful of cryptic interviews, the most prominent of which was with the *Sunday Times* in May 2011 at a restaurant on the island.

'I want to talk to the police in SA, but I don't think I will get a fair trial,' Louca told the newspaper. 'If I go under, I will not go down alone; a lot of important people will go down with me. I will pay the consequences, but they will as well. I am alive because I am not a betrayer.'

In March 2012, Louca was finally arrested in Cyprus. He made numerous court appearances and spent two years fending off extradition attempts by the South African government. The Supreme Court in Cyprus rejected a final appeal from Louca, which gave authorities the green light for him to be flown back to Johannesburg. An Interpol team was dispatched and Louca was escorted from the plane directly to prison in Johannesburg.

He appeared in the Kempton Park magistrate's court looking considerably leaner than when he left. His hair was trimmed and he had grown a moustache. He was facing a battery of charges, including murder and money laundering. Two prior cases of possession of stolen goods worth approximately R1.8 million were also revived. Fighting his corner was the eccentric attorney Owen Blumberg.

The Cypriot was keen to turn state witness and spill the beans on his former associate. Under the watchful eye of Blumberg, Louca deposed to a series of explosive affidavits detailing crimes involving Krejcir. One of these statements revealed in extensive detail the events of the night of

3 May 2010 when Lolly Jackson was murdered. For the first time, Louca gave a version of events on the record.

In his statement, Louca explained that the dispute between Krejcir and Jackson had its roots in the 'cash swap' agreement between the two men and Cypriot banker Alekos Panayi.

After the arrangement with Panayi fell through, Krejcir approached Jackson and said he and Cyril Beeka were in a position to make funds available offshore using a similar arrangement to the 'money swap' scheme operated through Laiki Bank. Jackson agreed to use their services and two or three transactions involving 'small' sums of money between R80 000 and R120 000 were successfully concluded.

Then, in April 2010, Louca says Jackson contacted him urgently and told him that he had arranged a 'transfer' of approximately R740 000 through Beeka and Krejcir. He had given the money to Krejcir but the equivalent amount of funds had not been transferred to his account despite receipt of a document in the form of a 'Swift transfer'. It turned out that the Swift document was fake.

Jackson was angry and requested that Louca set up a meeting with Krejcir. Louca claims he did, but that neither Krejcir nor Beeka showed up. Shortly after, Krejcir asked Louca to meet him at the Harbour. He arrived and, while speaking to him, Beeka walked towards him and punched him on the side of the head. He fell to the floor and was kicked several times on his head and face. Louca was hospitalised and missed a court appearance as a result.

On discharge, Louca tried again to set up a meeting between Krejcir and Jackson. The Czech refused to meet at Jackson's home or office and insisted that it be held at Louca's house in Kempton Park. The meeting was scheduled for the afternoon of Monday, 3 May.

Louca met Jackson on Modderfontein Road, outside Greenstone shopping centre, in the late afternoon. Jackson was driving his Jeep and followed Louca in his Peugeot van. Along the way to Kempton Park, the van broke down. Louca jumped into the Jeep and together they went on to Joan Hunter Street.

When they arrived, Louca says he invited Jackson into the living room and stepped behind the bar to offer him a beer. Krejcir arrived five or six minutes later and he also offered him a drink. Almost immediately Jackson began to shout at Krejcir.

Louca picked up this version of events when he testified in dramatic fashion at the Palm Ridge court in April 2015. By this stage his health had deteriorated considerably. He was bringing an application to be sent home to Cyprus to die because he was suffering from stage-four lung cancer. Louca was in a wheelchair and breathing with the assistance of an oxygen mask and a tank by his side. As he finally gave his account of events, he was a shadow of his former self. I sat in the public gallery as he gave his testimony in a Godfather-esque moment, with his raspy, wheezing voice. A translator was required to repeat everything he said. In all the years I have spent witnessing trials, this was some of the most compelling, dramatic testimony I have experienced.

Radovan came inside to the house. Lolly he took from his pocket a Swift money transfer that has been transferred to Lolly account. But it is Lolly he find out in two weeks' time he was a fake one that's why he was so upset. Proof of payment. And Lolly, he was swearing, very bad. By that time, things start getting very, pushing each other. Radovan and Lolly he was having touching each other, pushing each other. And Lolly he called Radovan, you don't know motherfucker who I am. Lolly said to Radovan. At that time, Radovan he put the gun and he shot him. I was in the bar … Lolly he fled back. He was alive. Me I came out from the bar and I say to Radovan what have you done. He said to me relax. Don't panic. And Lolly he raise his hands and he was asking for help. Radovan, I went to Lolly, Radovan pushed me back. Lolly he was lying down the body, Radovan he went on his side and he kick him twice on the ribs. And he said to him, now you know who I am. When he told him now you know who I am, he carry on shooting, I think in the chest, I don't know. And Lolly I couldn't see. He was passing. He ask me I must take him to the garage. I said to him why. He said to me relax, don't panic, I'm responsible for everything. [Pause while Louca takes oxygen, struggling to breathe.]

And he ask me to pick up Lolly and take him to the garage so I pick up Lolly but when I pick him up I was full of blood. And I said to him no,

I can't do that. So he ask me if I have a blanket. I said to him yes I have. When I went to the garage, he ask me, Radovan, to reverse Lolly's car so when I open the garage doors I saw Cyril Beeka outside with another person which I don't know. Soon as I open the door, Cyril he came inside so when I reverse because I reverse too much, the door of the car he couldn't open, he was touching the wall, the boot, the door of the boot. So Radovan he asked me to go further so I opened the doors and it is where I make my decision to left from the scenes. To leave from the scenes.

Louca says he was horrified and frightened as he fled the scene, having exchanged his bloody shirt for a clean one. He wanted to get away as quickly as possible and exited through the boom at the entrance to his suburb. This is when he called General Mabasa by phone and told him he had just witnessed Krejcir killing Jackson and asked for his help. Louca says Mabasa asked who had been present at the time of Jackson's murder and where he was. Louca says the policeman suggested they meet at Bedford Centre and that he should speak to Krejcir as soon as possible.

What followed was a series of calls and fleeting rendezvous between the key players: Louca, Mabasa, Krejcir and Beeka. First, Louca met up with Krejcir at Yannis Louca's garage near Linksfield, where they had a brief but heated conversation. Then he made his way to the Harbour restaurant where he was to meet with Mabasa. There he encountered Beeka and Hein Metrovich, but there was no sign of the general. It wasn't long, however, before Krejcir himself showed up. Krejcir took Louca's cellphone and gave him another, and – warning him to speak to no one – instructed him to drive to the Nicol Hotel in Bedfordview, and make his way to the second floor, Room 26. There he found Krejcir's friend from the Czech Republic, and the two were joined at 10pm that night by Krejcir. Krejcir told Louca that he had no choice but to leave the country. As he put it: Lolly was murdered in your house. You were there when it happened. You are fucked and there is nothing you can do about it.

Louca was told he should leave as soon as possible for Cyprus because it had no extradition treaty with South Africa. Krejcir also undertook to send him money. Louca says he called his friend Yannis and told him the truth about what had happened. Yannis drove him across the border to Mozambique from where he travelled to Cyprus via Lisbon.

In his court testimony Louca explained how he 'slipped' over the border by putting $1000 on top of his ID book when he handed it to customs officials. They pocketed it and he crossed into Mozambique.

Louca said that while in Cyprus, he was threatened several times after Krejcir asked him to become an 'agent' for receiving and selling drugs but he had refused. He also revealed how he had contacted the police and repeatedly stated he would come back to South Africa if they could guarantee his safety.

Louca alleged that Mabasa and Krejcir were in a corrupt relationship. 'Joey Mabasa and Radovan, they have big business together and Radovan and Mabasa, they have corruption business together so Radovan, very simple, is a rich one. I am poor.'

Sucking on his oxygen nebuliser, Louca begged to be allowed to go home to his wife and children to die. Judge Geraldine Borchers denied his request. Three weeks later George Louca, the only one able to piece the puzzle together, was dead.

In response to Louca's version of events of what happened the night Jackson was killed, Krejcir's lawyers described the account as 'absolute rubbish' and 'total nonsense' devoid of any truth.

Mabasa told the *Sunday Times* that Louca was being 'economical with the truth' and questioned why he ran away if he really wanted to clear his name. During a court appearance the day after Louca died, Krejcir told my colleague Mia Lindeque that he was not celebrating Louca's death. He said that Louca had made a confession to him while he was still in Cyprus. In a recorded phone call, Louca apparently admitted that Krejcir had nothing to do with the murder but then he changed his story.

'I have his confession, over the phone. In a 20-minute call he told me exactly what happened here when he ran away from South Africa; I even offered my DNA to the police so they could go to the scene. At the time George Louca died, I was 40 kilometres away, with my cellphone records to show,' said Krejcir. He claimed Louca went behind his back and made a plea bargain with the state to ensure his freedom.

GENERAL JOEY MABASA WAS FRUSTRATED. HE STOMPED AROUND the parking lot at the Rosebank Mall looking for the man who had stolen his police-issue firearm. A week earlier his car had been broken into and his gun taken. It was a Monday evening in May 2010.

Mabasa was speaking to the security guards in the hope that they had witnessed the crime. The policeman was very, very angry. A colleague at Eyewitness News had got his hands on the police docket and it looked like Mabasa was, at best, incompetent and, at worst, corrupt. How could the Gauteng head of Crime Intelligence be robbed of his service-issue pistol?

Mabasa's phone rang. He halted in his tracks. He didn't recognise the 072 number. When he answered, the panicked voice on the other end of the line told him it was George and that he had 'shot him'. The caller was police informant George Louca. Mabasa vividly recalls the phone call that changed his life.

It is now 2017, and it is the first time Mabasa has spoken out about the events of that night. We are sitting in a boardroom, coincidentally just a few hundred metres from where he was standing when his phone rang and George Louca was on the other end. I have finally convinced Mabasa to tell me his version.

'He said he wanted to meet me because he wants to hand himself over. He said we must meet at the Harbour. I told him to go to the police station to hand himself over. He said, No, I am a good man, he will hand himself to me. I said he should go to the police station and tell me at what police station he is at; I will go there. I didn't want to go there alone so I phoned two members from Crime Intelligence Johannesburg Central; I asked the commander for two members who can accompany me.'

Mabasa is adamant that he followed procedure and acted according to the book. He immediately called his commanders at head office, including General Lebeya, General Taioe and General Mdluli.

'I realised there was a problem. I'm an Intelligence person, so I decided to report it. From Rosebank I phoned head office, I phoned everybody. That area falls under Kempton Park so I phoned the head of the detectives there. I said this man said he has killed Lolly but his phone is switched off. Taioe then came back to me and asked what we should do. I told him to give me two members from the detectives.'

Mabasa drove from Rosebank to the provincial SAPS headquarters in Parktown where he met up with two Crime Intelligence officers, whom he recalls being a 'Hlongwane' and 'Rikhotso'.

'We waited for the detectives at the provincial office. They didn't come so I made a decision to go. We couldn't find George, and his phone was off. I said let's go to the Harbour because all the criminals meet there. The three of us went into the Harbour; it was full and Krejcir was also there. We asked him where George was.

'It was between 7:00 and 8:00 in the evening. He said he hasn't seen him that day. Beeka was also there. Krejcir said he didn't know where George stayed. One man – I think he is a Greek – told us he thinks he knows where he stays. I asked him to go with us but he refused. Beeka said the Greek guy will get in our car and we followed them; Cyril, Krejcir and two big guys.' The two 'big guys' were Jason Dominguez and Hein Metrovich, two heavies allegedly on Krejcir's payroll. The 'Greek guy' was Michael Arsiotis.

Cyril Beeka was driving a 4x4, Krejcir alongside him, Dominguez and Metrovich in the back seat. Mabasa was following behind, accompanied by his two CI officers.

'That boy got lost; we drove until we arrived in a suburb around Kempton Park. It was dark by that time. When we arrived in the house there was nobody in the house. My members said we must break in to check. I said no because I didn't want any liability to the police. If we break in and don't find anything, then what? If you break in and find something inside – no one can sue you, there was a crime committed. The Greek guy said he knew the owner of the house; he was the owner of the Spar in Randburg.

I asked him if he had his number so I phoned from my own phone. The owner told me he was still busy and he couldn't come. I threatened to arrest him and told him to come home straight away. We waited outside for him.

'We waited more than two hours,' remembers Mabasa. His phone was ringing off the hook with his superiors wanting answers.

'After some time the owner arrived and opened the gate. I introduced myself and said I got a call from George; I asked him if he knew George and he said yes, he was staying there with George. When he opened the garage door we saw the body.'

Mabasa has a vivid recollection of the scene in that Kempton Park garage.

'He was on the floor in the garage. He was on top of the blanket with his pants pulled down. It was a garage with a passage going into the house. You could see blood as he was dragging him. We walked into the house; there was a small bar. We found two glasses half full, showing they were drinking together. The blood started there at the bar, so you can see on the floor he was dragged to the garage. What we thought was that he pulled him to put him in the car and dump him somewhere. Lolly was heavy so I think he couldn't do that.'

Mabasa then asked Beeka to identify the body as that of Lolly Jackson. 'We wanted to be sure it's him. I closed the garage and told everyone to leave the property. We closed the gate so that no one could interfere with the scene. The investigating officers phoned to say they were on their way. The scene was not tampered with at all; it was as it was. I closed the garage and the gate; everybody was outside.'

Mabasa handed the scene over to the investigating officer and insists he then left and has no recollection of speaking to Teazers spokesperson Sean Newman or even sitting in a car with him. 'He is lying.'

The former head of Crime Intelligence in Gauteng says he has considered the possibilities of what happened that night. He says it is possible that Krejcir shot Jackson and that Louca took the fall for him. That, however, was not the obvious explanation. The fact that there were only two glasses in the house when he arrived tells him a lot.

He believes that Louca killed Jackson as a result of the fallout with

Kalymnios over the stripper. In fact, head of detectives General Taioe was investigating numerous cases linked to this fight.

'George was a hit man for Lolly. What happened is that there is a Greek guy [Kalymnios]. He deals with diamonds and gold. He stole one of the girls from Lolly and she became his wife, so this Greek guy and Lolly was fighting. Taioe had a case where George shot the Greek guy. Taioe told me that they know George was paid by Lolly to kill the Greek guy. He took a lot of money from Lolly. It had nothing to do with money laundering. Lolly sent George to go kill him. There were three dockets; Taioe was investigating them. There were three attempts.'

Returning to Parktown that evening, General Mabasa apparently thought about how 'these criminals were killing each other'. It wouldn't be long, however, before he would be directly implicated, with allegations that he was complicit – a corrupt top-level cop covering up the involvement of a global fugitive gangster in the murder of one of the country's most iconic, if sleazy, individuals. 'They wanted to pin me. In the beginning I was also a suspect for Lolly. People said I was the one who killed Lolly. I realised that I was now the suspect. I wanted to get him so he could talk because he was the one who phoned me. I wanted him to be in prison.'

Mabasa says that he made it his mission to try to bring Louca in so that he could prove that he, Mabasa, was in no way involved in the murder. He followed his tracks like a dog with a scent. He says he started with 'the syndicate', the network of criminals operating in Bedfordview. Mabasa's version of these events differs significantly from the version given by Louca in court as well as the facts gathered by Colonel PW van Heerden.

'He was involved in the syndicate of drugs and a lot of groupings. They still operate. They are Greek and Bulgarian. They told him he was stupid; he mustn't hand himself over, he must run. The syndicate found him outside the parking lot of the Harbour and they talked to him. From here they took him to Nelspruit.'

Mabasa tells me that while the cops were hunting for Louca, the Cypriot was holed up on a farm belonging to 'the syndicate' just outside Nelspruit. He was waiting for a new passport to be prepared, reading and watching the news about Lolly Jackson's murder. He spent four days there. Van

Heerden, however, also suggests that this version does not tie up with the facts, such as the records at the border post.

Mabasa says he went to the farm himself, with the intention of arresting Louca. But by the time he got there, Louca had already skipped across the Mozambique border. So he chased after him into the neighbouring country but was always just one step behind.

'He was in Maputo; I went there but he was gone already. I've got contacts in the police there. We went to the airport and found that from the airport to Cyprus he was using his name. He didn't use the false passport – he used the real one. When Interpol got there he was already in Cyprus. They never did their job. From Maputo to Cyprus he used his real passport. What surprised me that this man was wanted all over, but they didn't tell Interpol. That bothers me. How is it possible that a person uses his real passport from Maputo to Cyprus?'

Mabasa, the surveillance expert, a tracker with a nose like a hound, had failed to catch up with George Louca before he fled to Cyprus and sought refuge on the island. He knew that it looked like he had helped escort him out of the country and that the dominant narrative in the public domain was that he was a corrupt cop on the payroll of organised criminals. He is adamant that this is not the reality.

IT IS 48 HOURS AFTER LOLLY JACKSON'S MURDER WHEN I PULL UP IN the driveway to his Beaulieu mansion. There is a massive aviary holding the Jacksons' pet monkeys and they chatter away as I walk through the front door. The Teazers boss was a keen collector of gaudy celebrity artwork and memorabilia and there are images of Michael Jackson and Elvis Presley, amongst others.

Jackson's widow has agreed to sit down with me and talk about his death. While she was hysterical on the scene of the murder, when I greet her Demi Jackson is far more composed, but evidently still in shock. The striking brunette is candid about her fears that her husband would be taken out in a hit.

'Every single day he got out that door and got in his car and he rode, I worried. There's always stories that there's lots of people who didn't like Lolly; there's lots of people that loved Lolly. I was scared of the people who didn't like Lolly because they weren't very good people. I was always scared about that, that was my fear.'

Demi last spoke to her husband on the morning of his murder on 3 May. Clutching a tiny picture of Jackson between her manicured fingers, she's desperate for the public to know the gentler side of the brazen businessman.

'You see these gangster movies when people have got drugs, money, money laundering; it's always portrayed in a strip club. With Lolly, no, it wasn't like that. He was a loving person. His family came first and his animals came in between. My emu got attacked by the dog and he was playing a poker tournament … He dropped everything to take the bird to Joburg Zoo because I was in tears. And that was Lolly Jackson. No one knows that side of him. He was never the sleaze,' she assures me.

Demi featured in many of his controversial campaigns and fully supported his tactics. She says she went so far as faking their divorce for publicity in the weeks before his death. Tabloids speculated that Jackson was having an affair with model Christina Storm, his co-star in two soon-to-be-released movies. Storm denied the 'stubborn rumours', insisting they were just 'special friends'. Demi agrees it was just a publicity stunt. 'We drew up divorce papers and then we started fooling around on Facebook. I would put on "not married" and then he would put on "open relation-ship", and then I would put "complicated". We were playing it. We were very open with each other. I always told him, "I don't mind, if you want to have another girl, I mean you have a hundred chicks naked around you all day."'

But it later emerged that the divorce talks were very real and that the couple were literally days away from signing the papers when he was killed. Several sources close to Jackson told me how he was planning on giving her a house as well as a R2-million settlement.

Whatever the state of the marriage, 48 hours after the shooting Demi was set to take on the mantle of the 'Queen of Teaze', and was likely to inherit the reins of Jackson's empire – which she ultimately did. 'I know the business inside out. I've been in the industry for 15 years. I know Lolly inside out and how he wants the club to be run. There's lots of people that want to change stuff. I'm still going to keep it like Lolly Jackson, but where the girls have a mother figure,' she says with a glimmer of determination in her eyes.

Demi has no idea as to a possible motive for her husband's murder. 'It's a shock. Lolly discussed everything with me. I have question marks all over the place,' she laments. I'm surprised at how little she seems to know about Jackson's business partners-cum-friends. She doesn't seem to have a clue about the money-laundering allegations or any criminal activity. 'I don't know George Smith at all. I've never even heard of the name. Radovan. I know Radovan as a friend of ours. Him and Lolly's never spoken deals. He's like a friend who's actually stood by me even when Lolly was in jail. Now coming out with all these stories, I'm sitting back and going, "Oh my word." I know Lolly inside out and I didn't even know about this – that's what's really puzzling me.'

LOLLY JACKSON'S MURDER EXPOSED ONE OF THE COUNTRY'S MOST senior Crime Intelligence officers as being in an allegedly corrupt relationship with organised crime, much in the same way that Brett Kebble's murder had exposed Jackie Selebi five years previously. Just one month after Jackson was killed, Selebi was convicted of corruption and defeating the ends of justice in the High Court in Johannesburg. In the end, prosecutors were only able to prove that he pocketed less than R120 000, but that was enough to send him to prison for 15 years.

Selebi's conviction and Mabasa's alleged corruption fed into the public perception that the top level of the SAPS was riddled with graft. The swashbuckling commissioner at the time, Bheki Cele, was working hard to disabuse citizens of this notion. He was talking tough about crime during the 2010 Football World Cup hosted in South Africa in July.

But despite his 'stomach in, chest out' mantra, Cele's reign at the SAPS arguably caused even more damage to the reputation of the police. In August 2010, news broke that Cele had signed a R500-million SAPS headquarters lease with his friend and businessman Roux Shabangu. Cele had signed the rental lease in June, one that would see police headquarters move to the 18-storey Middestad Sanlam Centre in Pretoria, which was co-owned by Shabangu. Police headquarters at the time were around the corner at the Wachthuis building where Selebi had sat while at the helm. The new lease would run for 10 years.

Then it emerged that while Shabangu signed the lease agreement on 1 June 2010, the businessman actually only purchased the building in late July for R220 million. In other words, he had signed a deal for a building he didn't technically own. According to the *Sunday Times*, the deal was also not treated as a tender, violating Treasury regulations that all government contracts over R500 000 need to go through a bidding process.

This deal would ultimately cost Bheki Cele his job as national police commissioner just one year later.

Even worse, under Cele's command, the wound at Crime Intelligence scratched open under Selebi was festering. While former CI head Mulangi Mpegho was facing criminal charges for the role he had played in trying to protect Selebi, Richard Mdluli was now in charge of the unit, and it didn't take long before allegations against Mdluli began to emerge. They came thick and fast and there was soon a clear division between two distinct camps in the organisation: for Mdluli and against him. In effect, I would argue, for Zuma and against him.

Between 2010 and 2011 the allegations against Mdluli piled up. They also mounted against Crime Intelligence chief financial officer Solly Lazarus and head of procurement, Colonel Hein Barnard, known as 'Barries'. These allegations ranged from nepotism to fraud to attempted murder.

According to a top-secret document titled 'Allegations made by CI Officer in Witness Protection', Mdluli was accused of hiring and paying family members of senior intelligence officials.

'During January/February 2010, CI advertised through a covert advertisement process 250 posts for Crime Intelligence. Most of these posts were filled by friends or family of high-ranking police officials. Lazarus was driving this process and before these posts were even advertised, individuals were already earmarked for the above posts. Family and friends I personally know gained by these promotions, including myself,' the CI member is quoted as saying.

Amongst those who were hired as CI agents without any experience or requisite skills was Mdluli's girlfriend, Theresa Lyons, who later became his wife. She became a colonel. Her sister was appointed as a warrant officer. Mdluli's son, ex-wife and daughter all received posts too. Mdluli allegedly gave a list of names containing individuals to Lazarus for appointment to the agent programme.

Some were supposed to set up and run an undercover internet café in Cape Town but they had limited computer skills so basic training had to be arranged for them. Others were appointed to the loss management unit, although it was unclear what they were actually doing there. All received advances on their monthly salaries, and state vehicles were also delivered to these so-called agents.

According to the CI top-secret document quoting the anonymous source, expenditure on these seven agents linked to Mdluli – which included the cost of vehicles, salaries, cellphones and the hiring of premises from March 2010 – exceeded R5 million.

Lazarus and Mdluli also allegedly sought to appoint five employees at the level of colonel as part of the covert appointment process. They were to be deployed as undercover police agents in the covert environment and could, therefore, not be identified nor take part in any appointment process. One of these included an old colleague of Mdluli, a cop he had been close to at Vosloorus and who would feature prominently in the controversy around Crime Intelligence for the coming years, his protégé Colonel Nkosana 'Killer' Ximba.

Ximba had worked as a community constable in Vosloorus and, in 1999, Mdluli recommended that he be permanently appointed to the SAPS. However, in March 2005, Ximba resigned and it was only when he applied to be reappointed in 2007 that the full scope of his past came to the fore. Mdluli instructed that he be reappointed, but the SAPS personnel services opposed this.

In 2001, Ximba was investigated for possessing an unlicensed firearm, but the docket went missing. Personnel services stated that Ximba had a previous criminal conviction for reckless and negligent driving. According to the *City Press* newspaper, personnel services said Ximba 'has already embarrassed the SAPS' and his re-enlistment 'bodes badly for the future'. *City Press* also stated that it was in possession of an affidavit, dated July 2009, in which a Boksburg businessman, Vusi Msimango, claims he was 'brutally tortured' by Ximba. The cop was later also implicated in the alleged torture of detained striking mineworkers at Marikana.

Despite the torture allegations against Ximba, Mdluli controversially promoted him from constable to colonel in March 2010. 'Killer' would play a pivotal role in the Radovan Krejcir story.

Mdluli and Lazarus were also accused of looting Crime Intelligence's slush fund and abusing covert offices and safe houses. According to declassified intelligence reports, Mdluli had the exclusive use of a safe house in Clearwater Estate in Boksburg. Crime Intelligence also rented Mdluli's property in Gordon's Bay as a safe house. Lazarus was accused of signing off on monthly rental instalments of R8500 from the secret account to pay for Mdluli's private home. This meant that Mdluli essentially leased his private dwelling to Crime Intelligence, under the guise that the house was to be used for intelligence-related purposes. They also allegedly used state vehicles to go on family holidays to a covert facility and expenses were claimed from the Secret Service Account (SSA) as an operational expense.

The alleged looting didn't stop there. It got even more complex when it came to cars. Mdluli and his family members had seven cars, part of a fleet of luxury vehicles purchased for more than R47 million over a period of five years by a Crime Intelligence front company. The elaborate scheme is laid out in affidavits authored by Hawks investigators as part of a criminal investigation into the allegations.

The statements detail how Mdluli had the use of an Audi, three Mercedes-Benzes, a BMW, a Jeep and a Lexus. Mdluli wasn't a fan of the Jeep, so CI bought him the Lexus. A number of these cars were illegally registered in his wife's name.

In the affidavits, the investigators carefully break down how the state was allegedly defrauded of tens of thousands of rand when Mdluli's 7-series BMW was traded in for a 5-series BMW.

In brief, Crime Intelligence allegedly bought two cars it didn't need so that it could use the discount from the vehicles to cover Mdluli's shortfall on his trade-in. According to the Hawks' affidavits, Mdluli benefited fraudulently because the money was intended for the state and was not for his personal use.

The Hawks affidavits also accuse Major General Solly Lazarus, head of the secret slush fund, of furthering his 'own agendas within the broader police structure by handing senior personnel luxury state vehicles'. They claim that Lazarus kept a pool of vehicles – a Mercedes Viano, a Volkswagen Caravelle, a Nissan Pathfinder and a Nissan King Cab – for the exclusive use of Crime Intelligence members close to him. At least two of Lazarus's family members were appointed as lieutenant colonels in the police. One of Lazarus's nephews became a captain.

There were also overseas trips for top brass and their family members, allegedly paid for out of the slush fund used for secret operations. Mdluli, his wife, Lazarus and Barnard and their respective spouses flew business class to China. They apparently went to purchase official equipment but, according to an anonymous CI official who accompanied them, 'We only spent two days buying equipment; the rest of the time we were sightseeing and personal shopping.' In December 2010 there were also trips to Mauritius as well as other flights for personal use paid for from the secret account.

It was over this period, between 2009 and 2011, that allegations also emerged that, under Mdluli's watch, the SSA was plundered to pay for upgrades at then Police Minister Nathi Mthethwa's private residence in KwaZulu-Natal. *City Press* revealed that the minister had benefited from the CI 'slush fund' to the tune of some R200 000.

Top police brass began to appoint investigators to look into these allegations against Mdluli, and Deputy National Commissioner General Godfrey Lebeya authorised an official probe. Initially Gauteng-based investigators were appointed but then, as concerns were raised about interference, two senior Hawks officers – Kobus Roelofse and Piet Viljoen – were brought in from Cape Town to lead the investigation.

While the allegations of corruption and fraud began to solidify, a far more serious charge against Mdluli lurked in the shadows. This time there was quite literally a skeleton involved. An old case docket that was shelved in Vosloorus was dusted off and reopened. It was a murder file. Mdluli was accused of being behind the death of his ex-girlfriend's husband, Oupa Ramogibe, who had been killed in 1999. At the time, Mdluli was the station commander at Vosloorus.

While he was married to his first wife, Mdluli had had an affair with a young woman, Tshidi Buthelezi. The affair started while Buthelezi was still in school. Mdluli claimed that he had paid for her education and that he also paid R12 000 lobola to her parents. Together they had a son, Siphiwe.

But then Buthelezi fell in love with Oupa Ramogibe and married him at the Boksburg magistrate's court. Buthelezi was scared of her former boyfriend Mdluli so the couple told none of their family members about the marriage. And it appears she had good reason to be terrified.

According to an affidavit signed by investigator Kobus Roelofse, Mdluli along with three other police officers, including Killer Ximba, went knocking on the doors of family members and attempted to intimidate them into putting pressure on the couple to stop their relationship. Buthelezi and Ramogibe fled and went into hiding in Orange Farm in the south of Johannesburg.

Mdluli was persistent, and eventually he tracked the couple down. Together with his colleagues, he allegedly kidnapped Buthelezi's friend Alice Manana and forced her to take them to Buthelezi's home. Soon afterwards, in December 2008, an attempt was made on Ramogibe's life. Shots were fired at him while he was driving in Vosloorus, and two 9mm casings were found on the scene.

Two months after that shooting, Ramogibe returned to the scene of the attempt on his life to assist the investigating officer in the case by pointing out where the incident had occurred. It was 2pm on 17 February 1999. Ramogibe was standing with a police officer on a street corner in Vosloorus when two unknown individuals walked up to the cop and pointed a firearm at him. He was ordered to hand over his service pistol and forced to lie down. The officer heard shots and a while later he ran to the nearest house to get help. Only when he returned to the scene did he find Ramogibe's body. He had been shot several times. Nine bullet casings and a projectile were collected from the scene of the crime.

Mdluli was immediately a suspect in the murder, but within a year he had been promoted to director and transferred to the Southern Cape. When the investigating officer travelled to Oudtshoorn to interview him, Mdluli declined to state his version of events and instead opted to supply a written affidavit, which never materialised. No one was prosecuted for Ramogibe's murder and the docket was shelved for over a decade.

Although Mdluli was long suspected of interfering in the case and sabotaging the investigation, nothing was done until he rose to the powerful position of CI commander and someone went looking for that file.

While investigators were busy trying to build a case against Mdluli, he was investigating those who were probing him. He was also busy shoring up his own personal political capital. Before he even became head of CI, when the rumours that the Ramogibe docket was being unearthed again first reached his ears, Mdluli took pre-emptive measures. He tasked a little-known deputy commissioner in Limpopo with investigating who was behind a plot to prevent him from becoming CI head. That deputy commissioner was Mthandazo 'Berning' Ntlemeza, who subsequently became head of the Hawks and a close ally of Mdluli. Ntlemeza produced a report that exonerated Mdluli of any wrongdoing in Ramogibe's death and found that the allegations were part of a smear campaign to prevent Mdluli's appointment.

In October 2010, Mdluli then penned a bizarre, lengthy, poorly written 22-page 'Ground Coverage Intelligence Report' to President Jacob Zuma. The report detailed an alleged plot to unseat the president by what was loosely referred to as the Estcourt grouping. Mdluli claimed that the cabal, headed by then Housing Minister Tokyo Sexwale, included senior politicians Fikile Mbalula, Paul Mashatile, Zweli Mkhize and National Commissioner Bheki Cele. The document oozed paranoia, the stuff of spy fiction.

Initially, it was thought that the report emanated from an unauthorised investigation into Cele, but it later emerged that the information had actually been fabricated by spies who had sold the intelligence to the police for R200 000. Some of this faked intelligence also found its way into the report Ntlemeza had compiled for Mdluli. Years later, Mdluli denied authoring or declassifying the controversial 'Ground Coverage' report.

On 1 November 2010, Mdluli sent a secret letter to Zuma claiming 'victimisation and abuse of state resources'. He was convinced that senior figures in CI had been trying to frame him for the murder of Ramogibe since 2007 and he was worried that the Hawks were taking up the investigation. He appealed to Zuma to intervene, claiming that the spies behind this campaign were aligned to former President Thabo Mbeki. He compiled a dossier in which he pledged his loyalty to the president and provided the so-called intelligence report that implicated Zuma's alleged political enemies. He noted: 'The question arises — how do they want to use the intelligence environment to affect the 2012 build-up to the ANC conference?'

The ANC's elective conference in Mangaung was just over a year away and already the fight was getting dirty. As was the case in the run-up to the Polokwane conference, battle lines were drawn early on and state agencies were used to fight these factional battles within the ruling party. The most powerful weapon to wield was the police's intelligence unit. It would later be claimed that dozens of spies were deployed to the conference and a budget of over R50 million was allocated for bribes to delegates paid by CI agents.

Also in November 2010, an application was allegedly signed off by Mdluli to tap a number of phones. This included the line of National Commissioner Bheki Cele. In other words, Cele was being bugged by his own intelligence officers. According to the *Mail & Guardian*, one of Cele's phone numbers was allegedly put on an interception application that was filed under a false name. It was suggested that the phone intercept application was actually aimed at journalists who had revealed the dodgy building-lease deal Cele had signed. It was a convenient cover to slip in Cele's number and listen to his calls.

At the time it was widely held in political and media circles that everyone's phone was being tapped. It wasn't uncommon for us to jokingly greet Mdluli first when we answered our calls, before beginning our real conversation. Any meeting with a source meant removing the battery from our personal devices and leaving them in the car before walking into an office or restaurant because it was believed that phones could be bugged even when switched off. It was a time of great fear, anxiety and paranoia.

Over that period – between 2009 and 2011 – CI was crippled by corruption, resources were being abused, investigations were being conducted, slush funds were being looted and nests were being feathered.

Mdluli wasn't sitting back, but neither were the Hawks. Kobus Roelofse and Piet Viljoen were busy compiling a thick docket of evidence against Mdluli on both the corruption and murder cases.

Then the *Mail & Guardian* reported that the Hawks were investigating Mdluli on yet another case and this one had to do with his links to Radovan Krejcir:

The Hawks are probing senior members of police crime intelligence over allegations that they interfered with the Hawks' investigation into Czech fugitive Radovan Krejcir.

Hawks spokesperson McIntosh Polela would not comment. However, a source close to the Hawks, an intelligence source and a prosecuting authority official have all confirmed that the investigation centres on former Gauteng crime intelligence boss Joey Mabasa and the head of crime intelligence, General Richard Mdluli.

The probe is understood to focus on allegations that crime intelligence engaged in extensive phone-tapping of Hawks members and others involved in the Krejcir investigation.

It is alleged that in at least one case, intercepted conversations found their way to targets of the Hawks' investigation, which includes not only Krejcir but a number of his associates.

City Press also reported on the intra-police battle and how Krejcir was at the centre of it all:

Fugitive Czech millionaire Radovan Krejcir allegedly 'bought' influence and protection from police, and top cops are now spying on each other amid an investigation to identify the allegedly corrupt officials. The alleged 'mob boss' is currently the subject of a wide-ranging probe by the Hawks into a number of corruption cases involving senior police crime intelligence officers in Gauteng.

Krejcir is alleged to have paid top cops to make criminal cases 'go away' and to intimidate members of the Johannesburg underworld.

In short, the newspaper reported that Hawks investigators had evidence that their phones were being tapped by police CI operatives, and that information about their investigation into Krejcir was being leaked.

It was evident that Radovan Krejcir was using cops to feed him the phone records of the people who were investigating him and to tip him off about whatever evidence they thought they had against him. He was being protected by the very people who were supposed to be bringing him down.

UWE GEMBALLA'S BODY, BOUND IN A BLACK SHEET OF PLASTIC and duct-taped, was found in a shallow grave. When his remains were exhumed, a bullet wound was discovered at the back of his skull. It was Thabiso Melvin Mpye who led police investigator Ludi Schnelle and his colleagues to the old cemetery in Lotus Gardens in September 2010, seven months after Gemballa disappeared. Police had turned Mpye state witness after linking him to the cellphone data. The 29-year-old admitted stealing the car dealer's iPhone after he had been killed.

The wheels of the criminal justice system have a reputation for grinding frustratingly slowly in South Africa. It can take weeks for a court date to be set, months for a trial to be actually heard and years for a verdict to be delivered. Yet in the case of Mpye, the entire process was rushed through in a flash, likely expedited because of the profile of the victim.

Within 24 hours of confessing to the crime, he had entered into a plea deal with the state and appeared in court in Johannesburg. In exchange for pleading guilty to kidnapping and murder charges, he agreed to sell out his associates and testify against them for the prosecutors.

In the deal, he set out that he had acted on the instructions of others and he had been paid two instalments of R25 000 and R10 000 respectively. He detailed how he and three others had kidnapped Gemballa from the airport, taken him to the house in Edenvale, held him there for several days and then killed him by covering his head in duct tape and sitting on his chest.

In his plea statement, Mpye pointed to a much broader conspiracy and to the fact that he and his associates had acted on instructions. He said that two men who called themselves Kizzer and Madala offered him and his three accomplices R50 000 each to kill Gemballa.

In his statement, Mpye described Kizzer as being 'very tall with big muscles and long Afro hair' and Madala as 'between the age of 50 and 60, with blond, neatly trimmed hair and a full beard and moustache'. Mpye said he did not know whether Madala was South African, but Kizzer was not as he spoke 'dirty English with an accent'.

After taking Gemballa to the house, Mpye said: 'Madala and Kizzer were very happy; they said that they were looking for this guy for more than five years. I heard that they were communicating with him on computer. I then suspect that these guys were making messages with Gemballa to bring him this side to South Africa. They were saying, "Well done, good job," to us.'

Mpye's description of the murder reads like a scene from a crime thriller:

In the room I saw Gemballa lying on top of the bed with his clothes and shoes on, he was not moving. I saw his feet was tied with tape, I cannot remember if they were tied with the brown or the silver tape. I saw that his hands were now tied behind his back with tape, I cannot remember if the tape was the brown or the silver tape. His mouth was taped closed. He was still alive, he looked at us. The four of us, myself, Thabo, Kagiso and Garland then put on the gardening gloves that we kept from digging the hole. I did not notice Madala wearing any gloves. Madala then brought a large black plastic sheet to us, I think this is a sheet you use for roofing. Madala put the sheet on the floor in the passage at the door of the room. Madala stood to one side when we picked Gemballa up from the bed and placed him on the sheet of plastic. We all helped put extra tape around Gemballa's feet and hands. Kagiso was at his head as he is not very strong and has a bad hip so the rest of us were at Gemballa's body to stop him if he tried to fight. He however never put up any resistance, his body was only shaking. Kagiso put a black plastic packet over Gemballa's head and the plastic was then taped onto Gemballa's head. Kagiso completely taped up Gemballa's whole head with the tape so that he could not breathe. While Kagiso was holding his head, Thabo was sitting on his back as he was the biggest and heaviest of all four of us. I was holding Gemballa's legs. Garland and Madala were standing

watching us as we could not all fit on Gemballa in the small space of
the passage. After a few minutes I could feel that Gemballa had no more
power in him, so I stood up. Kagiso felt on Gemballa's neck and he said
'he is gone' meaning that he is dead.

For the truth, Mpye was sentenced to 28 years in prison: 20 for murder, five
for kidnapping and three for theft.

Mpye did not name Radovan Krejcir in his plea deal, nor did he reveal
who the people were who gave the order for the hit on Gemballa. But
Krejcir's shadow loomed large over the case from the outset. A list of
potential witnesses attached to the plea agreement gave an indication of
the direction in which the police were looking.

The *Mail & Guardian* reported at the time that at least eight of the 27
people on the witness list were associates of Krejcir and the Czech himself
was number 15 on the list.

A number of key associates also implicated Krejcir in Gemballa's murder and yet, despite this, he was never actually charged with the crime. The
gold refiner Juan Meyer claims he overheard a conversation during which
Krejcir angrily threatened Gemballa and told him he would 'get trouble'
and he would 'organise a surprise for him'. Meyer also linked the two men
through a money-laundering scheme.

Meyer revealed that Krejcir had told him that Lolly Jackson and Gemballa
were moving money into South Africa for him. Krejcir would allegedly
buy Porsches from the German and the car would arrive on South African
soil with bundles of foreign currency stashed inside the panels of the car
and the money would be sold on the black market. However, according to
plan, in September 2009 Krejcir bought a vehicle but when the car arrived,
there was no money hidden inside it. That's when Krejcir allegedly phoned
Gemballa and threatened him.

'I was present when he told Uwe Gemballa that he will kill him. They
would use those compartments and boxes to transport euros for Radovan.
Radovan bought himself a Gemballa Porsche Cayenne, which he brought
into South Africa. In consignment of that vehicle Uwe owed him €1 million. The money never arrived. That's what led to the argument and

Radovan told him if he finds him he will kill him. He lured him here with a so-called business deal that someone wants to open a business franchise here. It was just to get him here.

'We were at the Harbour café, he started speaking German to the guy on the phone and I could hear that he was threatening someone. Radovan likes to boast as to guys working for him or involved with him. I asked him what the conversation was about and he told me that he warned the guy he was going to kill him if he doesn't get his money within a certain period of time.'

Krejcir's doctor, Marian Tupy, also gave police a statement in which, among other things, he spoke about how his patient had suggested he was involved in Gemballa's murder. Tupy explained that he had asked Krejcir about the incident. 'He smiled. I then asked what had happened to Gemballa and he put his hand to his throat and drew his hand across his throat, making a cutting sound with his mouth and then he pointed to his own chest and said, "It was me." I realised that he is a very dangerous man.'

In his book *The Godfather African*, Krejcir's lieutenant, Milosh Potiska, sketches out a story very similar to that described by Meyer. Potiska paints Gemballa as a desperate man who was looking for money because he had taken a knock in the economic crisis. He was in such a fix that he was willing to enter into a dangerous deal with Krejcir – he would send a car to his client in South Africa and it would be used as a secret deposit box for €1 million in cash. According to Potiska, the agreement was simple. Gemballa would allegedly build secret boxes into the door of a tuned Porsche and the cash would be hidden in the panels. Krejcir would escape paying taxes on the money and, in exchange, he would have a branch of Gemballa's tuning company established in South Africa, which would 'supply rich Afrikaners with your scented cars'. Krejcir would also allegedly pay Gemballa the remainder of what was owed to him in diamonds to assist him with his new endeavour, making cars with a diamond coating.

Potiska claims that at the last minute, Gemballa crumbled and backed out of the deal. He sent the Porsche to South Africa without the money in the secret compartments. He doubted whether Krejcir would keep his end of the bargain. According to his lieutenant, Krejcir was furious and set up

Jerome Safi to lure Gemballa to Johannesburg and take him out. He goes so far as to claim that someone in Krejcir's circle began spreading outrageous rumours about Gemballa's disappearance to throw up a smoke-screen around the murder.

Potiska wasn't in the country at the time of the Gemballa incident, so this account is essentially second-hand. 'If I had been there, Gemballa would probably have never been found. As I don't like slapdash work. I like to get the details perfect,' he writes in his book.

He wasn't the only one of Krejcir's right-hand men to offer up a conflicting theory on what led to the German's kidnapping and death. George Louca also deposed to an affidavit in which he put forward another version of what might have happened. In Louca's account, Krejcir held an old grudge for which he sought revenge and patiently held out for years to seek that retribution.

'He explained that before his arrest in the Czech Republic, he had sent a Porsche GTS owned by him to Gemballa's workshops in Germany for modification. He told me that after work on the car was completed, Gemballa refused to release the Porsche to him because of a disagreement over certain costs, which, as I understood it, had not been paid by Krejcir. Krejcir said that he had insisted Gemballa return the vehicle, but Gemballa would not do so, and kept Krejcir's Porsche. For this reason Krejcir was angry with Gemballa and sought revenge,' claims Louca.

He states that Krejcir asked him to persuade Gemballa to visit the country to consider opening a branch here. He knew that the plan was to have Gemballa kidnapped and to ask for €2 million in ransom. However, Louca refused to be complicit in the crime. 'I believed that it was more than likely that Krejcir would want Gemballa killed after the transfer of the ransom money and I was not prepared to play any part in such a scheme.'

The standoff between the two became a point of contention in their relationship and Louca believes it was the catalyst for their fallout. 'He became extremely angry and told me that if I refused to cooperate with him I could "go to hell".'

While Krejcir was never directly implicated in the murder, the hit certainly highlighted the nexus between organised crime and police in South

Africa and entrenched the Czech as a mobster-type figure who had laid down roots and established himself in the local underworld. With questions being raised by the Hawks about whether or not Krejcir had corrupted the cops who were investigating him, the police officers investigating the Gemballa case were also under scrutiny.

Just two months after he had turned Mpye from accused to state witness, lead investigator Ludi Schnelle was abruptly removed from the case. A laptop seized from the murder scene, the Edenvale house, had mysteriously vanished from his office.

Hawks spokesperson McIntosh Polela stated that video footage showed that Schnelle had failed to book the laptop in as police evidence and it then went missing. The officer was facing a disciplinary inquiry and was transferred out of the Hawks. Polela said Schnelle was removed in line with a standing order to combat high levels of evidence and docket theft. 'Schnelle lost a very important exhibit in a massive case, so he had to go,' Polela said.

This, however, was not a clear-cut case. At the time, it was claimed in the media that Gauteng Hawks head Shadrack Sibiya had interfered in the murder investigation and had appointed Colonel Patrick Mbotho to oversee the case. Reports suggested that Mbotho was close to the controversial Joey Mabasa and he might have been placed there to protect Krejcir. Sources claim that, in fact, it was not Schnelle who had lost the laptop, but that Mbotho or Mabasa had had a hand in making it disappear. The computer allegedly contained information regarding Krejcir's financial affairs in South Africa. Schnelle's removal also considerably slowed the police's investigation in the Gemballa case.

Despite the swiftness of Mpye's confession and conviction, it still took another five months before the three other men were taken into custody. In March 2011, Thabo Mohapi, Garland Holworthy and Kagiso Joseph Linken, aka Thabiso Lincoln Ledwaba, were arrested. All three were professional criminals with long histories of breaking the law. All had spent time in jail for violent crimes and Linken had previously been charged with murder following a cash heist in Soweto in which a cop was killed.

Mpye had been convicted and sentenced in 24 hours. It took over five years for a verdict to be delivered in the trio's trial. True to form, the trial itself was not without high drama and was punctuated by surreal, unpredictable events.

When the trial actually began in Palm Ridge in 2013, Mpye shocked prosecutors and journalists when he did an extraordinary about-turn on the witness stand. The man who was meant to be the state's key witness against the three accused suddenly claimed the trio had absolutely nothing to do with Gemballa's murder. In a refrain so prevalent in criminal trials, Mpye claimed that his statement had been obtained through torture. It was an embarrassing spectacle for the state.

All three men were convicted by Judge George Maluleke but it was something of a pyrrhic victory for the state. It was evident throughout that these were only the foot soldiers of the crime, the 'button men' as the shooters are often referred to in mafia lore. Others had ordered the kidnapping and the murder. However, it seemed that there was simply not enough evidence to put those responsible on trial.

To add to the state's woes, three days before sentencing, Linken escaped from the Palm Ridge court. He managed to get his hands on a firearm, pointed it at a policeman in the holding cells, forced the colonel to hand over his service pistol, and took the keys from the cells and freed himself.

CCTV footage showed a police constable, an orderly, placing a bag containing a weapon in the parking lot outside the court and then making a phone call. The person he was talking to was Linken, who had a cellphone on him in the Correctional Services truck carrying him to court. When the truck arrived in the parking lot, Linken waited for everyone to disembark and then inconspicuously retrieved the bag containing the gun.

This exchange is the perfect illustration of the systemic nature of corruption within the SAPS and the symbiotic relationship between organised crime and the police. In this particular case, you have an experienced, violent criminal who is able to wriggle his way out of prison and escape justice because a low-level cop, a constable, has been paid off. The escape wiped out the five years, money and energy it took for this case to wind itself through the criminal justice system, only for the convict to escape from custody on the eve of the final chapter in the trial.

Linken was arrested seven months later in Sunninghill. Police found him and his associates in possession of two rifles, a handgun, ammunition and Police Service reflector vests, a cap and radio, among other items. Police suspected he was on his way to commit a crime. It's unclear what other crimes he may have been involved in while on the run.

Gemballa's case also illustrates how potential corruption at the top of the food chain might have ensured that key figures in the organised crime structure, those responsible for ordering the hit, were never brought to book. It stinks of suspicion. A crucial piece of evidence in the case, a laptop recovered at the house in Edenvale, conveniently went missing – stolen from inside a police station.

Mpye's arrest and Schnelle's removal from the case also came at a time when the Hawks were investigating alleged corruption between Krejcir and CI officers accused of meddling in investigations targeting the Czech. In fact, Gemballa's murder and the subsequent trial were a marker for Krejcir. It put his name on the map in the public domain as a dominant force in the underworld – though he has always firmly denied any involvement in the crime.

'I saw Gemballa once in my life for a couple of minutes at a car show in Prague in 1995,' Krejcir told amaBhungane, in response to the allegations. 'It was by accident because it was the big car expo and I love my cars, you know what I mean. So I like these toys and I like the conversions for the cars … This is how I met him and the first and last time I saw him, not only saw him, even talked to him. But maybe it is the reason why I want to kill him, because I saw him 15 years ago?

'… If I were in touch with Gemballa, his wife must know, his friends must know, his business partners must know that he's talking to Radovan or somebody from Radovan. It's obvious. So let's speak to these people, ask them if they ever heard about the fucking Radovan. I'm sick and tired of this explanation.'

In an extended interview, Krejcir claimed that it was Jerome Safi's idea to open a Gemballa franchise, not his.

'The whole story was that I ended up with this idea from Jerome. He came to visit me and he offered me if I am willing to support financially the business with the conversion of the cars and I told him if he will organise the exclusive contract with Gemballa ... I am willing to [invest].'

Safi initially agreed to an interview for this book but then never made himself available, despite numerous requests.

Krejcir also rubbished suggestions that he was responsible for ordering the hit because Gemballa was murdered at Ivan Savov's house and Krejcir was linked to other witnesses in the case.

'What I know about Savov is that he's a project manager working for a hundred people, actually he's not working for me, but he's working for my wife, she's got the ... companies, and Savov what he's doing only is take care of these companies which belong to my wife, from the accountant point of view and [legal] point of view ... I know Ivan is the family man, is the businessman, is the guy who never will be involved. The whole story is from these 27 people – I know five, including me.'

As far as Krejcir was concerned, Gemballa's gruesome murder had absolutely nothing to do with him.

IT WAS A TIP-OFF THAT LED AUTHORITIES TO THE 'UNUSUAL' CONTAINER at the Port of Ngqura near Port Elizabeth in the Eastern Cape in August 2010. Through a joint operation, the Hawks, customs officials and foreign law enforcement agencies tracked the container to a ship that had travelled from South America. It was en route from Asunción in Paraguay to Bulawayo, Zimbabwe. The container looked like a petrol tank but had construction-type pillars holding it together. Inside the container, authorities found 22 000 litres of used cooking oil. But inside the pillars was where the bounty was hidden: 250 kilograms of pure cocaine. Police couldn't believe what they had found and drained the oil from the tanker to ensure there were no more pillars holding drugs inside.

There was immediately some dispute about the quantity of drugs actually seized, with some claiming that the full shipment was 250 kilograms, but only 166 kilograms were booked in by police as evidence. According to media reports, there was also a break-in at the police laboratory in Port Elizabeth, apparently targeting the cocaine haul in an attempt to steal the drugs back after they had been confiscated. Five men, including a police constable, were arrested following the break-in.

Two months after the Port Elizabeth bust, the man thought to be responsible for the tip-off lay dead outside a wedding venue on Johannesburg's West Rand, murdered in what appeared to be a hit. At the time, word in intelligence circles was that Chris Couremetis was suspected by some of his partners of orchestrating the bust so he could recover part of the cocaine for himself.

'Mr Big', aka 'Mr Cocaine', 35-year-old Chris Couremetis was taken out by two men on the back of a motorbike clutching an AK-47 and a 9mm pistol. Twelve shots were fired, two hitting Couremetis and the rest striking his luxury vehicle. Mr Big was about to get into his Porsche Cayenne at around 7:30pm, having just been best man at a wedding at the Cradle restaurant in Muldersdrift.

The gunmen made off with his expensive Rolex watch and a moonbag he was wearing, containing R10 000.

Investigators established that the gunmen had arrived at the wedding venue, set a few kilometres off a main road in the savanna bushveld, by posing as guests dressed in suits. Two men arrived in a stolen blue Volvo hours before the shooting and signed in with their ID numbers and vehicle registration details. A third man arrived some time later on a motorcycle, claiming to be delivering a wedding present. Couremetis's murder appears to have been premeditated and professional.

It was only once his body was cold that the true extent of Mr Big's involvement in the criminal underworld emerged. It seemed to come as a shock to some of those who knew him best.

Couremetis was an intriguing individual who kept questionable company. Many of his close friends were also friends with Radovan Krejcir. He moved in drug-dealing circles and was known particularly amongst those with links to South American cartels. Despite his low profile locally, Couremetis led an ostentatious lifestyle. He owned a five-star villa in Thailand, a nightclub in Brazil and numerous upmarket properties. He owned multimillion-rand properties in Fresnaye on the Atlantic seaboard in Cape Town, in Hyde Park and in Bryanston. His home in Bryanston was in the lavish Savoy Estate, his neighbour was convicted drug dealer Glenn Agliotti. On the day after his death, Agliotti tweeted, 'Lost a dear friend in a shooting yesterday at a wedding. Say a prayer for Chris. Grazie.'

Another of Couremetis's closest friends was the owner of Sandton Gold and Diamond Exchange, Djordje Mihaljevic – the same Mihaljevic who had introduced Juan Meyer to Krejcir and who was a business partner of the Czech. In the wake of the hit, the *Weekend Argus* revealed just how close Couremetis and Mihaljevic were.

According to the newspaper report, Couremetis had kept a low profile following the massive Port Elizabeth drug bust, living a clandestine existence in Spain. He feared for his safety in South Africa, but wanted to return home to attend the wedding. He kept the news of his visit quiet and only planned to be in the country for a short period. Mihaljevic knew his friend was in town and the two arranged to meet on the side of the highway en route to the wedding venue in Muldersdrift. Mihaljevic reportedly left the wedding venue with Couremetis's parents, Judy and Costa, prior to the shooting.

The *Weekend Argus* pointed to whispers in police circles that the hit had something to do with a massive illegal diamond deal. 'Some informants – saying that as much as 10 000 carats of the illicit stones were at stake – have claimed that the trade-off was sealed during the wedding reception. When Couremetis was lying next to the vehicle, dying, one of the attackers, according to bystander testimony, leaped into the car shouting: "Where is the bag, where is the bag?"' This link to diamonds was never publicly confirmed by police.

Crucially, the final text messages on Couremetis's phone also highlighted another friendship that firmly planted him in the underworld. The last SMSes he sent were to alleged Cuban drug lord Nelson Pablo Yester-Garrido. Couremetis confirmed he was on his way to Yester-Garrido's Morningside house where he and his Italian girlfriend were hosting a party to celebrate the birth of their first child.

Nelson Pablo Yester-Garrido's name is not widely known in South Africa, but he is a fascinating character. As journalist Stefaans Brümmer wrote in the *Mail & Guardian*, his story has all the elements of a spy thriller, including intelligence networks, submarines, fast cars, Russian mobsters, escapes and a strip club. Not to mention cocaine cartels.

Following a string of arrests in the United States, the Cuban citizen fled to South Africa in the late 1990s after he was indicted in Florida. An undercover operation by authorities there had implicated him in a sensational plan to buy a diesel submarine from the Russians to be used by Colombian drug suppliers to transport cocaine to the west coast of the United States and Canada.

In South Africa, he created a fake persona, posing as a Mexican dealer in aircraft spares, and went by the name Antonio Lamas. He made friends with strategic individuals – including Agliotti.

In 2002, Yester-Garrido was living in upmarket Sandhurst with his girl-friend and their young child. Incredibly, a local viewer of the US television show *America's Most Wanted* recognised Yester-Garrido as 'Lamas' and tipped off the cops. The Cuban was arrested by the police, who acted on an Interpol warrant for charges including racketeering and conspiracy to import narcotics to the United States. A Mercedes-Benz SL500, US$30 000 and fake passports were seized at his house.

Attempts were made to extradite him to the United States but Yester-Garrido retained the services of senior advocate Laurance Hodes, who later successfully defended Agliotti on a murder charge. He was also later represented by Ian Small-Smith and advocate Anton Katz. Ultimately, Yester-Garrido remained in South Africa.

But then, in March 2011, nearly a decade after his first arrest, Yester-Garrido was taken into custody again. This time it was for his alleged involvement in the massive Port Elizabeth drug bust. Authorities car-ried out a simultaneous transnational operation involving the police's Organised Crime unit and the Brazilian Federal Police in São Paulo.

During the raid on the Cuban's Johannesburg home, officers report-edly found a Smith and Wesson Desert Eagle revolver registered in Couremetis's name. Yester-Garrido faced an additional charge for posses-sion of this weapon. The *Mail & Guardian* reported that although there was no evidence linking Yester-Garrido to Couremetis's murder, the police were convinced that the two cases were linked. 'We can't divorce the mur-der from the cocaine bust. We have made the links,' a source told the *Mail & Guardian*. The cops also connected Krejcir and his business partners to Couremetis, but not to his murder.

Yester-Garrido was released on R600 000 bail by a Motherwell court and the case against him was utterly bungled. At one stage, astonishingly, charges were even withdrawn against one of the most wanted drug lords in the world because no one was available to translate Brazilian official docu-ments from Portuguese into English. Yester-Garrido was later arrested in Rome on an Interpol red notice and remains in custody there although he is expected to be extradited to the US.

Then, in early 2017, news broke in the Port Elizabeth newspaper *The*

Herald that the National Prosecuting Authority was probing claims that a member of the prosecuting team was paid off to ensure that the case disappeared.

'The National Prosecuting Authority (NPA) is investigating allegations that a briefcase containing R700 000 was dropped off in Port Elizabeth to stop a drug prosecution in its tracks. Implicated in the alleged bribery is a former Cuban spy linked to Czech mob boss Radovan Krejcir,' *The Herald* reported.

The claims arose from an affidavit supplied by a former Krejcir employee, who had been a driver for the Czech, and who had supplied authorities with a range of allegations about payments, bribes and transactions. The driver claimed under oath that Krejcir had sent him to Port Elizabeth to bribe the prosecutors and, a day after the payment was made, the charges were withdrawn.

While Krejcir was never directly linked to Couremetis or to the Port Elizabeth drug deal gone wrong, the two moved in the same dubious circles. They shared many mutual friends, all with connections to the illicit world of drug dealing. When Couremetis was shot dead, Krejcir's name was immediately attached to the murder. To this day it remains unclear whether that connection was warranted or not. After the deaths of Trytsman, Jackson and Gemballa, here was another name to add to the growing list of Krejcir associates who had been killed: Chris Couremetis, aka Mr Big. In this particular case, the link might be tenuous and the Czech unfairly implicated. There is no evidence to suggest that Krejcir had a hand in the shooting.

However, Mr Big's murder served to add more fuel to the belief that Krejcir was establishing himself as the man calling all the shots in the underworld. The bodies were piling up.

CANDICE COETZEE, WITH HER WRIST TATTOO AND COIFFED SHORT hair, is an unlikely looking spy. But a short conversation on the public benches of a court will leave you with no doubt. She is a career cop through and through. Some in more nefarious circles used to refer to her as 'Cyril's cop', others more endearingly call her 'James Bond's mom'. In the months leading up to Beeka's death, Coetzee was often seen in his company and it is widely known that they were close. There have been suggestions of a romantic relationship, but Coetzee denies this.

As a young woman, Coetzee joined the cops, mostly because her husband was a cop. Naively, she thought she could make a difference, although experience has since disabused her of that notion. In 2003 she joined Crime Intelligence and was responsible for inspections and evaluation. From what I've been told by cops, this meant going to undercover offices, checking their vehicle logbooks and comparing their informer files with payments made for information. It was a system susceptible to corruption and she had to cast a keen eye over it.

For several years she served under Mulangi Mphego, head of CI at the time. Mphego put together what became known in the police as a 'hit squad', a tactical team aimed at curbing violent crimes, particularly cash-in-transit heists. During the mid-2000s, cash-in-transit heists were rife and becoming increasingly brazen and violent. In 2006, three SBV guards were burnt to death and another shot in the Waterberg region in Limpopo, south of Polokwane. It was a particularly brutal attack and police were under pressure to react. Being on Mphego's squad meant intense physical training and tactical courses. It was a hefty investment for Coetzee, who had to rely on DStv and PlayStation to act as babysitter for her three children.

It was through her pursuit of cash-in-transit gangs that Coetzee's path crossed Cyril Beeka's. The cop was chatting to State Security Agency contract agent George Darmanovich about her frustrations at how arrested suspects were repeatedly being let free, when the Serb suggested she speak to someone else experiencing the same problem. At the time, Cyril Beeka was head of security at RAM Hand-to-Hand Couriers. It was late 2009 and RAM's hijacking numbers were concerning.

Coetzee met Beeka at Doppio Zero restaurant in Greenside. The two clicked immediately. It helped that Beeka was charming and charismatic. Coetzee knew nothing of Beeka's legend or history and when she got home that night she began to Google. What she found online about the man known as the Rottweiler from Kuils River shocked the CI officer.

She read how he traversed the upper- and underworlds with one foot in the ganglands of the Cape and the other in intelligence structures, guaranteeing himself immunity from prosecution through the protection of well-placed political contacts.

She learnt how in 1994 he allegedly attacked a suspect in a murder case in court, how in 1998 charges of intimidation were laid against him by the head of the presidential task team in the Western Cape, how his companies Pro Security and Red Security were running protection rackets in Cape Town's nightclubs, about his links with mafioso and Sicilian businessman Vito Palazzolo, his associations with former MK operative Robert McBride and his business dealings with Yuri 'The Russian' Ulianitski, who was shot dead with his four-year-old daughter in a hit in 2007.

She also got some understanding of just how politically connected he was, with reports that Beeka and Moe Shaik owned the company that controlled the voting process at the ANC's electoral conference in Polokwane in 2007.

Coetzee was under no illusion that Cyril Beeka was capable of being a dangerous and volatile man, but it appeared that he had since put the brakes on the behaviour that had earned him such a terrifying reputation. He had left Cape Town a few years previously and settled in Johannesburg, taking a respectable job in a corporate environment. However, she was not naive enough to believe that he didn't still have a hand in that world and suspected that he could still be doing dodgy, illegal deals on the side. His friendship with Radovan Krejcir was evidence enough for Coetzee. But Beeka never broke the law in front of her; he was discreet and respectful of her position, and wasn't afraid to trust her, allowing her to accompany him to meetings on a regular basis.

In the meantime, Beeka and Coetzee worked together fighting criminals who were targeting RAM trucks. They recovered stolen goods and notched up successes with their shared intelligence. Their relationship flourished and Beeka's trust in the cop grew. She became an 'insider', navigating the fine line so many intelligence officers have to negotiate between immersing oneself in the criminal world to gather information and still maintaining the objectivity and independence required of a law enforcement official.

Coetzee got a handle on what was going on in Beeka's circle. As far as Krejcir was concerned, Coetzee was Cyril's cop who tipped him off when investigators started looking too closely at his activities. Beeka and Krejcir discussed business prospects: potential gold mines in Zimbabwe, diamonds they wanted to bring in from Angola and gun running off the coast of Mozambique. Coetzee had to look the other way when the men met with her colleagues, dirty cops who were on the take from Krejcir, even though she knew that ignoring corruption was making her complicit. She saw the Bedfordview officers drive into Money Point. Coetzee knew that sounding the alarm over relatively petty bribery was nothing in comparison to the broader case being slowly built in the background.

Beeka continued to travel regularly to Cape Town to do business. Many sources say he still had his fingers in the clubs as he maintained an uneasy truce amongst the key players in the city, the most notable being former military man and head of Professional Protection Services, André Naudé; Sexy Boys gang leader Jerome 'Donkie' Booysen; and Sea Point businessman Mark Lifman.

Beeka always knew his position was not entirely secure and his life could be under threat. He realised this even more so after 'The Russian', Yuri Ulianitski, was gunned down. After arriving in the country in the 1990s, Ulianitski had established himself in the Cape Town underworld. He had partnered Beeka in the extortion business and also had close ties to Lifman. At the time of his death, 'The Russian' was widely considered the boss of the city.

Beeka knew that if someone as powerful as Ulianitski had been taken out by his rivals, there was nothing stopping the hammer men from coming after him too. For months before his death he felt that his position was tenuous. The threat could come from a number of quarters.

In the weeks before Beeka's death it was rumoured that a turf war was brewing between various players in Cape Town. According to a report by Media24 Investigations, Beeka was understood to have held a meeting two weeks prior to the shooting at a restaurant in Monte Vista with a leader of the notorious Americans gang. The meeting was to discuss apparent efforts by the Americans to encroach on 'territory' in the central business district that Beeka regarded as his.

But it was a fallout with his most recent associate, Krejcir, that truly had Beeka worried. The two had come to blows in a Cape Town nightclub in November 2010, their relationship irrevocably damaged. The incident had occurred at the Casa Blanca club in Green Point and witnesses say Krejcir was horribly embarrassed.

According to a source with intimate knowledge of the incident, the blow-up occurred because another underworld player, Nafiz Modack, 'got wise assed with one of Krejcir's girls, Marissa'. Marissa Christopher, a *Playboy* cover model, was Krejcir's mistress at the time. 'Nafiz was drunk and he was apparently passing comments about her. Krejcir with his drunken ass – he's a pig when he's drunk – they wanted to come to blows and the more Cyril told him to stop, stop, stop, Radovan wanted to bliksem Nafiz, Cyril stepped in so he wanted to bliksem Cyril. Cyril split Radovan's lip open.'

Another source told the *Weekend Argus*: 'Cyril hit him right through the chairs and tables, and Krejcir had to go to hospital to get stitches.' However, Krejcir denied to the newspaper that Beeka had beaten him, saying it was a big bar fight involving about 20 men.

There were even rumours at the time that Krejcir had put a hit out on Beeka and, in turn, Krejcir heard that Beeka had put out a hit on him. There were also allegations that Krejcir owed Beeka a few million and again, vice versa, that Beeka owed the Czech money. Typically, in the murky after-math of murder, it's hard to tell where the truth lies. But it was certain that their relationship had deteriorated.

IN HIS METHODICAL, RELENTLESS MANNER, FORENSIC CONSULTANT Paul O'Sullivan kept chipping away at Project 'Czechmate'. O'Sullivan's instincts told him that Krejcir was a gangster who was polluting the police service with his toxic corruption. He wanted him behind bars. While he was carefully weighing the pieces of the murders to which Krejcir had been linked, the real evidence he was looking for presented itself in connection with a much less serious crime: insurance fraud.

O'Sullivan was contacted by a terrified doctor of Eastern European descent who had explosive information on Krejcir. The Slovakian urologist was frightened for his life and, in desperation, was turning to the Irishman for help. Dr Marian Tupy had become Krejcir's personal physician and confessed to O'Sullivan that he had been complicit in submitting a false insurance claim for his patient. He had swapped Krejcir's samples with another person's to give the impression that Krejcir was suffering from cancer. He handed O'Sullivan Krejcir's medical file and made a full statement about what had happened. O'Sullivan took this information to the authorities.

On Wednesday, 16 March 2011, Dr Tupy appeared in the Wynberg magistrate's court in Johannesburg and pleaded guilty to a charge of fraud. In exchange, he agreed to make a full disclosure to prosecutors and to testify against Krejcir. Finally, O'Sullivan and the Hawks had a solid witness who could testify about Krejcir's illegal conduct with the potential of a conviction and jail time. As part of the plea deal, Tupy was sentenced to seven years in jail, suspended for five.

That week News24's Investigations Unit published details of Tupy's affidavit and revealed how Krejcir had allegedly engineered the R4.5-million insurance scam by coercing the doctor into falsely diagnosing him with cancer.

According to the report, R4 579 600 was paid out to Krejcir by Liberty Life after pathologists' reports confirmed in 2010 the presence of secondary stage cancerous cells. Discovery Health also suffered losses of around R250 000 through the scam. Tupy stated that Krejcir intended using the false cancer diagnosis to secure asylum in South Africa and to avoid extradition through a presidential pardon.

Tupy, who practised at Flora Clinic in Florida in western Johannesburg, first met Krejcir in 2008, shortly after he had arrived in the country on a false passport. He did some enquiries and established that his patient was not simply a regular guy.

'I ascertained that he was alleged to be either the first-, or second-in-command of a mafia-type organisation based in Eastern Europe, with its headquarters in Prague. There were also stories about persons that had mysteriously "disappeared", or been murdered, but no bodies found. Although I had never done anything like this in my life, I was now quite worried that I might be subject to unlawful "pressures" by this man,' Tupy wrote in his statement.

Tupy was terrified and hoped that if he dragged the process out long enough, Krejcir would pack up and leave the country for his next destination. However, the exact opposite occurred. Krejcir allegedly entrenched himself and began leaning on his doctor more and more, calling him at all hours and showing up at his rooms unannounced.

Ultimately, and although he never intended to comply with Krejcir's plan, Tupy did a biopsy on a cancer patient, took the sample to his rooms and swapped it with a sample that Krejcir had provided. He sent it off to the labs, sealing his fate.

Tupy found out just how deep Krejcir's reach into the SAPS was when, he claims, Krejcir forced him to hand over the original medical file and obtain the samples from the laboratory for him. Then, in January 2011, Krejcir met him at a pub near the Flora Clinic where he showed Tupy his own statement that he had made to the authorities. Incredibly, Krejcir – as an accused in the case – had managed to get his hands on an affidavit made by a key witness, implicating him in the crime.

'Krejcir showed me a statement I had previously made and told me that, if he can prove I made that statement, he will kill me and he also said he would kill Paul O'Sullivan.' Tupy had visions of being bundled into the boot of a car and executed, much in the same way Uwe Gemballa had been. After all, Tupy also claimed that Krejcir had admitted to him that he had been behind the German's murder.

According to a News24 report the week that Tupy entered into the plea bargain with the state, investigators probing Krejcir had tightened security around key witnesses. The reports suggested that a Czech national, 'identified as "Milash" and described as "a professional hit man" is in South Africa, allegedly to kill O'Sullivan'. This is likely a reference to Milosh Potiska, Krejcir's right-hand man.

The news website also reported on how Krejcir had allegedly bought influence and protection from police and how top cops were spying on one another amid an investigation to identify the allegedly corrupt officials. This was a reference to the ongoing war between Crime Intelligence and the Hawks, and concerns that CI operatives were leaking to Krejcir like a sieve.

With Tupy in their arsenal, the Hawks felt that they were ready to move on Krejcir. The net was tightening.

'CAN YOU DRIVE WITH A TRAILER?' COETZEE HEARD BEEKA'S voice on the other end of the line.

'What do you mean?' she asked perplexed.

'This is going to be a nightmare. I want to drive to Cape Town. I want to pick up a dog. We are going to leave just after lunch on Friday. Monday is a public holiday,' Beeka explained.

It was an unusual request, but she had become familiar with Beeka's idiosyncrasies. She had been concerned about him lately. Since he had got into that brawl with Krejcir in the club in Cape Town a few months back, things had been in flux. She thought Krejcir owed Cyril money and it must have been a couple of million, not just a few thousand. There was friction between the two men and it was tense. She had also noticed a change in Beeka's behaviour. Usually, when she picked him up, he fell asleep in the passenger seat in a matter of minutes. Lately, he was always on edge. He wouldn't sit in the car and sleep. He was constantly glancing around, looking out for a potential threat.

Beeka knew that he had to tell someone in authority about his concerns for his life. Coetzee knew this too. So they called Shadrack Sibiya and asked to meet him for dinner before the trip to Cape Town.

Shadrack Sibiya has a presence about him, an aura of strength and solidity. He is the type of man others follow. He oozes power and over the past few years I have spent a great deal of time trying to determine whether the authority he exudes is corrupted for ill intent, as many have told me, or if it is an unwavering pursuit of evil that drives him, as others have proclaimed.

Sibiya is not shy to promote his own achievements and capabilities and talks a tough game, rattling off his successes first at the Scorpions in the Free State and then as head of the Hawks in Gauteng.

He joined the SAPS in 1989 in Rustenburg. Initially he wanted to be a magistrate but realised that he would never progress far beyond his career as a court interpreter and then a clerk of the court. After all, he was not white. But policing was a natural fit for him and he quickly climbed the ranks, bringing down cash-in-transit heist kingpins, criminal syndicates and other high-flying gangsters.

In March 2011, as the head of the Hawks in Gauteng, General Sibiya was juggling several glass balls. He was in the middle of the simmering battle between the Hawks and Crime Intelligence, as he was essentially overseeing the investigation into Richard Mdluli and the abuse of the secret source fund at CI. As a result, he had been receiving threats – but nothing he was too unfamiliar with.

He was also keeping a close eye on the other significant investigations being run by his unit, one of the most notable being into a spate of underworld killings. Radovan Krejcir was firmly in his sights.

'When I was appointed as a general in Gauteng, as a head of the Hawks in Gauteng, you come across many people, who will come and inform you about crime that is being committed, murders that are taking place in organised crime, you know, your top ten people that are actually crime lords you know in the province,' Sibiya recalls.

As is typical in the world of law enforcement and organised crime, the individual suspected of being the criminal was apparently desperate to become a source, wanting to work with the cops in order to ensure his own protection. Krejcir was one such man. He had sought out Sibiya, offering to work with the Hawks on the Lolly Jackson murder case. It was this effort to turn state witness that had so incensed Interpol and the Czech authorities.

'I have met him once or twice but at that point in time he was actually offering to work with me to bring the killers of Lolly Jackson to book. He wanted to work with me to bring George Louca back to South Africa. What he wanted us to do then, he wanted me to agree to the fact that I will assist him in his extradition fight.'

Sibiya had a handle on who the key characters were in the underworld at that time, so it didn't surprise him when Cyril Beeka and Coetzee asked to come and see him on a Thursday evening that March.

'I think a week before he was killed, it was on a Thursday, when he came to my office,' Sibiya tells me. 'I was still in the provincial office of the South African Police Service in Parktown. He came to see me there. He was accompanied by Candice Coetzee and then he actually was on his way to Cape Town, where he was going to attend a meeting between the different gangs there apparently to stabilise Cape Town.'

Beeka told Sibiya he believed there was a bounty on his head and that his life was in danger. 'When he came to me he said to me he understands that there is a million over his head, that he will be killed and those who will be killing him will get a million,' says Sibiya. The general adds that Beeka believed the threat was a spillover from the fight he had had with Krejcir.

'Beeka knocked him down and Radovan said to him, "You'll regret this, I'm going to kill you." As we all know, Radovan Krejcir, once he says he's going to kill you he means exactly that. All those that crossed him, he made sure they died and then he was also worried. Now Cyril Beeka came to me looking for some other ways of being able to make Radovan Krejcir get out of that story. He wanted us to start the process of investigation and then check who's actually going to be killing him and that we should warn Radovan Krejcir that should this happen he should know that you'll be the suspect.'

Sibiya also shared his own experiences with Beeka, revealing that he too had received death threats, apparently because of his ongoing investigation into Mdluli and his associates. Ironically, Beeka apparently offered the provincial head of the Hawks security. Sibiya declined and the two men agreed they would meet the following week so that Beeka could depose an affidavit and the Hawks could investigate whether his life was in fact in danger. That meeting never took place.

MONDAY, 21 MARCH 2011, WAS MY WEDDING DAY. IT WAS THE FIRST time in nearly a decade of hard news journalism I had switched my phone off. 'It's just a few hours, what could possibly happen?' I reasoned. When I switched it on that evening, it exploded with messages and missed calls.

Cyril Beeka had been gunned down in an apparent hit on Modderdam Road in Bellville South, Cape Town. Two men on a motorbike had pulled up alongside the 4x4 he was travelling in and opened fire, shooting over 30 times at the vehicle. Beeka was struck in the arms, chest and head. He died on the scene.

An event like this can lead to a string of revenge attacks, strategic assaults on power and manoeuvres to take over the person's domain. This could spell real trouble.

Immediately there was speculation about who was behind the hit and why it had gone down. Slowly information seeped out about the circumstances surrounding the shooting and Beeka's movements in the run-up to his death.

Candice Coetzee never did get to drive to Cape Town to bring back a dog for Beeka. He phoned to cancel just after lunchtime on Friday. Instead, he got on a plane and flew down alone. On the Saturday, he received more information about a hit that had been issued. He had a bodyguard accompanying him to his meetings in the Mother City – Sasa Kovačević, a Serb who had been in the country for a few years and was fairly familiar in Joburg poker circles. He co-owned a few businesses in the city and was also looking to open a pawnshop in Parow in the Cape. Kovačević had also got to know Krejcir and his circle of Eastern European associates.

The incredible truth about Kovačević's real identity only emerged after the shooting, although South African police had been aware of it for around six months. Kovačević was, in fact, Dobrosav Gavrić, a Serb fugitive allegedly responsible for the high-profile assassination of paramilitary commander and warlord Željko Ražnatović aka 'Arkan the Tiger'. Ražnatović was a bodyguard to Slobodan Milošević and had been indicted for crimes against humanity. Gavrić, a police officer with links to Serbian intelligence, was convicted of the assassination but vanished into thin air before he could be arrested. It later emerged that he'd arrived in South Africa in 2008.

For over three years, a highly sought-after international fugitive was living under an alias in South Africa with no one any the wiser. He secured business, driving and gun licences using his fake passport. He was able to open a restaurant in Joburg and buy a luxury apartment overlooking the V&A Waterfront in Cape Town. But towards the end of 2010, his identity did become known to intelligence agents and I'm told he was working with the state to provide information.

In a statement he gave to the police after Beeka's death, published in part by the *Mail & Guardian*, Gavrić detailed his friendship with Beeka. 'We often used to meet at clubs such as Cubana, Trinity and the Casino.' He explained that he was having trouble getting the renovations for his Parow pawnshop approved by the City of Cape Town and Beeka offered to phone a friend who could help.

That friend was Jerome 'Donkie' Booysen, a leader of the Sexy Boys gang in Cape Town, who also happened to be a former municipal building inspector for the city.

On the Monday morning, Gavrić went to meet Beeka at the Primi Piatti restaurant at the V&A Waterfront. Gavrić arrived at around 11am, accompanied by Sailor van Schalkwyk, another of Beeka's associates. Van Schalkwyk had previously served time in a New Zealand jail for drug smuggling.

A little later, Beeka told Gavrić to drive him to the airport where he had another meeting scheduled. As they headed out of the city towards their destination, Beeka chatted to his bodyguard. Once they were on the N2 highway, Beeka decided on a change in plan and instructed Gavrić to turn off the highway towards Booysen's home in Belhar.

Beeka and Booysen chatted for around 45 minutes, mostly in Afrikaans. Gavrić couldn't understand the language but later told the police that the meeting was amicable, although investigators would later suggest that the mood was not quite so 'hunky-dory'.

Gavrić says Booysen and Beeka said goodbye and they set off again towards the airport. Beeka was chatting away to Gavrić, reminiscing about his youth, when the gunmen struck as they stopped at a traffic light not far from Booysen's house.

'I was the driver and Cyril was seated in the front passenger seat. Cyril had turned in his seat with his chest almost facing the driver's side window. Cyril was explaining to me about his younger days. I saw something stop, but it was out of the corner of my eye. The next thing I recall was hearing two loud bangs going off. I was hit in my right arm as well as my left one and I noticed that Cyril had been hit in the chest. It sounded like a shotgun went off. There was smoke and glass and I was confused.'

Muscle memory and training immediately kicked in for Gavrić, a professional assassin. He fought back, opening fire on the assailants.

'I then came to my senses and I noticed a motorbike on my right-hand side. Then more shots were fired in succession,' he recalls. He slammed the car into reverse, a tactic he cleverly employed to gain the upper hand because it was so difficult for the motorbike to follow. Gavrić then pursued the motorbike, firing several shots at the hit men, despite his own injuries.

'The next thing I recall was my motor vehicle lifting from the ground and I lost control,' he remembers. The 4x4 had flipped. Beeka died on the scene and Gavrić was airlifted to hospital in a critical condition.

According to some reports, Jerome Booysen was the first person on the scene of the shooting. Although the incident had taken place not far from his home, some have raised questions about just how convenient it was that Booysen was there so quickly. One source even claims that Gavrić heard Booysen's voice while he was lying in the overturned wreck.

As the news broke about Beeka's death, speculation immediately went into overdrive around who could be behind the hit. The shooting was almost an exact replica of the hit on Yuri the Russian – could the same killers be responsible? European professional assassins perhaps? There were far more questions than answers, and the man known as The Rottweiler from Kuils River was dead.

IT WAS JUST AFTER 5PM WHEN CANDICE COETZEE'S PHONE RANG. She was at home with her kids when the news she had been dreading came: Beeka had been taken out.

She immediately called Shadrack Sibiya, who happened to be in Cape Town at the time. He was in parliament with a delegation of high-ranking police generals and prosecuting authority officials. They were briefing the then Justice Minister Jeff Radebe and Police Minister Nathi Mthethwa about the imminent arrest of Richard Mdluli. The delegation included the national director of public prosecutions at the time, Menzi Simelane, the prosecutors on the case, National Police Commissioner Bheki Cele, head of the Hawks Anwa Dramat and Provincial Commissioner Mzwandile Petros.

'As we are busy with the briefing session, that's when an SMS came,' Sibiya tells me. 'I saw Candice calling me desperately, continuously, and she was crying actually, because I answered and she said to me, "Cyril Beeka's been killed, he's been gunned down in Cape Town" and she even sent a text. Then I showed one of the ministers an SMS. I showed General Petros. I showed all of them and we suspected that it was Radovan Krejcir. They then released me, I left parliament and flew back to Gauteng.'

Sibiya had no doubt that Krejcir was behind the hit on Beeka and he wanted to act swiftly. There was no evidence yet to link the Czech to this latest murder so he would have to arrest him on something else. Fortunately, Sibiya had just the case: it involved Krejcir's bladder, his personal doctor and a fake R4-million insurance claim. He even had a warrant to act on and figured that once he had Krejcir behind bars on this charge, all the others would swiftly follow.

Meanwhile, Coetzee was devastated at the loss of her friend.

She felt compelled to do something about Beeka's murder, so the following morning she flew down to Cape Town and reached out to Beeka's inner circle, which included Sailor van Schalkwyk, Hein Metrovich and Nafiz Modack. There was fighting talk of retribution and justice for Beeka but she wondered whether anything would ever come of it.

Cape Town cops led the investigation and there was no room for Coetzee. In any case, she was probably too emotionally invested. It was best for her to fly home and focus her attention on Krejcir in Johannesburg, where things were beginning to hot up.

DRESSED IN FULL COMBAT GEAR, PROTECTIVE GUARDS ON THEIR knees and elbows, gloves on their hands and helmets on their heads, the officers rode into Kloof Road on the back of an armoured police Nyala at midnight. A helicopter hovered overhead, its beam of light leading the way through suburbia. It was a full-blown military operation as stun grenades exploded and members of the National Intervention Unit stormed through the front door of the house, tearing the security gates off their hinges and ransacking each and every room. The wooden garage door was crumpled and a ceramic pot at the entrance lay in pieces. Journalists trailed behind with broadcast cameras perched on their shoulders.

Alphius Matshavha and Christina Modutoane woke with a start when they heard the commotion, the house being raided and the stun grenades cleaving the silence. Terrified they would be shot, they didn't move. They were employees in Simon Guidetti's house and lived on the property. It was the day after Cyril Beeka had been killed and the cavalcade of cops was hunting for Radovan Krejcir.

The problem was they had stormed into the wrong house – 54 rather than 54a.

In the mansion perched on the ridge where Krejcir did, in fact, live, his son Denis heard the helicopter and saw the chaos outside. He phoned his father's employee, Potiska, who also lived in the house, and asked him if he could see what was going on. Potiska looked out of the window and saw people with torches and guns running around. He thought it could be an armed assault, but then he saw the beam from the helicopter lighting up the neighbour's house.

When it dawned on the Keystone cops that they had the wrong house, they fetched ladders and scaled the wall between the two properties. It occurred to Potiska that he could just open the gate for them, but he was having too much fun watching them struggle. Denis told Potiska to call the family's lawyer. As the heavily armed police officers rushed into the house and cuffed the security guards and pointed their submachine guns at the dogs, Denis and Potiska walked down the stairs with their hands in the air. The two men were forced onto the ground, their faces stuffed into the floor, as white cable ties were used to cuff their hands behind their backs. Officers scurried around the house, desperately searching for Krejcir, shouting questions at the two men about where he was. Within moments, Paul O'Sullivan appeared, apparently part of the police operation. Journalists were not far behind, photographing and filming the raid and the arrests. But where was Krejcir?

General Sibiya was in charge of the operation that night. He explains what happened. 'We launched an operation and I called Paul O'Sullivan to find out if he knows his house, 'cause we didn't know where Radovan was staying. He said, "Yes, I know and in fact let me speak to one of my guys in there," because Paul O'Sullivan had one of Radovan's security as his informer. So he always knew where he was and what is happening. So, Paul O'Sullivan then said to me, "Yes, I know where the man is, he's at his house now and this is the address and I am even prepared to go show your guys." He took our guys of National Intervention Unit, he went and pointed the house and they came back for a planning session. When they went on their own now to hit the house, they hit the next-door neighbour.'

But how did they get it so wrong, I want to know. He laughs sheepishly. 'I don't know, but what I know, I was not there. The gate is strategically positioned in such a way that as you see the gate in front of the house is not actually that of the house. It's that of the neighbour. For you to get to the house, there's a way you drive up to get to the house. So it was strategically built.'

Sibiya is almost certain that Krejcir was inside the house that night, but managed to evade the dozens of cops crawling around the property. 'We found three glasses, you know, on the kitchen table and then we found his friend and his son but there was a third glass. Because we came there knowing that he's there, the security said that he is there and then we hit the house. It took quite some time before they could go into the next-door house and then when they got there he was nowhere to be found.

'We even searched, there's a sort of a bunker, there's a big pipe under the house. Right under,' he demonstrates, using his arms and ducking down. 'It's built under the foundation and we went through that pipe. We searched all over. In the main bedroom as you open the main bedroom window, you are just onto the mountain. We then went into the mountain and there was a helicopter also that we used to hover around there looking and assisting but we couldn't find him.'

It later emerged that while a veritable battalion of heavily armed officers were occupying his house, Krejcir was actually inside the building – hiding inside a secret compartment behind a wine rack. Several insiders with knowledge of the house and Krejcir's movements have told me about this secret room and how you need to jiggle the wine rack in just the right way to gain access to the hideout.

'He was somewhere in the house but we didn't know at that stage,' admits Sibiya. 'We got to know that he was in the house because the engineer who was responsible for building the house, who assisted and said there is this thing in the house. It was late already, but I've seen that now because I went there also at the later stage and we found out there was that thing.'

Potiska, however, contradicts this version of events. Instead, he says that Krejcir was never in the house at all; he had got wind of the raid and had holed up in a hotel.

'He told me he had some confidential information that there was going to be a house search and that it was "the muck O'Sullivan" who was responsible for it. And that he was trying to get him with the help of bribed cops from Cape Town. In Johannesburg, Radek kept a check on it but as soon as the cops from Cape Town started meddling in it, he knew it could be bad. In such situations Radek was pragmatic. He followed the basic rule, which was to secure his safety and to observe "radio silence". This meant that his relocation to a nearby hotel was prepared. It wasn't the divulged Nicol Hotel where he put up his guests. It was another hotel a short way down the street from Radek's residence. Radek could see his villa from there. So he could keep good track of what was going on at home.'

While Denis Krejcir and Potiska were shepherded out of the house and away for interrogation, Sibiya and his officers continued to hunt for Krejcir. For days he was hiding out under the noses of his pursuers.

However, news columns were full of reports that the officers who carried out the raid on his house had found a 'hit list' scribbled on a piece of paper in Krejcir's safe. The list included the names of four people whom the Czech allegedly wanted rubbed out. These were Cyril Beeka, Paul O'Sullivan and prosecutor Riegel du Toit. Krejcir's urologist Marian Tupy, who had turned state witness against him in the insurance fraud case, was also on the list.

It's unclear whether or not the hit list ever did exist. The origin of the claim seems to be O'Sullivan, although Hawks spokesperson McIntosh Polela confirmed that it had indeed been found. 'The suspect had drawn up a hit list of four individuals. Cyril Beeka, who was allegedly at the top of the list, was gunned down in Cape Town a couple of days ago,' Polela told reporters. However, those close to Krejcir deny that the hit list ever existed and allege that it was a fabrication, giving police ammunition to go after Krejcir. Potiska has described it as 'bullshit'.

While the cops scrambled around the rocky mountainside in the dark looking for Krejcir, on the road below bystanders were watching as his luxury vehicles, including a Lamborghini and a Ferrari, were being removed from the property. Meanwhile, a few kilometres away in Germiston, officers were raiding another house belonging to Krejcir's business partner, Michael Arsiotis. He and his girlfriend, Stacey Swanepoel, were at home when heavily armed policemen stormed into the house. Swanepoel later told *The Star* newspaper that Paul O'Sullivan, who had 'orchestrated' the raid, slapped her with a backhand and told her to 'Shut the fuck up' when she asked what right he had to be in their house. Arsiotis was taken in for questioning along with Denis Krejcir and Potiska, but was later released.

For nearly three days the Czech stayed one step ahead of the police, helped by information channelled to him by informants. When police got wind that he was at Rosebank Clinic seeing doctors, they raced there. He was gone by the time they arrived.

'He has counterintelligence and, unfortunately, some of them are in our employ. We knew he might have been warned and might not be at the house. Now he is playing a game with us through his lawyer,' said Hawks spokesperson Polela at the time.

O'Sullivan was convinced that Krejcir had been tipped off about the impending raid and other ongoing cases. He knew there had to be a reason that Krejcir couldn't be taken in for the Lolly Jackson and Uwe Gemballa murders. 'We looked at all these investigations and wondered why we have not been able to get convictions. We realised they had all been frustrated by crooked cops,' said O'Sullivan.

Police wanted to arrest Krejcir on a raft of charges linked to several murders, corruption, money laundering, fraud, human trafficking and smuggling. Finally, after three days of stating that their client would cooperate with authorities, Krejcir's lawyers at BDK, Piet du Plessis and Ian Small-Smith, arranged for Krejcir to be handed over to the Hawks. On Friday, four days after the raid took place and five days after Beeka was killed, Krejcir surrendered to the head of the Hawks, Lieutenant General Anwa Dramat.

So deep was the distrust between the Hawks and Crime Intelligence at the time that reports suggested Dramat had insisted that all cellphones had to be switched off and batteries removed for the duration of the handover. Dramat believed their phones were being tapped by CI and information was being leaked by intelligence officers to Krejcir.

After the handover and all the frenzied media attention surrounding the cat-and-mouse game of the week, Krejcir was questioned in connection with Beeka's murder and multiple other crimes. But despite the rhetoric from the Hawks and the allegations mounting in the press, they were only able to charge him on the solitary case of insurance fraud.

TWELVE DAYS AFTER BEEKA WAS MURDERED, HIS FUNERAL TOOK place at the Good Hope Christian Centre in Athlone under heavy armed guard. Members of Beeka's own security company scanned guests with handheld metal detectors. Security officials in dark suits and wearing earpieces patrolled the venue and journalists had to provide their identity documents to register to attend. City traffic cops were stationed at major intersections along the route followed by the funeral procession to the cemetery where he was buried.

Beeka's coffin was draped in an ANC flag, testament to his years spent in MK, the ruling party's armed wing, and potentially also a nod to his less official affiliation to the country's intelligence services. Photographs of Beeka's eventful life were displayed on big screens around the centre to the soundtrack of Frank Sinatra's 'My Way'. The minister officiating at the service, the Reverend Neville McDonald, told the eclectic crowd, 'I'm glad to have so many people in this building who would be rejected by man but not by God.'

Americans gang boss Igshaan Davids and Jerome 'Donkie' Booysen were among the mourners.

Booysen's presence at the funeral was curious considering that, months later, Paul Hendrickse, the investigating officer probing Beeka's death, named him as a suspect in the crime. Hendrickse was testifying in Gavrić's bail application. Gavrić had handed himself over to the Hawks after his identity was confirmed and Serbian authorities requested his extradition. Hendrickse said that the hit was motivated by organised crime. 'I do have evidence and statements under oath to back me up,' he testified. He found it odd that Booysen was on the scene so quickly after the shooting. 'Not long thereafter, Booysen arrived … It's very suspicious because they'd just left his place and coincidentally he was the first person on the scene,' he testified.

Hendrickse told the court that at the time of Beeka's killing, the police's organised crime unit in Gauteng had been investigating Beeka for murder, drug trafficking and trade in illegal diamonds. Hendrickse also testified about Beeka's links to other underworld characters and how Gavrić played cards with both Lifman and Krejcir. 'Mark Lifman is also being investigated by [the] organised crime [unit],' he explained. His testimony was merely a peek into the complex web of relationships at play and what might have been the true motive for the killing. Beeka's murder remains unsolved.

In October 2013, two years after Beeka's death, a key piece of the puzzle in the hit was also lost. Leon 'Lyons' Davids, who was believed to be the driver of the motorbike in the incident, was shot dead while at a braai in Belhar. Davids was allegedly a hit man for the Sexy Boys gang. At the time of his death, it was believed that he was cooperating with authorities in the investigation into the killing. There were suggestions that he had also been in the police's witness protection programme but the Hawks denied that he was in any set-up linked to the unit.

Beeka's murder was a cataclysmic moment in South Africa's underworld. It unravelled the uneasy truce that had been in place for years. Six years later, the full effects of the disruption are now being felt in Cape Town in particular, but are also spilling over into Johannesburg, as warring factions fight for control of turf in the Cape Peninsula.

The initial instability in the nightclub security industry, spawned by Beeka's death, was brought under control by the establishment of Specialised Protection Services. SPS was essentially a joint venture, a unification of previously opposing groupings in the industry. Mark Lifman and Jerome Booysen were the key players in SPS, although André Naudé provided the muscle, backed up by the Sexy Boys gang.

Within months, SPS controlled security at the bulk of venues across Cape Town and employed over 400 bouncers, most of whom were Congolese. However, in early 2012 there was a crackdown on SPS when the courts declared the company illegal because it had not been properly registered. SPS bosses Lifman and Naudé were arrested and faced dozens of criminal charges. They were ultimately acquitted.

The vacuum left first by Beeka and then by the SPS players created a rush for power, with underworld factions jockeying to take control of the lucrative bouncer and drugs business. Throughout it all, Krejcir's name skirted the narrative and it was never entirely apparent what, if any, role he was playing in the scramble for control or where his allegiances lay.

For the record, Krejcir denies being behind Beeka's death. He insists that they were friends and that he was upset he could not attend Beeka's funeral because he was in jail at the time. Lifman also emphatically denies any involvement in the hit.

While no one has been arrested for Beeka's murder, it certainly appears as though it was a strategic assassination, orchestrated by consensus, to manipulate the balance of power in the world of organised crime.

Krejcir's involvement did not end with Beeka's death. He still had unfinished business with the man and made significant claims against his estate and from Beeka's family. This contributed to speculation that Krejcir, motivated by money, might have been behind the murder.

A settlement was finally reached, which the Beeka family hoped would keep Krejcir at a distance. In any event, the Czech had other problems he had to deal with: primarily, keeping himself out of jail.

FOLLOWING THE RAID ON HIS HOUSE AND THREE DAYS OF CAT-and-mouse, Radovan Krejcir finally made an appearance in the Johannesburg magistrate's court. It was exactly a week after Beeka had been killed. Krejcir was released on R500 000 bail.

Prosecutor Riegel du Toit appeared shell-shocked by the magistrate's decision. The investigating officer had told the court that Krejcir might threaten or intimidate witnesses as he knew who they were and where they lived. In a statement, the investigating officer also claimed that Krejcir had flown three Serbian assassins into the country on 18 or 19 March, two days before Beeka was murdered. The reason for this was to take out those named on the hit list. In response, Krejcir and his legal team suggested that the state's case was not to be trusted and that Tupy was dishonest and motivated to accuse him falsely.

Krejcir was a free man and returned to his mansion on the hill in Bedfordview. Before going home, he commented in his thick European accent to journalists outside court: 'I always believed in the justice system in South Africa so I was not surprised because I always believed that all these rumours and lies must come out. I think I'll relax a little bit and play with my son.'

On the day after Krejcir handed himself over to police, O'Sullivan took television cameras to Krejcir's headquarters at the Harbour restaurant in Bedfordview so he could be filmed drinking a Guinness at his target's favourite table, behind the bulletproof glass screen he had installed to protect him from potential assassins. After Krejcir's release, the Czech made a point of going back to that very table to raise a glass to O'Sullivan and shout 'Salut', to rub salt in his wounds.

At the time of his arrest, it certainly appeared as though the walls were starting to close in on Krejcir. Over that two-week period in March 2011, three men appeared in court in connection with Uwe Gemballa's murder, his personal doctor turned state witness against him in the fraud matter and the Hawks raided his house, apparently triggered by the hit on Beeka. News had also been made public about the fact that he had senior CI cops on his payroll, cops who were leaking him evidence and information about the very cases in which he was a suspect and there was an investigation into this.

Krejcir, however, was not to be underestimated. He deserved his reputation as a Teflon don. For months he continued galvanising his empire, occasionally making the odd court appearance. He easily dealt with the insurance fraud charge against him and police struggled to make anything else stick.

Then, just a few months later, out of the blue, the state's key witness against Krejcir made an astonishing about-turn, backtracking on his plea deal arrangement with the state. Dr Marian Tupy wrote to the Health Professions Council of South Africa, stating that he was planning on launching an appeal and review of his conviction. He said that Krejcir did indeed have cancer. He had realised that, as a result of his criminal record, he could no longer practise as a doctor and needed to do something about it.

According to the *Mail & Guardian*, Tupy claimed he had signed the agreement while 'under duress' and that he was 'unduly influenced' by Paul O'Sullivan and misled by the Hawks.

The full details of Tupy's grievances were laid out in his affidavit in the review application. These included sensational claims and allegations that O'Sullivan had stolen Krejcir's medical file from his offices, that he had forged evidence and that he stole a biopsy sample. Tupy also alleged that O'Sullivan got him so drunk that he didn't know what he was signing and was set up to sign the guilty plea.

At a meeting with O'Sullivan, the investigator allegedly produced Krejcir's missing medical file.

The urologist claims he was taken into custody, held in the police cells and appeared in court for just 12 minutes during which he signed the guilty plea. He also alleges that O'Sullivan hired and paid for his attorney.

O'Sullivan vehemently denied Tupy's allegations, responding that he believed that the doctor was back on Krejcir's payroll and that he was an alcoholic and addicted to Valium. The suggestion was that Krejcir had 'got to' Tupy, and that he had backtracked out of fear or out of greed for a payoff.

Whatever the truth behind Tupy's about-turn, the net result was that the state's case against Krejcir collapsed and the Czech was off the hook. Again.

O'Sullivan was incensed. He continued to dig away at Krejcir and his lawyers, travelling to the Czech Republic to meet with potential witnesses and investigators. He employed his brash, abrasive tactics, sending inflammatory emails to Ian Small-Smith and Piet du Plessis, Krejcir's attorneys.

O'Sullivan threatened to take 'in-your-face actions' against Du Plessis, in the presence of his wife and son. He mentioned Du Plessis's home address. He referred to the lawyers as 'crooked' and 'liars' and said he would 'leave no stone unturned in ruining' the law firm. He accused them of pocketing 'blood money' from their client. In response, BDK Attorneys successfully sought an interdict against O'Sullivan.

O'Sullivan, in turn, received abusive and threatening phone calls from a person he believed to be Krejcir.

'Hello, clown, you want to fuck with me? I will show you who is Radovan. When you will come to South Africa, I will make you suck my cock, then I will kill you, to show you you fucking with the wrong guy,' is what O'Sullivan claims the individual on the phone said to him. Then another call … 'It's Radovan, you fucking poes. You fucking finished, I'm gonna kill you very soon, you fucking poes.'

O'Sullivan also brought legal action against cellphone network provider Vodacom because he believed that the company had handed his personal information to criminals. Krejcir had apparently bragged to a number of people that he had O'Sullivan's phone records.

O'Sullivan says that in 2011 Krejcir sat down with O'Sullivan's apparent 'sources' at a café across the road from the Bedfordview police station. He alleges that station commander Colonel Sambo was also there. Krejcir allegedly interrogated people about why they had been in contact with O'Sullivan on the day of the Hawks raid. 'He brazenly admitted having my cellular records, which he obtained from corrupt cops, who had illegally obtained my records from Vodacom,' O'Sullivan later alleged.

Former Teazers spokesperson Sean Newman has largely corroborated this, claiming that he too was summoned by Krejcir to explain why he had been speaking to O'Sullivan.

'I walked into Harbour, sat down at the table and Radovan was sitting next to me, talking to me, and Marian Tupy was sitting with a lawyer, deposing an affidavit with Jerome Safi in the left-hand corner, recanting everything that Paul had said to him. I knew who he was because he says, "You see that doctor over there? Lying piece of shit." Wasn't hard when photos came out to put two and two together of who had been sitting there. It was a whole Paul O'Sullivan showdown and I got asked, "Why have you been phoning O'Sullivan?" I said to him, "What do you mean?" He said to me, "Here's your records, here's his records, here's everyone's records."'

Newman says Krejcir didn't explain how he had got his hands on the documents.

'Fuck knows, but he had them.'

In October 2014, O'Sullivan secured an order forcing the return of all his call records. The court also ordered Krejcir to pay all O'Sullivan's legal fees. However, O'Sullivan never saw the money because Krejcir was declared insolvent. So, in 2017 O'Sullivan brought an application to get Vodacom to carry the costs of R2 million. He argued that had the cellphone giant acted lawfully, his records would not have been handed over and he would not have incurred the massive legal bill.

'They can't hand my records over to the mafia and expect to get away with it,' he told me after filing the application. In response, Vodacom told me that it had released his cellphone records under a lawfully issued subpoena as it was obliged to do under the Criminal Procedure Act.

Despite the Hawks' and O'Sullivan's best efforts, Krejcir was more in control than he had ever been. He had warded off the threat of fraud charges and evaded arrest in connection with any murder. In fact, at that point, he was not facing a single criminal charge despite his name being linked to a litany of crimes.

Krejcir also had a network of high-ranking and low-ranking police officers supplying him with information and there was the belief that they were manipulating cases on his behalf. Krejcir's words about the South African justice system when he left the courtroom resonated. He had taken a look at the criminal justice system in the country, evaluated where the loopholes and weak spots were, and manipulated them to work for him. He employed a battery of the best defence lawyers to fight on his behalf. Krejcir was also buoyed by the arrival of his mother, Nadezda Krejcirova, who brought with her R40 million to invest in the country and Krejcir's operations in South Africa. This meant even more cash with which to buy influence and freedom. Krejcir's empire was growing in reach and in reputation. The future looked bright from Bedfordview.

THE SYMMETRY BETWEEN KREJCIR'S AND MDLULI'S CASES PLAYED out in the last week of March 2011 and the first week of April. Just days after Krejcir handed himself over to police, so too did the country's head of Crime Intelligence. A warrant for Mdluli's arrest had been issued and he appeared in the Boksburg magistrate's court in connection with the 1999 murder of Oupa Ramogibe, his ex-girlfriend's lover.

Coincidentally, this happened in the same month that the two were linked in newspaper reports on allegations that Mdluli and Mabasa were in a suspect relationship with Krejcir and had been feeding him information. The one common denominator in both cases was Major General Shadrack Sibiya, the Hawks boss who oversaw the investigation into Krejcir and who had apparently 'revived' the Mdluli murder investigation in September 2009.

And Krejcir and Mdluli applied for bail on the same day in April, one in the Johannesburg magistrate's court and the other in Boksburg. Both were released. Mdluli was granted bail of R20 000 while his three co-accused were released on bail of R10 000 each. Court orderly Samuel Dlomo, Colonel Nkosana 'Killer' Ximba, Lieutenant Colonel Mthembeni Mtunzi and Mdluli were charged with Ramogibe's murder. The magistrate stated that while there was no direct evidence linking them to the murder, there was circumstantial evidence. A witness had seen three or four people running from the scene. They were also charged with intimidation, kidnapping, assault, attempted murder and conspiracy to commit murder. Mdluli faced an additional charge of defeating and obstructing the course of justice for attempting to conceal the docket.

The CI head was suspended from the SAPS as a result of the case.

Mdluli's arrest sent shock waves through the police and intelligence community, sparking fears of a dirty propaganda campaign and reports of covert investigations, abuse of agencies and malicious leaks of top-secret information.

The *Mail & Guardian* reported that before Mdluli was suddenly arrested and charged with murder, he had obtained a secret intelligence report detailing extensive allegations of corruption against then National Police Commissioner Bheki Cele. This was a reference to the 'Ground Coverage' intelligence report on the Estcourt grouping.

Before Mdluli was arrested, an internal memo emanating from the NPA was also leaked. The document apparently detailed grounds for his prosecution. A *Mail & Guardian* report quoted experts as saying that the propaganda war could get worse following Mdluli's arrest. 'One highly placed security source said: "Mdluli is likely to bring out things on other people. This could make the fight between the police and the Scorpions look like a crèche picnic by comparison."'

While the SAPS was adamant that Cele was not the subject of a corruption investigation by CI, the national commissioner was feeling the heat from another quarter. Then Public Protector Thuli Madonsela had been investigating the building-lease claims against Cele.

During her probe, Madonsela's offices were raided by CI officers in an attempt to intimidate her and search for evidence. In a display of how severe the breakdown was between CI and the Hawks, spokesperson McIntosh Polela told reporters that the Hawks had not sanctioned the raid and, in fact, condemned it.

Madonsela ultimately found Cele guilty of 'improper and unlawful conduct' in relation to the Middestad lease in Pretoria. Cele was suspended in October 2011, having served just over two years of his term. But, in the strange way South Africa's washing machine has of spinning people back to power after controversy, Cele was appointed police minister by President Cyril Ramaphosa in February 2018.

A police service that was already reeling from one corrupt, jailed national commissioner was now left rudderless again. Organised crime bosses such as Krejcir were making the most of the situation.

However, a committed career cop named Nhlanhla Mkhwanazi was appointed to act in the post of national commissioner. As the former head of the Special Task Force, Air Wing and National Intervention Unit, he was seen as a tough guy. He had grown up in the notorious township of Edendale outside Pietermaritzburg during a time of brutal political violence in the late 1980s.

Mkhwanazi's appointment by Zuma was a surprise. He leapfrogged five deputy commissioners and nine divisional commissioners, as well as nine provincial commissioners. So junior was Mkhwanazi that his epaulettes had to be quietly delivered to him on the morning before he was announced as national commissioner by Zuma.

But if Zuma and Mdluli were hoping for a naive, malleable commissioner, they were in for a surprise. 'Lucky' Mkhwanazi was about to show that he was his own man, committed to the cause and independent of any kind of political influence and capable of avoiding the dangerous tentacles of corruption.

SOMETIMES THE MYTH OF A MAN CAN FAR OUTWEIGH THE reality. Radovan Krejcir had built a considerable reputation. He had manoeuvred himself into the position of head of a mafia-esque network in Johannesburg with dominant control over underworld operations. His name had been directly and indirectly associated with at least four commissioned murders and it was widely reported that he had corrupted senior police officials. Yet he remained entirely free to savour a lavish life-style in Bedfordview.

'He's the real deal. Be careful,' I was warned by a source when I told them I was on my way to the Harbour restaurant to meet Krejcir for lunch. It was August 2011.

This was the first time I sat across from him, face to face, outside a court-room. At the time I was riding the crest of the *Killing Kebble* wave, the book having been released six months prior, and I pretty much thought I was bulletproof anyway. I was fascinated by him and wanted to hear his story.

The week before my meeting with Krejcir, there had been another article in the *Mail & Guardian* by Sally Evans, pointing to the Czech's obvious association with violent and organised crime, and I was under no illusion that I was about to lunch with an angel. The story unveiled a secret cache of weapons buried on Beeka's smallholding in Mnandi in Centurion. Krejcir was allegedly attempting to gain access to the property so that he could get his hands on the guns.

Paul O'Sullivan had signed an affidavit about the cache and handed it to the Hawks. According to the article, O'Sullivan stated in his affidavit that the gardener recalled that 'In or about early or mid-2009, he had been asked to dig a hole at the back of the stables, wherein he assisted the late Beeka in placing a "bundle". He described the bundle as about a metre long, wrapped in heavy-duty plastic and bound with red string.'

The bundle was dug up and O'Sullivan apparently handed it over to the Hawks. He 'subsequently learned that the bundle contained two rifles, one AK-47 and one shotgun'.

No one buries an arms cache and then desperately goes looking for it without being involved in some dodgy stuff. I was a little apprehensive about the meeting but intrigue rode roughshod over any warning instincts. I pulled into the parking lot at the back of the 'old side' of Bedford Centre and parked outside the Harbour restaurant.

Besides the imminent meeting, I had a lot on my mind. It had been a busy news cycle and, as a daily radio news reporter, I was rushing from deadline to deadline. There had been chaos on the streets outside Luthuli House as then ANC Youth League leader Julius Malema's disciplinary hearing was under way; the ruling party was mooting a ludicrous 'secrecy bill' that would muzzle the media; and Mogoeng Mogoeng was about to be announced as the country's new Chief Justice amidst serious doubt and cynicism about his capabilities and his impartiality. That morning, before I drove out to Bedfordview, I had interviewed apartheid-era cabinet minister Pik Botha from his hospital bed. He had told me in a raspy voice, 'I've had a good life. I have no complaints.'

I walked through the parking lot, past Krejcir's cars with their DKR number plates and onto the patio of the restaurant.

Dressed in his trademark black shirt and jeans, Krejcir was holding court at his usual table behind the bulletproof glass he had had installed after assassins supposedly tried to shoot him from the high-rise apartment blocks overlooking the parking. He was seriously concerned about his safety and believed the Czech government was sponsoring the attempts on his life.

I waited for Krejcir to finish another meeting before sitting down with him. A group of men sitting at a table near the stairs to the deck were arguing loudly about something or other. They were uninhibited and their debate was punctuated with raucous laughter. I didn't recognise any of them but they appeared to be of European or Middle Eastern descent. One man stood out – he looked to be of Arab origins, was slender and walked with a crutch. I didn't know who he was then but I remembered him two years later when his body lay riddled with bullets on a nearby street.

Krejcir greeted me with a charm offensive. He was humorous and charismatic. As he fiddled with his silver bangle and watch, we spoke about the cases to which he had been linked and his astonishment at how the media kept perpetuating the belief that he was a dangerous gangster and a 'big mafia boss'. He pushed a refrain that he would regularly roll out to the media about how he was 'Mr Banana Peel' in South Africa. The gist of his story was that if someone slipped on a banana peel, or if anything at all happened in the country, it was Krejcir's fault. As he regaled me with stories in his thick accent and broken English, I amused myself with the thought that the waiter's name was 'Witness' and at least he could bear testimony to my presence here if anything were to happen to me.

Through it all, there was obvious evidence of Krejcir's ostentatious lifestyle. The Louis Vuitton keyring on the table. The plates of sushi. But it was the cylindrical bottle of artisan Voss water that really gave the game away. At a hundred bucks a pop, the water comes from an aquifer in the pristine reaches of southern Norway. It's deliberately pretentious. There was a new boss in town and he was living large.

That was my first of many personal encounters with Krejcir. Over the years I got to know him as well as I thought appropriate. We spoke on the phone and chatted outside and inside courtrooms. The charm was always switched on and he was always ready to offer a quip or a funny one-liner, made even funnier by his mispronunciation or mauling of the English language.

But despite the front he presented to the press, the reality behind the scenes was very different. While Krejcir was a free man, innocent of all charges against him in South Africa when I first met with him, it did not remain that way for long. More criminal charges were coming. The myth of a man can't last forever: eventually reality will catch up.

HE LOVED THE RUSH OF THE RIDE AND THE FREEDOM THAT CAME with the wind hurtling against his body. Given the option, Ian Jordaan would ride his motorbike from the estate he lived on in Beaulieu near Kyalami through to Louis Botha Avenue in Norwood where his legal practice was situated. It helped with the traffic too. His Aston Martin was a plaything for weekends and his fiancé, Joanne Rizzotto, drove his silver Colt bakkie to the office. She worked as an articled clerk at the same firm. Handsome, rugged and sun-kissed, 55-year-old Jordaan had a reputation for being something of a playboy. He had been married twice before and 25-year-old Joanne was set to become his third wife.

Tuesday, 20 September 2011, was a full day for Jordaan but there were two specific tasks that stood out for him in his diary. The first filled him with a sense of foreboding. For the past few months, he had been trying to wrap up his client Lolly Jackson's estate. It was a messy business. Jordaan had met Jackson a few years previously – they lived near each other in Beaulieu and shared a passion for cars and motorbikes. Jackson had turned to Jordaan to deal with his frequent run-ins with the law and counted on the attorney to keep him out of jail. On one occasion, a photograph in the newspapers captured a laughing Jordaan in the driver's seat, with Jackson throwing a thumbs-up sign to photographers as they drove away from court after the Teazers boss was granted bail.

Jordaan was dealing with a huge outstanding tax bill, monstrous debt and a variety of claims on the estate. One such claim had been by the Durban boss of Teazers, Shaun Russouw, who argued that he owned half the Teazers logo and brand. Others also wanted a piece of the estate, but there wasn't much money to go around. Just about all of it was going to the taxman.

The claim that most worried Jordaan was one submitted in May 2011 on behalf of a company in the name of Krejcir's wife, Katerina. Jordaan believed Krejcir was behind the move. Essentially, he was arguing that Jackson had signed numerous acknowledgements of debt before he died and the estate now had to repay these loans, which amounted to R11 million. Jordaan was not willing to sign off on the claim because there was no paperwork to back it up – the money had all been channelled through off-shore accounts and there was no supporting evidence to prove that money had actually been paid over.

At 12:45pm on that Tuesday afternoon, Jordaan sent a fax to Karla Strydom, the lawyer handling this particular matter for Krejcir, and informed her that the claim had been rejected. Jordaan was under no illusions about what he had just done and he didn't expect Krejcir to be thrilled with his decision. He knew about the rumours swirling around the Czech and what he might be capable of, but Jordaan was principled and ethical. He was a good man, true to his values.

With that task out of the way, Jordaan turned his attention to the second big job of the day. He had been asked to do something a little unusual. A new client wanted to meet with him but because the person was a paraplegic, he had to go to them. The person had cancelled once before but the meeting was fixed for the Tuesday afternoon. Jordaan often kept his firearm on him, but that day he opted to leave his gun in his drawer in his office. He also considered taking Joanne with him, but then decided against it. He left the office of Jordaan & Wolberg on Louis Botha Avenue in his bakkie at 2pm after mentioning to his colleagues that he was on his way to a meeting.

Jordaan steered his bakkie from Norwood towards Balfour Park shopping centre and through into Johannesburg Road in Lyndhurst. His destination was apparently an apartment in a block of residential flats. None of these details have ever been confirmed before a court of law, nor have they been made public in sworn affidavits, but sources close to the investigation and to Jordaan have pieced together the likely events of that day.

The person who had lured Jordaan to the non-existent 'meeting' was

Mark Andrews, who was not a paraplegic but a former protégé of Lolly Jackson who had been engaged in a legal battle with him over the Cresta branch of Teazers.

Thickset, with receding, spiked blond hair, Andrews was a keen poker player who had been involved in Teazers since 2008. He and Jackson were close. They travelled to Europe together to recruit strippers for the business and the boss even allowed his protégé the use of his sports-car collection when he was out of town. But almost inevitably in this business, there was a personal fallout – and it was over a woman. Andrews fell in love with a stripper named Micaela. Lolly was unwavering in his one key rule in his clubs and this relationship was completely against the company policy. According to reports, Jackson had previously fired Micaela from the Cape Town Teazers after she got involved with another business partner.

Andrews knew he was out in the cold so he took action, freezing Jackson out of the Teazers Cresta bank accounts and squeezing him out of the club, renaming it Decadence. Jackson turned to the court. He was granted full control of the club and Andrews was ordered to vacate the premises. At the same time, the court did give Andrews permission to sue Jackson. The court also ordered that R1.8 million be held in a trust account in the event that Andrews's application was successful. The money was put into Jordaan's trust account and he was the caretaker of the cash.

Of course, Andrews knew the money was there. He had found himself in a tight spot of late and had racked up some serious debt. According to a Media24 Investigations report, Andrews had accumulated credit card and other debts of close to R1 million, the bulk of which had been written off by creditors. He had relocated to Thailand and spent some time there before returning to South Africa to sort out his legal wrangle with Jackson. 'Andrews was on the bones of his ass and Lolly told him to jump in a lake,' says one of Jackson's former associates.

The police believe that Andrews wanted the money left in trust with Jordaan, so he lured Jordaan to the flat in Lyndhurst under false pretences to get him to transfer the cash.

At around 4pm, the secretary at the law firm received a call from Jordaan. He told her that a man in a pink shirt would be coming to collect his laptop and a 3G dongle he used for internet banking and it would be in order for her to hand it over.

CCTV footage shows a black man in a pink shirt walking into the office, taking the laptop and leaving. He was Thabo Maimane, Andrews's side-kick. Maimane had worked as a police reservist and sources say he had been involved in a shooting at a Harrismith music festival in which multiple people were killed. At the time of the Jordaan incident, he was running a coffee shop in Newtown.

While Maimane went to Norwood, Andrews was holding Jordaan inside the first-floor apartment in Lyndhurst owned by his parents. He lived there with his girlfriend. When Maimane returned with the laptop, Jordaan then apparently called a woman in charge of finances for the firm and asked her to release the funds in the trust account. However, the bank then phoned Jordaan's business partner Matt Smith and asked him whether he was aware that Jordaan wanted to transfer the money into an unknown Bidvest account. Smith knew nothing about this and stopped the transfer.

Andrews was furious that the money hadn't gone through. They were also under pressure to conclude the transaction as quickly as possible because Andrews's girlfriend and her child were due to arrive back at the Lyndhurst flat after work ended at 5pm. Andrews and Jordaan got into a fight. It ended with Jordaan being rolled up in a carpet and placed in the back of his silver bakkie. It is unclear whether the lawyer was dead or alive at this stage.

According to sources, there are two differing versions about what exactly happened next. Maimane would later turn state witness and give police a 40-page statement in an attempt to receive indemnity from prosecution. Maimane told police investigators that two unidentified coloured men were involved in Jordaan's death. He says he drove Andrews's Mini Cooper, Andrews got into the bakkie and the two coloured men followed behind in a red Golf.

In rush-hour traffic, they drove out to Hekpoort, west of Pretoria, and with Jordaan's body inside the bakkie, it was set alight. Some say the burnt corpse, unrecognisable, was found lying on top of the overturned bakkie, on the chassis. Others say he was inside, burnt to a cinder. His teeth were smashed out and his hands bound together with cable ties.

Maimane told police that he had sat in the red Golf reading messages on his phone while Andrews and the two other men took care of Jordaan. Police sources say they don't believe Maimane's version of events and the two coloured men are fictitious creations dreamed up by him because, in truth, he was the one who did the job with Andrews.

That night, Andrews made several attempts to draw the money they thought had been transferred, but was unsuccessful. Police found the burnt-out wreckage at around 9pm, and traced the owner of the vehicle. Although Jordaan drove the bakkie on a daily basis, it was registered in the name of his partner Matt Smith. By this point, Jordaan's fiancée had become concerned that he had not returned from his meeting and had gone to the Norwood police station to open a missing-person docket.

It wasn't immediately possible to establish whether the burnt body belonged to Jordaan, but the bakkie was his and he was missing so it was an obvious conclusion to draw.

The following morning Paul O'Sullivan became involved. He was work-ing for Demi Jackson at the time, assisting with the wrapping up of Lolly's estate. He went to Jordaan's law firm in Norwood and helped to ensure that the payment was not made to Andrews's account.

I received a call about Jordaan's apparent murder the next day. Sources quickly let on about the trust fund money, the failed transaction and Mark Andrews's involvement. That afternoon I spoke to Demi, who confirmed that Jordaan was winding up her late husband's estate and had been over-seeing the trust of R1.8 million. Those who knew Jordaan were devastated and shocked by the brutality of his murder; all described him as a 'good guy', who wasn't in any way involved in the murky underworld.

A week after Jordaan was killed, I broke a story on EWN. 'Lolly Jackson's former protégé and business partner is the prime suspect in his lawyer's apparent murder,' it read. It was full of the details about the trust-fund money and the failed transfer and how police were searching for Andrews. Within 24 hours he was dead.

I got the call about Andrews as I was stepping onto a plane heading to Cape Town. His body had been found next to the R59 highway in Brackendowns, south of Johannesburg. His hands had been bound with cable ties and he had a bullet wound to the back of the head. Execution-style. He lay face-down in a pool of blood.

The corpse was spotted by the police officers patrolling the area at 3am. His white takkies and light pants had caught the car's headlights as they drove past.

It was an excruciating two-hour flight with no cellphone or internet connectivity. I wondered whether my story had been the catalyst for his murder or if I was simply suffering delusions of grandeur. Had I unintentionally put a target on his back? It was likely that whoever wanted him dead was paying little attention to the radio or Twitter and was streets ahead of the news cycle anyway.

As I landed in Cape Town, I scrambled to switch on my phone and confirm the story. It was a mad news day in the Mother City. A shark had attacked a woman, there was a shootout at a court and a widespread power outage had hit the city. Amidst the mayhem of all this, then, I tweeted the news that Mark Phillip Andrews had been executed.

Within only seven days, two people had been murdered in what were clearly underworld hits. They were ruthless and brutal. But for a story that had moved so quickly, information quickly dried up. The assumption was that Andrews had been taken out because the money hadn't made it into his offshore account and whoever he was indebted to had killed him since he couldn't pay up.

There is a version of the events that occurred in the week between Jordaan's death and when Andrews was killed. This was the one supplied to the police by Maimane. He says that after Jordaan was killed, the two coloured men disappeared and he went to a hotel near the Vaal River before returning to Joburg. On the evening of Andrews's shooting, Maimane says he was driving with Mark Andrews in his Mini Cooper on the M2 highway and they picked up the same two coloured men from the week before. According to his version, they were on the R59 towards Vereeniging when one of the coloured men put 'the boss' on the phone and told them that Radovan Krejcir wanted to speak to them. The suggestion was, then, that Krejcir was behind the murders and had been giving the coloured men instructions.

Maimane says that they pulled over to the side of the road and their arms were bound with the same black cable ties used on Jordaan. Maimane says they were being held at gunpoint, but claims he was able to kick the weapon out of the hand of one coloured man and make a run for it. He fled from the highway, ran towards nearby houses in Kliprivier and managed to get away. As he ran, he heard the gunshot that killed Andrews.

Police have, however, picked multiple holes in Maimane's version of events. Investigators interviewed the security guard at the Lyndhurst complex, who confirmed that Jordaan had arrived there and that Andrews and Maimane were there, but there were never any coloured men and no red Golf. The investigators also went to the hotel near the Vaal where Maimane claimed to have been drinking wine. There were no bills for any wine ordered on that day and no record of him having been there. Police also analysed Maimane's cellphone records, as well as his movements. They found that Maimane was in the vicinity of Krejcir's Vaal holiday home on the day in question.

The biggest problem they had with his version was how Andrews's car, the Mini Cooper, found its way back into the garage at the Lyndhurst apartment block after he was shot. If Maimane was telling the truth, the two coloured men would have had to have returned it after killing him. Police sources I've spoken to say it was far more likely that Maimane did the shooting himself and then threw the gun in the river. Despite their doubts, Maimane was admitted into the police's witness protection programme. Towards the end of 2017, there were attempts to have him thrown out of the programme and charged, but he brought an urgent court application to be reinstated.

Because Jordaan had turned down his claim against Lolly's estate on the morning of his murder, Krejcir looked like a suspect. Speculation was that he was so enraged by Jordaan's decision that he orchestrated the plan to get him to transfer the money and then have him killed. It was possible that Maimane knew this and attempted to frame Krejcir as the mastermind.

To date, no one has been prosecuted or convicted in connection with these two killings.

Some time after Jordaan and Andrews were killed, a man arrived at my office at Primedia Broadcasting in Sandton. He was jumpy and said he had information he wanted to share with me. He told me his name and claimed to be a close friend of Mark Andrews. He was dressed in a T-shirt, camo pants and heavy boots. He carried a bag containing a small video camera and tapes. I met him twice more, once at a police station in Honeydew and once at a Sandton hotel, along with my editor and his wife. He showed me the tapes. They were videos of Andrews talking about how he feared for his life. The man told me he was the guy in the pink shirt who had gone to Jordaan's office to collect his laptop. He was Thabo Maimane. He wanted me to know that people were after him. I got the impression that he was working with the police and he mentioned a general, but that was about it. I never heard from him again. I had no idea if what he was saying was the truth or a fantastical creation constructed to indemnify himself.

THERE IS NO DOUBT THAT GEOFF JORDAAN WAS IAN'S BROTHER. They share an uncanny resemblance and the minute I walked into the lounge in a lovely townhouse in Lonehill, I recognised the smile. Geoff is more low-key-retired-family-man than playboy-petrol-head-lawyer, though. I've been speaking to Geoff's wife, Corrina, for years and meeting them feels familiar. The walls of their home are adorned with colourful local art, their eager poodles yap at my ankles and there's tea neatly set out on a tray. The poodle pram is parked at the door. In my experience, these are not the kind of people who meddle in organised crime or have any affiliation with dodgy, underworld characters.

Ian's murder brought them to the fringes of this world, but they found it much safer and more comfortable in their townhouse in Lonehill. That doesn't mean they have forgotten. Every few months, Geoff phones the investigating officer in the case, nudging him along, asking for an update. On the anniversary of his brother's death, he always makes a point of calling, just to remind the police that there are people out there who still want answers.

Geoff is matter-of-fact as he talks about how Ian 'got nailed'.

Ian was the laatlammetjie of the family. The Jordaans were happy, middle class and moved around quite a lot while he was growing up, the consequence of his father being a civil servant. Ian chose to study law and went off to Wits to do an LLB. He wrote his Latin exam while battling testicular cancer. He won the fight, but as a result could never have children.

Geoff describes his brother as 'quite a complicated person', who was dedicated to his work, his family and his friends. 'We never knew what he was doing in his work. We knew he was reputable and he was well known for his ethics in the law profession. You couldn't bend him.'

Although Geoff didn't know the intricacies of Ian's business, he did know that his baby brother was doing work for Lolly Jackson and this worried him.

'He told me after Lolly was shot,' Geoff says with some consternation. 'They both were passionate about motorcars and Lolly lived close to him. We never spoke business, but after Lolly was nailed he phoned me and said he was a little concerned because he was acting for Lolly and he got shot, so he said he is bailing out now. My understanding of what he did for Lolly was keeping him out of jail. I think Lolly had the heavyweights to do the other stuff.'

Despite wanting to get out, Jordaan was then roped in to handle Lolly's estate and Geoff thinks this might have put him in danger. Previously, tax attorney Alan Allschwang had been responsible for all Jackson's SARS affairs. Around two or three months after Lolly died, Ian apparently received a call from Krejcir.

'I understand that Lolly's wife spoke to Ian about handling the estate. We started talking a bit and he said Krejcir phoned him and told him that Lolly owed him R11 million – because Krejcir heard that Ian was handling the estate – and he wants it back. He phoned Krejcir back and said he can't find it. He was worried; for him to phone me to say that he was a bit concerned now that Lolly had been taken out, that was something.'

Corrina pipes up at this point to share what she knows. She's effervescent and a real talker.

'Ian told me, categorically, that he knew who killed Lolly Jackson!'

'When was this?' I ask.

'After the murder.'

'A day or week?'

'I can't remember, but his exact words were "I know who killed Lolly".'

Corrina had been in regular contact with her brother-in-law during this time and knew a little more about what was going on in his life. 'I was talking to him a lot. We were planning on going out that weekend to have a big meeting to meet his future wife's family at his home. Saturday after Saturday, building up to Ian's death on the Tuesday, we always had something going on, so we never met her family. We were chatting, but it was nothing to do with work.'

Because she barely knew Joanne, Corrina was surprised when she woke up one morning at 5am to see that she had a missed call from her on her cellphone.

Geoff sighs heavily. 'One never expects it to happen. He never led a shady life; he was upstanding and known for that.'

Jordaan was so badly burnt that forensics experts struggled to identify him. His teeth were smashed in and dental records weren't helpful.

'They didn't have enough DNA to identify him because there was nothing on his body, just a bit of hair,' explains Geoff. He gave his DNA but, for some reason, it didn't work. 'They said it didn't work as well with a sibling as with a parent. I took the dental records and that didn't work either because there were no teeth left. I went to his office; he wore these scarves for bike riding and there were some hairs on it. I took it to the doctor and from that it took two weeks.

'While I was sitting there in the mortuary, these big Afrikaans gentlemen came in, the one bigger than the other. With their little bags, they took my brother's arm and said, "Don't worry, Oom, we're going to find these bad buggers."'

No one has been brought before court on the matter, and all that Geoff and Corrina know comes from conversations with police officers. Sometimes their information collides, sometimes it corroborates. They've both been speaking to different cops at various times and get muddled in the details. They've been told 'Nigerians' were involved, not two coloured men, and it's all quite confusing.

Initially, Geoff and Corrina received efficient updates from the Hawks but then the case was moved and the stream of information slowed. Their memories of the early days after Jordaan's death feature family feuds, confusion and the presence of one man, forensic consultant Paul O'Sullivan.

'He came to the practice and collected the Krejcir files,' adds Geoff. At the time, O'Sullivan had been hired by Demi Jackson and he set about interviewing people, including Jordaan's fiancée and his business partner.

O'Sullivan is not evasive about his involvement in the matter and again believes Krejcir played a role in these murders.

'After the murder of Lolly Jackson, Radovan Krejcir filed a claim against the estate so I carried out an investigation into that and opened a substantial case. The fraud docket implicated Radovan Krejcir in forging documents to make a false claim against the estate. You ended up with a situation where Radovan Krejcir was claiming and the figures kept changing. One minute it was R8 million, then it was R7 million, and his mother was claiming.'

O'Sullivan explains that at one point, Krejcir walked into the Teazers headquarters in Rivonia and tried to manoeuvre a hostile takeover. 'They tried to take over Teazers. Remember Radovan Krejcir never had money; he tried to portray himself as a wealthy individual but he had nothing. The only money he ever had was money that he stole from people and he conned criminals.'

O'Sullivan lays the blame for the lack of progress in the case with the cops investigating.

'Go ask the investigating officers, because they fucked up the case,' he says with disdain. I ask him if he believes that Krejcir corrupted these cops in order not to be arrested for murder. His response?

'Absolutely!'

Ian Jordaan's brother is more circumspect. While he initially thought that Krejcir might have been somehow involved, he now thinks it's unlikely.

'My view is that it was two independent actions – that's my view. Mark wanted his money back from Lolly, Lolly was dead and Ian had the money. I think the Nigerians didn't get paid for doing what they did to Ian so they took him out afterwards. That's my perception of the thing.'

Ian Jordaan's family aren't vengeful. They're not driven by a pursuit for justice like so many other relatives of murder victims I have interviewed. They're more realistic about their prospects and the criminal justice system.

'I suppose everyone wants to go sit in court and say, "There is the bugger that killed my brother,"' says Geoff, resigned to the outcome. 'But it's not; I'm quite fatalistic about these things. I would like answers. I would like to know who they are.'

ABOVE: The view from Radovan Krejcir's Kloof Road mansion.

MANDY WIENER – MW

LEFT: This image once hung in Krejcir's mansion. Now it hangs in Paul O'Sullivan's office. MW

Veselin Laganin, Jason Dominguez and Krejcir in court in Pretoria on armed robbery charges. MW

Krejcir speaking to his lawyers, Eddie Claasen and Ulrich Roux, in court. MW

Police officers at the house in Edleen where Lolly Jackson was shot in 2010. MW

Ambulance outside the Edleen house where Lolly Jackson was killed in 2010. MW

Cape Town security boss Cyril Beeka who was shot dead in 2011. IAN LANDSBERG/ AFRICAN NEWS AGENCY (ANA)

Celebrating the life of

Ian Jordaan

11ᵗʰ August 1956 - 20ᵗʰ September 2011

Ian Jordaan's funeral programme.

Radovan Krejcir's black Mercedes-Benz following the Polo incident in 2013. EYEWITNESS NEWS – EWN

The red Polo vehicle used in an apparent assasination attempt on Krejcir at Money Point in 2013. EWN

Police cordon off the road outside Money Point in Bedfordview the morning after the bomb blast in 2013. MW

Emergency services officials enter Money Point following the bomb blast. MW

The scene of Sam Issa's murder in Bedfordview in 2013. EWN

Denis Krejcir and Katerina Krejcirova waiting to go into court in Palm Ridge. MW

Krejcir appears in court with lieutenant 'Mike' Grigorov. MW

Heavy police presence as Krejcir appears in court in Palm Ridge. EWN

Krejcir speaks with lawyer Anneline van den Heever. MW

Krejcir speaks to his co-accused in the High Court. MW

Ivan Savov appears in court in Joburg. MW

Forensics experts at the Road Lodge in Rivonia in 2013. EWN

General Vinesh Moonoo at the Road Lodge in Rivonia in 2013 following the arrest of suspects allegedly planning on killing Paul O'Sullivan. EWN

RICHARD MDLULI CAUGHT WIND OF HIS IMPENDING ARREST ON corruption and fraud charges by the Hawks before it could be carried out. He handed himself over on 21 September 2011, to appear in the Commercial Crimes Court in Pretoria. It was the same day that the news of Ian Jordaan's murder broke; the two stories competed for space in the headlines.

The Hawks did not disclose the full details of the charges, but newspaper reports made it clear that Mdluli had allegedly used a Crime Intelligence fund to pay salaries for lovers and family members and buy houses and cars for himself and others.

The *Sunday Times* carried part of the charge sheet, which alleged that Mdluli 'illegally, dishonestly and without authority carried out some police work; misused or sold information or material acquired during the course of his duties; abused his position of authority; breached the trust of the police; and tried to conspire with others to commit offences.'

Mdluli was released with a warning, despite also being an accused in the Oupa Ramogibe murder case.

Facing two separate serious cases in two courts, Mdluli sought political intervention in a move that demonstrates the influence and power at his disposal. On 3 November 2011, Mdluli wrote a letter to President Jacob Zuma, claiming there was a conspiracy to oust him because he was seen as a 'Zuma man'.

'It is alleged that I support the minister of police and the president of the country. In the event that I come back to work, I will assist the president to succeed next year,' Mdluli wrote in reference to the ANC's Mangaung conference, set for December 2012.

The letter was seen as a blatant attempt to ingratiate himself with the president – and it paid off. A month after sending the letter to Number One, the charges against Mdluli miraculously disappeared.

THE BIG FELLA. SCARFACE. AMERICAN MOBSTER AL CAPONE RULED a crime empire known as the Chicago Outfit in the Windy City. He is without doubt the most famous gangster of the Prohibition era. Under his watch, during the Roaring Twenties, his men were responsible for a reign of terror that included murder, protection rackets, gambling, prostitution, drug trafficking and bootlegging. All of this was done with the assistance of dirty cops who were on the take. Capone topped the list of the Chicago Crime Commission's list of public enemies and his reputation, coupled with his charm, made him a celebrity. In many ways, there are similarities between Capone's story and that of Radovan Krejcir.

In the 1920s, the streets of Chicago were wild. Drive-by shootings were a regular occurrence. Rival gang members and public servants were gunned down in full view of the public. But despite the spike in the murder rate and the violence between the mobsters, Capone remained a free man. Federal prosecutors couldn't get anything to stick. They spent years building a case, but couldn't find any firm evidence directly connecting him to any of the crimes.

This was largely because Capone was very, very careful. The Treasury Department described him as 'possessing a natural Italian secretiveness'. He placed enough distance between himself and the perpetrators of the violence so that the actual crimes couldn't be tracked back to him. He also created 'plausible deniability' by ensuring he had an alibi.

On St Valentine's Day in 1929, seven members of the Bugs Moran gang were shot in the back when they were misled into believing they were being arrested by the cops. Instead, Capone's men – who were in disguise – had lured them into a trap. Officials could never pin the St Valentine's Day Massacre on Capone because he was at his beach house in Miami at the time and he also had a doctor's note saying he was bedridden.

Capone was also very careful about how money could be traced back to him. He had no bank account in his name and barely ever wrote or cashed cheques. In fact, he only ever endorsed a cheque once. It was all untraceable cash.

Everyone close to him was either too terrified to testify against him or they were too loyal to do so. Those who were willing were bribed not to. According to reports, in 1927 Capone spent an estimated US$30 million in bribes alone to politicians, prosecutors, police and other city officials.

While Capone did face minor charges for concealing a weapon and failing to appear in court for questioning, prosecutors couldn't catch him on any of the major murders or violent crimes. But it was because he didn't turn up in court in Chicago to be quizzed about the St Valentine's Day Massacre that the Feds could get involved in his case. Up until that point, none of the crimes was of a Federal nature.

This triggered an intense investigation into his business operations and officials were able to piece together a substantial paper trail. Working together with the Treasury Department and the Internal Revenue Service, the FBI was able to convince people to testify and found enough dirt against the mobster to secure a conviction. They used that one cheque that Capone had endorsed, along with witness testimony from a handful of people, to finally put him away.

Al Capone wasn't convicted of murder or drug running or gambling or racketeering. Scarface, the Big Fella, was convicted of tax evasion. He was sentenced to 11 years in prison. Ultimately, the jail term proved to be his death warrant. He contracted syphilis in jail, suffered brain damage and died in 1946.

It was increasingly obvious that the only way South African authorities would be able to bring down Krejcir would be to 'Capone' him.

By the mid- to late 2000s, as Radovan Krejcir was landing on South African shores, the South African Revenue Service had established a mean reputation for 'Caponing' big fish in the organised crime game. Well-known drug lord and Western Cape gang boss Colin Stanfield could testify to this. A joint effort by SARS, the Scorpions, the NPA and the Office of Serious Economic Offences saw Stanfield jailed in 2000 after a conviction for tax evasion of R2.5 million, 'Al Capone'-style. Stanfield, known as Moses of the Cape Flats, was one of the founding members of the drug cartel The Firm, and his name was linked to a number of violent gang-related crimes. However, it was tax evasion that brought him down. He contracted cancer while in prison and died soon after being released.

Unfortunately, the excellent working relationship between the various law enforcement agencies that saw gangsters such as Stanfield put behind bars deteriorated in the mid- to late 2000s. Significant SARS investigations such as that into businessman Dave King stalled. So, too, the probe into Zimbabwean Billy Rautenbach. A rift formed between SARS and the NPA, and it only deepened over the Agliotti–Selebi case.

In around 2005, then National Police Commissioner Jackie Selebi asked SARS to investigate a number of controversial individuals, including his friend Glenn Agliotti and members of his clique, Cuban Pablo Yester-Garrido, Carnilinx boss Adriano Mazzotti and Martin Wingate-Pearse. This was before Brett Kebble had been shot, and Agliotti and Selebi's relationship had hit the headlines.

But while SARS was looking at Agliotti, it was also looking at his various business partners. There were multiple projects running parallel to one another but they were all interlinked – as were the business relationships. Project Lollipop was the longest-running of them all: an in-depth probe into Lolly Jackson and the Teazers group. In fact, it was through Project Lollipop that Krejcir had come onto the radar of SARS and, in particular, became a focus of attention for the group executive for tax and customs enforcement investigations, Johann van Loggerenberg.

With his salt-and-pepper hair, olive complexion and penetrating eyes, JvL – as he is known – is an enigma to many. He spent time as an undercover agent in the police in his youth, diving deep into the world of drug dealers and, well, rogues. JvL was impenetrable. He was known to be inscrutable and beyond reproach. Unbribable in an industry full of crooks.

Officially, the investigation into Krejcir was called 'Project K'. While it was a spinoff of Project Lollipop and Project PAR into Lolly Jackson and Juan Meyer respectively, Project K was an entirely separate probe. Van Loggerenberg was concerned about scope creep, so he assigned it to a particular team.

Van Loggerenberg had a number of different units reporting to him. In fact, the so-called Rogue Unit, the High-Risk Investigation Unit (HRIU), which led to his termination at the revenue service, took up less than 5 per cent of his capacity. It later became known as the National Research Group (NRG), which Van Loggerenberg describes in his book *Rogue* as 'a small, low-maintenance outfit comprising fearless, hard-working civil servants, who were prepared to work day and night, with little or no support, to fight real crime'.

The biggest unit he oversaw was National Projects. The team had offices across the country in all major centres. The other important unit was Central Projects, which formed the core of the people who worked on the long-running cases. The so-called Rogue Unit mostly did support work for both Central and National Projects.

Typically, Van Loggerenberg would have handed Project K to the Central Projects team. It was the obvious choice because tax inquiries were second nature to them – they had cut their teeth on tough cases and were familiar with the complexities.

However, Van Loggerenberg took a deliberate decision to place Project K with National Projects. His plan was to increase the capacity and skill of the team there.

Like all SARS projects, Project K started off with what has become a legendary 'JvL' drawing. He called the managers on the project into his office, set up a whiteboard and noted what they knew about the subject so they could establish gaps in their information. He wrote the name 'Krejcir' in a little circle in the middle of the board and then asked questions so they could visualise the enterprise they were dealing with. Where were its weaknesses? He wrote down the names of other people and businesses with links to Krejcir. What were the names of the companies of which he was a director? Was he registered for income tax? Did he owe SARS money? Were all his tax returns in and on time? Did his assets show up on any third-party databases? Who were the other directors of his companies? Were their VAT returns in? Did they have customs codes? It was a basic preliminary investigation and by the end of it there was a clear picture on the whiteboard.

It was a very interactive, workshop-style meeting and at the end of it Van Loggerenberg drew up a to-do list. He explains the process in *Rogue*:

> In 2010, we developed a JvL drawing about Krejcir. It was evident that there were many gaps. We didn't know this man at all. Our first stop was to ask law-enforcement agencies, both locally and abroad, to help us fill those gaps, but they weren't of much use, so I asked permission for Paulina, Tall Pete and some other investigators to go to Europe to glean first-hand information about Krejcir from the authorities there. This was the first time in the history of SARS that investigators had travelled to Europe for an investigation of this nature. They came back with a veritable treasure trove of information, which helped us to complete one part of the JvL drawing on my whiteboard and contributed greatly to our asset-freezing order that was to follow. The units under me began to engage all the third parties we had managed to identify and in the years that followed we slowly completed the rest of the JvL drawing.

After that first JvL drawing, investigators set about collating as much information on Krejcir as possible. The team asked banks to pull their records to see what was going on in his accounts. They compared that with what Krejcir had declared. They then began to look at the value chain of the enterprise and established that the primary vehicle through which the money was moving was Groep Twee Beleggings. Van Loggerenberg wanted to know all about the bank account. The team concluded that the entity was the recipient of money from foreign funds and distributed money to other companies.

Investigators were looking at his business framework, his transactions, who he was operating with, as well as his companies. By late 2010, JvL's team had a pretty good understanding of his operations. Money came into the country in large sums, to the total value of roughly R110 million, from foreign bank accounts controlled by Krejcir's mother. The money was recorded as loans, but SARS believed it was the proceeds of crime, earned during Krejcir's time in the Czech Republic. Krejcir and his wife set up 'sub-companies' such as a beauty parlour, property holdings, Money Point shops, etc. Each of these companies had inter-company loans with Groep Twee Beleggings.

A SARS insider explains: 'They would need start-up capital, so they would borrow money from Groep Twee, or they would buy a house and the house would be bought in the name of the property holding company and that money would be borrowed from Groep Twee. So Groep Twee was the feeding account and then the money would be inter-company loans to the various companies, and these companies would either be a means to hold assets, cars and properties and that sort of thing, or they would be business ventures like the Money Points for instance. That was the piggy bank. The piggy bank gets fed by the mom and this money then gets distributed into all these different companies and they serve one of two purposes. One is either a business enterprise to generate more money, or to hold assets [like] cars and properties, the homes they lived in, the cars they drove, etc.'

Krejcir also ran 'off-the-book' operations, such as his potential venture with Juan Meyer and his attempted hijack of Meyer's Pan African Refineries, which investigators believe was intended to become a vehicle for money laundering. When that failed, he used the Money Point instead, buying legitimate and illegal gold, melting it down and selling it on. Once the SARS investigators worked out his business model, they could identify where he planned to expand and could shut him down before it happened.

It was a few months after Lolly Jackson's death that the SARS investigators had a breakthrough in their Krejcir probe. This propelled the investigation forward and allowed them to connect the dots.

Van Loggerenberg was sitting in his office on the second floor of 'A' block of the face-brick SARS headquarters, Lehae la SARS, in Brooklyn. His phone rang. On the line was an advocate he had dealt with on previous matters. The advocate asked for a meeting, but was vague. All he said was that it concerned a tax matter that SARS was busy investigating. The men scheduled a meeting.

Van Loggerenberg had absolutely no idea who he would be meeting with or which investigation it concerned. It could have been any one of the dozens of projects his team was working on at the time. The advocate arrived along with his client, a well-known commercial attorney.

Over coffee, the advocate asked whether the conversation could be off the record. He explained that his client was in trouble, but he was vague so JvL pushed him for details. The advocate finally relented and explained that the matter concerned Lolly Jackson and Radovan Krejcir. Up until that point, the lawyer had not featured on the SARS radar, despite the in-depth audit that was ongoing. His fingerprints were not on any of the paperwork.

But JvL was an old hand at this, and he had a hunch. He knew a big breakthrough was rolling in over the horizon.

Sitting in the boardroom at Lehae la SARS, the lawyer was petrified. He genuinely feared for his life, but felt compelled to come clean. He was far too scared to put anything on paper. The bulk of the discussion was around how JvL could assure him that, if he spilt the beans, he would be safe. They hashed out an agreement and the lawyer went off with his advocate to write down his story.

Throughout the process, there were concerns that the lawyer would pull out. The SARS team was worried that fear would overwhelm him and he would make a run for it. When they saw the first draft of the statement, they realised that the lawyer could deliver the complete inside picture of Krejcir's money-laundering scheme. But the lawyer was panicky; he wouldn't come to their offices again and wouldn't speak on the phone. As a result, the final version wasn't perfect, at least by JvL's standards, but it was done and signed. This affidavit was crucial to understanding Krejcir's operations and proved vital during his subsequent tax inquiry.

Van Loggerenberg kept a beady eye on Project K, closely monitoring developments and instituting strict deadlines. Every Monday he chaired an operational management meeting in which he ran through all his projects.

From time to time, he would also drop in on specific projects. He would literally go into the office and use the team's whiteboard to ascertain where they were. He had a central view over the various projects and how they intersected. In that way he could advise one team to speak to another if he believed their information overlapped.

By this stage, Krejcir had been in South Africa for close on four years, yet law enforcement authorities still had very little information on him. SARS formally asked the NPA, the Assets Forfeiture Unit, the Hawks and the police's Crime Intelligence unit for any information they had that could be shared. Not one was able to tell SARS a single thing. Krejcir was an unknown entity. He had no history in South Africa as a conventional taxpayer would, so they could not establish where he was born, how he accumulated his wealth, how he acquired his assets.

In order to gather more information, Van Loggerenberg sent the so-called Rogue Unit out onto the streets of Bedfordview. They set about asking people about Krejcir and his business. They frequented the Harbour restaurant, chatted to waiters and watched who Krejcir met with. When a person left, they would follow them to the parking lot and take down the details of the car they were driving. They would attend his court cases and take note of who accompanied him to these appearances and what cars they were driving.

There was a man who I assumed was some kind of government agent at every court appearance that I attended. He was very friendly and inter-ested in everyone else there, but would not say where he was from or why he was there. In retrospect, I think he must have been one of the SARS High-Risk Unit members.

They periodically did a drive-by past Krejcir's house. This was a useful technique that the unit regularly employed. They would drive by his house and take down the registration numbers of cars parked there. They went past the Money Point in Bedfordview and took down the details of the cars there, too. In this way, they were able to build up a chart of individuals associated with Krejcir.

It was through this process that the team dealt their first blow against the Czech. They identified Krejcir's fancy cars, which were ultimately seized in early 2011 during the botched Hawks raid on his mansion. The investiga-tors looked at the import papers, did a compliance check and found that

Krejcir had attempted to undervalue the declaration to SARS.

Throughout 2011, the SARS team continued to put together the missing pieces of the puzzle around Krejcir, and slowly the gaps in the JvL drawing began to close. Over the next year, SARS accumulated more information on Krejcir's operations than any other law enforcement authority, which ultimately resulted in a classic 'Caponing'.

IN OCTOBER 2011, GENERAL JOEY MABASA, WHO WAS UNDER investigation for bribery and corruption in connection with Radovan Krejcir, was given a golden handshake and paid R3.5 million to walk away into the sunset. He was also apparently given credit for an additional 14 years of service to boost his pension. Officially, the police stated that Mabasa had been discharged because 'his services were no longer needed and because it was in the interest of the service to discontinue his job'. Mabasa had refused an offer to be a station commander in Limpopo – not surprising for a man who had once held a powerful intelligence post at a national level. At that point, he had already been removed from the position of Crime Intelligence boss in Gauteng and was loitering around the intelligence unit's head office doing nothing.

Mabasa's golden handshake came during a time of upheaval in the top echelons of the police. It was less than a month after Richard Mdluli had been charged with corruption and the same month in which Bheki Cele was removed as national commissioner and replaced with Nhlanhla Mkhwanazi. It also came in the same month that newspapers finally broke stories about how the Crime Intelligence secret fund was plundered and how an anonymous senior member of the unit turned state witness about the malfeasance and fraud within the ranks.

In the same report revealing Mabasa's golden handshake, *City Press* detailed the fallout that had been spurred on by the Hawks investigation and the growing feud between Crime Intelligence and the Hawks.

According to the report, the investigation had put enormous pressure on Hawks head Anwa Dramat, who had indicated that he might leave his position because of the interference from above. There were claims that Dramat had received an email from the State Security Agency stating that Hawks investigator Piet Viljoen's phone was being tapped by Crime Intelligence. It was already known that CI cops were tapping the phones of Hawks investigators.

City Press reported that investigating officers Piet Viljoen and Kobus Roelofse had found several examples of top police officers caught in a web of criminality. This included allegations that Crime Intelligence members had bought a Harley-Davidson motorcycle, a quad bike and a farm in KwaZulu-Natal from the secret fund; a group of policemen spent R22 000 on a dinner at a fish restaurant in Johannesburg paid for from the fund; and two Crime Intelligence policemen were held up and robbed of R2.2 million in the middle of the day in downtown Johannesburg after they had drawn money from the secret fund.

There was a battle raging for the heart of Crime Intelligence. Another explosive article by De Wet Potgieter in the *Daily Maverick* in 2012 detailed the extent of what was going on behind the scenes during that period. There were allegations of large-scale shredding of evidence that linked global organised crime syndicates to top politicians.

According to intelligence sources, Operations Dante and Snowman were two top secret intelligence-driven investigations into the links of South African crime bosses with, in particular, the dangerous crime syndicates operating from the Balkan countries – with the main focus on Serbia and Montenegro.

'There were at least 30 targets whose telephones were legally tapped in these operations,' sources closely connected to these deep cover operations said.

Some of the key 'targets' the agents were eavesdropping on were, among others, the slain gangland boss, Cyril Beeka, the murdered king of sleaze, Lolly Jackson, the Czech fugitive, Radovan Krejcir, one of his Serbian business associates, Veselin 'Vesco' Laganin, and convicted drug dealer, Glenn Agliotti.

According to well-placed sources, within days of Mdluli's arrest, [Major General Mark] Hankel withdrew particular crime intelligence material from the vaults at crime intelligence head office in Pretoria, and the frantic shredding started around the clock, destroying vital evidence regarding international organised crime syndicates. Hankel, who is regarded as 'very knowledgeable', with a lot of sensitive information, including the criminal activities of influential people, declined to comment.

The Crime Intelligence unit was a hot mess. It may have been a blessing in disguise for Mabasa that he was able to walk away, with no criminal charges against him and R3.5 million in his pocket.

I T'S JULY 2017 AND AN INYANGA IS SITTING ACROSS FROM ME AT the boardroom table. He wears beads on his wrist and speaks with the gravity of a man who has accepted his calling. He has had the time to put distance between himself and the events for which he made headline news. Six years after the event, he is ready to tell me what he believes was behind the campaign against him.

He was never corrupt, insists Joey Mabasa; rather, he was being targeted by a faction because of politics. He has many stories to share about why he believes this. They are tales of honeypots, espionage and double-crossing.

The first story is about a trap that was set for him, but he was far too wily to be ensnared.

'One day I was going home. It was around 18:00 and I got a call from Luthuli House that there was a woman with good intelligence. They said they were sending someone to bring that lady to me. I said, "No, I'm going home." I went back to my office, but I knew I was going to be targeted so I called two female officers to arrive with me. At reception I asked them what the problem was and that woman told me something unbelievable that wouldn't even happen in a movie,' Mabasa tells me.

Because she was female, Mabasa had arranged for female officers to come and take her statement.

'I brought the officers, she must give them everything and they will write it down and we will operationalise the information. They questioned her and she didn't want to answer so they told her to come back the following day. They phoned me to say there is something wrong with the woman because when they ask her questions she doesn't answer. The following day when they had a meeting with her she forgot what she had told them the previous day. She was lying. They reminded her what she said and she realised she was caught. She told them she was going to the toilet. When she came back she was pretending to be on the phone and asked, "How are you, Comrade Fikile? I'm coming." She said Fikile Mbalula was looking for her and she left.'

The woman returned to the ANC headquarters and never came back to speak to the policewomen. Mabasa had no doubt she was sent as a honeypot to lure him into a compromised position. 'Two weeks down the line I heard that I fiddled with the woman; there was an allegation that I'm being investigated for harassment. I was laughing because I didn't talk to that woman,' he says incredulously, insisting that he hadn't taken down her statement but had handed her over to his colleagues. 'A guy from head office came to get a statement from me. I told him I won't give a statement because I didn't talk to her. He needs to get a statement from the two officers.'

A week later, another trap was allegedly laid; this one also involved a woman who phoned him, claiming she had secret information to give him. She attempted to lure him into a hotel room at the Balalaika Hotel and when surveillance officers followed her home, they watched as she debriefed a senior police officer about her meeting. Several cars parked strategically around her house were also registered to Crime Intelligence. She had insisted that Mabasa give her a lift back to Mamelodi, but he had seen the trap and avoided it.

'My heart was shivering. What the hell is this? I'm a trained operator, I know. I started to get phone calls from private numbers with males telling me that I think I'm clever, but they will get me and I will be killed. I went to Dramat and opened a case.'

He speculates that a pro-Zuma faction was behind the attempt to smear him and bring him down. 'We fought because they wanted me to do something that I saw as wrong.'

Mabasa shares two more stories with me to support his claim that he was being targeted. The first is an incident at a Makro store from which his bakkie was stolen. The second is about the infamous episode at the Rosebank Mall when his service pistol was taken. Both occurred in the weeks before Lolly Jackson was shot.

'I got a call from somebody, also on a Saturday, and they said they had some information. I said I will send somebody to you and he said he doesn't trust the members – they are corrupt – and that we must meet. I said if he wanted to meet we must meet at my office. He insisted that we meet at East Rand Mall. So we agreed to meet at the office. When I arrived at the office I phoned him but his phone was switched off. I parked my car and told the security guard to watch my car. I couldn't find that person and thought I cannot go underground; they can shoot me any time – maybe they are hiding there. So I parked my car outside and walked through reception. That person was nowhere to be found so I got back in my car.'

When Mabasa drove off, he realised he was being followed. 'I saw two cars behind me and realised it's a police car. My mother wanted something to make sorghum beer, so I thought I'll go to Makro to get the things she needed. I wanted to see the cars that were following me. I drove to Makro and parked my car; I saw the cars passing me and parking in the same row. I walked past the cars and the security guard said they jumped out. I don't know how they didn't see me passing them. They jumped out with guns and went to my car, but they couldn't find me. Remember, the people who phoned me said they will kill me. One of them broke the window on the right-hand side and opened the car. According to the statement of the security guard, he said one went underneath the car. It was a 4x4 and they started the car and drove off. When I came out I found a lot of security guards and another car was parked in my parking bay. I called the police and opened a case.'

That Monday he received a call from his insurance brokers asking him to bring the key in. Apparently, someone from the police had tipped them off that he had sold the vehicle. To this day, he has not received a pay-out from insurance for the stolen car.

Two weeks after that incident, he was attacked at the Rosebank Mall.

'When I went there I saw a bakkie. For me, even if there is 10 cars, I use my mirror. I took a street and saw two cars following me, so I knew I'm being followed. I came back to Oxford and they came back with me. I parked at the section where the banks are at Rosebank. I walked on foot,' he recalls. He was packing his service pistol, a Z88, at the time. It was about

6pm as he walked through the open-air parking lot at the mall towards the ATMs.

'I walked to the machine and withdrew money for petrol. When I was walking, from nowhere I had a gun here,' he says pointing to his head. 'Both sides; I couldn't do anything. You can't do anything even if you are a good shot. Two guys, I saw them. On my statement I said one is a cop but I don't know where I've seen him. They just said, "Don't move." They searched me and took my gun and wallet. The security guard was there. When I arrived at the car, the car was broken into. They've opened the dashboard.'

The firearm was recovered soon after in the possession of criminals in Kagiso, near Krugersdorp. Despite this, the *Mail & Guardian* later erroneously reported that Mabasa's gun was the one used to kill Lolly Jackson, despite it being a different calibre from the murder weapon.

'They were trying very hard, but I was one step ahead of them. When they got the gun [found in Kagiso], they told me to take the gun; I said, no, I won't take it because I don't know what the gun has done during this time. The gun might have shot someone, so I refused to take it.'

Mabasa's stories are compelling. But what about the allegations of corruption? His wife was in business with Krejcir's wife. There were claims that he had received payments and a car. How does he explain all of that?

At the time of the allegations, he says he was already divorced from his wife, Dorcas. But because they share children, they maintained a relationship. He explains that the genesis of his ex-wife's relationship with Katerina Krejcirova started, believe it or not, at the Wimpy at Eastgate shopping centre.

I'll let Mabasa tell the story and you can decide whether or not you believe him.

'I was in the East Rand, working with a team. I met the team outside the shopping centre there. This guy, the one who shot Lolly Jackson, George, he phoned and said there is something he wants to discuss concerning information from the airport. I told him we are at Eastgate; he can come there. We were four people, sitting at the Wimpy in Eastgate. He came with Krejcir and an entourage. They were about six and he said he was coming alone. Luckily one of the handlers of George was with me. He gave the handler all the information. I cannot remember what the information was all about. My ex phoned me for money for the kids. I told her I was at Eastgate and she came there. We were sitting at the table with my members. I was never alone, that is why they could never get me; there was no time I was alone with them. When she arrived she wanted money. I didn't know there was a woman; Krejcir also came with this wife. The Wimpy was full. I said to her I will talk to her; she must sit there. Krejcir said, no, his wife should sit with her. The wives never talked for more than 15 minutes. Maybe they exchanged telephone numbers.'

'So Krejcir's wife and your wife were sitting in the Wimpy?'

'Yes.'

'Where was Krejcir at this time?'

'We sat at a big table for a debriefing.'

'When did this meeting happen?'

'It was during that time but before Lolly Jackson was killed. After that I had another meeting. We told George Louca and the rest that we were going. My wife was also gone and we left. We left them there at the Wimpy. At a later stage, I think at that time my ex was working for herself selling protein shakes or something. When the story came up I asked her what it was; she told me the woman wanted to join in the business. She said they could work together and make it a big company. She said to create another one.'

'So you weren't involved?'

'No, I wasn't.'

'Did you know about it?'

'No.'

'Were you cross when you found out?'

'There is a word stronger than that! You must understand I was under pressure at that time and here is something I didn't know. I asked her if there weren't any other people she could start the company with. At that time we didn't have any information on Krejcir. The company she had didn't work at all.'

'They opened a company together, registered it together?'

'Yes, but they never operated from that company. When the story came out I went to her house. I was so angry I gave them a tough time.'

'Did your wife take money from Krejcir?'

'No, she says no. She told me that that company didn't operate.'

'Did you ever take money from Krejcir?'

'Nothing.'

'There are a number of witnesses who say that they saw you taking money.'

'You see me, I'm even willing, you can bring those witnesses. I'm prepared even to do a polygraph openly. Never. I've heard the story about a bag which came to me, but I'm still waiting for that bag.'

'Somebody from SARS told me they saw in your bank account ...'

'No, they're lying. I can print it from 2000 up to now. I'm telling you the Hawks have investigated everything.'

'Did they do a lifestyle audit?'

'Yes. There was nothing. They told me I'm a clean man. They got an officer from the East Rand to check the open account if maybe I stole one cent. It was a white guy. He called me the one day; we met in the evening. He shook my hand and said if all policemen could be me. He said he checked everything, not even a cent.'

'So you never met Krejcir alone?'

'Never ever. That person, I saw one day on TV they put a photo and say it's me. It was not me. It was my name but the photo was wrong. It was not me. Up to today, I have never ever ...'

'Did you ever go to the Harbour?'

'No. Since a long time ago the Harbour is a place where the criminals meet. If we want to recruit somebody we'll go there. I don't drink or smoke; my members will drink or smoke and then we will recruit one or two. That is how I know the Harbour. In the newspaper they say they saw me in Sandton at this big hotel as well. I told them there's cameras there – they must check it.'

'Did you ever go to his house?'

'No, I know his house is somewhere there on top.'

'You were never corrupt?'

'Never, ever.'

Joey Mabasa is unwavering. According to his version, he was never on Krejcir's payroll. But the allegations against him, whether true or not, had a catastrophic impact on his career. Just weeks after Lolly Jackson was shot, he was transferred from his position as the head of Crime Intelligence in Gauteng to head office. It was downhill from there. He says he was never given a reason for his transfer. He received a phone call from General Mdluli informing him of the decision.

'He said I must transfer to head office. I asked him what the reason was; he said they didn't give him a reason. When I arrived I didn't have an office, I didn't have a job for a year. They were trying to frustrate me so that I could buy this charge. It was difficult. In the morning I would go to work, walk in the passages and greet everyone. At 10am I would go. For a year. I like working, but I realised those people wanted me to buy those charges. I was frustrated. They wanted me to quit, so I knew what their plan was. I was going to work for a year without an office or anything to do. Mdluli came to me and said they told him to suspend me. He asked them what he should suspend me for because I have nothing. It was very difficult.

'After a year they wrote me a letter. Before that I heard that they cannot get anything from me because I'm connected in Gauteng; whatever they tried to do I knew before. In every area I have my own sources, so what-ever they planned I knew about it. I wasn't scared, I was ready because I knew they had nothing to produce in court. I knew they were coming and wanted me to be transferred to Tzaneen.'

In order to get rid of him, he says, they wanted him to become station commander of the Tzaneen cluster. Mabasa believes their motive was more sinister. 'The information was that in Tzaneen they will be able to assas-sinate me because it was in the bush. When the letter arrived, I told them to go to hell. If they wanted me to work, there are clusters in Gauteng, they can post me anywhere. After I told them to go to Kilimanjaro and throw themselves on the ground. When I know I'm right and you're telling me I'm wrong, I'm very strong, I'll tell you to go to hell,' he says, growing increasingly impassioned, his brow furrowing.

'I told them I'm not going there. I was born in Soweto, I don't know any-one there. I can serve anywhere in the country, but not if it is to punish me. If there is any allegation in the police they must open an inquiry, a departmental trial. That was never done because on what would they open it? There is no evidence; it was just to get Joey Mabasa down. After that Mdluli told me the people are on his neck to suspend me. I said he must suspend me, but then he said I will sue them because he didn't have grounds to suspend me on. After that I got a letter telling me my services were no longer needed.'

Mabasa says he went to speak to lawyer Ian Small-Smith about the letter. Of course, at the time Small-Smith was also acting for Krejcir, which immediately raises further suspicion.

'We talked about it and he said it is better for me to go. It was very hard. I'm still young and hard-working. In the whole country Gauteng Crime Intelligence was the best. No one can come near to my expertise but if you get a letter that your service is no longer wanted, meanwhile the person behind you can't even write his name. I accepted and said, let me go.'

While media reports broadcast that he got R3.5 million, he downplays the golden handshake saying he got 'very little'. 'Yes, they said R3 million. It was not the truth. I got R1 million.'

It is obvious to me that he is still angry about how he was worked out of the system. But he also has a sense of calm about him and seems to have come to terms with his fate. 'I have anger but, no, I've let it go for my health. I realised that when I look in the police, the people who are behind it are corrupt to the core and they are still there. In my career I didn't even have a disciplinary hearing; I have a clean record. So now to be told that my expertise isn't needed, it is difficult.'

Like so many police officers, prosecutors and civil servants I have interviewed who have been kicked out of their jobs, for whatever reason, I hear how the process has taken a toll on his health and on his family.

'I was finished, like I was sick with Aids. On my last day I called all Crime Intelligence members of Gauteng to say goodbye. I told them that nobody is going to arrest me because I have done nothing. I have never even stolen one cent. I have arrested a lot of cops and criminals where I've been given cash, but I didn't take it. I was a good commander.'

In the years since he left the SAPS, Mabasa has spent time in Mozambique studying to become a traditional healer. It is a journey that seems to have helped him process what he went through. 'The calling is something in the family. In the history of the family there must be one who has a calling for that generation. When I pass from this world there must be someone else. I was refusing my calling when I was a cop. The whole family knew I had a calling from an early age, but I didn't want to do that. After all these things – there is a belief in the African culture – if you refuse you will have bad luck. So when I look at the things that happened to me, I realised it must be the calling. I went to the north of Mozambique to train. It was hard; I mean if you were born in Soweto and you go to the bundu, there is nothing. When you want water you must go to the river. Because I'm strong I stayed there for two years until I was finished.'

He now practises as an inyanga. He also does forensic investigations for private interests.

With his skill in the intelligence and surveillance environment, and his newly achieved qualifications, I ask him whether he has ever thought about seeking revenge on his enemies. He is philosophical in his response.

'Some of them got revenge of their own. Even though I am an inyanga, I still believe in God as the mighty one. I believe if you do something wrong, your time will also come, and when your time comes it will be very difficult for you.'

He is still not entirely clear about who was behind the campaign against him. He believes it was a political faction, but is loath to attribute it all to one individual.

'I don't know who it was, but because I'm not a comrade, I'm a career policeman and I didn't want to take instruction from anybody. I didn't take any instruction from Luthuli [House], so I had to be removed.'

He's been watching from the sidelines as the police force has been rocked by one scandal after another. I want to know his views on how Crime Intelligence has been captured, corrupted and grossly abused for personal and political interests.

'I've dealt with the slush fund for the past 28 years. You need to be disciplined. It is tempting,' he admits.

Mabasa is scathing about the current state of the country's intelligence capacity. He actually doesn't believe it exists at all and reveals that some operatives are still coming to him for help and direction.

'There is no intelligence!' he exclaims. 'They know nothing. In intelligence you need to know what is going to happen next week, even next year. They get their intelligence from the newspapers now. That is not intelligence. Intelligence needs to infiltrate certain groupings so that you can get first-hand information.'

Mabasa believes the entire resources of the intelligence community are being focused on politics and factional battles. 'You must go when there is an ANC rally. They have this operational plan, but they are not doing that for the DA. Everything will be concentrated on the ANC conference. What they are doing is concentrating on political issues. Then they forget about their core function. They must protect the country, they must get rid of the criminals. We must see to it that our country is safe. If there is a bombing we can all die in one minute because our borders are porous.'

I ask whether there is any intelligence being gathered on terrorist organisations or organised crime syndicates or any other grouping that could pose a threat to the country's safety.

'Very minimal,' he tells me. 'You know what kills intelligence in the country? If you know about something like maybe drugs coming into the country, the first thing they'll ask you is how you got the information – it means you are corrupt. You find members who are scared because if you come with something that is tangible they ask you how you got it. Members are now scared. At that time I told them to go inside and not to be scared; you need to get dirty in order for us to achieve what we want. Tell me now, in the past five years, which big syndicate has been crushed in the country? Nothing.'

'If you can't trust the intelligence of the country and you open your own intelligence [that] is unknown, it shows we are in trouble. Who are those people? Who is paying them to do the intelligence? And as the head of the state you rely on those people. It shows that we are in trouble.'

What about Mdluli? Was he the bogeyman everyone thought he was, tapping phones and pulling the strings in favour of Zuma?

'I think that they were lying. I think Mdluli has been made a monster by them.'

At heart, Joey Mabasa remains a policeman and I am sure he always will. I do not know if what he has told me is the truth or not, but as I have learned along this journey, there are many versions of the truth. Investigators who probed Krejcir's activities and forensic consultant Paul O'Sullivan will read his story here and laugh out loud. Or weep. They will point to apparent evidence such as bank statements and company records to prove he was corrupt and that Krejcir had him on his payroll.

Mabasa has not faced criminal charges and none of the allegations were tested in court, so it is difficult to know who to believe. On one version, he is a corrupt cop who colluded with and protected one of the most dangerous crime bosses the country has ever seen. On the other, he is an experienced officer at the top of his game with mountains of skill who was worked out of the police service for factional political motives. Either way, this story has no happy ending.

Whether corrupt or not, he still has insight that comes with nearly 30 years of working in the organised crime sector. He leaves me with his comments on how crucial it is for syndicates and people like Krejcir to have complicit cops as part of their network.

'In order for the syndicate to survive, they need someone from the police. If that person is in organised crime, they need to inform them if there is any investigation. The syndicate cannot operate without having two or three members. The cops are very cheap; they don't get a lot of money: R500 and the cop is excited for the rest of his life. That is what the problem is – our recruitment is wrong. I hope they will realise that they will have to put the right people in the strategic posts.'

WHEN GLYNNIS BREYTENBACH WAS A YOUNG PROSECUTOR, SHE believed that all people were inherently bad. But after 26 years of putting people in prison and working in the criminal justice system, she changed her mind. She now holds the view that people are inherently good and, in some instances, behave badly. They 'knowingly give up on being decent and choose to become assholes'.

Breytenbach is in the unique position of understanding how the NPA and the police provide the perfect breeding ground for organised crime. Having spent nearly three decades prosecuting criminals, she's the ideal person to speak to about how the underworld has been able to flourish because the NPA and the police have been distracted by internal turmoil. Having now become a politician herself, she also understands the nexus between politics, the criminal justice system and organised crime.

I get the impression that Breytenbach defines her life as 'BM' and 'AM'. Before Mdluli and after Mdluli. In 2010, she was the head of the Specialised Commercial Crime Unit (SCCU), which was handling the case against Richard Mdluli. The two Hawks officers investigating the case, Piet Viljoen and Kobus Roelofse, were working with senior advocate Chris Smith. He in turn was reporting to Breytenbach's deputy Jan Ferreira, and she was keeping a watch over the case. She had developed a strong instinct for cases like this and sensed that it was going to attract trouble.

It was at an office Christmas braai in Pretoria in December 2010 that Breytenbach first met the two Hawks investigators. At that stage, she says, it was a smallish docket and wasn't a 'big thing'. While Smith and Ferreira were braaiing meat, she chatted to the two cops. For the time being, they were only investigating the fraud and corruption case, not the murder docket.

'I asked them how the investigation was going. They were making progress and they were getting ready to place it on the roll. It was going okay. I didn't know Roelofse at that point. They told me about the murder docket and I told them I would like to see it. They were having trouble getting it going and getting it on the roll. They were asking for help with the docket to get it moving. They asked if I could speak to the guys in Johannesburg and could I take this thing seriously.'

Breytenbach insists that there was no political motive behind the prosecution as Mdluli has suggested. 'There was no political thing behind it at all – Kobus Roelofse is an old policeman with years and years of experience. They're just straight-up cops, there's no motive there, just work to be done. We spoke about the docket and they said they would bring it – the other docket we discussed the status of, where it was, what they were busy doing, and Ferreira joined us at some point.'

She arranged a meeting with her direct superior, advocate Sibongile Mzinyathi, to update him on the situation. 'He was happy and they placed the matter on the roll in the Regional Court in Pretoria initially. He was aware of it and he approved of it and he was happy that there was a case. I saw the docket several times, and as it developed I was absolutely convinced that there was a case. There was really damning evidence.

'There was certainly prima facie evidence that he'd appointed family members as covert agents who were doing no work but were getting paid a lot of money – much more than ordinary policemen, for instance, who were actually doing their job. There was a big issue with the cars; they had bought BMWs and used the covert funds to supplement the ability to pay. There was a lot of other stuff about Mdluli and the way they conducted themselves and what the money was being used for. They were slowly gathering evidence on all of those things. There was an audit done on a portion of the covert funds – the portion on which they were allowed to do an audit – which was shocking. They were using it like their own little bank account. It became very clear that they were not doing proper Crime Intelligence work but they were using the Crime Intelligence infrastructure to do other kinds of work.'

If this is true, it seems very much like they were running an organised crime racket off the back of the very institution that was meant to be combating that kind of operation. The money that was supposed to be used to fight crime was being used to bankroll crime. 'Run organised crime rackets and to investigate people with political motives. To gather information on people that were not singing from the same hymn sheet as everybody else,' Breytenbach rattles off. 'Crime Intelligence – because of the nature of the work – has always been ... the checks and balances are very frail because it has to be, and so you have to be very careful how you deal with it and you need a strong leader with integrity. You need a particularly strong leader with a particular determination to do things right, which isn't always possible. It's always been dodgy. The difficulty is that the work they do is covert and the reporting is flimsy. The control of funds is flimsy. The fund doesn't get audited in its entirety by anybody – not the auditor general, not anybody.'

When the Hawks carried out a search-and-seizure raid on Crime Intelligence, Breytenbach began to take more of an interest in the case. She read the docket and was happy with the warrant application. The matter was placed on the roll in the High Court in Pretoria. With the increased interest, it became obvious that trouble was coming. She knew that both Smith and Ferreira were competent, so she didn't interfere. But then people whom they didn't expect to be making inquiries were suddenly very interested.

In November 2011, out of the blue, the president appointed Lawrence Mrwebi as the national head of the Specialised Commercial Crime Unit. Up until that point, the SCCU was being whittled down and its resources had become depleted. 'They intended to destroy the SCCU, but when they needed it to protect Richard Mdluli, they resurrected it,' explains Breytenbach. Mrwebi believed that Breytenbach reported to him, but she vehemently believed otherwise. She was adamant Mzinyathi remained her direct boss. 'Days before the announcement, Mrwebi was already asking for stuff on Mdluli – this was before his appointment was officially announced. And he wasn't asking for anything else. The minute I got that letter from Mrwebi, I knew that that was what he was going to do.'

There is no doubt in Breytenbach's mind that Mrwebi was placed in that post mainly to protect Mdluli and scupper the case against him. His appointment made no sense to her otherwise. '[Nomgcobo] Jiba's appointment as acting national director of public prosecutions was equally rapid, but was not quite as implausible, because she is smart and Mrwebi is not. Mrwebi had been specifically appointed to do Jiba's bidding in the SCCU.'

Breytenbach received an instruction to provide a summary of the investigation and to give Mrwebi the docket. She advised her team not to hand it over but to send a summary and make an electronic copy of the docket. She knew that the trouble she had expected was now coming. In her book *Rule of Law*, she describes this moment. 'I discussed this with Smith and Ferreira. I said to them, shit is coming. It's obvious. Smith said he didn't have the guts for the fight. I could see he was taking strain. I told him to hand the docket over to me, and I told Ferreira I would run interference for a time, and after that he should also disappear from the case. Which is what he did.'

Between 17 November and 14 December 2011, the shit came.

First, Mdluli's lawyers handed written representations to Lawrence Mrwebi asking for the fraud and corruption charges to be withdrawn against their client. They wrote to him even though Mzinyathi and Mrwebi were on the same level within the NPA and the representations should have gone to Mzinyathi as he was Breytenbach's direct report.

Four days later, on 21 November, Mrwebi forwarded the representations to Breytenbach and asked for a full report on the case within a few days. Breytenbach, along with Ferreira, went ahead and prepared a report for Mrwebi. It goes without saying that they recommended that the prosecution of Mdluli should definitely go ahead. A few days later, on 24 November, the report was forwarded to Mrwebi and Mzinyathi.

While this had all been going on, Breytenbach had been fighting fires on another front. She was also the prosecutor in a complex mining-rights case involving Kumba Iron Ore and the politically connected company Imperial Crown Trading (ICT). She had been accused of improper conduct in that case. Just one day after sending the Mdluli memo, Breytenbach withdrew from the ICT case following a meeting with the NPA's acting CEO Karen van Rensburg.

On 28 November, Mrwebi sent a memo to Mzinyathi and Breytenbach in which he said he was dissatisfied with the report they had provided. Again, he wanted the full Mdluli docket to be handed to him, but Breytenbach dug in her heels. She was adamant that he wouldn't get his hands on the docket so she sent him an electronic copy.

Things were really starting to heat up – according to Breytenbach, Mrwebi appeared to be determined to scrap the case against Mdluli. On 4 December, he instructed Breytenbach that the fraud and corruption charges against Mdluli be withdrawn immediately. Breytenbach was beside herself with rage. She took the docket to Mzinyathi to get his opinion and he too believed that there was a prima facie case against Mdluli.

Mzinyathi consulted with the inspector-general of intelligence and was given an assurance that nothing in the case compromised state security. They agreed that the prosecution should proceed. Meanwhile, Breytenbach was not willing to comply with Mrwebi's instruction to withdraw and so a showdown ensued.

Breytenbach, accompanied by Mzinyathi, went to see Mrwebi. When they arrived in his office, he said to them, 'Colleagues, I suppose you are here to test my powers.' This immediately got Breytenbach's back up and she again refused to drop the charges. Mzinyathi made it clear to Mrwebi that he had taken an autocratic decision without consulting with him or the prosecutor as required by the NPA Act. According to the law, both Mzinyathi and Mrwebi had to be in agreement about the decision to withdraw charges.

But then Mrwebi pulled his trump card. He informed them that he had already written to Mdluli's lawyers telling them the charges would be dropped.

Breytenbach picks up the story:

> We were scheduled to go to court two days later. Either we had to proceed with the matter or withdraw. And the other attorney would have a letter on paper, from my boss, stating that the charges had been withdrawn. The NPA was already in so much shit. We couldn't air our dirty laundry in public. It is unbecoming. To save that situation, I agreed to withdraw

the matter provisionally until we could sort out the impasse. We got to court, and I withdrew in order to avoid an ugly scene. Then I sent a memo to Jiba. Ferreira and I wrote the memorandum together, but everybody knows the person calling the shots was me. The 19-page memo set out the matter, the history, the facts, the merits, the chances of success, and why I thought it should go on. 'I am asking you to review the matter and to give an instruction to re-enroll,' I wrote to Jiba. Then I added that if it was not re-enrolled, I would take the matter on review. I had absolutely no idea how I would do that, but a decision like that must be reviewable. It was not a threat, it was a promise to Mrwebi and to Jiba: if you don't reconsider Mrwebi's decision, I will take you on review to the High Court. Four days later I was told that I was being suspended, for made-up shit.

On 14 December, the fraud and corruption charges against Richard Mdluli were provisionally withdrawn in the Specialised Commercial Crimes Court. No reason was given. Two months later, in February 2012, the NPA announced that the murder and related charges against Mdluli and his co-accused would be withdrawn and a formal inquest set up. It flatly denied that there was a link between the suspension of Breytenbach and the dropping of charges.

For MONTHS, I SAT THROUGH GLYNNIS BREYTENBACH'S DISCIPLINARY hearing in the sweltering stuffiness of a sealed-off room in the NPA's Victoria & Griffiths Mxenge building in Silverton. It was clear to me from the outset that it was not just Breytenbach on trial. Rather, it was the mission statement of the NPA, so obviously emblazoned on the orange banners beside the chairperson, which was really being tried and tested in the hearing.

The banners featured an illustration of Lady Justice, photographs of prosecutors in action, police officers dutifully taking down statements, courthouse pillars and a South African flag in full flap. But it was the NPA's mission statement that dominated: 'Guided by the Constitution, we in the National Prosecuting Authority ensure justice for the victims of crime by prosecuting without fear, favour and prejudice and by working with our partners and the public to solve and prevent crime.' The key words there were 'prosecuting without fear, favour and prejudice'.

The hearing was swallowed by elaborate evidence about an astonishingly complex mining dispute and it became increasingly difficult to keep track of events and wade through the detail of it all. On Twitter, we battled to keep it straight and simple as our followers were lost in the intricacies of an ugly mining brawl. I took to adopting the hashtag #SAsMostComplicatedStoryYouShouldCareAbout

When you stripped it all down, this was the essence: Glynnis Breytenbach was arguably the country's top graft and economic crime prosecutor. Until her suspension she was prosecuting numerous headline-grabbing cases, including that of Julius Malema, ponzi scheme accused Barry Tannenbaum and the Arms Deal. She was also prosecuting politically connected mining company ICT for fraud. It was her handling of the ICT case that her bosses at the NPA used as grounds to suspend her. But Breytenbach wasn't buying it. She didn't believe she was suspended because of her handling of the ICT matter – rather, she thought it had everything to do with Richard Mdluli.

Breytenbach was adamant that the cabal at the top of the country's prosecuting service was colluding to stop her from prosecuting their mate. But there was more than just Breytenbach's career at stake. Rather, the entire ethos underpinning free and fair prosecutions was at risk.

If Breytenbach's version was correct, then those in charge at the NPA were going after the best commercial prosecutor in the country in order to get rid of her. The reason they were doing so was to stop the prosecution of not just Mdluli, but others like him – those with power, like President Zuma himself. They were doing so using trumped-up charges.

What was at stake for the country was the creation of a National Prosecuting Authority that had neither the capacity nor the will to prosecute those with political power. Others in the corridors at the VGM Building would have seen what happened to Breytenbach when she attempted to speak truth to power. There was the risk that it would create an NPA consisting of prosecutors who couldn't and wouldn't touch people in power. The deeply vaunted value of prosecutorial independence would have been compromised and the ideal of prosecuting without fear, favour and prejudice trampled upon.

At the end of it all, the chairperson, advocate Selby Mbenenge, acquitted Breytenbach of all the charges against her. It was a joke to watch as the NPA's bumbling witnesses attempted to make a case against the advocate. She didn't care. She played chess on her phone and watched the US Open tennis tournament on her laptop.

Breytenbach returned to her job at the NPA but it was never the same. They didn't give her any work to do and she sat idly by, unable to do anything with her considerable skills as criminals looted the state. Criminal charges were brought against her for allegedly deleting information off her work laptop and leaking stories to journalists, all charges for which she was acquitted in her internal disciplinary hearing. (She was later acquitted of these criminal charges too.)

So when Helen Zille called Breytenbach and asked her to get involved in politics, it didn't take her long to decide to do just that. South Africa was one prosecutor poorer – and the NPA's integrity was in tatters. But the true cost of losing Breytenbach was so much higher than the value of just one staff member. The entire saga around her had cost the NPA its integrity.

Glynnis Breytenbach is now the shadow minister of justice for the Democratic Alliance in parliament. Despite her new role, her desire for Richard Mdluli to face justice still burns strongly. We meet to talk about it over a chilled glass of Sauvignon Blanc at an Italian restaurant in Oaklands in Johannesburg.

Breytenbach believes it is crucial that Mdluli be prosecuted and face the allegations against him.

'The covert funds are made up of taxpayers' money and it's not there to be used for every little flight of fancy of Crime Intelligence and it's his job to see that it was not done. Instead of doing that job that he was supposed to do, he became the biggest abuser of the fund. For that reason, I was determined that he would be tried. You can't be a general and be corrupt. If you want to be in that kind of leadership position, especially in the police and more especially in Crime Intelligence, you have to be honest. You have to be completely and utterly, scrupulously honest, have bucket loads of integrity and lead by example. It's the only way to keep a thing like that more or less on the straight and narrow. That was his job and he wasn't doing it.'

There is no doubt in her mind that politics were at play in this case and that Mdluli was being protected.

'When it became clear to me that there was an agenda ... When I looked at the murder docket, there was more than enough circumstantial evidence to charge him for the murder at the time,' she says. I ask why she thinks the case stalled for a decade, gathering dust in a safe in Boksburg.

'He was clearly being protected. There was a family that lost a husband, father and a son. In the new South Africa, where we have a great Constitution, that kind of thing isn't supposed to happen. I would have been happy if they prosecuted him for murder and I am confident that I would've gotten a conviction.

'Now he's being prosecuted for assault and I think kidnapping or something. It's crazy; it isn't right. When I saw how the situation had been manipulated to protect him in that docket and Mrwebi – bless his cotton socks – started showing an interest in the corruption docket, it was very clear what was happening. I was absolutely determined that that was not going to happen.'

Breytenbach is hitting her stride. She has often spoken about how much she hates bullies and how she feels the need to protect the innocent.

'If we prosecuted Richard Mdluli and he was acquitted, fine, I would've walked away, no problem. But Richard Mdluli is just like you and me and everybody else in this country. If there's a case to be answered, you must answer it. If you're found guilty, you're guilty and so be it. If you're found innocent, then so be it. You can't bastardise the process. Due process and the rule of law are important, especially with people who are in positions of power – they must be seen to be upheld. And I was determined that that was going to be the case with Richard Mdluli.'

I want to know who Breytenbach believes was protecting him. Who in the NPA does she think was doing his bidding?

'On the Johannesburg murder matter, clearly [South Gauteng Director of Public Prosecutions] Andrew Chauke protected him. He made the decision,' she laments. 'He was supposed to be prosecuted by, I think, Zaais van Zyl, then Zaais fell off the roof of his house and nearly killed himself and the whole thing went to hell in a hand basket and Chauke referred it for an inquest. What happened with the corruption docket, there was pressure on Roelofse. They tried to prevent him from gaining access to the building at Crime Intelligence, having to run around for months, and we really had to do a lot of hard work to make sure that the investigation ran its course. It meant forcing people to do their jobs; it meant forcing people in higher positions to ensure that the matter didn't become subverted. Anwa Dramat took all the pressure and allowed Roelofse to do his investigation. Roelofse finished the investigation, followed it through and Dramat was the buffer – he allowed Roelofse the space and he took all the political pressure. He was under enormous pressure.'

From whom?

'From Zuma, is my opinion. That's certainly the impression that I got from Dramat. He was getting pressure from the commissioner of police and he got pressure from Zuma and probably other cabinet members as well, and probably the minister of police as well, I don't know. Dramat was under a lot of pressure and he was shielding Roelofse to allow him to do the investigation and it was hard. Then they started fiddling with the NPA component of the case; Jiba was acting director and she wouldn't call Mrwebi to account and it was clear that they had moved Mrwebi into that position of special director at the SCCU, in order to do this thing for Mdluli.'

Breytenbach is at her most derisive and disparaging when speaking about Mrwebi. It is as if she is spitting flames.

'Lawrence Mrwebi and Jiba were instrumental in the dismantling of the SCCU. The SCCU was in its last days. We were reporting to the office of the director of public prosecutions. Because the SCCU was independent, it was staffed with outstanding prosecutors. We did all the high-profile commercial crime matters. More importantly, the prosecutors were old prosecutors. We all had experience. They were not available to be stuffed around by anybody. All of a sudden they appoint Lawrence Mrwebi as special director when for months we'd been moved – everything was dismantled, our administrative component was so to speak gone; they had no office space for us. It was very clear. Mrwebi and Jiba were instrumental in doing that. Mrwebi especially was saying it's elitist and tried to make the point that we were all old and white, which wasn't the case – it was a very well-balanced office with very competent black prosecutors. Overnight Mrwebi was taken out of the DPP's office where he was doing nothing at all and made a special director at the SCCU, for what? And the only reason for doing that was to kill the Mdluli matter.

'He used to write me letters with instructions and I used to ignore him. I would attach his letter to my own letter and take it to Sibongile [Mzinyathi] and say, "This is my answer to that; if you want to answer him you're welcome to, I'm not." I never ever acknowledged him; I ignored him,' Breytenbach says. When I suggest that her conduct might have upset a superior, she lets me have it.

'I don't give a flying fuck what pissed him off. He's useless. I initially said in my own book that he had the intellectual capacity of a sock. The publishers made me take it out. I thought I was being flattering. If I have to be entirely honest, he has the intellectual capacity of a week-old dog turd!' Seething, she takes a sip of her Sauvignon Blanc.

Breytenbach says she will ensure that Mrwebi and Jiba never get their hands on the original Mdluli docket. It would be unlikely anyway as they have both since been suspended from the NPA following a High Court ruling that removed them from the bar of advocates, although they are appealing this decision.

I ask who has the docket now, considering Mdluli has still not been prosecuted for fraud and corruption.

'I'm not telling you either. That would be an offence,' she chastises me.

Breytenbach went through hell after her suspension. Shots were fired at her at night while she was driving on the highway. She used an armoured vehicle. She lost her job as a prosecutor, which she lived for. During her disciplinary hearing, both her mother and her father died. I wonder why she fought so hard. Why was the principle so important to her? It was never really about Mdluli for her, was it?

'It has got nothing to do with Mdluli. It has got everything to do with prosecuting without fear, favour or prejudice, which the NPA is constrained to do in terms of the Constitution, and to uphold the rule of law. Everybody in this country is equal before the law. It shouldn't matter if you're rich or poor, or weak or strong, or well connected or very powerful, or not connected at all with no power; everybody's equal before the law. That is the only way that the Constitution can work. And that is how the NPA has to function. I don't give a fig for Richard Mdluli. This particular matter, there's a prima facie case against him – it's a strong case – it's absolutely winnable. But he's in a position of enormous power. He's a general, he leads hundreds, thousands of policemen and what he does, they think it's okay. It's not okay. He needs to be prosecuted so that everybody can see it doesn't matter who you are, you cannot behave like this. That is why we are in the trouble we are in because some people are more connected than others. If you are well connected, you can buy injustice, which is a scary concept.'

Breytenbach has an opinion on why Crime Intelligence officials are so susceptible to corruption and why they become so greedy. 'It is because of the
nature of the environment – it happens everywhere; it happens in covert
sort of secret things everywhere. The DSO [Scorpions] had a private fund;
we had the same problem. I had to prosecute the people who stole the
money. In the Defence Force you have problems with the covert people.
In every organisation where there is something covert there is a problem
because of the nature of the environment, and in the police even more so
because they are really not well paid. If the general is stealing, why the hell
shouldn't the constable steal? It's a problem.

'The NPA is a different dynamic. The NPA ordinarily isn't susceptible to
corruption and I'm happy to say that in the first 15 years of my life as a prosecutor you would not have convinced me that any prosecutor that I knew,
or knew of, was corrupt. Nobody took bribes, as far as I was aware. I would
have staked my life on it that you couldn't bribe a magistrate and certainly
not a judge. Unthinkable! That's no longer the case as far as magistrates
and prosecutors are concerned. I sincerely hope it is still the case as far as
judges are concerned. Prosecutors have a different dynamic; they have a
lot of power and they are well paid – they earn a lot of money. I earn just a
little over half as an MP of what I did as a prosecutor. What prosecutors are
susceptible to is they have no position as a prosecutor. It's not a status symbol to be a prosecutor, so when somebody who is well connected and who
has a lot of power taps them on the shoulder and says come to my house
and have some Johnnie Walker Blue, it's easy to fall for that. It's a different
kind of thing; it's a new-found social status. It was never a desire before; I
don't know why prosecutors would desire social status.'

She explains that someone like Krejcir, who was already an expert in the
field, would have enjoyed easy pickings in South Africa.

'The Eastern Bloc countries are masters in the art of corruption and
organised crime. It's what they do. I think people in South Africa were like
babes in arms, they had no idea. You just have to get a policeman drunk
enough once to get a photograph of him in a compromising position and
say you'll give it to his wife and you've got him. You don't even need to pay
him after that; you just have to get them drunk once and then set them up

to get caught for drunken driving once and get them off.'

She points to the weakened state institutions as examples of how susceptible the country is to masters in the art of corruption. 'It's got a lot to do with the president [Zuma], of course, who chose to weaken all these institutions because it didn't suit him to have a strong police force and a strong prosecuting authority and a strong revenue service.'

Does she think the weakening was an intentional project by Zuma and his acolytes? And if so, for what purpose? It's quite a thing to go about eviscerating the state's capacity to fight crime just to protect a handful of powerful individuals. She absolutely believes it was intentional.

'After Zuma came so close in the Arms Deal and because there were so many other people implicated in the Arms Deal and powerful people who still have a lot to lose should it ever go ahead, and after Travelgate, they intentionally set about dismantling those institutions that could effectively investigate and prosecute them. Anything that could hold them to account, SARS, anybody who had the power to force them to operate in the parameters of the law. It was a cynical, intentional, planned project.'

And I point out to her what she already knows, that this kind of situation is the perfect breeding ground for organised crime.

'Organised crime is absolutely unchecked. They have no Crime Intelligence. Things happen on a daily basis that Crime Intelligence should know about, but nothing happens. People getting murdered in their beds, farm murders; there's no Crime Intelligence. These things would've happened on a much smaller scale if they had proper Crime Intelligence. Cash-in-transit heists, I mean, we all know who's doing it and why they're doing it and nothing gets done about it, and the reason for that is where the money goes. Nothing is ever going to get done about it because you need a lot of money to buy an election …'

By the end of our meeting, I was ready to drain the entire bottle of wine.

A LOUD CRACK BROKE THE AWKWARD SILENCE IN THE DIMLY LIT courtroom and the three men collapsed onto the floor. I struggled to stop myself from shrieking with laughter. It's not every day you see a big bad guy, accused of armed robbery, stumbling around trying to keep his footing. To his credit, Krejcir saw the humour in the moment and laughed out loud too. So did his strongman Jason Dominguez and sidekick Serb Veselin Laganin. Krejcir was looking hefty and we joked that it was his weight that had broken the court bench. Dominguez, with his brushcut, bulging muscles and thick gold bracelet, was everything a heavy was meant to be but he was amiable and friendly, not menacing at all. Laganin looked the most out of place, with his man bag and loafers and broken English. The three were accused in an armed robbery case in the Pretoria magistrate's court. It was February 2012, but the alleged armed robbery had occurred three months earlier.

In October 2011, I got wind that Dominguez had been shot in the arm in Pretoria West on a Sunday afternoon. Details were sketchy but I knew that he was apparently 'on the run'. His lawyer, however, denied this. It took us a while to piece together the events of that day and it was only when Krejcir and his two accomplices were arrested and brought to court that the picture became clearer.

There had been a showdown between the trio and some Pakistani business owners over cash. Laganin, who moved to South Africa in 1989, had gone to the electronics shop to collect money the owner apparently owed him. Laganin had allegedly left R900 000 packed in a box in the shop, but the money – the proceeds of a property sale – had disappeared. The Serb was sure that the Pakistani man who owned the shop had taken the cash because he was supposedly the only person who knew about it. Laganin returned to Joburg to fetch his mates and, together with Dominguez and Krejcir, who was in shorts and flip-flops on a Sunday afternoon, went to see the Pakistani about the money.

Faced with the trio standing in his shop, the Pakistani handed over an initial payment of R105 000 and agreed to pay back the rest. As the three were walking back to their cars, all hell broke loose. A group of men stormed them, attacking the trio with bricks and stones. Dominguez drew his gun and fired warning shots into the air. In the moments that followed, a gun battle ensued and Dominguez was wounded in the arm. His bakkie took a number of bullets. Krejcir, still in his flip-flops, scrambled into his vehicle and sped away.

Laganin opened a case of theft and attempted murder against the Pakistani man at a Pretoria West police station. In turn, the Pakistani alleged that he was being extorted and that Krejcir and his cohorts were attempting to rob him at gunpoint.

The three spent a week in custody before being released on bail. Advocate Mike Hellens acted for Krejcir in the bail application, insisting that the entire arrest was driven by retribution for the legal action Krejcir had instituted against then Police Minister Nathi Mthethwa. Krejcir was suing the minister for the botched police raid on his Bedfordview mansion. 'Armed robbery is a very serious offence, always accompanied with immediate action from the police. They only decided to arrest the three accused after the minister was served with a summons,' Hellens told the court.

The case fizzled out and ultimately the three men were released and charges were withdrawn. It was a mere blip in Krejcir's operations; he continued with his various business interests from his Money Point headquarters.

Outside the courtroom, after he was released, he gave me a brief interview. It was classic Eastern European gangster.

'The reason is that I was suing two ministers in South Africa. It was just an exercise to teach me a lesson,' he said in his thick Czech accent.

So what was it about then – was he involved? I ask.

'Never, I will be never involved,' he insists. 'Me as a billionaire … Do I really need to go on Sunday morning with my flip-flops, shorts and a

T-shirt to rob the people for R20 000? I don't think I need this.

'It was just moral support because I went there with my friend because he was robbed for R900 000. I never speak to nobody. I never take any gun. I do nothing. Fuck all.' He laughed and apologised for his language. 'They teach me a lesson that I misbehave here in this country against the two ministers.' He walked outside to face a bank of cameras, reinforcing his image as a mafioso who kept getting off.

NHLANHLA MKHWANAZI IS NOT A MAN OF POLITICS. HE IS A man of action. As head of the Special Task Force and the police's Air Wing and the National Intervention Unit, he was used to operating under immense pressure. He was also required to have guts, be courageous and stand his ground.

From October 2011 until June 2012, his resolve was tested as he babysat the SAPS. It was a tumultuous time dominated by politics. Mkhwanazi, despite his tough-guy exterior, was out of his comfort zone. Yet he stepped up and performed.

Central to his focus was Richard Mdluli and his battle with the police management. Mdluli was waging a fight-back campaign. At this stage the fraud and corruption charges had been withdrawn, but a departmental inquiry was still ongoing. Mdluli had returned to head Crime Intelligence and was still in charge of the slush fund. He was also given increased powers, having been placed in charge of the VIP police unit, which meant he knew all the details of the protection plans of all cabinet ministers. The murder charges had been withdrawn and it had been recommended that an inquest be held instead.

Mdluli was firmly of the view that he was the target of a smear campaign and that former National Commissioner Bheki Cele was behind the plot to unseat him. Mdluli believed that this campaign was an officially sanctioned project and it even had a name: Project 'Ulibambe Lingashoni', loosely translated as 'Don't let the sun go down'. Mdluli also translated it as 'let us wage a relentless campaign to see to it that he [Mdluli] does not survive'.

This resulted in a period of chaos within the police and the NPA, with Mdluli and Breytenbach featuring as the main protagonists. On 12

March 2012, the Inspector-General of Intelligence Faith Radebe advised Mkhwanazi to reinstate the fraud and corruption charges against Richard Mdluli. The police had written to her and provided her with the Hawks corruption docket on Mdluli. Despite this recommendation, it did not happen.

Within Crime Intelligence, officers were filled with fear that when he returned to his office Mdluli would target those who had investigated him for fraud and murder. It was widely known that he was vengeful and was fighting back. Mkhwanazi had to attempt to get a handle on the situation.

Mkhwanazi was making a genuine attempt to stop the chaos raging around him. It emerged that Mkhwanazi had stood up to his political principals and threatened to resign over the alleged political protection Mdluli was receiving. At the height of the standoff with Mdluli, Mkhwanazi appeared in parliament and dropped a bombshell. He revealed that there was political interference in the police.

He told MPs that 'powers beyond us' had been telling him 'to release some case dockets to the inspector-general for intelligence'. This was, of course, a reference to the Mdluli investigations. Mkhwanazi said that 'we have been told in many instances of late that we don't have the right to investigate certain case dockets'.

'There are powers beyond us that are going to decide whether there is a conviction or not. It's all good that we say we want to achieve this target of conviction, but we are not prosecutors. We are not judges,' he said. Mkhwanazi would not go further and did not reveal who had given him these instructions.

At the time it was known that Mdluli had appealed to President Zuma for help with the campaign against him. But presidential spokesperson Mac Maharaj denied that Zuma played any part in the decision to drop the charges against Mdluli. Police Minister Nathi Mthethwa also denied any involvement.

In a surprising move, the minister of police announced in parliament a month later, in May 2012, that Richard Mdluli would be moved away from the Crime Intelligence division. Mthethwa stated that the shift was to allow for an investigation into the allegations of a conspiracy against Mdluli by his colleagues. The next morning, Mkhwanazi went on SABC radio and explained that Mdluli had, in fact, been moved to a post in an operations division so that the allegations into fraud and corruption could be investigated.

A couple of weeks later, Mkhwanazi set himself on a collision course with his political masters when he decided that Mdluli and the financial head of Crime Intelligence, Major General Solly Lazarus, should be suspended. The *Sunday Independent* reported that the move was part of a massive clean-up of Crime Intelligence. 'I am a cop. I want the police environment to have clean cops. If we want to fight crime we must rid the SAPS of criminals and stay with clean cops,' Mkhwanazi told the paper.

A letter of suspension was sent to Mdluli's lawyer on a Sunday. The following Friday, Mdluli brought a late-afternoon application at the Labour Court to have his suspension lifted. It was so sneaky that no SAPS lawyers were even present to oppose the application. The following Sunday, another urgent application was brought by the police in the Labour Court to set aside the lifting of Mdluli's suspension. It was getting ugly and complicated.

Then in stepped civil society. Lobby group Freedom Under Law applied for an urgent interdict to stop Mdluli from performing any functions in the police pending a judicial review of the decisions relating to his reinstatement. On 6 June, the North Gauteng High Court interdicted Mdluli from executing his duties as a policeman.

Judge Ephraim Makgoba said in his ruling:

> *The allegations against the fifth respondent [Mdluli] are no ordinary allegations of misconduct. Murder, defeating the ends of justice, fraud and money laundering are serious criminal acts which go to the fabric of public order and security. While these allegations remain unresolved the fifth respondent's very presence in the senior echelons of SAPS will necessarily erode the function he and SAPS as a whole are entrusted. Hence such allegations need to be attended to diligently and promptly.*

In my view, this matter is of considerable public importance. The sooner this saga is brought to an end the sooner the credibility of the police, security service and the justice system as a whole can be restored.

Mkhwanazi had stood up against his political masters and against Mdluli. Writing in the *Daily Maverick*, Ranjeni Munusamy explained the importance of this:

In a sea of deceit and contempt for the public by his political bosses, Mkhwanazi has been a breath of fresh air by speaking out and taking action against the rot. This cannot be good for his career and he may not succeed in his goals if he is confronted with further political pressure. But Mkhwanazi is helping to restore public confidence in the police service. And he is showing that maybe, just maybe, there are still a few good men.

Two weeks later, President Jacob Zuma removed Mkhwanazi from the post of acting national commissioner and returned him to his day job. In the official, permanent position he appointed a businesswoman, with no police experience – a 'hasie' as this is known in police parlance, a rabbit caught in the headlights.

THERE IS A PLUSH, HIGH-BACKED, BLACK LEATHER CHAIR IN THE national police commissioner's office on the seventh floor of the Wachthuis building. Its dark wooden arms are polished to a gleam and the silver-studded buttons stretching the shiny leather into finely shaped diamonds glint in the hazy, yellow light. The chair is flanked on either side by metal poles, holding up two unfurled flags that drape down to the floor. Gold- and blue-framed portraits of President Jacob Zuma and his deputy, Kgalema Motlanthe, peer down from the cherrywood-panelled walls over the black leather chair and those who occupy it.

When I see it, in mid-2012, it dawns on me that over the past dozen years, no fewer than five people have claimed that seat as their own. Two have done so in acting capacities under dubious circumstances. Jackie Selebi, Tim Williams, Bheki Cele, Nhlanhla Mkhwanazi and now, the first woman to do so, Riah Phiyega.

On the day that I walk into that office, General Riah Phiyega has been national police commissioner for only 18 days. She was appointed to the position by President Zuma on 13 June 2012 to replace her suspended pre-decessor, Bheki Cele. There is little in the room that identifies it as her own – there are brown cardboard police dockets on the desk, an official-looking green folder and a bland blue file. The visible lack of anything of the personal is indicative of the fact that the occupant of the space is rarely a permanent one. Phiyega is statuesque and imposing as she stands to greet me, dressed in a stylish suit, sensible heels and pearl earrings. Despite the business attire, she is warm and embracing. Not quite what one would expect from a chief of police.

The position of national commissioner is a poisoned chalice, mired in controversy – why would Phiyega, a largely respected business executive with no experience in policing, voluntarily accept it?

'Can we shelve the safety and security of South African citizens? No. Do we want to leave it to chance? No. So when the clarion call was made and I started understanding the challenge, I thought if some of the skill set that I'm having can make a difference then let me answer "Yes", she says. 'I believe any other South African, if the finger was pointing at you, Mandy, and you understood the challenges that are before us as a nation, you would have said "Yes". It's not about *who* but about *what* we need to do for the country and I believe I do have something to offer.

'We don't have a broken police service. We have a police service that requires to be continuously improved,' she assures me in her measured, confident way. 'We need to be very clear about those priorities. In what areas do we need to bolster? In what areas do we need to maintain? In what areas do we need to completely restructure? We have a working police service. I do want to say to South Africans that. Are we perfect? Absolutely not. Are we willing to learn and listen? Yes, we are. And I want to say to citizens of this country, I take them up to come to my office, to guide us, to give inputs and always to criticise us where they have to criticise us because that constructive criticism is fodder for growth and improvement.'

But while the new commissioner is upbeat, she appears to be ignoring an important voice: the police doing the real, grim, thankless work. No one knows the true state of the SAPS better than the members themselves – the uniformed constable who patrols dusty township streets by night, the specialised tactical response officer who is jumping walls and banging down doors in pursuit of armed assailants, the drained detective who spends hours on end chasing down leads and working dockets, piled high on a desk. They are the ones who can testify to the levels of morale within the service, the degree of respect shown to them by the members of the communities they serve, and the quality of the equipment they are provided with in order to fight crime.

Not long after speaking to Phiyega, I meet with a cop at his home in Johannesburg to get some thoughts on what the rank and file thought of the new commissioner. He sits across from me in his slippers on his couch. He is part of a specialist task team and has nearly 30 years' experience on the ground in nearly every facet of policing. He reckons he's made 'four, maybe five, thousand' arrests during his career and has been in 'too many, way too many' shootouts to count. He doesn't say how many people he's shot, but yes, he has been shot himself. He regales me with spectacular memories of car chases, gun battles and manhunts. He is one of the good guys, deeply passionate about safeguarding citizens and getting the bad guys off the streets.

'I do it because I believe in the country. We've got a good future over here. South Africa's a great country and I want to do my bit, hey. I truly believe in this country and I believe we can make it great. I believe there are some animals out there and they need to be brought to justice. I haven't been affected by any personal tragedy or anything like that. I just believe in it,' he assures me.

Every day he comes face to face with criminals and I ask him if he thinks the perspective of the criminals towards the police has changed over the years? 'Oh, they're straightforward. They'll drive into a suburb. They're not looking for a uniformed vehicle. They're looking for unmarked vehicles. They've got no fear of the uniformed police officer. According to them, they can "talk" their way out of it. They can bribe their way out of it. It won't work every time; not every police officer is like that. You're going to try it with the wrong one and get nabbed, but they don't have the fear of the uniformed guys. Their perception is these guys are doing it as a job. The plainclothes guys are the career policemen. The guys in uniform get up every morning and go to work. It's a job. They do the bare minimum to get through the day and then collect their pay cheque.'

Corruption amongst his colleagues is a very real problem. 'Every shift the guys come on duty, they do parade, they get given profiles of what suspects they're looking for and, most of the time, it's two to five black males in this car or walking on foot, it's the reality of it. That's the profile. They drive around with blinkers on unless it's a flashy car that they can probably get something from. Then they're alert. I see it every day, pulling over vehicles that have no bearing on crime prevention whatsoever. Expensive

Mercedes-Benz, elderly male or a young lady, and they're soliciting bribes. They're accusing and intimidating people, they're thuggish.'

While he can't be bothered about the scandals rocking the top structures of the organisation, he says it does have implications for officers on the ground. 'Look, as far as I'm concerned, leave me alone and let me get on with my job. But it affects public confidence in the police, though. Every time one of these bigwigs has a finger pointed at him, it's going to have a negative effect on the way the public views the police.'

It's easy to assume that it's only the old white career cops who are quick to complain about the state of the organisation, but things are not quite so simple.

It's early in the morning on a freezing winter's day when I walk into the face-brick police station in the heart of Soweto. Already the service centre at the charge office is heaving. An elderly woman, wrapped in a thick coat and scarf, sits on a chair against one wall, clutching a pile of dog-eared papers. She has settled in for a long day of waiting. Plainclothes detectives stroll up and down the corridors, walking from room to room, stopping in for a brief chat with colleagues. Constables in blue uniforms make a point of looking busy.

The overweight detective plods over to me and beckons me to his office with a nod of his head. I follow him down a passage of doors and into a grimy room that overlooks a parade ground. He heaves himself into his worn chair with a grunt and sits behind a desk, stacked high with brown files. Dockets are piled high on every possible surface in the office. On windowsills, on top of cabinets, spilling out of drawers, on the floor. There appears to be absolutely no sense of order and nothing to indicate what category each docket falls into.

'You can see how many dockets there are here. These are all my dockets,' he shows me with a wave of his arm. 'The others, they're stopped because of the forensic report, then you must get the PM [post-mortem] report, then if the pathologist is not yet ready, what must you do? You just wait for the report. Hey, hey, stressful. Traumatised!'

He became a police officer in his early twenties and has been a detective for nearly 30 years now. He is tired from a lifetime of chasing criminals.

'I get two or three new dockets every day. Usually it's theft, robbery, malicious damage to property. I'm sure there are about five murders here, rape I've got three,' he tells me, thumbing through the files on his bulging desk. 'You read it and you see the instruction from court or instruction from officer, what must you do urgently, you must do this urgently. The new one you check it. Sometimes the suspect is around, then you must attend to it the same time. It's too much. Too much work. There is no solution because most of the people, when they come from the College, they don't want to be a detective. They just want to work with uniform because detectives are overloaded. You knock off now but they can phone you even at eight o'clock. You work 24 hours. They can phone you any time and say there's a suspect you're looking for from two months or three months ago and you must go and arrest the suspect.'

He informs me that corruption at grassroots level is endemic and the way it's being handled by management is equally problematic. 'Corruption is a big problem. Lots of officers. It's a big problem.'

The more I speak to cops, the more evident it becomes that Phiyega's primary challenge in her new post is going to be boosting morale on the ground.

In her office in the Wachthuis building, Riah Phiyega stands between the two flagpoles and poses for a photo shoot. She smooths the skirt of her business suit and sits down on the plush, high-backed black leather chair. We chat a little more, and as I leave I quip that we've had too much to report over the past few years about the occupants of this room. 'Please', I say, 'don't give us anything to write about this time around.'

Less than two months later, the bodies of 34 mineworkers lay dead on the country's platinum belt, their blood seeping into the dry earth of the Marikana mine. They had been cut down by police bullets and Phiyega would be held responsible.

DESPITE THE MOUNTING ALLEGATIONS AGAINST HIM, RADOVAN Krejcir remained a free man. By 2013, he still was not facing a single charge. He insisted he was a family man, a businessman and an all-round good guy. A billionaire who had no reason to be running around in his flip-flops with a gun holding people up. The police were doing very little, if anything, about him.

But SARS was still quietly chipping away at Krejcir's publicly created persona, looking for every chink to exploit. They found a few.

The first was a fake Facebook profile under the name of Russel Knight. A member of the investigating team found the profile and worked out that Krejcir was using it to communicate with his associates. This led them to a number of other individuals they didn't know about and more information was gathered about his network.

SARS also got a tip-off that a man who had just returned from Swaziland had been arrested by the police. The man was Brendan Harrison, a former employee of Krejcir. Harrison had met Krejcir in 2009 when he was working at the Harbour restaurant. In 2011, he was given a job by Krejcir's lieutenant Michael Arsiotis. In his position as a manager at Money Point, he witnessed many things. In his affidavit before court, Harrison recounted how four men came into the shop one day and began threatening Arsiotis. These were Jason Dominguez, Ronny Bvuma and two Congolese men. Arsiotis told Harrison to report the threats to the police, which he did. Not long after, it was alleged by Harrison that he got a call from Krejcir's financial manager, Ivan Savov, telling him that he had 'picked the wrong side'. He began to receive death threats.

Harrison fled. He went to Swaziland and cut all ties with Krejcir. He kept a low profile and didn't make contact with anyone, including his family.

But when he returned to South Africa on a business trip in mid-2013, he was stopped at the Oshoek border post and placed under arrest. The charge – conspiracy to kill Krejcir.

It seemed that the Czech had rustled up some cops on the take to nab Harrison and get his revenge. The investigating officer on the case was none other than Colonel François Steyn, the same Germiston cop who had taken a loan from Krejcir. It also later emerged that police had allegedly allowed Krejcir to see Harrison after his arrest, intimidate him and hold him at gunpoint while in their custody.

In his bail application, Harrison told the court that a Warrant Officer David Mothibi had driven him to Gauteng and threatened him, saying if he didn't cooperate, 'he will make [his] life difficult' and also would oppose any future bail applications.

He was taken to the Bedfordview police station and then moved again to Germiston for his court appearance. Harrison alleged that on the way there in the car, Mothibi took a phone call. He told the person on the other end that they could not meet at the Bedfordview police station but rather en route to Germiston. As they drove past Kloof Road, Mothibi apparently remarked to Harrison, 'There is your boss's house.'

Harrison said the police vehicle came to a stop near a Pick n Pay store en route to Germiston, and Krejcir and Ronny Bvuma pulled up behind them. Mothibi allegedly unlocked the door for Krejcir and Ronny to enter the police car. Harrison was handcuffed at the time. He claims Krejcir then pulled out a gun and began harassing him about gold and diamonds that had gone missing. He also wanted to know where Arsiotis had disappeared to.

During the interrogation, Krejcir allegedly turned to Mothibi and said: 'See, I did not hurt or bruise him; your job will not be in jeopardy.' Eventually, Krejcir got out of the car, leaving Harrison unharmed. Police were so convinced that Krejcir wanted to kill Harrison that they opposed bail because they believed he was safer in jail than out. Harrison denied having anything to do with an alleged plot to kill Krejcir. He wasn't even in South Africa at the time the plan was said to have been hatched. He was eventually released and the charges were withdrawn.

While Harrison was being held at the Boksburg prison, members of the SARS High-Risk Investigation Unit (HRIU) got wind that he was there and went to see him. They took an affidavit from him and it was pure gold for the investigators. He had the inside track on how the Money Point shops were organised and how they operated.

All of this kind of information received from the field was fed into Project K. Investigators also scoured Krejcir's bank accounts and pieced together a picture of how he was operating. They noticed that he was using his lawyer BDK's trust account to transfer funds, which made it more difficult for investigators to access. They needed a warrant to look at lawyers' trust accounts.

Van Loggerenberg and his team took the decision to hold a formal tax inquiry and informed Krejcir of the decision. 'That's the advantage of a tax investigation – you don't have to look for your suspect. You engage them from day one,' explains a member of the SARS investigation unit. 'It's different from how the police functions. When you deal with the taxman, you're obliged to answer. If you fail to answer, that's a criminal offence. So, if we say to you we want you to explain to us the origin of this foreign funding, we want you to explain the payments to these different companies, blah, blah, blah.'

The tax inquiry was held from September 2012 until January 2013. Officially the inquiry was not only into Krejcir, but also into his wife Katerina, his son Denis, and into a litany of entities associated with them. A total of 23 people appeared to give evidence, including the three Krejcirs, Glenn Agliotti, Juan Meyer, Ian Small-Smith, Djordje Mihaljevic, Ronelle Engelbrecht, Ronny Bvuma and a series of other people with Eastern European names who had entered into some kind of business relationship with Krejcir. The full list is detailed in Van Loggerenberg's High Court affidavit.

SARS used the inquiry to glean as much information as possible from those who appeared and to fill in the final gaps on the 'JvL' drawing. An investigator who was at the inquiry told me one story about how they were watching every single move made by every single person there.

Members of the HRIU, which became known as the so-called Rogue

Unit, hung around at the chambers in Brooklyn where the inquiry was being held. They were checking to see who arrived with whom and who spoke to whom during the breaks. If there were any new characters, they could build a hierarchical picture of Krejcir's network, who his henchmen were and who slotted in under them.

On one of the days, a particularly attentive member spotted a piece of paper changing hands. An individual subpoenaed to testify had handed a note to the next person to testify as they crossed paths in the parking lot. The second man read the piece of paper, crumpled it up and threw it in the dustbin before walking off. The so-called Rogue Unit member walked straight over to the bin and dug out the crumpled note.

The note had nothing to do with the inquiry. But it had everything to do with their investigation. Krejcir wanted to pass a message on to someone who wasn't anywhere on the JvL map. SARS didn't even know he existed. Krejcir needed cash and it had to be delivered to Money Point on a certain date at an exact time. There was a phone number scribbled on the note.

The investigators did a background check on the phone number, saw who it belonged to and rang him up. The call went something like this: We're from SARS, we've got this note, we know you've been given an instruction to collect R100 000 from somebody to deliver it to Money Point, we want you to come in and tell us about it.

The man voluntarily went into SARS, met with Van Loggerenberg and shared what he knew. He had one crucial piece of information: a lot of the gold that went into Money Point didn't go through the books of the company. He revealed that a lot was stolen. It came from zama zamas (illegal miners), from house robberies and theft. This included jewellery stolen in hijackings and during violent home invasions. The precious stones were removed and pawned or taken out of the country and converted to cash offshore, but the gold went off to small smelting plants Krejcir had set up all over town. The gold was smelted down, made into gold bars and then sold on or taken out of the country. It was a gold washing machine. Crucially, the informant handed over the address of one of the smelting plants.

The HRIU members went to check out the address, but it was little more than a residential house. They thought that the guy must have been talking nonsense. But Van Loggerenberg kept the address on record and frequently sent the HRIU past to keep an eye on the place. They were scratching around trying to see where it fitted into the bigger picture. They knew that money was collected from the address and taken to Money Point, but that was all. They had also been talking to the neighbours and had established that the occupants of the house, the Bezuidenhouts, were running a full-fledged operation of their own, and when Krejcir was in trouble and needed cash, he would get money from them as a last resort.

Several months later, the HRIU did a routine drive-by and noticed that the house was for sale. The investigators didn't have enough basis for a warrant so they had to be smart about it. The house was on show that particular Sunday so they strolled into the house and the agent assumed they were prospective buyers and took them on a walkabout. As they went past the kitchen, they noticed an inside door that led into a double garage. The door was closed so one of the men asked the estate agent if they could open it. She apologised for the mess in the garage but showed them around. The HRIU member snapped away on his cellphone, capturing images of gas bottles and other paraphernalia.

That afternoon they took the photos to an expert, who confirmed that what they'd seen in that garage was a rudimentary smelting plant. They sent the Tactical Intervention Unit straight in and closed the place down overnight.

SARS was tightening the screws on Krejcir. What they really wanted was to shut down his ability to operate financially. Following the tax inquiry, they had established that Krejcir and his family and companies owed the taxman R110 million. Their plan was to apply for a preservation order. Van Loggerenberg knew that preserving Krejcir's assets would stem the flow of cash and change his life dramatically. A curator would take control of absolutely everything. An inventory would be taken of his house and other assets, banks would be notified, cards would be stopped. It would be practically impossible for him to operate.

IT WAS THE END OF JULY 2013, FREEZING COLD, AND I WAS SITTING on the hard court benches of the High Court in Pretoria listening to dense legal argument. The Democratic Alliance was attempting to get the National Prosecuting Authority to hand over the elusive 'Spy Tapes' and the record of the decision by Mokotedi Mpshe to withdraw corruption charges against President Jacob Zuma. I was straining, listening to eccentric advocate Kemp J Kemp argue his case. It was pretty dreary stuff and I was struggling to concentrate. I could never in my wildest dreams have imagined what happened next.

My phone rang and I stepped outside the courtroom to take it. It was a contact. And I could not believe what I was hearing. It was the stuff of James Bond movies. I immediately dialled the number saved under 'Radovan Krejcir' in my contacts. I had to hear this first-hand to believe it. He answered the phone sounding shaken. He told me what had happened and he sounded genuinely incredulous. I tweeted out the breaking news:

#BREAKING EWN Czech businessman Radovan #Krejcir has survived an apparent attempted hit on his life in Bedfordview.

#Krejcir has just told EWN – he parked his car outside his office near Eastgate when several shots were fired at him from a red Polo.

#Krejcir says a 'mechanical device' from behind the licence plate of the car opened fire with 'twelve barrels'.

I phoned my colleague Alex Eliseev. He was en route to the scene at Money Point in Bedfordview. I had to work hard to convince him that the story was not fiction. Alex arrived to find a burnt-out shell of a car, smouldering and grey, parked in the Money Point premises. Gun barrels were exposed where the licence plate should have been. Krejcir's matte-black Mercedes was parked a short distance away, riddled with bullet holes. The place was teeming with cops. Alex wrote up the events of that day for *Daily Maverick*, emphasising, of course, that this was Krejcir's version of what happened:

> He arrived at work at around 11:30am and parked in his usual spot. He climbed out of his matte black Merc and, while talking on his cellphone, moved away from the car and towards the front entrance. Barely a metre into his walk, he heard what sounded like a loud explosion. Then 'firecrackers' began to go off, or at least that's what he thought until he saw that the side of his car was riddled with holes. His colleague ran out to help get him inside the building while a car in the parking lot exploded into flames.
>
> Krejcir is unharmed. 'I'm a lucky man,' he says. But he has just survived what is clearly an assassination attempt. Upon further investigation, it turns out the car parked nearby, a red VW Polo, was in fact a weapon. Its back number plate blew off to reveal a dozen gun barrels aimed directly at where Krejcir parks each and every day. Although it seemed like bullets were being fired, the more likely scenario is that the car was modified with home-made shotguns, which sprayed pellets in his direction.
>
> Amazingly, the VW Polo was empty all along, and Krejcir's theory is that it was being operated by someone lurking nearby. 'I suspect it was like somebody had a remote control and when he saw me from a close distance he pressed the remote control and the bullets came out.'

Speaking to journalists afterwards, Krejcir delivered one of his trademark lines. 'All my life is like James Bond stuff,' he said, 'so it's usual stuff for me … It's how I live my life.'

He was not forthcoming about who might have been behind the incident. 'Nobody knows. I don't have any suspect … And even if I have some idea, I'm not going to tell you.'

For days after the bizarre 007 shooting, I tried to get to the bottom of what had happened. Police confirmed that the VW Polo was reported stolen in April of that year. From what officials could establish, the vehicle was positioned in the parking lot the previous night but it was unclear by whom.

The most popular theory was that, incredibly, Krejcir had been behind the whole thing. It was believed that he had set it up to make himself appear to be the victim. The dramatic flair and the attention-grabbing pizzazz had his fingerprints all over it. It would assist with his refugee application and help him avoid extradition back to the Czech Republic.

Sources told me that the car had been rigged up by a mechanic in Wynberg near Sandton, but had originally come from Cape Town. Speculation was that it could have been a revenge attempt by those close to Cyril Beeka who wanted to take Krejcir out.

The other theory was that it was a turf war boiling over. It might well have been the work of international agents brought in to assassinate the Czech, although the plan had failed spectacularly. But maybe it was someone closer to home, someone in Krejcir's inner circle who knew his movements and who had grown aggrieved.

At the end of the day, there were no factual explanations. But it made for one helluva story.

THERE'S A VIDEO ON MY LAPTOP THAT I WATCH OCCASIONALLY. IT'S 39 seconds long. It's raw and gritty and graphically tells the story of how the underworld spilled into the overworld in the upmarket suburb of Bedfordview.

It's cunningly shot from a distance, through the gap left between an Ekurhuleni Metro Police vehicle and the tar of Bradford Road. At least half of the horizontal screen is consumed by a clear image of a truck with bold, capital letters reading EMPD and blue chevron lines stuttering across the bottom of the vehicle.

You can see four sets of feet from the knees to the ankles. One pair is particularly active. The individual is wearing a blue pathologist's coat and blue gloves. One of the other men is wearing running shoes and short white athletics socks.

The men are rolling around a body. The corpse is wearing beige chinos and a black belt and a short-sleeved, grey button-up top. It's hard to tell what colour it actually is because it is so saturated in blood. The shirt on the person's right shoulder has been completely shredded by bullets and so has his body. Rivulets of blood run down his arms as the forensic experts flop them to one side and then to the other. As they roll him over, his face comes into near-full view. If you know the man, it is not difficult to identify him, with his sharp features, angular forehead and dark, receding hairline even though his face is almost entirely covered in blood.

What you can't see off-screen is the shot-up black Audi Q7 that came to an abrupt stop, its rear wheels awkwardly perched on the pavement and its nose facing into the street just metres away from the traffic light. There are at least two dozen little snippets of white tape pasted onto the car's front right window showing where bullets struck the driver's door. Police found a .38 revolver, 9mm rounds and a silencer in the car, as well as four cellphones.

The entire intersection is cordoned off with yellow police tape keeping back the crowds of rubberneckers, and yellow cones litter the tar, marking out where the shells fell. The cops counted 33 shells that had spilled out of the semi-automatic weapons. Tyre marks stretch across the road, an illustration of just how quickly the getaway car screeched off.

The soundtrack to the short clip serves as a little window into the context of the crime scene. You can hear the busy din of the street outside a bustling Bedford Centre on a Saturday morning. Two women are talking. They are exclaiming at what they are witnessing with 'Yoh, yoh, yohs' and 'Eh, ehs'. And then they start to ask questions. 'Why didn't they take the car? This couldn't have been a hijacking then? But this must be somebody's husband and father?'

They have no idea that the body being rolled around methodically on the tar is that of 'Black Sam', aka 'Cripple Sam' Issa, and that this is a mafia hit. They also have no clue that the man lying dead on the ground had a phenomenal tale to tell of terrorist cells, church bombs, international drug syndicates, gangsters and cut-throats.

At around 5:45am, Sam Issa climbed into his Audi somewhere around the nearby Mercure Hotel opposite Eastgate. He drove towards Bedford Centre and came to a stop at the intersection of Bradford and Smith roads. A white Ford Ranger bakkie with blue police lights pulled up next to him. Suddenly the sound of automatic gunfire shattered the early-morning silence, startling nearby residents awake. They described hearing a flurry of shots, silence, then more shots.

Issa slammed his car into reverse but didn't get far. The driver of the Ranger did a U-turn. The tyres screeched loudly, leaving skid marks on the road. They switched on the flashing blue lights and blaring sirens and raced off back towards Eastgate, Money Point and the highway.

It didn't take long before my phone rang with news of the hit. I was told it was Sam Issa who had been killed. I remembered seeing him at the Harbour a few years before. The man who walked with a limp:

#Breaking Shooting near Bedford Centre this morning. A man with underworld connections has been killed in an apparent hit.

#BedfordShooting The man, whose name is known to EWN, is believed to have been an associate of Czech businessman Radovan Krejcir.

I immediately tried to call Krejcir, but his phone was off. It stayed off for a while. Finally, he answered. I told him about the shooting and, because it was a few hours later, I assumed he was fully up to speed with what had happened in his neighbourhood. Instead what I got was 'I couldn't believe actually what you're telling me. I'm shocked.' Krejcir seemed to have not heard the news. I asked him about Issa.

'I knew this guy from Bedfordview. He was a little bit strange. I can't understand what's going on,' he said. 'I didn't know him so well. I just knew he was a very private person. Nobody knows actually what he is doing. We never been so close and I don't believe it was linked to me or connected to me. I feel sorry for him but, ja, what can we do ...'

This was the ninth murder to be added to the list of individuals somehow connected to Krejcir who had been killed since he arrived in the country. It didn't take long for investigators and associates to come out and publicly correct Krejcir about his relationship with Issa. It was no secret at all that the two were doing business together. All fingers pointed to him. The very next day after Issa was shot, another Krejcir associate, Jerome Safi, received an ominous SMS message reading 'You're Next.'

When I look back on this Krejcir interview years later, knowing what has come out in sworn testimony in the High Court in Johannesburg, I can't help but laugh.

From time to time when I'm in the High Court on Pritchard Street, I pop into the Sam Issa murder trial. It's still running in March 2018. It's the only floor in the court that has security guards and an X-ray machine stationed outside. There are invariably dozens of heavily armed Correctional Services officials in the courtroom and a scattering of lawyers. There's rarely anyone from the public in the gallery. It is probably one of the worst-run trials I have witnessed. The legal representatives are puffed up, ranting and raving about continued delays and stomping around in fury about how they're never coming back. But they always do.

The trial never starts on time, and has been postponed something like 40 times. One of the advocates has read so many crime novels waiting for something to happen he could stock a library. Everyone sits around for a couple of hours before things get going. It runs for just long enough to get some momentum rolling and then someone brings some kind of nebulous application that brings the whole thing rumbling to a halt. It's laughable. Talk about the wheels of justice grinding slowly.

There are four accused in the matter. There used to be five.

Siboniso Miya is slender and affable with a clean-shaven head, mani-cured goatee and a big smile. He goes by the nickname Zuluboy. Then there's the relatively unremarkable Nkanyiso Mafunda. Short and stocky, Simphiwe Memela is known as 'Baba kaJesu', translated to mean 'Father of Jesus'. In other words, God.

These three men are part of an entirely different world from the one publicly known about Krejcir. Having given the perception of a slick, Eastern European mobster living a glamorous, expensive lifestyle, Krejcir kept the part involving these three, and others in their network, largely hidden. As one police officer explained it to me, the theory was that Krejcir

248

had different criminals doing different things for him. For example, if he hypothetically needed a gold smelter, he went to specialists, such as the Bezuidenhouts. If he wanted to perpetrate VAT fraud, he used a finance expert such as Ivan Savov. If he needed a fixer, he used someone who was connected, such as George Louca. But if there was violence to be meted out, he had to access the killers from a world far deeper. He looked to professional assassins, mostly from the taxi industry, with reputations for ruthlessly killing for a fee. It was a similar modus operandi in the Gemballa case. And potentially with Ian Jordaan. This was the world allegedly occupied by Baba ka Jesu, Zuluboy and others.

Krejcir is Accused Number Four but he hardly ever actually appears in the courtroom. He got permission to stay in prison for medical reasons. Bulgarian Borislav Grigorov was an accused for nearly two years before he flipped, doing a 'Section 204' deal with the prosecution and turning state witness. Grigorov, known as Boris or Mike, is a small man with deep-set, sunken eyes and a large forehead. He was allegedly the middleman who liaised with the shooters on behalf of Krejcir.

Through the course of stop-start court testimony and a half-baked partial affidavit handed into court with missing pages, Grigorov has provided a version of events. To date, it is the only version that exists in the public domain about what happened in the lead-up to Issa's murder. Other members of the criminal network have also turned state witness and are expected to give evidence in the trial. The accused are yet to testify in their defence.

I was in court for some of Grigorov's evidence and I've read the partial transcripts. Despite all the technicalities and potholes in the case, this is what I've managed to piece together from the evidence given about what Grigorov says happened.

Lyubomir Borislavov Grigorov's main line of work when he met Radovan Krejcir was running foreign-exchange services at casinos across the city. But he was looking for something else to do. He heard about Radovan Krejcir and set up a meeting with him. Grigorov had something to sell to the Czech: two jet engines.

They met at the Harbour restaurant and Grigorov found Krejcir friendly and cordial. Krejcir liked Grigorov because he did not drink or do drugs. He felt he already had too many people around him who were addicts. It's unclear whether they ever concluded the jet engine deal.

Grigorov began to work for Krejcir, looking after his fleet of luxury vehicles. He renewed licence discs and took the vehicles for services. He moved up the hierarchy and found himself responsible for locking up the Money Point shop in Bedfordview and acting as a driver for Krejcir. He fetched him from his home in the mornings and the two men had a coffee and shared a cigarette or two before going about their day. Grigorov was often around Money Point and could see who was coming and going.

It was at the shop that he met Krejcir's co-accused, Memela, Mafunda and Miya. Miya spent the most time at Money Point, working as a runner for Krejcir. When Grigorov met Memela, he was introduced as a 'taxi boss hit man'. He also met Lucky Mokoena, a self-confessed hit man and robber who has also turned state witness. Grigorov claims that Krejcir was introduced to Mokoena by Glenn Agliotti.

Not long after Krejcir met Grigorov, he also met Sam Issa through Veselin Laganin. The two men became friendly and they partied together at clubs such as The Grand and Taboo. It was around the time that Krejcir was arrested for the cancer insurance-fraud case involving Dr Marian Tupy and Krejcir asked Issa for a R500 000 loan to pay his bail. Issa agreed and the money was given to attorney Piet du Plessis. Krejcir undertook to pay the money back when he was set free. Only, that never happened. Issa was persistent about asking for his money but Krejcir didn't budge. The relationship began to deteriorate. 'Their relationship started getting sour with Krejcir saying he thinks he must kill Issa because he demands his money back,' says Grigorov in his affidavit.

Krejcir was sure that Issa was responsible for the bizarre attempt on his life involving the rigged red Polo. 'After this attempt Krejcir started telling me that he has information from reliable sources that Sam Issa was assisting the following people who were trying to kill him namely – Cyril Beeker's [sic] brother, Alexandra Govrich and Jerome Safi as well as George Darmanovich,' says Grigorov.

'Govrich' is a reference to Sasha, aka Gavrić, the Arkan slayer. George

Darmanovich is a known underworld player and State Security contract agent who now lives in Serbia.

There were showdowns and fallouts, but the two still hung out and Issa and Krejcir were seen around Bedfordview together. Krejcir was brooding. According to Grigorov, he had plots and plans about how to get rid of Issa. This included getting his son Denis and his girlfriend to lure Issa to a club in Sandton and to take him out there or to make it look like a botched robbery.

Enter Lucky Mokoena.

'It is at this stage that Krejcir requested Lucky Mokoena to go and rob Issa's house and then kill him after he takes all the firearms and jewellery that will be found in Issa's house,' says Grigorov. Krejcir apparently sent the Bulgarian to buy two throwaway phones from 'Mohamed' in Bedfordview so that Krejcir and Mokoena could communicate inconspicuously during the planned robbery and murder. Grigorov allegedly bought the cellphones and gave one to Krejcir and another to Mokoena.

The robbery went down around two weeks before Issa was finally killed. Issa's relatives later told the media how four men wearing balaclavas had forced their way into his house, covered his head with a hood and cable-tied his arms and legs and then beat him.

Grigorov says Mokoena made off with jewellery, an AK-47 and a Glock 9mm handgun. 'The AK-47 was given to Siboniso Miya by Lucky in my presence after the robbery, however the jewellery was taken by Lucky as he refused to give it to Krejcir. Lucky Mokoena did not kill Issa because after he robbed Issa's house and tied him up he tried to phone Krejcir … to get a go-ahead to kill Issa but Krejcir did not answer as he was drunk. When Lucky came to report back to Krejcir about the robbery I was also present,' explains Grigorov. Mokoena had allegedly left Issa cuffed in the back of his car outside the Bedford Gardens Hospital around the corner from the Bedford Centre and just a stone's throw from where he ultimately met his death.

Krejcir also leveraged his police lackeys. According to Grigorov, he 'instructed' Colonel Steyn from the Germiston Organised Crime unit to carry out a raid at Issa's house. He told Steyn that the police would find 3 kilograms of cocaine as well as R88 000 in cash.

'Krejcir was very excited when Stein [sic] went to do this operation at

Issa's house. Issa still came to our office to complain but Krejcir said he will help him but he should not worry. After this incident Krejcir said we should now kill Issa as he has already stripped Issa of all the monies he can get from Issa. It is at this stage that Krejcir informed Miya, Nkanyiso to kill Issa in the presence of the above people whom I listed,' says Grigorov. 'On the evening of the Friday before Sam Issa was killed, Krejcir called us to his coffee shop in Money Point where he told us that he will kill Issa this night. He told Miya to get Nkanyiso ready to kill Issa.'

In the run-up to this, Krejcir had briefed the shooters on who they would be targeting. At one point, Issa arrived at the shop with expensive AMG Mercedes mags worth hundreds of thousands of rand. He wanted Krejcir to sell them. Krejcir allegedly asked Nkanyiso to collect them from Issa's car so that he could identify Issa when he had to shoot him.

He also bought a tracking device to use on Issa's car. In the weeks leading up to the shooting, a white Ford Ranger bakkie had been brought to the shop. Krejcir's son Denis took it away for a week and then brought it back. Krejcir then gave Grigorov R20 000 to have the vehicle fitted with blue lights and a siren. It was Miya's responsibility to have these fitted.

That Friday evening, Krejcir called Issa and invited him to a party at Money Point. Despite their recent fallouts, Issa decided to go, arriving in his black Q7. The booze and cocaine flowed. Senses – and tensions – were heightened. In the early hours of the Saturday, Krejcir and Issa began to argue about something or other. According to Grigorov, Krejcir grabbed Issa's silver revolver and stuck the barrel in his mouth. Krejcir said to Issa, 'I am God and your life depends on me from now on.' Issa panicked and apologised for whatever he had done. Krejcir stopped short of pulling the trigger. He knew that Issa's time would come soon.

The party started to wind down at around 5am and the sun began to rise. 'Before Issa left Krejcir told him to sniff the cocaine and then said to Vashi in my language "Vac'cu Toba enocreajha nuhug", which means "Vashi this is as last time for this man in his life". Issa did not understand this and indeed it was the last one for him,' Grigorov recounts in his statement.

The men prepared to leave. Grigorov says that Krejcir told him not to lock the gate and to ensure that Issa was the last person to leave. 'As they were all living [leaving] I saw Nkanyiso driving with the bakkie with Baba kaJesu where Miya jump into it. The bakkie was a white Ford Ranger and they drove away but shortly returned where they parked the bakkie right next to the end of the fence but inside the Money Point. We all left and indeed Issa was the last one to live [leave] followed by the bakkie of Nkanyiso, Miya and Memela.'

Grigorov and Krejcir drove in convoy in the other direction, towards Linksfield. Krejcir was en route to his mistress Marissa Christopher's house. He has always maintained that he was at her house in Linksfield at the time that Issa was shot. Grigorov says Krejcir told him that they should wait at the house, and half an hour later he decided that he was ready to go. Just enough time for an alibi.

Grigorov went home to sleep. At around 10am his wife woke him and gave him his phone. It was Ivan Savov telling him that Issa had been killed. In his statement Grigorov says, 'I was shocked.' It's unclear why he would have been surprised by the planned hit.

The Bulgarian tried unsuccessfully to call Krejcir to let him know that Issa had been killed. 'I was not sure if they will kill Issa as Siboniso was drunk. Siboniso Miya also came to the office on the same Saturday after we all went there but I could see that he was still drunk a bit.'

All the main players gathered at Money Point later that Saturday morning. Grigorov says Miya bragged about how they had opened fire on Issa using his own stolen firearm. 'Siboniso told us including Krejcir that he was driving the Ford Ranger bakkie while Nkanyiso is the one who shot at Issa with the same AK-47 given to him by Lucky. Siboniso said Baba kaJesu was sitting at the back holding a R5 rifle. Krejcir celebrated and everyone continued to drink except me as I do not drink.'

Krejcir denies any involvement in Issa's murder. So, too, do his co-accused. As is the case with underworld hits such as these, theories abound about who else could have been responsible.

The main defence of the accused in the trial is that eyewitnesses saw two white men in the bakkie who then fled the scene. They're adamant they weren't responsible and instead it was these two European hit men who had done the job and then fled the country.

Black/Cripple Sam/Issa was known to be a player in Johannesburg's drug game. He served as a middleman, bringing narcotics into the country from Brazil and distributing them to dealers in the city. It was believed that in the run-up to his death he had a fallout with a Brazilian cartel and was in deep trouble. He had also been involved in the purchase of a large consignment of cocaine being brought in via East Africa. There was a problem with the payment and this could have been the motive for his murder. A drug deal gone wrong.

It's also believed that Issa was desperate for cash to pay the cartel for the consignment, which is why he was pushing Krejcir hard to repay the loan. It is possible that Krejcir got irritated and took care of the problem.

'Issa was caught in the middle. In the underworld, the last man who handles the goods carries the bucket, and if something goes wrong, they also kick the bucket,' an intelligence source told amaBhungane.

In the weeks leading up to his death, Issa received numerous warnings that his life was at risk. But he thought he knew better. He knew his way around this world and how to play the game.

In *The President's Keepers*, Jacques Pauw writes about an alleged meeting between Glenn Agliotti and key players in the illegal cigarette industry, including Yusuf Kajee. One of the men present at the meeting recorded it and handed the tapes to SARS. In one of the recordings, Agliotti speaks about Krejcir and the Sam Issa murder:

> Agliotti: *Radovan, he's gone, boy. And I warned him. Radovan's a fucking blast. The nicest guy. Brother, did you kill him? We talk like this. He would go after you till you pay him. For your protection, you will pay him. Sam Issa, we called him Penguin. We were having drinks with him. The night before. I had drinks with him. Him and Sam. Next morning, I get a call saying Sam has been shot. He and Radovan carried on drinking until one in the morning. Fuck, let's have a drink on poor Sam. Radovan had him taken out.*
> Kajee: *Why?*

Agliotti: *Because a drug deal went wrong.*

This transcript supports the notion that Issa's murder was indeed related to a drug deal. It also then raises questions around the motive suggested in court – that it was related to the R500 000 loan Issa had made to Krejcir.

But when I ask Agliotti about the events of that Friday afternoon and Issa's murder, his take is very different.

'It was like a Friday afternoon, they were drinking vodka, I had a double espresso. I said goodbye to them and I left. It was so friendly like fucking kissing and cuddling. Very friendly, no hostility, nothing whatsoever. It was 4pm in the afternoon; they used to drink right through the night. Krejcir could do a bottle of Jägermeister on his own. I think Sam had just arrived when I arrived. I had a coffee and I left. There were a lot of black guys. Just sitting ... meeting with him or having coffee or whatever. Guys were friendly. "Hi, howzit. Hi, howzit." Shake each other's hands. I left and the next morning I hear the shit on the news so I fucking phone Krejcir and say jeez what happened to Sam? He said, "Can you fucking believe it?" I said what the fuck happened and he said he didn't know; he was going to get his guys to find out.'

I ask Agliotti about the transcript in the Pauw book and whether or not he believes Krejcir was behind the hit. 'No, bullshit. The day before, I got there, I had a coffee and I left. I wasn't there for more than 10 minutes. So where [Pauw] came with that I have no fucking idea.'

Agliotti says he was interviewed by police investigators about whether or not he was involved.

'I was interviewed by the Hawks in the Sandton police station. The Hawks called me in; I was coming back from Swaziland. I got this call from a colonel in the Hawks and I said, sure, no problem. He said he wanted to interview me about Issa, Krejcir and Mokoena. I went there and asked what they wanted. He said, "Lucky Mokoena." I said that Lucky Mokoena was a two-bit gangster so he's trying to implicate me and Sibiya. I don't even know Sibiya – I've never met him. I said this is what you guys are after, he is a two-bit hustler. Look at all the cases against him and they're talking to me; they should go and arrest him.'

Agliotti also denies that he introduced Mokoena to Krejcir. He says he barely knows the man and tells me a story about how he first met him.

'He's a hustler. He's got like 60 cases against him – drugs, theft – all sorts of shit. You'll always see him driving in a Ferrari with the best labels, but he scams. If you look at his cases they are either robbery or armed robbery or whatever. I bumped him in Sandton. He said, "How are you, Glenn Agliotti? Can I have a picture?" I was sitting there having breakfast with Ronny [Bvuma] and this guy walks up. He stands in front of the table with his sunglasses on and says, "I know you from TV." Normally, I say I'm Pastor Ray McCauley and they fall for it. I said, no, Glenn Agliotti. He walked away and came back to ask for a photograph with me.'

Krejcir's former right-hand man Milosh Potiska also suggests that Issa's murder had everything to do with a drug deal. He came to know Issa well during his time working for Krejcir in South Africa:

> K never released his money unless he ensured complicity with someone who would take the greatest share of responsibility. He agreed with Sam on a partnership. Sam Issa put his money into the business with meth and expected a lot of money coming back. After some time Sam became annoyed, though. He got into trouble with a Brazilian gang he had got some cocaine from as he could not pay for the whole consignment. Sam felt like in a vice. So he started to push on K pretty hard. He wanted him to pay off at least a part of the money. Well, you know K. He is not easy to be blackmailed. K and Sam fell out really badly. Radek apparently counted on the Brazilian drug dealers to settle things with Sam finally. They ran out of patience … Two weeks before the murder some masked men broke into his house at night. They tied up Issa with cables. And robbed him. Cripple Sam got even more pissed off. He tried to contact the cops. He offered to reveal something about K to them. You know the rest.

If, indeed, it is true that Issa was talking to the police about Krejcir, there is no doubt the Czech would have heard about it. Potiska's right: you know the rest.

THE MONDAY MORNING AFTER SAM ISSA WAS GUNNED DOWN, RIAH Phiyega sat down in the boardroom adjacent to her office. She was 'gatvol'. She wanted answers from her generals about why someone with a public profile like Krejcir was able to operate with impunity. The police were looking either incompetent or corrupt or both. She was also reeling from a series of PR disasters, including the Marikana massacre and the appointment of Mondli Zuma. Hours after announcing him as the new Gauteng police commissioner, she had to withdraw her decision because he had skeletons in his closet that he hadn't disclosed: a pending criminal case for drunk driving and escaping from custody.

In the meeting with her was the head of the Hawks, Anwa Dramat; Brigadier Ebrahim Kadwa, who was in charge of organised crime for the Hawks; the country's head of detectives, General Vinesh Moonoo; and divisional commissioner for policing, General Khehla Sitole. Interestingly, four years later, Sitole was appointed commissioner to replace Phiyega. Phiyega's spokesperson General Solomon Makgale was also at the table.

Brigadier Kadwa did most of the talking. Because he was responsible for organised crime, he had the detail around Krejcir's operations, who he was connected to, his history with the SAPS and why it was so difficult to arrest him. The generals explained to Phiyega the obstacles to arresting people involved in organised crime because they rarely engaged in the dirty work themselves. There were also real challenges because there was such widespread corruption in the system. They briefed her on the insurance fraud case, the armed robbery matter and other cases in which he was implicated.

By all accounts, it seems Phiyega was not satisfied with the overall performance of the Hawks in terms of targeting Krejcir. They had been making

257

arrests, but there were no convictions. Cases were dragging on and no one could explain why. She suspected that this was probably because of corruption. Krejcir had cops on his payroll and he was walking free as a result.

She was under no illusion that corruption was endemic in the SAPS. She recalled attending the funeral of a junior cop and couldn't help but notice the Maseratis and other luxury cars at the event. How could low-ranking officers afford such cars? she wondered. She had also heard all about generals in her ranks who were themselves involved in organised crime, such as cash-in-transit heists, running gangs as a side business. She was deeply worried.

Phiyega listened to what the generals had to say and then she tried to understand. What would it take for Krejcir to be arrested? Was it a question of resources? Did the officers not *want* to take action against him? She also wanted to know whether lifestyle audits had been done on the investigators. She was suspicious as to why no lifestyle audit had yet been carried out on the head of the Hawks in Gauteng, Shadrack Sibiya, since he was leading the investigation. She wanted answers.

At the end of that lengthy meeting, Phiyega held a separate meeting with only General Moonoo, General Sitole and General Makgale. They decided to set up a special multidisciplinary task team to focus on Krejcir. They were evidently worried about the Hawks and their potential involvement with Krejcir. Phiyega was profoundly distrustful of the Hawks. They had made little progress thus far and some of them must, she felt, be on his payroll. Moonoo gave his boss an undertaking that day. 'Give me three months and I'll have Krejcir behind bars,' he told Phiyega.

A few days later, it emerged that Major General Mxolisi Dladla, head of the presidential protection services responsible for security around VIPs, had information that could assist in nailing Krejcir. Dladla knew someone who might know something about Krejcir that could help the investigators. At this point, police management were desperate for any new leads in the case and a meeting was set up at a hotel at OR Tambo International Airport.

Who was the man who had info on Krejcir? 'Killer' Ximba, the close ally of Richard Mdluli who had served alongside him for decades. At the time, he was a colonel in Crime Intelligence. It was a top-level delegation that met with Ximba, and included the national commissioner, the acting head of Crime Intelligence, Bongiwe Zulu, General Sitole, General Moonoo and General Makgale.

Ximba's eyes were big and darted around as he spoke. He had intel on Krejcir to share with the top cops. He knew who the Czech was doing business with, as well as the names of the Hawks officers on his payroll. He mentioned one case in particular that was 'hot' because Krejcir was personally involved in the crime. He was sure it was the one that could be used against the Czech, but it wasn't one that was high profile or in the public domain: a kidnapping case registered in Katlehong on the East Rand. It had been inexplicably closed.

The police only needed one case to get Krejcir behind bars and keep him there. Once he was out of the picture, they hoped witnesses would be emboldened and come forward with information. If they could arrest him, the other cases might solve themselves.

The Katlehong case was ripe for the picking but police management then had to make a decision. Who would they get to investigate the case? They needed someone who was competent and beyond reproach, someone who had no connection to Krejcir and who had not been corrupted by him.

General Sitole had previously been the provincial commissioner in the Free State and he suggested a crack detective with whom he had previously worked. Captain Mashudu 'Freddy' Ramuhala had experience in investigating murder and robbery and used to report directly to Sitole in the Free State. He had made a name for himself solving an SBV heist case in Limpopo in which four guards were burnt alive. He was the guy they needed.

Ramuhala is not what you would expect a crack detective to look like. He's jovial and funny, with a propensity for loud, baggy suits and garish ties. He is a character.

And so the Free State captain set about investigating the Katlehong case. A new docket was opened. Fresh statements were obtained. A team of 30 to 40 people was working on the case around the clock. A lot was at stake. Ultimately, it was this case about a 'Doctor', a drug deal and a kettle of boiling water that landed Krejcir behind bars.

BHEKISIZWE DOCTOR NKOSI, KNOWN TO MOST AS DOCTOR, WORKED as a clearing agent at OR Tambo International Airport. This meant he knew the ins and outs of security at the facility, which was an invaluable commodity for a drug-smuggling syndicate. He had found a weakness in the system that he was able to manipulate to get drugs on board an aircraft. This involved generating and attaching a label to a piece of baggage and then pretending that the baggage had been left behind at the airport by a passenger who had already flown out or who was due to fly. It was a skill needed by Krejcir's network of drug traffickers. Krejcir had big plans to smuggle R25 million worth of crystal meth to Australia and Doctor was perfect for the job. The full details of this elaborate cross-border drug-smuggling operation were laid bare in the South Gauteng High Court and a subsequent guilty judgment.

The drugs had been organised through Krejcir's dealer, Desai Luphondo, who had met Doctor in 2012. Luphondo told Doctor that he was involved with a white person who would change their lives forever, though he didn't mention the person's name. The network referred to him as only as 'Baas John'. Luphondo asked Doctor to assist with getting a parcel through the airport. Three trial runs were set up to test the system and a five-kilogram batch was handed over to Doctor. In return, he gave Luphondo a receipt bearing a serial number. In the first two trial runs the drugs failed to reach their destination Down Under. The third one was successful. Five kilograms of crystal meth made it to Australia. For his efforts, Doctor was paid R70 000.

Having tested the system, Krejcir and his associates decided that the fourth consignment would be the real deal and they would send five times the amount of the previous shipment. The drugs were again handed to

Doctor, he was paid another R70 000 upfront and stood to make between R250 000 and R350 000 if this consignment was successful. However, Doctor decided that instead of exporting the bag he would try to sell it himself. He put the bag into the vehicle of his friend 'Sobaba'. Inside were small parcels, roundish in shape and wrapped in silver tape. Naively, Doctor thought that the small parcels that contained 'Ice' – a street name for crystal meth – would melt because they were literally ice. That's what he had been told and he believed it.

Luphondo realised that his stash, along with Doctor, had disappeared. Twenty-five kilograms of crystal meth with a street value of R24 million was gone. Luphondo went knocking on Doctor's door. Doctor told him that he had been searched by police, who had taken his money as well as the bag of meth. Luphondo didn't believe a word of it so he got Krejcir on the phone. Doctor was put onto the call with the 'white man'. Krejcir told him to sort the matter out because the 'Hawks' from Pretoria had been to the airport and had found that no one had been arrested. It didn't take long for Doctor to disappear.

Krejcir and Luphondo were both furious. Krejcir was desperate for Doctor to hand over the merchandise, and recruited Peter Vusi Msimango to help search. Msimango, in turn, asked Paul Mthabela to assist with the manhunt. They would receive two kilograms of tik if they could find Doctor. If they sold a gram at R300, they stood to make a small fortune. Both Msimango and Mthabela ultimately turned state witness against Krejcir and Luphondo.

On the witness stand, Msimango recalled how he and Luphondo did actually manage to track down Doctor.

'Desai told Doctor when we finally met up with him at a filling station [in Tembisa] that the boss [Krejcir] understood that the consignment went missing, but wanted him to come and take a lie detector test,' Msimango testified. But Doctor refused. 'He told Desai there was no guarantee that he would come back alive should he go with him to see the boss.'

Doctor finally agreed to go the following day, in the company of a relative. But in the interim, he met his brother, Bheki Lukhele. He confided to him that he had to go into hiding because he had done something that could get his family into trouble.

The following day Luphondo, Msimango and Mthabela met at the Eastgate Mall, and then travelled in Luphondo's Mercedes-Benz to fetch Doctor. But Doctor had already fled to Ermelo and was giving them the run-around.

'Desai called the boss and told him Doctor was giving him problems and was being evasive,' Msimango said. Krejcir's response was to have members of Doctor's family targeted. He wanted his brother, Bheki Lukhele, to be kidnapped.

'I then asked him how the kidnapping was going to be carried out … Desai said the boss said he would send his policemen to do the job,' Msimango testified.

What had always been speculated about Krejcir turned out to be frighteningly true. Not only did he have Hawks members on his payroll, but also a crew of what was supposed to be elite crime-fighting members operating at his behest. Hawks members were active participants in his criminal schemes, using their badges, their uniforms, their guns and their marked vehicles to commit crimes on Krejcir's instructions. They were not just taking money to turn a blind eye to crime – they were criminals themselves.

Samuel Modise Maropeng was a warrant officer, but lived a life far exceeding the R160 000 annual income of his rank. He drove swanky cars and had been seen around town in a Maserati, a red Ferrari and a Range Rover. Because of his bad-boy reputation, he had earned the nickname 'Saddam'. Paul O'Sullivan described him as a 'real bad dude'. Saddam was stationed at the Germiston Organised Crime unit, under the leadership of Colonel François Steyn, who we know took a loan from Krejcir. Warrant Officer Jeff Nthoroane and Jan Mofokeng were also officers on the East Rand who worked with Saddam.

These were Krejcir's 'police', the ones doing his dirty work for him.

Bheki Lukhele was at home in Katlehong on the evening of 25 June 2013 when he heard knocking at the gate. He looked through the window and saw people outside. They were looking for his brother, Doctor. He told them that his brother wasn't home. One of the men showed him his police ID and explained that he was a cop. He asked to speak to Lukhele's grandmother. 'They showed a police identity card and because of my experience I did not completely trust them,' he testified.

He opened the gate to allow them in. The men began to quiz him about when last he had seen his brother. He told them it had been days before, but still they continued to interrogate him. They knew he had met him at a shopping mall much more recently. The cops grabbed, manhandled and slapped Lukhele. There were six people in total, and they had arrived in three cars: a white BMW, a Mercedes Vito and a 4x4. Lukhele was forced into the BMW, his shirt was used to cover his face and he was told to look down. His hands were tied behind his back with a cable tie.

Lukhele's neighbour watched the action as it unfolded. The following day he went to the police station and opened a case of kidnapping.

Lukhele's captors took him to 'a house', which turned out to be Money Point in Bedfordview. At the house he was slapped, punched and kicked. During the interrogation, he was forced to sit on the floor facing a corner. One of those doing the beating told him that his brother had robbed him of money and that they were looking for Doctor and the money. Lukhele testified about his assault in court.

'They were kicking me on my stomach and on the side of my torso,' he said. He explained that when the blindfold was taken off, he could see a man with a white kettle who again asked where his brother was.

'I told him that I don't know and then he poured the water over my head. I felt pain. I screamed but with a low voice. As he was pouring the water over my head he again asked where my brother was and I said I don't know and he kicked me with a booted foot. Twice.'

Lukhele could taste blood in his mouth. The skin began to peel off his scalded head.

Msimango was present when this assault took place. He gave testimony about it in court, describing how Krejcir, Luphondo, Miya and the three cops took turns to beat Lukhele.

'They all took part in asking him where his brother Doctor was ... He told them he did not know and last saw him two days earlier.' Krejcir ordered that the bag be removed from Lukhele's head and then said to the man: 'Look at me ... Do you know who I am? Why are you lying about your brother? You want to die like a soldier? Well, that's fine then.'

He describes the moment when Krejcir poured boiling water from a kettle onto his head. 'The boy gave out an excruciating scream ... stopped and then started shaking,' Msimango said.

Lukhele asked to call Doctor.

Krejcir instructed his men to drive him to a place far from the office so he could make the call. Msimango accompanied them to somewhere near Alexandra where a cellphone was assembled and Lukhele called his brother.

'He said, "Doctor, my life is in your hands. Return whatever you owe these people. If I die, this is all in your hands,"' Msimango said. Luphondo took the phone and told Doctor to make it easy for everyone and return the consignment. 'Doctor told Luphondo that what they did was a provocation and that they would be arrested for kidnapping.'

Lukhele was then taken to a safe house where he was held for four days under the supervision, primarily, of Luphondo. At one stage, the men heard that Doctor was in Ermelo. Krejcir instructed them to take Lukhele, with the 'police', to find his brother. They drove in convoy together with the three police officers. At their destination they found Doctor's father, but not the man they were looking for. They returned to Joburg and at Money Point the debate began. What should they do with Lukhele? Krejcir wanted him killed. His plan was that a funeral would lure Doctor out into the open. The other men were not eager. Eventually, it was decided that he would live.

Lukhele was released and dropped off near a stadium in Katlehong. He ran for his life.

OVER THE SECOND HALF OF 2013, A SERIES OF EVENTS OCCURRED in Bedfordview like a set of dominoes toppling into one another in Krejcir's game of strategy and survival. The first was the bizarre red Polo incident, followed by Sam Issa's dawn murder. The next was another murder less than three weeks after Cripple Sam's. And it took place just one block from where Issa was gunned down.

Remember the short, thin Serb with the satchel and loafers who was 'robbed' by the Pretoria Pakistanis? Veselin 'Vesko' Laganin was one of the two men arrested alongside Krejcir for armed robbery. He worked for Krejcir but was also involved in his own dealings, allegedly along with Issa in the drug trade. He was always quiet, skittish and aloof, but I put that down to a language barrier. Like Issa and so many others who had sought refuge in Krejcir's circle in Johannesburg, Laganin had a dark past. There were suggestions that he had fled Serbia because of his involvement in war crimes there. He had a wife and son who lived with him in a townhouse complex on Smith Street, just behind Bedford Centre.

On 2 November 2013, in the middle of the night, two men used a ladder to enter Laganin's bedroom window. There had been a break-in at the complex two weeks previously and they wanted this to look like a house invasion gone wrong. The Serb was shot in the stomach and died in his bedroom. Two watches and two phones were stolen. Police found two 9mm pistols in a bag on the scene. A resident who lived nearby told me that she hadn't heard a thing during the night and only found out the following morning about the shooting.

Former bouncer and private investigator Mike Bolhuis was vocal about the incident. He believed that Laganin was killed for shooting his mouth off.

'From the information that we have received from the underworld, Veselin was a character with a very loose mouth,' said Bolhuis. 'He spoke very openly about affairs of the underworld and many people weren't happy with that. We have questions surrounding the murder of Veselin Laganin. It could be a hit staged as a robbery because once again his name is linked to other people who are involved in organised crime,' said Bolhuis. 'According to my information and my investigators, nothing of extreme value was taken. That is why I do not think it was a robbery. Mastermind criminals do not break into a secure premises to steal watches and cellular phones.'

Like Issa, Laganin was killed on a Saturday morning. When I heard about it, again I dialled Krejcir's number. Again, he seemed not to know about the death of his close associate. He sounded genuinely shocked.

Ten days later, another domino fell and two more Krejcir lieutenants were dead. The circle was closing.

TUESDAY, 12 NOVEMBER 2013, WAS A BUSY AFTERNOON IN THE newsroom. There was breaking news and it got my colleagues and me joking about 'WTF' moments in South Africa. The new head of the police watchdog Independent Police Investigative Directorate (IPID) had been announced and we couldn't quite believe it. Robert McBride had once again come back from the wilderness into a position of power and influence. McBride had repeatedly hit the headlines for the wrong reasons but, technically, he had never been convicted and there was no reason he shouldn't be appointed to the job. He had a long track record in law enforcement and the Institute for Security Studies' Johan Berger even applauded the appointment, stating that when he lectured him during his policing degree, McBride was 'hardworking and intelligent'.

I was on my way home just before 5:30pm when my phone began to buzz with tweets and messages. There had been a massive explosion in Bedfordview. Eyewitnesses were describing a loud blast at the Money Point offices across from Eastgate shopping centre. The glass windows and doors had been blown out and police and emergency services officials were streaming to the scene. There were reports of casualties and injuries. I turned onto the N3 highway and raced to Bedfordview.

It wasn't long before I found myself waddling towards a bomb scene, heavily pregnant, with my editor, Katy Katopodis, in heels alongside me. She lived nearby and had arrived quickly. We watched as police with dogs ventured inside looking for a potential secondary device. A cloud of smoke was rising from the building. Police had closed off the busy road during peak traffic and the cops tried to keep us on the opposite pavement in the event that there was a second blast.

We established that Krejcir hadn't been inside when the bomb exploded but he had been nearby. But he wasn't talking and his lawyer, Eddie Claasen, didn't know much about what had happened. As dusk fell, the bright yellow sign bearing a large blue 3D diamond shone brightly above the wreckage of the building. Debris lay scattered on the bonnets of the luxury vehicles in the parking lot. Officials were milling about behind red-and-white police tape, searching the scene for forensic clues. Finally, the pathologists came to collect the bodies.

A few hours later, we were told that Krejcir was at home and in shock. Two people had been killed and three critically wounded. One had lost a leg. Anxious relatives gathered at the nearby Bedford Gardens Hospital. Dressed in white pants and a striped shirt, Krejcir visited the hospital the following day to see his injured associates.

Two of his closest men had died in the bombing.

Politically connected Ronny Bvuma was known to his friends as 'Ronsta'. He acted as the owner of Money Point after it was transferred into his name in 2012, although authorities believed he was merely acting as a front. Bvuma, also known as Ronny Smith, lived in Morningside and was the director of Sivuma Holdings. He was schooled at Damelin College and Fourways High School in northern Joburg and was popular in his circle of friends. The day after his death, his Facebook page was full of posts mourning his passing.

Czech national Jan Charvat was a man with a past. He had been convicted of tax fraud in the Czech Republic and sentenced to five years in prison there, but he had fled. He was also facing other pending court cases. There was a post on the Czech police's website carrying a photo of him and a description of the crimes he had committed.

Hours after the bombing, I was on the phone to Czech journalist Jiří Hynek, who told me that Charvat's death had shocked his country because no one knew where he was hiding out. 'The man who was killed, Mr Charvat, was known in the Czech Republic as a criminal sentenced to five years in prison for tax fraud, so it's a big surprise in our country and local news is full of this story,' he told me.

Krejcir had allegedly brought Charvat to South Africa to assist with his meth-brewing operations. In *The Godfather African*, Potiska describes

Charvat as a remarkable figure in the Czech underworld:

> *Honza Charvat was a beefy guy. We called him Dumpling as he was*
> *short but weighed about 150 kilos. He came to business meetings dressed*
> *as a scarecrow in his shorts. So when he got out of his gorgeous Rolls*
> *Royce Phantom worth six million crowns in just a T-shirt and shorts on*
> *Parizska Street in Prague and went shopping at the Cartier jeweller's,*
> *people must have thought that a film was being made there. Most prob-*
> *ably a comedy. However, Dumpling was canny and smart. In business he*
> *was in his element. He was involved in VAT frauds worth hundreds of*
> *millions of crowns. Ranging from issuing permits to ordinary deals with*
> *telephone cards. And then also drugs.*

In 2012, with the police on his tail, Charvat fled his home country and popped up in Johannesburg. A year later, he bled out on the floor of the Money Point shop.

Speculation was rife in the wake of the bombing that Krejcir had orchestrated the explosion himself. It is alleged that he had fallen out with both men shortly before the bombing and he owed them both money. None of this was grounded in fact, though, so it was difficult to ascertain where the truth lay. Officially, police were saying that an unknown man had walked into the shop and left a bag containing the explosives on the floor. There were holes in this theory, though, as Money Point had a bulletproof divider preventing unknown individuals from gaining access to the main office. This meant it would have to have been a man known to the others who had left the bag behind.

There was also a theory that the explosives had detonated accidentally. They were apparently meant for the SARS office where Van Loggerenberg and his team were based in Pretoria. Krejcir knew that the SARS net was tightening around him and he was literally days away from being cut off from his finances.

A witness statement then emerged via Paul O'Sullivan that revealed details about Bvuma's and Charvat's involvement in Krejcir's network and, in particular, Bvuma's desperation to escape his clutches. It was as if he sensed an imminent threat to his life. According to the statement, Bvuma was responsible for handing over 'bags of money' to senior policemen on behalf of Krejcir.

The statement was authored by a Johannesburg businessman, Keith van der Spuy. He had met Bvuma around 2006 through Bvuma's uncle, Vic Davidson, who was interested in getting involved in Van der Spuy's diamond-cutting business. At the time, Bvuma was working as a nightclub bouncer and doing debt collection on the side. Van der Spuy bumped into Bvuma from time to time, often at the Food Lover's Market in Rivonia. They would greet one another and chat, but it was only in 2012 that they explored the possibility of a business venture together. Van der Spuy says Bvuma called him and asked him to meet with him and a 'partner' who was interested in buying his car.

Van der Spuy is laid-back and loves to shoot the breeze. He tells stories about how he became a millionaire four times and lost all his money three times, including once to Barry Tannenbaum's ponzi scheme. He finds his entire episode with Krejcir surreal, kind of amusing and scary all at once. He's happy to tell me about it.

'Ronny was a complete coconut. Lovely guy, sense of humour – I mean he could compete with Trevor Noah in terms of personality and jokes. Stocky guy, went to gym. Everyone wanted to use him as their BEE partner and Radovan approached him and asked if he wouldn't be his front.'

Van der Spuy recalls how he first met Krejcir when the Czech wanted to buy his Rolls Royce Phantom.

'He walks in with all these burly guys and his offer to me was that he would pay me with shares in the company. I told him I can't pay my ex-wife in shares, I need greenbacks – give me notes. I've got four kids and the court won't allow me to give her shares. He then phoned me about a week later and asked if I've thought again and I asked him if he had the money. He said, no, he was still with the same deal. He phoned me a subsequent time and then he phoned me a third time, at which point in time I didn't make a well-thought-out comment and said is he either effing deaf or effing stupid because if he didn't have the cash there was no deal.'

According to Van der Spuy, over this period Krejcir was cooking other plans in which he wanted Van der Spuy to get involved. These included arranging sham refinancing deals involving cars and another venture acquiring distressed property portfolios. Krejcir and his associates had apparently managed to infiltrate the big banks. They had found dormant accounts that still had large amounts of money sitting in them. It is alleged that the plan was to get the money from these accounts and move them into the trust accounts of a lawyer they were using. Van der Spuy claims that Krejcir was the architect of the scheme, but he didn't know enough about the South African banking system and wanted Van der Spuy to assist him. He needed someone to front the operation, by paying the cash and getting the deals rolling. The profits would be shared. Van der Spuy says that Krejcir also asked the businessman to draw up 'fake contracts' to make the deals appear authentic but Van der Spuy was concerned about the legalities and wasn't keen to get involved. so he didn't.

Van der Spuy alleges he was coerced into lending Krejcir R500 000 to pay his lawyers, specifically advocate Mike Hellens. If this happened, it was a classic Krejcir move. He asked for a loan from a terrified acquaintance who paid over the cash, never to see the money again. When Van der Spuy asked Krejcir when he would be paid, he was told that Bvuma had taken over the obligation of the loan. 'He said if I did not like the arrangement it was tough, because that's the way it would be, whether I liked it or not. I was afraid to argue with him.'

During the course of their meetings, Van der Spuy says he also noticed that Krejcir had some kind of 'device or computer, where he can put in anyone's cellular phone number and can then see exactly where that person is and listen to their calls. For this reason, he would know where anyone is, just by putting in the number. I know this because there was someone that had tried to fiddle another guy out of a few rand and he gave the number to Krejcir and Krejcir told him where the guy was.'

According to Van der Spuy, in April 2013, Krejcir summoned Van der Spuy to another meeting at Money Point. This time, Krejcir was looking for funding for his Australian drug-smuggling plan involving Doctor.

He told the businessman all about how a dummy package had been sent through the airport and how he had 'some coloured guys' who would cook the drugs into crystal meth. Krejcir asked him for R2 million and promised he would get double the money in return. Van der Spuy told him that he didn't have the funds to get involved because he was still owed the half a bar that he had lent Krejcir. 'We left it there. As I recall, the senior cop, whom I would describe as a black male in his forties and not too tall, came through to fetch his packet. Krejcir described it as his weekly pay.'

Van der Spuy's affidavit also details other incidents that he witnessed at Money Point including accounts of police officers collecting large bags of cash there. 'In the course of the meetings I had with Krejcir I had seen a policeman come there twice. Once in a marked police car, with a uni-formed driver and once in a plain car, I do not recall which. On both occasions the cop left with large bags of money given to him by Ronny in Krejcir's presence. It was clear to me that Krejcir had plenty of cops on his payroll, so going to the police might be a way of getting myself killed, if Krejcir found out.

'Apart from the regular payments being made to senior cops, Ronny also bragged that Krejcir was "untouchable" as he told Ronny he had made a donation of R1 million to Jacob Zuma's re-election campaign at Mangaung. I believed this as I heard Krejcir saying that he was untouchable as Krejcir was "connected to No. 1", which everybody knows is Zuma.'

There is, however, no independent verification that Krejcir did make a payment to Zuma's campaign or that he did, in fact, have direct access to the president.

Not long after he had told Krejcir to 'eff off', Van der Spuy experienced the full reach of the Czech's influence.

'Probably a week or 10 days later, I was at Grosvenor Crossing [shop-ping centre]. A police van stopped me and said I must come with them because there was a road rage incident and I was apparently involved in it. He showed me his white card and they arrived in a police van. The guy who got out of the car walked around and I was parked in my Volvo. He asked if I will accompany him and he then got into the passenger seat in my car. We followed the vehicle for a while and then he said we can just drive.'

They drove towards the highway and headed to the south of Joburg. Van der Spuy grew concerned. 'I asked him if I should take that turn-off and the next thing I just felt a gun against me and said I should just keep on driving. They took me out to the Sharpeville area. When we got there they put me in a house. The moment we got there everyone scattered away from the house. They started questioning me and they took my wallet and my cellphone. They asked me what my PIN number was and I said they must be joking. The next thing I had the gun back at my temple here.'

He was held for over seven hours as his kidnappers attempted to draw money from various ATMs. Finally, in a Nedbank in Lenasia, he was able to alert a bank manager to what had happened and he was rescued. He later worked with the police to set up a sting operation to catch the kidnappers.

'I then phoned Ronny and said he has underground connections, could he find out who kidnapped me and why. I mean I'm not a flashy, *windgat* kind of guy. I asked him who and he said, "We did." I asked what he meant by that and he said, Radovan said I'm lucky that I'm still alive. He said no one tells Radovan to eff off and lives. He said I am only alive because of my relationship with him [Ronny]. He said Radovan wanted me killed. He said instead of that they tried to get me to draw R750 000 out of that account.'

Van der Spuy was so shaken that he moved to a farm in Christiana in the Free State. He would never take his phone with him there, in case he could be traced.

Things then fell quiet until October 2013 when Van der Spuy became aware that Bvuma and Krejcir had fallen out. This occurred around three weeks before the Money Point bombing. Van der Spuy claims that Krejcir wanted to carry on stealing from the banks, but Bvuma was getting worried. He told the Czech to take him off the company records as the front for all his businesses and to let him go. This resulted in a huge row. Bvuma continued to get SMSes from the bank showing large deposits into the Cross Point account and he knew that Krejcir was still stealing. He was enraged.

'On the day of the bombing, when Ronny was killed, he was sitting at Vasili's Restaurant in Rivonia. He got a call from someone who said he should come through to Money Point, as Radovan Krejcir wanted to meet with him, Jan Charvat and others. This call would have been sometime just after 16h00.'

Although initially reluctant to go, fatefully Bvuma relented. 'It seems he went there anyway, to meet with Krejcir, and the bomb went off and he was killed. It was fully meant for him.'

Van der Spuy's account of events contributes to the theory that it may have been Krejcir who was behind the blast and that he had orchestrated it in order to take out former lieutenants who could sink him. He knew that the police and prosecutors would be looking for close associates to flip to state witnesses and these were ideal candidates, individuals who would sell him out to save themselves.

KREJCIR WAS LIKE A TIGER BACKED INTO A CORNER. HIS DECISIONS were becoming irrational and his behaviour erratic. The string of murders in Bedfordview and a wave of violent underworld-style crime had culminated in a bomb blast on a busy road during rush-hour traffic. It was the breaking point for the neighbourhood. The affluent suburb had been dubbed 'Deadfordview' or 'Gangsterview' and it had earned a reputation as a haven for the mafia. Residents began to sign a petition calling on Krejcir to get out.

More and more of his associates were dying, the SARS net was closing in and the police investigators appointed by Phiyega were building a watertight case against him. Now his neighbours also wanted him out. The public reputation Krejcir had carefully cultivated over the years was beginning to collapse. He couldn't be a mafia boss and a celebrity.

Forty-eight hours after the bomb blast in Bedfordview I was sitting face to face with the country's most renowned 'gangster'. The setting could not have been more ominous. The walls of Krejcir's advocate Mike Hellens's chambers at the Island Group were lined with gleaming swords and a vast collection of metal armour. It was as if the ghosts of war were readying themselves for battle. The gloom of dusk was rolling in across Sandown. Radovan Krejcir had arrived for our scheduled interview dressed in a black T-shirt and black jacket. He was at his heaviest, bulky and tall, an imposing presence. I was in front of the lift doors as they unexpectedly rumbled open to reveal Krejcir, sending my heart into my throat. He had gone to ground over the two days since the deadly explosion at his office, and the events of the past few weeks had added to the enigma of the man and the associated danger he posed. But, true to his nature, he attempted to break the tension with his charisma and humour.

He had requested the sit-down exclusive interview with me in an effort to respond to the media reports around him, the bomb blast and the murders of Sam Issa and Veselin Laganin. Krejcir was concerned about public perception and he wanted to tell the country that he was not a mafia boss, an evil gangster or a bad guy. He found these descriptions 'disgusting and disappointing'.

As part of the agreement, Krejcir began by delivering a prepared statement that had been drafted in collaboration with his lawyers. He began by explaining that he had been in the country since 2007, was very happy and proud to be living in Bedfordview and that he wanted to stay there permanently. He said that he had remained silent about the allegations against him because he did not want to affect his extradition application or his refugee application in any way, but the time had come for him to speak out.

The time has now come for me to at least say something about the wild and irresponsible speculation in the press about my involvement in the recent murders that have taken place of my friends. I must immediately point out that there have been two attempts on my own life and also point out that someone is presently under arrest and in prison for conspiracy to murder me.

The two attempts on my life had been well publicised. The first was outside the offices of Money Point. This involved a motorcar that had been rigged with crude guns and operated by remote control. The other was a recent bomb blast which I assume was aimed at killing me. Unfortunately two friends of mine died and another friend of mine was severely injured.

It is highly irresponsible of the media to speculate, on the one hand that I have any involvement in the incidents in which my own life was or could have been at risk, and on the other hand to link the death of any of my friends in other incidents to me.

I want to categorically state that I have had no involvement in any of the killings that the media have been so freely speculating about. The South African Police Service is, in particular in relation to these sorts of crimes, very capable of conducting sound investigations. I am sure that if there were any evidence of my involvement, the South African Police would have found such evidence by investigation. There is no evidence because I am not involved and have not been involved in any murders of anyone.

I do not know if there is some common thread between the deaths of my friends and the attempt on my own life. I am as puzzled as the public should be about these deaths. I am not even certain if there is actually any connection between any of these incidents.

Krejcir's message was clear. He was a good, family man who had not been involved in crime and who was the target of attempts on his life by unknown individuals. I could hear the cynics already as he went on to gush about the South African people and the country's democracy.

I am very disappointed that the media continuously paint me as the 'bad guy' and seem to relish or enjoy painting me as some sort of evil gangster or outright criminal. I am none of these things. I am a family man seeking refuge in a country that I have come to love and respect and in which I wish to remain. I find its society to be cosmopolitan and democratic. I have in my time travelled a lot and it was with great delight that I discovered the wonderful nature of the South African people in general and of the strength of the democracy in this country. I think many people in this country should take a look around themselves and appreciate the very great merits that South Africa has to offer as a country with its climate, its unique society and its strong democracy. I think many South Africans do not appreciate the wonderful country that they live in. In my view, South Africa is the best country in the world to live in.

My suburb Bedfordview is very close to my heart and it pains me greatly to hear the various wild and unjustified allegations being made against me.

For those people who have got to know me personally, they know that they have a close and loyal friend who goes out of his way to help his friends. I am friendly and a steady person. Those who know me even slightly are as amazed as I am at the unjustified and wild speculation in the press about me. In fact, I am by nature a polite and humble person.

I repeat, I have not been involved in any of the crimes about which there has been such unreasonable and unjustified speculation. All of that speculation is based on gossip and rumour and is without any foundation.

Krejcir used the opportunity to lay the blame for the campaign against him on Paul O'Sullivan, stating that the investigator had an agenda he found inexplicable. He finished by appealing to the South African public to look critically at the unbalanced reporting taking place about him.

Once he was done reading, we got to the heart of the interview. I wanted to hear Krejcir speak for himself, without the intervention of lawyers. He had allegations to answer and explanations to give. The claims were racking up and we wanted to know his truth.

'How are you feeling? Obviously it's been a difficult few days for you,' I asked.

'Well, I'm not happy. I lost two of my closest friends, so I'm very sad about it,' he said, very seriously.

'Are you under attack?'

'I believe so. I'm under attack because so far there's already two attempts to murder me.'

'Who is behind this?' I wanted to know.

'I really don't know. I was trying to think about it, but I don't know,' he told me, seemingly oblivious.

'Why does your name keep popping up? You've been linked to 12 murders.'

'It comes from the speculation of the media and this rumours, gossips from people like Sullivan. Unreasonable informations. What the people fabricate, stories.'

'Are you a gangster and a mafia boss? Are you that? What are you?'

'No, I'm not. I'm the family man who is trying to enjoy his life in the country I love and trying to help everybody. That's all,' he assured me.

'Should the people fear you?' I pushed him.

'Of course not,' he insisted. 'I am every day on public. I don't know why they would fear me. There is no reason!'

'Should they be worried for their safety?'

'Of course not!' he chuckled awkwardly. 'Do I look like evil? I done nothing wrong in my life!'

I asked him about public sentiment and the dissatisfaction from his neighbours in Bedfordview. Krejcir said he's not going anywhere. 'Well, I have no reason to change my place because I have done nothing wrong. The reaction of the people are from speculation and from fabrication story what media serve to them,' he said.

Mockingly, Krejcir had begun to refer to himself in interviews as 'Mr Banana Peel'. I wanted him to explain why he thought he's being unfairly linked to everything that happens in the underworld. Was it wrong for him to be associated with the gangland-style killings happening around him?

'Look, I feel like that because whoever will slip on banana peel and break his legs is Radovan fault. I believe so before I come to South Africa there is so many killings and dead people but now for some reason it suit to some people like Sullivan to blame me for everything. You can see the media never ask me for the comment but with the last incident with the bomb blast they're saying some business went sour with me and Ronny, my friend, so I must be behind; it's ridiculous, it's disgusting.

'Look, you cannot stop anybody to fabricate any story. Anybody can create a story in one minute. It's the professional people what I can see who are wants to sell newspapers and stories. So they like to fabricate this stories. So I am selling newspapers now. They need somebody like a bogeyman in this country, so they choose me and I will be happy if somebody else will come and take my place.'

While he had said in the past that his life was like a James Bond movie, he was not so quick to crack a joke about it now, suggesting that it had escalated more into terrorism than spy-novel stuff.

'This week, it's even worse. We're not talking now about any hit on the person. We're talking about serious terrorist attack because they use the explosions and they don't care in this office if there are 20 people, there was kids there or whoever, they will blow all this people, we talking different level, we talking al-Qaeda-style terrorism.'

He was worried about his own safety and that there might be another attempt on his life, but was also circumspect about what action he could take to prevent it.

'I am worried obviously. There was two attempts on my life now so I have to be scared. I have to worry. My mother is very worried. My mother would love to move here to this country. Obviously, she's not happy. She doesn't want me to go home. She knows if I go home I will be killed for political reasons.'

But he admitted that if whoever was after him really wanted him dead, they would succeed and he's not increasing his security. 'I don't believe in more security. Look, they killed JFK, so if these people want to kill me I will be dead. Security is not going to help you.'

Krejcir was on the PR offensive, selling himself as a patriotic South African who loved the Springboks, loved to braai, wanted to meet Madiba and would pay his etolls. His problem was that absolutely no one believed him.

The next morning, Friday, 15 November, Krejcir's exclusive interview led the front page of *The Star* newspaper with a headline reading 'Krejcir Breaks Silence' and a subheading stating 'Czech fugitive thinks he was deadly blast target'. It was accompanied by a picture of the very serious-looking Czech in his advocate's office. It was just three days after the Money Point bomb blast. With Krejcir headlining news that Friday, SARS finally made its move.

Johann van Loggerenberg applied for, and was granted, a preservation order against Radovan Krejcir, his wife Katerina, his son Denis, and a list of companies. These included Groep Twee Beleggings (Pty) Ltd, Cross Point Trading, Intaglio Trading, Tiger Falls Diamonds, Libraline, DKR Auto CC, Matis Institute, Woodhill CC, Scara Technologies and several other entities, all of which were in one way or another affiliated to Krejcir.

As part of the application, and based on years of investigation that made up Project K, Van Loggerenberg authored a lengthy affidavit setting out Krejcir's business operations. When it hit the public domain, it was the most detailed description of how Krejcir operated, who he was dealing with and what exactly he was up to in South Africa. Until this point, most of this had been left to speculation and conjecture, adding to the myth of the man.

According to the affidavit, Krejcir and his family possessed a number of assets in their own right. This included the Kloof Road mansion bought for R13 million, a sectional-title property and a motorcycle. From the records of Groep Twee Beleggings, SARS had established that the business had eight different sources of income.

The records also showed that a number of loans had been made to individuals from Groep Twee Beleggings. An amount of R3.7 million had been lent to George Louca in terms of an undated written agreement of settlement that had been produced at the tax inquiry. Louca had agreed to repay a sum of R3.5 million to Groep Twee and pledged a number of assets to the company as security for the loan.

The same company had also been used to make loans to cop François Steyn and Glenn Agliotti. It would emerge in Agliotti's own sequestration hearing in court that he had borrowed R400 000 from Groep Twee, but Agliotti insisted that he had repaid the loan in full.

Similarly, DKR Auto was the entity used by Krejcir to hold his fleet of vehicles. These included a Lamborghini Murciélago, a Mercedes-Benz CL 63 AMG, Porsche 990 Tiptronic sports car, Audis, BMWs, Mercs, Jeeps, a Lexus, numerous Toyota Fortuners, several boats and various motorbikes. DKR Auto conducted no business and showed no income, yet it owned millions of rands' worth of top-of-the-range cars, boats and bikes.

The affidavit set out how Intaglio Trading, set up by Ronelle Engelbrecht before Krejcir arrived in the country, was ostensibly selling instant lawn. Krejcir bought it to demonstrate that he had business interests in South Africa, in support of his application for recognition as a refugee. SARS believed that Intaglio 'was used by Radovan Krejcir as a conduit or front to "launder" income'.

As far as Cross Point was concerned, SARS had established that Krejcir had sold the business to associate Ronny Bvuma as a 'sham'. Bvuma had bought the business in 2012, but when he appeared at the tax inquiry he didn't have any real knowledge of the day-to-day operations of Cross Point and it was still being managed by Ivan Savov. Cross Point was the holding company for Money Point, which lent money and purchased gold.

Tiger Falls conducted business from the premises of Rand Refinery. Krejcir bought it because he believed that the company possessed an import-and-export licence for gold and 'because the premises from which it operated were secure and not easily accessible'. 'Tiger Falls is clearly a company that was utilised by Radovan Krejcir for the conduct of business, which probably included the import and export of gold. Tiger Falls has not submitted any income tax returns since Radovan Krejcir acquired control of the company.' SARS held the view that assets and income were hidden in Tiger Falls in order to evade the payment of income tax.

Van Loggerenberg's affidavit also set out in detail a VAT scheme uncovered by SARS that involved George Louca's cousin, Yannis the motor mechanic, Krejcir's money man, Savov, and another company, Scara Technologies.

Ultimately, SARS was of the view that Krejcir had used Groep Twee Beleggings as a conduit to conceal the true nature of his business dealings. It decided to raise the companies' assessments against him personally. SARS contended that Krejcir had under-disclosed his taxable income to the amount of R114 763 692.64. Van Loggerenberg asked that Krejcir's assets be preserved and a curator be appointed. The order was granted.

Krejcir was served with the notice at 4pm on the afternoon of Friday, 15 November 2013. He was ordered to hand over all the books and records of all his companies. His Lamborghini and Porsche were attached. Murray Cloete from the Sechaba Trust was appointed curator to manage the assets.

'Czech-mate! The corrupt machine that is Krejcir has come to a grinding halt,' said an elated Paul O'Sullivan to IOL on the day. 'This is the culmination of two years of hard work by SARS and my four-year investigation. Just go back to the Czech Republic and face the music there – unless you want to go to a South African jail. I hope that from now on when he wants a packet of cigarettes, he has to ask his curator for R30.'

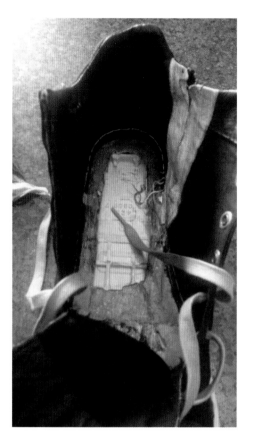

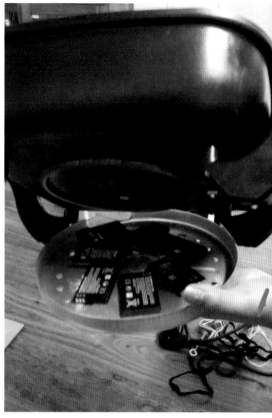

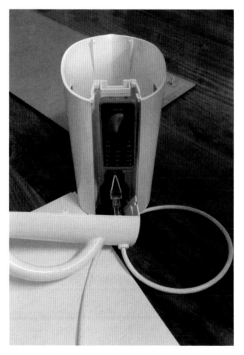

ABOVE LEFT: Contraband hidden in
Radovan Krejcir's shoe in prison.
SOUTH AFRICAN POLICE SERVICE — SAPS

ABOVE RIGHT: Phone batteries hidden inside
an electric frying pan in Krejcir's cell. SAPS

LEFT: Phone hidden in Krejcir's kettle in
prison. SAPS

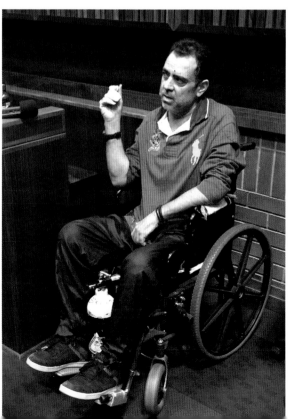

George Louca testifies in court in Palm Ridge shortly before his death. MW

Forensic consultant Paul O'Sullivan appears in court after being arrested.
GALLO IMAGES/NETWERK24/DEAAN VIVIER

A photograph released by Paul O'Sullivan of General Vinesh Moonoo with tobacco baron Yusuf Kajee. PAUL O'SULLIVAN

LEFT: Ralph Stanfield's car following the shooting in Melrose. EWN

BELOW: Convicted Krejcir in prison uniform in the High Court in 2018. MW

ABOVE: Shadrack Sibiya in his office in Johannesburg in 2018. MW

LEFT: Gauteng Hawks head Prince Mokotedi meeting with Nafiz Modack. EWN

ABOVE: Cape Town police officer Major General Jeremy Vearey. GALLO IMAGES/*DIE BURGER*/ LERATO MADUNA

LEFT: Controversial Cape Town businessman Mark Lifman, 2018. MW

Nafiz Modack at Cyril Beeka's graveside in 2017.

Nafiz Modack outside court following his arrest in 2017.

CASH-STRAPPED AND RUNNING OUT OF OPTIONS, KREJCIR PANICKED. SARS had cut off his lifeline and he could no longer fund either his operations or his lifestyle. With his back against the wall, he made silly mistakes, acting out of desperation. Up until this point, he had been infallible, believing himself to be immune from prosecution and acting with impunity.

'He was so strapped for cash that he started calling in little debts like R5 000 here and R10 000 there,' says a former SARS insider. 'This was when his mom came to South Africa with a briefcase full of cash. We took all his money here. So he couldn't pay his lawyers. He couldn't keep his organisation going; we just cut off his lifeline, which was the money, and that I think sparked the cops and everybody else to move. It was soon after our preservation order that all of a sudden there was this task team and suddenly there was a lot of investment into building cases against him.'

Van Loggerenberg's affidavit was used by state prosecutors in the other criminal cases against Krejcir that followed, substantiating the point that SARS had done far more work on the Czech than any other law enforcement agency. The police were so behind that Van Loggerenberg's statement became a guiding light for them.

'What we also then subsequently picked up was that he was busy with two other scams which were tax scams. So he had already diversified around the time when we were busy auditing him, and the one scam was a classic scam of changing bank account details on refunds, that was simply because he understood the SARS system so he just got proxies to go and act as if they are representative of a particular taxpayer and then change the bank account system so that when the refund comes through, it goes into that bank account and then you quickly take it out of the bank account and split it up. Now I've always wondered to this day how they knew which accounts to target because you've got to have access to the SARS system to see which taxpayers have big refunds due,' says the SARS insider.

The Anti-Corruption Unit at SARS was also investigating Krejcir on something entirely different, which had to do with him paying IT experts to hack the SARS system. They were still in the early stages of an investigation into that scheme.

At the same time, the police were getting a much clearer picture of the various criminal schemes Krejcir's network was running. He was using the Hawks officers on his payroll very effectively to knock, intimidate and rob people. Using Money Point as his headquarters, he was running a network of criminals, with the cops doing his dirty work.

'Krejcir would put it out there in the underworld that he's got Krugerrands that he was selling, as way of example, but that would be below the market price. So let's say for a million rands and he wants cash for it. So some "business person", in inverted commas, would go and buy these Krugerrands for R5 million and on his way back then he'll get robbed by the police and Krejcir's people,' explains one former policeman with inside knowledge of the investigation.

'The same with drugs. Nigerians would come buy drugs from him, then they would get caught, be taken to Germiston police station. They confessed they got the drugs from Krejcir. Krejcir is called to come to the station; he then tells these Nigerians that, "Look, you know, I'll talk to the police but they want to be bribed. They want a million rand so if you guys want I can pay R1 million for you and you guys owe me now a million bucks." So now what happened is they've paid cash for the drugs whatever they've paid; the drugs have been taken away by the "police" and now they owe Krejcir for being released.'

He had his own gang of cops at his beck and call, ready to commit crime on his behalf. How did he manage to do this? The answer is simple, says the ex-policeman.

'Money, money, money. With money you can do a lot of things. He had cops, he had magistrates. He had, well, not as in lots of them but, you know, a couple of them, prosecutors on his books because from time to time his people get arrested so he's got to get them out of there.'

The problem the police investigators had been facing was that there was an abundance of cases similar to the Bheki Lukhele one. In fact, there were so many that their resources were severely stretched and it was taking far too long to tie them up, allowing Krejcir to operate unhindered without any criminal charges pending against him. They needed to finalise one case with strong witnesses that would result in a conviction that would stick.

Priority number one for the cops was to get Krejcir behind bars. They knew that once he was removed from the system, people would start to come forward with information. Priority number two was to ensure a conviction and a lengthy jail term, preferably life. Third, he couldn't get bail because of the delaying tactics he had employed in the past. He would do this again and, out on bail, would delay a conviction forever. This is why they were zeroing in on the Bheki Lukhele case and largely ignoring most of the high-profile gangland murders, despite the public and media spotlight on them.

Krejcir, meanwhile, was managing the fallout from the bomb blast and the blow he had suffered from SARS. In the week after the blast and our exclusive interview, his mother issued a statement of her own. Nadezda Krejcirova, who at the time was the tenth wealthiest woman in the Czech Republic, offered a R2-million reward for information about the two separate attempts on her son's life. There was something oddly amusing about the alleged mobster's mother wading in asking who it was who had threatened her son. Krejcir's own funds were under the control of a curator so Krejcirova had to do it on his behalf.

In the same week as the blast and the SARS judgment, Krejcir's network had also taken another significant knock. Krejcir's main bagman, the guy who was doing all his finance work and business management, Ivan Savov, was arrested by the police, taken into custody while Krejcir was doing his interview with me at Mike Hellens's office. Savov was charged in connection with a R10-million fraud case. On the Monday morning after his arrest, I watched as he appeared in the Commercial Crimes Court in Johannesburg in a black collared shirt, dark-black stubble covering his face and his eyes heavy under dark brows. He had spent the weekend behind bars.

According to the charge sheet, an Absa employee had withdrawn millions from a bank account belonging to the Bloemfontein Correctional Services. The money was paid to a firm of lawyers, ostensibly as payment to Savov as the purchase price for gold commodities. This money was paid to the lawyers on behalf of Scara Technologies, which linked Savov to the two men killed in the Money Point blast, Jan Charvat and Ronny Bvuma. Interestingly, Charvat was also named as an accused in the fraud case. The description of the fraud mirrored what businessman Keith van der Spuy had described: corrupt bank insiders, dormant cash-stuffed accounts, lawyers' trust accounts being manipulated, and shady, fake company agreements. SARS and the cops had begun to piece it all together.

THE DOOR TO THE LIFT IN KREJCIR'S KLOOF ROAD MANSION opened. To Krejcir's surprise, he came face to face with a Tactical Response Team policeman in full riot gear.

'How did you get past security?' Krejcir wanted to know.

The cop was there to arrest him. It was late on the afternoon of Friday, 22 November 2013. Police vehicles were parked in the steep, narrow road outside his mansion. An ambulance was there too, just in case. There were also several unmarked cars and around 20 officers in plainclothes.

A few kilometres away, in Germiston, more arrests were being made at the Organised Crime unit on the East Rand. Officers had arrived to handcuff some of their own – the Hawks who were part of Krejcir's personal 'crime squad'. Amusingly, when they walked into the office to make the arrests, Colonel François Steyn stood up and began to pack his things. He assumed that they were there for him. Perhaps he had a guilty conscience from taking a loan from Groep Twee Beleggings. The story about the loan had broken in the *Mail & Guardian* that very morning and his blood must have been running. Flustered, he settled down and watched his colleagues being handcuffed.

Just after 6pm that afternoon, I began to get calls about the police action outside Krejcir's house and tip-offs that he had been arrested. What followed was half an hour of complete confusion. At that stage, we had no idea about the so-called Ermelo case involving Doctor and Bheki Lukhele. We also had no idea that Phiyega had appointed a Free State police detective, Freddy Ramuhala, to investigate the case. We knew that there was a Hawks task team probing the high-profile underworld killings and we were all expecting an arrest to come from them. The Hawks, on the record, denied that there had been an arrest. Paul O'Sullivan knew nothing about it and initially told me categorically that there had been no arrest. But I had impeccable top-level sources so I was sure that it had happened. Krejcir's phone was off and his lawyers knew nothing about it.

But later that evening both the police and O'Sullivan confirmed that Krejcir had been taken into custody.

BREAKING #Krejcir EWN has learnt that Czech fugitive Radovan Krejcir has been arrested for kidnapping and attempted murder.

#Krejcir It's unclear at this stage what incident the arrest warrant is related to – understand it's a case in Ermelo.

#Krejcir The arrest warrant was executed by the SAPS and not by the Hawks special unit investigating Krejcir.

Throughout the night there was confusion about where Krejcir was being held, as his lawyers had been unable to contact him and he hadn't been checked in at any police station. That night, his attorneys went to the High Court to get an urgent order compelling the police to allow Krejcir to exercise his rights to representation. The police had to tell them where Krejcir was and allow them to see him. We only got a sense of what had happened the following day when the lawyers issued a statement detailing alleged abuse and torture:

Mr Krejcir ('our client') was arrested at 18:00 on 22 November 2013 at his residence. Approximately 20 police officers attended to his home. Said officers were driving unmarked vehicles and were not in uniform. Upon request, the officers could not produce a warrant of arrest or a search warrant.

Our client's house was ransacked by the officers and numerous items unlawfully confiscated. He was handcuffed, forced into an unmarked vehicle without number plates and driven towards the direction of Kathlehong [sic], At least five vehicles were in the motorcade, which pulled over in a rural isolated area where our client was forced out of the *vehicle by an officer electrocuting him with a tazer [sic] gun. After being forced to his knees and asked several unanswerable questions, our client was tortured by having a plastic bag placed over his head and being suffocated until he lost consciousness.*

The lawyers went on to detail the extent of the abuse allegedly suffered by Krejcir:

Upon regaining consciousness, he was tazered, asked more questions and assaulted. He suffered cuts to his wrists and forearms, after which a chemical substance was poured over the wounds, causing him severe pain. This continued for approximately ninety minutes, with all members of the SAPS (approximately 20) being present during said torture. Our client lost consciousness on several occasions as a result of being suffocated with a plastic bag.

It later also emerged in court that notorious cop 'Killer' Ximba had allegedly played a key role in this abuse in an attempt to get Krejcir to confess. As mentioned, Ximba had a reputation for torturing suspects and the Hawks investigators probing Mdluli had picked up a number of instances in which Ximba faced similar allegations.

Krejcir's co-accused, Sandton businessman Desai Luphondo, also alleged that he had been tortured into making a confession. He claimed that he was brutalised into signing a statement that would be a key weapon in the case against Krejcir but ultimately not allowed to be used as evidence.

The day after the arrest, National Police Commissioner Riah Phiyega called a press conference. It was an unusual step to make such a public statement on a development in a criminal case and to name an accused before he appeared in court. But, following the disastrous reputational damage done by Marikana, Phiyega had latched onto the Krejcir case as an opportunity for good publicity. The police had made a breakthrough and she had to be seen to be applauding their apparent good work. She also felt the case had a high public-interest element and that required her to make a public address.

'We have indeed arrested Krejcir,' she confirmed to a room full of journalists. Phiyega said it took a combined team of officers a long time to crack this case but a warrant of arrest was issued and the police acted immediately. The police were hoping to arrest more suspects as the investigation continued. Phiyega refused to reveal where Krejcir was being held but stated that they would communicate with his lawyers. Phiyega also confirmed that police were looking at the involvement of their own members in Krejcir's crimes. She would, however, reveal no further info, saying, 'We will not trial Mr Krejcir in the media.'

Krejcir was scheduled to appear in court for a bail application the following Monday. That Sunday night, his lawyers again went to court on an urgent basis to have him taken to hospital. A doctor's report stated that he had sustained 'significant muscle damage' from being repeatedly shocked. The lawyers argued he was at risk of renal failure and had to be moved to a private facility urgently. Judgment was reserved after midnight, just hours before Krejcir would make his first appearance in Palm Ridge amidst great media interest and police protection.

FOUR POLICE OFFICERS IN FULL SWAT GEAR, REPLETE WITH BULLET-proof vests, elbow and knee guards, helmets, gloves and automatic weapons, flanked the magistrate as he took his seat in the Palm Ridge court. At least 40 others filled the courtroom, lining the face-brick walls and blocking the doors. The entire Palm Ridge court building was cleared out for this single case. Journalists were barred from entering the public gallery. It was an astonishing sight, one not witnessed before in a South African court. Even during President Jacob Zuma's court appearances, there was not this kind of police presence. Radovan Krejcir was making his first appearance following his arrest, but police had received a tip-off that he would try to escape. Incredibly, they had also received information that a weapon would be hidden in a television or photographer's camera, hence the media ban. His lawyers described it as a scene out of a 'dictator's palace', stating that it was window dressing to create grounds to oppose a bail application.

It was believed that Krejcir had plans in place to flee the country. He had already booked plane tickets and his exit strategy was in place to make his way to Argentina. His former home of the Seychelles was also an option. At the time of his arrest, his family was out of the country, on holiday in Mauritius, leading to further speculation about his plans to flee.

Meanwhile, in the High Court in Joburg, Krejcir won his urgent application to be transferred to a private medical facility. The state was also ordered to pay costs.

A few days later, again under extremely tight security, Krejcir brought the first of three bail applications. He was evidently desperate to get out. In his affidavit, he named 'Killer' Ximba as the officer who allegedly tortured him. He attacked Paul O'Sullivan for driving the case against him, labelling him an 'unstable vigilante', 'a self-appointed white knight' and a 'super policeman'. He insisted he enjoyed living in South Africa and that he wanted to stay. His co-accused, two Hawks officers, insisted there was not one iota of evidence against them. In its argument against bail, Johann van Loggerenberg's affidavit was a vital piece of evidence for the state. The court took its time making a decision and by the time it ruled in mid-December 2013 that Krejcir and his co-accused had to stay behind bars, the country was a different place and a Czech fugitive from Bedfordview was the furthest thing on most people's minds. Former President Nelson Mandela had died and South Africa was in mourning.

Over the next three months Krejcir went on to bring two further bail applications. He was desperate to get out of jail. He knew that if he didn't do so soon, it could be the end of the road for him. More cases were coming.

PAUL O'SULLIVAN WENT FOR A WALK. HIS NEIGHBOURHOOD IN Sandton is boomed off from passing traffic and it's relatively quiet and serene despite its location near the heart of the central business district. He liked to walk, but he also thought it necessary to do some counter-surveillance, just in case. Of course, he took his firearm with him. You never know what danger lurks in leafy suburbia. It was a hot day in early January 2014 and the streets were quieter than usual. Except for a black BMW. There were three men in the car and it was trailing him. O'Sullivan felt that he might be in danger. He drew his pistol and confronted them.

'Please, Paul, don't shoot! We are police and we are here to help you,' pleaded one of the men in the BMW.

The officers told him they were following him because they were aware his life was in danger and that a hit had been taken out on his life for later that morning. It was believed that Krejcir had given the order from his prison cell. They had been told that the assassination was planned to take place between 10am and 12pm, when the forensic consultant was sched-uled to leave his house for a meeting. A Toyota Fortuner would be used as a spotter vehicle and they would alert others waiting for him in another vehicle with an R5 rifle who would then do the job and 'plug him'. The cops told O'Sullivan to leave his phone in his house because it was being traced by the hit men with the help of Crime Intelligence operatives. Their information was that the hit men would first take out policeman 'Killer' Ximba, the cop who had been behind Krejcir's arrest, before going after the investigator.

At midday, the cops swooped on a restaurant in Sandton and took the first target into custody. Information he gave them led them to the Road Lodge on Rivonia Road. A task team arrived at the motel and arrested a man and a woman. All three were believed to be behind planned hits on O'Sullivan and Ximba.

I got a call late in the afternoon that the arrests had taken place and I went straight to the Road Lodge. It was already teeming with forensics experts in sky-blue clothes covers, masks, gloves and booties.

The boot of a white BMW X6 stood open and cops were sifting through items stashed in the back of the vehicle. There were balaclavas, gloves, six cellphones and blue lights. There was also a white Toyota Fortuner and a Nissan van, both of which had been reported stolen. Head of detectives Vinesh Moonoo was there, as was the investigating officer, Freddy Ramuhala, both dressed in casual short-sleeved shirts.

There were three weapons laid out on plastic on the tar of the parking lot: an R5 assault rifle and two 9mm pistols. The magazines had been removed and placed alongside the guns and the magazine for the R5 was wrapped with brown masking tape. The officers carefully examined the gun and checked the chamber, before carefully laying it back down on the plastic. This particular R5 had many stories to tell and the forensics team would unravel its tales in due course.

The arrests meant that the network around Krejcir was being exposed. The Hawks officers were already behind bars. Now the hit men were facing the law. Siboniso Miya, Jacob Nare and Owen Serero had been arrested along with Zoe Biyela. Biyela, the woman taken into custody at the Road Lodge, was believed to be Serero's girlfriend, who had simply been in the wrong place at the wrong time. But the other three were firmly entrenched in Krejcir's criminal network.

Serero was a hardened criminal with a long record. Police linked him to a litany of other crimes, including hijackings, robbery and motor vehicle theft. He had previously escaped from custody. Miya was also believed to be a serial criminal, linked to numerous crimes. But Jacob Nare was a plant. He was the police's man on the inside who had been feeding them information all along. He had been arrested purely to keep up his cover.

There was one more arrest linked to the planned hits: the Crime Intelligence cop who was working with the group. Sergeant Nandi Nkosi worked in the same office as Ximba. It was believed that she had supplied

GPS coordinates to the hit men planning to kill O'Sullivan and Ximba. Police even alleged that she had sent a picture of her boss to the group and had downloaded cellphone tracking technology on the targets. For this she was paid R30 000. When she was taken into custody, she was in possession of nine different cellphones. The SMSes found showed that she wanted her boss to be 'removed'. As is so often the case, the criminal network appears to have had a cop on the take who was complicit, corrupted to assist in what was potentially the murder of a senior CI officer, her boss no less.

Jacob Nare is not his real name. In 2013, Nare found himself thrust into a murky world where he witnessed the inner workings of a mafia hit squad. Having seen his fill, he went to the cops and became their inside man, feeding information on to investigators.

Nare told his story to Paul O'Sullivan and journalist Angelique Serrao. It is a tale that is truly stranger than fiction.

According to his version on transcripts of the interview, Nare met Siboniso Miya in 2004 and they remained firm friends. They saw each other every day. Miya was a successful entrepreneur in the taxi industry and Nare began to suspect that his old friend was dabbling in crime, but all was going along just fine until Phumlani Ncube walked into their lives in 2013.

Nare told O'Sullivan: 'This whole Krejcir thing started in January 2013 when Siboniso met a man called Phumlani Ncube in Sandton for lunch. At that lunch Phumlani introduced the whole business of being a hit man to Siboniso. Phumlani said he was looking for a guy who could do a hit "on some white guy in Bedfordview". To assassinate him. The man they wanted dead was Krejcir.'

The Sandton businessman who wanted him dead was paying R500 000 for the hit. But the assassins went to Krejcir and negotiated more money to walk away. Nare says one of the men in the businessman's family was then killed.

Nare recounts how Phumlani Ncube was 'taken out', his bullet-riddled body found near Heidelberg. It seems he too was speaking to the cops. 'I found out that Phumlani had been killed when a friend of his called me, asking if I knew where Siboniso was. He told me Siboniso had killed Phumlani the day before. I realised then how dangerous he was. Phumlani was killed because they found out he was talking to Colonel Ximba. He was giving information to the Crime Intelligence guys. They found out from a policewoman in Crime Intelligence, Nandi, who gave Krejcir information.'

Nandi is Nandi Nkosi, the Crime Intelligence sergeant who was arrested for helping the gang with GPS details and info on her boss. Nare reveals how Nkosi was hindering the police investigation from the inside, tipping off Miya about the investigations. They were homing in on him in connection with the Ermelo case involving Doctor's brother, Bheki Lukhele.

Crucially, Nare had also been party to the events surrounding Sam Issa's murder in October 2013, and provided a detailed account of this time in his statement.

His insider account also lays bare how closely the gang was working with the police, even impersonating police officers. He describes how blue lights were fitted to the Ford Ranger used in Issa's murder. Nare also says that Miya and his associates had police appointment cards supplied to them by a contact in Durban. They flashed the blue lights and the cards to give the impression they were legitimate cops.

'Just before Issa's murder, Siboniso asked me if I could buy two SIM cards for him from a shop in Sandton. He put them in a small machine and a Samsung S4. The machine was a tracking device that synced the phone. It was supplied to Krejcir by Crime Intelligence. You put the machine under the petrol tank of a car with a magnet. It was used to track Issa. After he [Issa] was killed, Siboniso came to my house. You could see something had happened. I hadn't heard any news yet. He said they had just done a job for the boss and went to sleep. When I came back around 3pm I heard it in the news. Siboniso said they would never find the Ranger. They had parked it at the house of a cop.' Miya was dropped off at Nare's house by a policeman driving a black BMW convertible.

At one point, Nare claims that the investigating officer allegedly contacted Krejcir to tell him to tell Miya to 'do away' with his iPhone because they had tracked his number and linked it to the crime scene.

So it was that Miya and two other men moved in with Nare, hiding out at his two-bedroom Illovo apartment. It became untenable for Nare, and he lived not only with the fear of harbouring criminals from the cops, but also that Miya's accomplices would take him out. 'They told Siboniso that "if this boy wasn't your friend, I would give him an AK-47", meaning they wanted to kill me. They came back to the house every day carrying bags with their AK-47s inside. They said they would never be arrested. Those AKs were for the cops. I kept on thinking that I could get caught in the middle of a shootout.'

Nare was facing a dilemma. He knew that if he snitched to the police, he ran the risk of Krejcir and his network finding out. 'I told another friend about it. I didn't know what to do. These people were very connected. I couldn't just go to a police station and report it.'

His friend knew a cop in Lenasia who was clean. That cop was Bongani Gininda, who would become one of the main investigators in the Krejcir cases. Nare was introduced to him, but it took him three weeks before he told Gininda the full story. Nare, though, knew he was running out of time because the planned hits on O'Sullivan and Ximba were drawing closer and they were going to use his flat as a hideout after the murders. Nare was living in the same house as the people he was selling out. It was terrifying.

'It was so hard to trust this policeman. After speaking to him, I had to go back to those people, sleep in the next bedroom. Every time Siboniso got a phone call from Krejcir, I didn't know if he was telling him what I had done. So many people are saying to me that I am a sell-out. But I don't know what they would have done in my shoes.'

Initially, the plan was that Miya and his team would take out three people: the witness Bheki Lukhele, O'Sullivan and Ximba. O'Sullivan's and Ximba's coordinates had been supplied by Crime Intelligence. Nare explained that Miya had also received an email showing Lukhele's exact location despite the fact that he was in witness protection at the time. It was clear to him that Krejcir had penetrated every organ of state, including the witness protection programme.

However, the plan was turned on its head when Krejcir's emotions got the better of him. Krejcir was furious that O'Sullivan had attended his court case and had provided documents to help the state oppose bail. Krejcir called Miya. He put him on speaker phone and Nare listened as the Czech complained that he hadn't heard on the radio that O'Sullivan had been killed.

All along, Nare was playing both sides. He was sitting in the car with Miya, going along for the ride for the planned hits, but simultaneously messaging Gininda, feeding him information. When the police swooped on Miya, they arrested Nare too. It was all part of his cover.

Gininda took Nare to Phiyega and Deputy Police Commissioner (now National Commissioner) General Sitole. 'He suggested witness protection. But I remembered Lukhele, who was in the witness protection programme, that Siboniso was supposed to kill. He had a map showing where he was. I said no to Sitole and he agreed and said it would be better I go outside of South Africa. I went to the UK.'

But after some time in the UK, Nare's fortunes turned. He was 'dropped' by the police, his life placed in mortal danger as he was kicked to the kerb by those who had promised to protect him. Nare specifically singles out the country's head of detectives at the time, Lieutenant General Vinesh Moonoo.

'General Moonoo brought me back to South Africa and just dropped me. I asked Sitole and Phiyega two years ago, what if I testify and you people just drop me in the street? I would be killed. They promised me it wouldn't happen. They said: "We will protect you until the end."'

He alleges that Moonoo first cut his living allowance. Then he brought him back to South Africa on the pretext that he would be visiting his child. This was December 2015. He was told he would not be returning to the UK. Nare believes this was done to flush him out into the open so that he could be killed. He had no doubt about Krejcir's ability to buy off officials who could assist him with his location.

Back in South Africa, Nare met with Dawood Adam, head of the witness protection unit, which falls under the National Prosecuting Authority. Transcripts of the meeting show that Nare expressed his concerns about his safety because Miya had been provided with electronic communication showing Lukhele's whereabouts whilst in the programme. Adam dismissed Nare's fears, insisting that there was no breach of the programme.

Nare's lawyer, Darryl Furman – who also acts for O'Sullivan – wrote to senior police officers in February 2016. In the letter he expressed that it was essential for Nare, as a key state witness, to 'be properly looked after, given

Krejcir's previous propensity to murder witnesses'.

Nare was particularly distrustful of Moonoo. In his statement, he made startling allegations about the extent of Moonoo's involvement in Krejcir's network. He believed Moonoo had been paid a substantial sum of money by Krejcir in order to 'fix' the cases against him. 'I have subsequently discovered that Moonoo was paid R5 000 000 by Krejcir to get him out of prison and out of South Africa. I also learnt that Moonoo promised Krejcir I would never give evidence against him.'

He also listed a number of incidents that, he said, pointed to Moonoo's questionable conduct. Nare said all of these put together suggested that Moonoo wanted him dead. The most obvious of these occurred on the day Nare was arrested.

'Whilst we were arrested and sitting in Ximba's car, Moonoo came to me and took a picture of me with his cellular phone. Later on, when I met Miya at the holding cells, he told me, "If the police come and book us out of the prison, we must not say anything about the boss [referring to Krejcir]." He then asked me if I saw the Indian guy at the crime scene and he named him "Moonoo". I said I did and that Moonoo had taken my picture with his phone. He then told me Moonoo is going to help us out, because he is "Krejcir's connection" and we had nothing to worry about.'

When Nare refused to go into the witness protection programme, Moonoo told him that he should 'stand on his own'.

Instead of leaving him on the street to die, O'Sullivan stepped in. He took responsibility for Nare, personally protecting him. Nare had no choice but to throw in his lot with the forensic consultant, who was in a similar position.

Nare isn't the only one accusing the former head of detectives in the country, Lieutenant General Vinesh Moonoo. Paul O'Sullivan has led a very public campaign against Moonoo, even holding press conferences at which he handed out a cache of evidence, including affidavits and tape recordings of conversations in which Moonoo features. The recordings have been particularly contentious – Moonoo believed that his phone was illegally intercepted. Crime Intelligence agents were accused of being behind it all, leaking the contents to O'Sullivan. Because these things are never simple, it is also alleged that O'Sullivan has been driving the campaign against Moonoo because Moonoo had been behind cases targeting O'Sullivan, particularly one involving former SAA chairperson Dudu Myeni.

O'Sullivan's allegations are extensive but they are summarised in a document 'Joining the Dots – Capture of the Criminal Justice System'. In it, he draws links between Moonoo and several controversial characters. These include Yusuf Kajee, a Pietermaritzburg-based co-owner of Amalgamated Tobacco Manufacturing who is a business partner of Edward Zuma, son of the former president, and who is facing multiple charges by SARS for customs violations. The document includes not only a photograph of Moonoo and Kajee at a social function in Pietermaritzburg, but also claims of paid overseas trips and bags of cash dropped off to be used as pocket money.

He also links Moonoo to Jen Chih 'Robert' Huang, a Chinese national and convicted murderer with links to the import and distribution of counterfeit goods and allegedly involved in various SARS violations. Moonoo's daughter was employed by Huang, and when O'Sullivan made this public knowledge, she went to work for the law firm that looks after Huang's interests. In December 2014, 15 months prior to going on early pension, Moonoo was in China, with Huang, where he was introduced as 'Vice President' of Huang's Mpisi Group. Moonoo apparently made several trips to China on behalf of the Mpisi Group.

O'Sullivan alleges that Moonoo 'blocked' criminal investigations into Huang's and Kajee's criminal conduct and he made it his mission to take ownership of the case dockets relating to them.

As part of the pile of documentation O'Sullivan handed out, there is a series of phone calls that allegedly connect Moonoo to Krejcir through a well-known Durban moneylender and businessman, Preggy Padayachee. The background to these calls and the details of their contents are also contained in a lengthy complaint penned by Crime Intelligence officer Candice Coetzee, which she wrote to SAPS management, IPID and the inspector-general of intelligence after she was suspended for allegedly leaking classified information to O'Sullivan.

In the complaint she explains that a decision was taken by the Krejcir team, who were reporting to Deputy National Commissioner Sitole, to intercept the calls of certain people close to Krejcir in order to obtain intelligence. At the time, he was planning on escaping and was apparently plotting to have several people murdered. One of those phones to be intercepted belonged to Padayachee, because the cops had established that he was in contact with Krejcir and Moonoo.

'There had also been allegations that Krejcir had paid a substantial sum of money to Moonoo to interfere with and possibly derail the Krejcir cases. The figure mentioned was R5 million,' Coetzee explains.

Coetzee believed that several generals and brigadiers targeted her because she had been gathering intelligence pertaining to the criminal conduct of Moonoo.

'I will show throughout this complaint that Moonoo has been assisting criminals for a number of years. That he has been exposed for this conduct by a certain Paul O'Sullivan and that, purely because of my "association" with O'Sullivan, I have been singled out to be silenced, along with O'Sullivan and others. I will also show that attempts to have O'Sullivan murdered by Radovan Krejcir, for his own account and also at the insistence of Moonoo, have been disrupted or thwarted by myself and other police officers that I have worked with over the last few years.

'During the course of my investigations I had come across information that Krejcir had a number of functionaries ranging from media, suspected foreign spies, as well as police officials (including generals) colluding with him in his criminal activities. I might add that both O'Sullivan and Moonoo featured prominently.'

Coetzee alleges that Moonoo deliberately attempted to scupper the Krejcir investigation and even went so far as to conspire with Krejcir to have O'Sullivan murdered. She goes on to claim that Moonoo actively attempted to derail the Bheki Lukhele trial and have the investigating officer, Freddy Ramuhala, arrested in court.

'It is clear that Moonoo is very dangerous. Given his obvious connections via the criminal associates with the Zuma family, it cannot be ruled out that he did not have a hand in the suspensions of Dramat, Sibiya, McBride and Phiyega, for the benefit of those Zuma connections,' Coetzee warns.

Given that Moonoo was the most senior detective in the country, the man responsible for investigating criminals, these are astonishing claims to make.

To this day, O'Sullivan remains adamant that Moonoo should be in jail. He wrote to police management several times about his concerns and has even opened criminal cases against Moonoo, but the man has never been charged with any wrongdoing.

'There are tape recordings of Krejcir phoning Padayachee and saying if he doesn't get his R5 million back he will kill Moonoo. So Padayachee gets him on the phone, like a conference call, and Moonoo says to calm down, they'll fix everything and neutralise the state witnesses, your cases will be dropped and you will be free. That is a lieutenant general in the police!'

'IT WAS ALWAYS MY DREAM. I LIVED IN DURBAN AND WE WOULD see the police vehicles and the police sorting out the illegal brewers and my friend and I said it's a nice job. As time went by, I realised that I wanted to serve the community. If I wanted to make money, I would've taken another job. You have to be corrupt to make money in the police. If I wanted money I was in the wrong job.'

Lieutenant General Vinesh Moonoo has come out of retirement to deny the allegations against him. He's spent the months since he left the SAPS travelling with his wife and spending time with his grandson, fetching him from school and watching him grow up. Moonoo doesn't want anything to do with the police any more. In fact, almost no one in the organisation has a current phone number for him. It's a substantial shift from the man who was once the police's 'Mr Fix-It', pulled in to take over every high-profile investigation that had caught the media eye.

Moonoo arrives to meet me with his long-time friend Preggy Padayachee at the Doppio Zero in Greenside. The two, who are accused of being in a corrupt triad with Radovan Krejcir, are complete foils: Padayachee is tall, boisterous, gregarious and literally has his name embroidered on his shiny collared shirt while Moonoo is understated, introverted and speaks in a near whisper.

'I know Moonoo about 35, 40 years. He got married to a very prominent family in Lenasia. Prior to them coming to Lenasia they were living in Newclare. My father and Moonoo's father-in-law and his family were all great friends. When Moonoo came into the family, that is when I met him. I was at Moonoo's daughters' weddings. I was on the stage and whatever I could do for the family I did it because his two daughters are like my two children as well. I know his entire family and he knows my entire family.

Further, his late father-in-law and his mother. I deny all allegations that they've made upon me. That is what I can tell you,' Padayachee rattles off, tracking the history of their relationship.

The two men don't deny they are old family friends, but they do strongly reject any allegation that there was any kind of collusion or corruption on their part. 'I didn't know who Krejcir was … I saw him on TV. I never ever met him or any of his associates and I had no dealings with Krejcir,' insists Padayachee. 'Absolutely, no. Never. I deny it 200 per cent. I haven't even met Paul O'Sullivan. I saw him on the TV and I've seen him in the media, but I haven't met him. I've heard about him and that's as far as I know him. I'll say it in front of the general – we had always met, but we never spoke about business, of his police things or my business. We met on a friendly basis and spoke about the family or children or whatever. Never ever did we speak about his business.'

Moonoo nods quietly. Once Padayachee has had his say, the general has his turn. He is considered and conservative with his words. He puts much of the animosity towards him down to what he calls 'professional jealousy'. Former National Commissioner Riah Phiyega trusted him and regularly asked him to take over high-profile cases and would then make a fuss about it in the media. The Oscar Pistorius case is a prime example.

'I think there was a bit of jealousy involved between myself and the Hawks when it came to these things. Where they fail, it comes to me. Unfortunately, some people call me Mr Fix-It. I don't see myself as that. When I joined the organisation I joined to serve the citizens, not to get recognition as a hero, and that is why I was angry with the national commissioner. She exposed me. I was undercover all the years, doing my work without anybody knowing. But this thing came that you had to go to the press conferences and I hated that.'

After Phiyega asked Moonoo to take over the Krejcir dockets in October 2013, the head of detectives had told her that he needed three months to get the Czech behind bars. He focused on two cases in particular: the Bheki Lukhele kidnapping and the Sam Issa murder. It was during this time that the allegations of corruption against him in connection with the Czech emerged.

'At that time, because of all these talks from other people about my involvement with Krejcir, in my team there was some reluctance to discuss everything with me and I said they are working with me; if they don't trust me they must tell the national commissioner so that she can take them off the case. I don't have any personal interest in any of the cases. I take what is given from my bosses.'

Although he was overseeing the investigations, he insists he did not interact directly with suspects in these matters.

'I haven't spoken to Krejcir. I have never spoken to him. I've met him a few times on the scene at Money Point. When Money Point was blown up, I was on the scene every day because it was part of the investigation that I've taken over. I was there every day until it was cleared up. I've never spoken to him. I haven't taken a blue penny from anybody on any investigations. I was leading that investigation. It's like Oscar – I haven't spoken to Oscar. I give the instructions, I look at the docket and see what needs to be tied up.'

He was on the scene the day police plant Jacob Nare was arrested alongside Siboniso Miya for the conspiracy to kill Paul O'Sullivan. He vehemently denies speaking to Nare in the car and taking his photo, as claimed.

'I deny that. I heard that allegation. I mean, they could've taken my phone and seen that I didn't take the photo,' he points out.

He also has an explanation for Nare's extensive claims that he lured him back from overseas and dropped him on the street, leaving him exposed to danger.

'You see when Jacob Nare was put into the programme, I was not informed. There were two people – I was in charge of the detective service, there was a deputy national commissioner who is now the national commissioner [Sitole]. He was in charge. Nare reported to him and at one stage it became a problem. When he was already in the programme, I was called. It was a long weekend or something. I was on speaker phone and that's when the national commissioner wanted me to take over the payment of this. We have to pay for him to be in protective custody. I've explained to her on the phone that I don't have the budget for it. I was told I will get the budget. I don't know who was around, maybe it was Sitole and them who sat around the table. I said it is wrong. Witnesses are supposed to be protected by the NPA, not by the police. I was told that this was different because this witness is now somebody that we require against Krejcir.

'I've explained to the national commissioner that we'll do it for six months, but if we can't finalise the cases in six months we'll have to look at alternatives because we cannot keep this witness outside the country forever because it's against policy and the cost was enormous. Then it went to a year. I said no. He said he met me there – I saw him at the scene but I haven't spoken to him. He phoned me, I was in the Kruger Park. I explained to him that he is not supposed to call me; he is going to expose himself. There's a handler that's handling him, I just deal with the embassy.

'Then I heard he was brought back. I've said that if Paul O'Sullivan had taken him in, it is bad for our case because in court if you have a good defence you're going to lose that case. I did not bring him and drop him. I had a meeting with Adams from the witness protection unit and I asked if we can see how best we can accommodate him; if it's not here, we can put him in one of the countries outside our borders, close by. He was demanding – if I'm not mistaken – 80 or 100 pounds a day. I told him we don't even pay our policemen that much salary. I refused to see him. He came to my office and I was angry that he was brought to my office because I do not want to see him. Let him go to court as a witness and then after that we can talk.'

Moonoo has heard all about Paul O'Sullivan's claims that he was is in bed with dubious characters and that he helped protect tobacco baron Yusuf Kajee, Chinese businessman Robert Huang and others. The former general laughs off O'Sullivan's allegations and lays out his explanation.

He starts with how, when Phiyega was national commissioner, she asked him to take over more and more dockets from the Hawks, including cases involving organised crime, truck hijackings and cigarette smuggling. This is how he became involved with individuals such as Kajee and Huang.

'I said I don't have the capacity. Every time someone failed, the dockets came to me. That's how I got involved with all the other people that you mentioned. You mentioned about Yusuf Kajee. He complained to the national commissioner and I was asked to take over. I don't take over the cases; I usually only monitor the investigation and give guidance. There were complaints, because Kajee laid complaints against the Hawks, so obviously they won't investigate themselves. Then the national commissioner told me to take over. There are many other cases where the provincial commissioners – whether they informed the national commissioner, but they alleged that they've spoken to the national commissioner – and then they send the dockets to me. Kajee is a complaint that came from Maritzburg. All I did was to ensure that the province investigated.'

What about the photograph of him with Kajee at a social event that features in O'Sullivan's 'Joining the Dots' document?

'I was invited by the Consulate General of India. I get a lot of invitations from all the embassies. If I'm available, I go. It was a celebration of the Indians' arrival to South Africa. Initially, that's what it was. I attend a lot of functions. It was initially said that I was at a casino with my wife with that photograph. But that photograph was taken there at this celebration. A lawyer came up to me and said he'd always wanted a photo.'

'So you didn't see anything wrong with it?'

'To take a photo? I take a lot of photos at functions.'

'But he was the subject of the investigation.'

'Not that I was aware of. I was not aware of any investigation against him. I was aware of a case where he was the complainant and the Hawks were suspects.'

Then of course there is the matter of Robert Huang, overseas trips, suggestions that he has taken a job with Huang's company and that his daughter is working for Huang.

'I deny going overseas and saying that I worked for Mr Huang. How I met Mr Huang was a complaint again that he addressed to the national commissioner and I was again asked to take over those investigations, but I didn't take over. Being the head of detectives, I must ensure that the investigation runs properly. There was a thing between SARS and him. I don't get involved with their issues – I make sure that the issues are being investigated thoroughly. My daughter is a professional, she's a lawyer – who she works for I cannot dictate. She works for him via a lawyer.'

'Did you get her the job?'

'I did not get her the job – she's a lawyer, she's married.'

'So it's pure coincidence?'

'She has her own practice now. Who she works for I cannot change, that's her life. I'm not going to tell my daughter to do this or that – her husband must tell her.'

'So you're saying you weren't involved in getting her that job?' I push on.

'No. If that was the case, I would be working for him.'

'Do you work for him?'

'No.'

'Have you ever worked for him?'

'No.'

'Have you ever purported to work for him?'

'No.'

'Did you ever go overseas ...'

'I went many times. Not with him. I pay with my credit cards. The state pays for my offical trips. The state paid me enough to live a comfortable life. I don't need anybody to pay.'

If this is the case, then why would O'Sullivan construct such an elaborate campaign against him, replete with audio recordings, photographs and documents. What does O'Sullivan have against him?

'When I took over the Krejcir investigation, I remember receiving an SMS from Paul O'Sullivan that he wanted to work with me. I don't work with anyone outside the SAPS unless you're a source. I will not do a joint investigation with somebody that is not in the organisation, so I refused. I still remember there was a meeting in the national commissioner's boardroom. The Hawks were there and she wanted to know who worked with Paul O'Sullivan and I said I didn't know. I work with people who are registered sources, but I don't work with people who want to piggyback on my investigation. I think that could've given him reason ... When it came to the SAA investigation, again that was given to me and he was a suspect in that investigation. I've taken that investigation and gave it to KZN so that I could monitor it from here. I wanted the case to be neutral so that he couldn't say I had a vendetta against him. Even that didn't work.'

Moonoo believes that his phone was being illegally tapped and that the recordings produced by O'Sullivan were the products of this. He's not happy about it.

'There was a recording of me and Mr Padayachee that was now in the public domain. I went to the inspector-general's office and laid a complaint. I said I don't have a problem with my telephone being tapped legally, but I have a problem with this recording being in the public domain.'

He vehemently denies the allegation that he wanted O'Sullivan dead and that he attempted to prevent Candice Coetzee or anyone else from tipping him off about the hit on his life. He claims it was actually the exact opposite.

'With the team that I led, we saved Paul's life. If I wanted him dead I would not have acted when there was an assassination attempt on him where we arrested those people. I deny it. I have no reason to want to kill people. I'm not about killing people. If I wanted him dead he would've been dead during that assassination attempt,' he says matter-of-factly.

Despite living and breathing the police, Moonoo doesn't want to comment on the current state of the organisation or its capacity to fight organised crime. 'I don't want to comment on police; it won't be right of me. I don't want to be like other members who leave and then criticise.'

Moonoo didn't leave the SAPS because of the allegations against him or because Phiyega, his political cover, was sidelined. Instead, he says, it was always part of the plan.

'It was always my plan to leave the police after 30 years. I got the post as divisional commissioner … and that also caused a problem because there were people who wanted the post but didn't get it. I got the post as divisional commissioner of detectives but I said I'll leave after five years, at 35 years [of service] I'll leave. When I came to 35 I decided it was time. I spent a lot of time away from home. I didn't see my two daughters growing up, thanks to my good wife – she has taken care of them. I have a grandson and I've decided I want to spend time with him. I have a family history where my brothers passed away at young ages. I've worked hard and I want to now reap the benefit.'

He lives in Lenasia with his wife and they regularly take holidays locally and abroad. 'I do a lot of travelling and I don't have to ask for leave. I don't need to worry about my phone.'

The ex-general insists, crucially, that for him it has never been and never will be about the money.

'I was offered a lot of jobs after I left and I refused all of them. In the private sector there is enough money. I was 35 years old when I was offered a job for twice the salary I got in the police and I refused it. Money is not the issue for me; I just need to live. Whether I drive a Toyota or a Ferrari, it takes me to the same place. Whether I live in Sandton or Lenasia, I've got a house that is comfortable. I totally deny that I ever took money from anyone corruptly.'

'YOUR CALL HAS BEEN PLACED ON HOLD. PLEASE WAIT. *BEEP-BAAP.*'
'Hello,' says the voice, deep and rich. He begins to babble, aware
of the constraints of time. I can hear voices echoing in the corridor behind
him. His words are punctuated by a regular beep on the line. Our conversation takes place over several dropped calls.

Siboniso Miya is speaking to me from prison. He has been convicted
alongside Krejcir for the attempted murder of Bheki Lukhele, kidnapping
and attempted drug dealing. He is serving 15 years in jail.

Miya is not what you expect. He is refined and well spoken. Although he
originally comes from KwaZulu-Natal, he attended the Mitzvah School in
Sandton, a Jewish institution run by the Bet David community for under-
privileged students from Alexandra.

His version of events directly contradicts that of Nare, his old friend.
He vacillates between describing Nare as a scammer, a fraudster and an
imposter, and as a victim and pitiful character whom he, Miya, saved. He
says he first met Nare in 2003, but that 'Nare' had a different name then and
originally came from Zimbabwe.

Miya first came to Johannesburg from KwaZulu-Natal in 1998 and finished matric before going into the taxi industry. He was in prison when
he met Nare, who had been convicted of fraud. He says Nare had been
assaulted in prison, so he took him under his wing.

'I protected him. Then he made a plea bargain; he went to the other side,
then I was able to, when I got out, I was able to pay his fine; his fine was
R20 000. By the time I paid it, it was December 2004. I paid his fine and
then basically I helped him to get wherever he is now,' Miya explains. Now
his old friend has turned on him.

'Ja, now I understand that he's scared of prison; he's traumatised by what happened to him in prison; I understand the deal he made – it was from fear and it was the easiest thing to get out of this mess as well,' Miya says with some sympathy.

Miya's path crossed that of Ronny Bvuma through rugby. 'Ronny went to Fourways High, so we played rugby together, so it's somebody I've known from way back. He was junior to me so we would meet up during our rugby tournaments or in clubs.' Along with the taxis, he started doing some debt collecting for Bvuma. 'I used to ask Ronny, with debt collecting, if he needed help to collect like jewellery in the shop. I was the one going around townships looking for people selling jewellery and everything, and I played rugby with Ronny, so that was our friendship.'

Through Bvuma he met Jan 'Johnny' Charvat, the Czech 'Dumpling' who wanted to invest money in his taxi business. He insists, though, that he barely knew Krejcir and never did any work for him.

'So basically I know Krejcir now since we're in prison that we became close since we're in this conspiracy together. I just knew him in passing like I didn't, we weren't say buddy-buddies. I just knew a man called Krejcir, but we were never close.'

Essentially, Miya's defence is that he was set up. He was in the wrong place at the wrong time and he's been stitched up as a fall guy to build a case against Krejcir by the state, the cops and Paul O'Sullivan. The key weapon used against him is his old friend 'Jacob Nare', who has woven a story about their alleged complicity in crime to save his own skin.

'Jacob Nare will say anything to stay out of prison and will basically collude with Gininda [the investigating officer] and the state prosecutor to say anything. Even to Paul O'Sullivan he will say anything, yet they haven't researched who is this Jacob Nare because that's not Jacob Nare. He's a fraudster basically, so he can say anything to implicate me and he continues frauding outside.

'I've been set up for I don't know whatever reason with some guys in Crime Intelligence,' he ventures. Miya's argument is that the cops needed to create a network around Krejcir to present an image of an organised crime gang and he fitted the mould. 'What happened is they take like, you know, there was a bombing in Bedfordview, Money Point. So most of Krejcir's right-hand men, they died there, so they trying to reinvent them by using me basically. That's how they're trying to say I'm his right-hand man but, you know, his right-hand people died in the bomb in Bedfordview.'

Why did he become the fall guy? Because he fitted the mould and it was convenient.

'Basically I'm in the taxi industry so with the bad reputation in taxi industry, so everything it'll suit me. I'm not sentenced for participating in anything; I'm just, you know, in the taxi industry it's, it's violent. I'm being criticised for being a taxi person, taxi owner. Basically I'm here, I'm not dead, so why not?'

I want to know what he thinks the motive is behind this conspiracy. He believes the prosecutor Lawrence Gcaba and O'Sullivan are working on behalf of Czech paymasters.

'He [Gcaba] has got an agenda obviously. I think he's getting paid because he's been to the Czech Republic; he's met people that want Krejcir behind bars forever so he's also getting paid for it. It's just the same, who pays Paul O'Sullivan to investigate Krejcir for so long and for so many millions in expenses? It's a million-dollar question, I promise you. I also need to know.'

Miya goes as far as claiming that there is a conspiracy against him and that he has been wrongfully convicted in a court of law because of collusion between the cops and prosecutors.

'These people they hide our alibis. We aren't given the particulars in court; they don't give us times and dates. I believe – I'm not a law expert – but I believe to prove a conspiracy you need to have dates, times, places of meeting where these conspiracies might have happened, but when you ask for that in court we ... we're not given anything and these witnesses are just sitting. If you see the statements of Jacob Nare and Lucky Mokoena, they basically talking about hearsay. I told them or Krejcir told them this; there was nothing that says I was there with him talking, because you know you've got cellphone records that can help us prove our alibis if you know the date and the time. I was sitting in Durban at that time, between July and September. I was almost every weekend in Durban because I was preparing for my wedding. So, if I'm not given the time, the date and the places, I can't ... I can't really prove my alibi. They've got our cellphone records. So you get my frustration at the moment.'

On the morning of our conversation, I had spoken to Miya in the High Court where he was appearing for the Sam Issa murder. The matter was trundling along at a snail's pace and he believed the prosecutor and the judge were incompetent at best, corrupt at worst. 'It's the prosecutor as well, like he knows his case has got holes so he's also opposing us getting all the particulars and the court is siding with him, you know how High Court is.'

It is obvious that Miya is frustrated by his position and is in a state of despair about his jail term. He has been convicted by a court of law that heard evidence over the course of a full trial. Nevertheless, he maintains his innocence and feels that he has been wrongfully incarcerated. All this, he says, is taking a toll on him and his family.

'Ay, I cry myself to sleep, hey,' he says desperately. 'I cry myself to sleep because whatever we do with Krejcir's stigma, nobody wants to listen to us, or nobody wants to take our side of the story. You know, because he, Krejcir's got this stigma, he's … he's this rough rider and basically, we, we're different, we're not him. Even the prison I'm in now, I'm getting ill treated because he was here before and he made rubbish here, so I'm getting ill treated for that. I'm not being properly assessed just because I'm Krejcir's accused … like I'll be searched every day, I wouldn't be allowed to go to the gym, I wouldn't be allowed to study because of Krejcir. I wouldn't be allowed to have a laptop because of him. I'm very disappointed in the system and, and I'll wish and pray that Krejcir would say and talk who did he step on because this thing is politically motivated.'

Miya has a 74-year-old mother, a wife and eight kids.

'It's sad, I'm taking treatment for depression as it is,' he admits. 'I haven't seen my kids in three years, like every time I think about them, like, I cry but it's, it's like we're fighting a losing battle; whatever we do we're sinking anyway and I'm … I just wish I had an opportunity to finish my small trials, which were created by this, this Jacob Nare guy. I just wanna finish those trials because I know for a fact that I'm gonna win and Krejcir is not involved in them so there's no influence of badness in them.'

The other matters he's currently facing are a conspiracy case in Kagiso and a robbery charge in Soweto. He claims he's innocent of those charges too.

Miya is interrupted by shouting in the corridor behind him and a beep on the phone. He assures me we still have more time to talk when I apologise for keeping him. The line drops and I phone back. After a 'Your call has been placed on hold, please wait', Miya comes back on the line. We talk about his co-accused in the Issa trial.

'Nkanyiso Mafunda. He's like a brother to me,' Miya tells me. They met in the taxi business. 'We're involved in the taxis in KZN, so I brought them up here to help me and to expand their businesses this side because it's less violent. It's peaceful basically.'

'Were the three of you involved in the Sam Issa murder at all?' I push.

'None of us were involved. The witnesses, the eyewitnesses in Sam Issa in the docket that I read, they say it was two white guys that killed Issa. So, I can't change overnight and become white,' he insists.

'And did you know Issa?'

'I knew him in passing, I didn't know him in speaking to him or whatever; didn't even know his surname Issa. I'd seen him in Money Point a couple of times.'

'And you were never hired to kill him?'

'Never.'

'Your car was never involved in that shooting?' I ask, referring to the white Ford Ranger.

'That car, I'm still looking for it as it is, and I've tried to help the Crime Intelligence and the police locate a car which is a Ford Ranger. I've never owned a Ford Ranger.'

In the week that I spoke to Miya, I was handed a large A4 envelope in a parking lot by someone unrelated to the case. It contained Miya's lengthy complaint to the NPA about how his case has been handled. It contains explosive allegations against the prosecutor, the investigating officer and the judge. Tales of bribes and payoffs. The NPA confirmed it had received the complaint from Miya.

I ask him about this and it sets him off.

'Basically, what I would like them to do, to review our cases, to review the prima facie evidence against us, but to take it objectively after what I've said about the witnesses and the status of the witnesses, especially Jacob Nare, being an identity thief, you know, being a fraudster himself. He will do anything to get out of prison, so I wanted the NPA just to review and investigate Gcaba.

'The system has failed us. The South Gauteng court is corrupt as a whole, judges and prosecutors. I just have no faith in it.'

According to Miya, he is an innocent man who has been conveniently stitched up as part of a carefully constructed conspiracy to ensure that a dangerous gangster, Radovan Krejcir, is kept behind bars at all costs. The allegedly malleable justice system has been bent and manipulated so that he cannot fight back. No one cares and no one will listen.

Over their time in prison, travelling to and from court, he has got to know Krejcir fairly well. And he believes the Czech feels the same way as he does.

'We're okay. We chilled. Krejcir is like, after these three years being with him, you can't really read him, what is he thinking or what is he going through or if he's frustrated. I just know he's frustrated being in prison, you know he's just frustrated of the whole conspiracy and he just can't speak out because nobody will probably listen to him.'

WHEN GEORGE LOUCA TOUCHED DOWN ON SOUTH AFRICAN SOIL, he was a different man from the one who had fled the country four years previously. He was half his size physically, he had grown a moustache and he was ready to talk. He also returned to a very different place from the one he had left in the hours after Lolly Jackson's murder. Radovan Krejcir was largely a spent force, behind bars and without influence or money. The risk of exposing him was greatly diminished. Louca was also overwrought with guilt, filled with a compelling desire to do the right thing so that his children would think him a good man.

Initially, however, it wasn't a done deal that he would testify against Krejcir as a state witness. He was still an accused and to the police he was the main suspect in Lolly Jackson's death. Investigating officer PW van Heerden was not having his mind changed. He tells me about it while chain-smoking Chesterfields and stroking his ginger-blond moustache at a News Café.

'I got the call the Friday afternoon saying that George would arrive the Sunday,' Van Heerden starts.

There were serious security implications as the court in Cyprus had been concerned around Louca's safety if he were to be extradited to South Africa. Louca arrived at OR Tambo on an Egypt Air flight.

'I got him there; it was a heck of a fight about where to keep him. There was a guy from Interpol who had made arrangements to keep him in Pretoria Central, at Kgosi Mampuru.' At that stage, Krejcir was also being held at Kgosi Mampuru and this would have been a match to a tinderbox. 'I said no ways. I phoned the head of the Pretoria area Correctional Services and he messed me around the whole Saturday. Van Heerden phoned his general, Taioe. 'Eventually I met with Taioe late that afternoon and he told me it was arranged at Zonderwater.'

When Van Heerden saw Louca at the airport, he was surprised. 'He had lost weight; he wasn't the guy on the photo we had. George was friendly. His attitude was quite okay. We took him to Pretoria and kept him at the police station overnight. We brought him through to Kempton Park court the next day, trying to duck the media. The media circus started and then it was a question of trying to get George a lawyer.' After a long process, eventually Owen Blumberg took the case and Louca couldn't have asked for a more eager attorney. 'Owen – we had our ding-dongs – he was very passionate, but he also had blinkers on. He had a personal axe to grind with Krejcir.' There was some debate around whether he took the case out of the 'goodness of his heart' or whether Paul O'Sullivan paid his fees.

Louca didn't tell Van Heerden his story because Blumberg didn't trust the cop. And so began a convoluted set-up in which Louca and Blumberg began to cooperate with a separate state agency from that actually handling his case. Louca authored several statements in which he set out his truth, but these were not made to Van Heerden. As far as the investigating officer was concerned, Louca remained his primary accused.

Van Heerden explains what was going on at the time. 'Whenever Owen wanted to see George, I had to accompany him. I would then go sit and wait in the car, waiting for hours for him to finish. I couldn't say straight out to Owen to put his cards on the table and then we could possibly work out a deal. You couldn't say that to him; it wasn't my prerogative – it's the prosecutor's prerogative. What I said to Owen was that he should put George's version in writing; and Paul Schutte, the prosecutor, also said he should give them a version in writing so that they could work on it. The promises came that I will get it, but it never materialised.'

Louca was making statements, though. He was working with Candice Coetzee from Crime Intelligence and the National Intervention Unit, the task team set up to investigate Krejcir. Paul O'Sullivan was also meddling, much to Van Heerden's annoyance.

'Then Mr O'Sullivan became involved and then it started popping out in the media and one of the statements that O'Sullivan made right at the beginning was that I was corrupt or gullible or both,' he says.

O'Sullivan had said straight out to me that he believed that Van Heerden was on Krejcir's payroll. I ask the investigating officer about this accusation and he tenses up immediately.

'I can show you emails that I've sent to my bosses and said that that was what was happening in the media and they could investigate me, do a lifestyle audit. I have never taken money from anybody. I've calmed down a lot over the years. The one thing that used to pee me off – you can call me a four-letter word and I'll actually tell you I'm one. Like this O'Sullivan saying that I'm stupid and gullible, I accept it. Nobody's perfect. When you say I'm corrupt, then I get angry. In my years in the cops I've never taken a cent from anybody. When I was still a greenhorn detective I messed up opportunities to knock guys for corruption. The accused would phone you to ask if we could talk about it and my whole manner on the phone would put them off. Later I learnt to just sound a bit more agreeable and try to set something up.'

Over this period, Louca was moved around from prison to prison. There were rumours of a hit on him and threats to his life. Everyone was really concerned that he could be taken out before he could tell the truth. In the end, he wasn't killed by an outside threat. It was his ill health that took him down. He had lung cancer and it was aggressive. It was a race against time as Louca's health deteriorated.

'We had him moved to Joburg prison, to Sun City. There we had a good working relationship with the guy. From the day that George flew in, I handed a letter signed by Taioe to Correctional Services stating that nobody except the investigating team may be allowed to visit him. If people wanted to see him, they had to contact us. After he became ill, when I went to collect him at Joburg, the head of the prison wasn't available and I spoke to one of the junior ladies. She asked me if I was going to inform Captain Coetzee that he is going. She said Captain Coetzee has been visiting him.'

Another of the few people who did have a face-to-face meeting with Louca in prison was the former Teazers spokesman, Sean Newman. He went along with Arthur Calamaras, a sex-industry businessman, who had once been to visit Louca in the cells in Cyprus. Calamaras had recorded his encounter with Louca at the time.

'We went to Sun City,' Newman tells me. 'We got there; Arthur bought him a whole bunch of smokes and chips and cooldrinks, chicken, all of that, and we stood around. I'd forgotten my ID book at home. They wouldn't let me in and eventually I said to Arthur, "Just go, just go talk to him, just go," and one of the female guards said, "Are you going to George?" I said, "Yes." She said, "Oh no, go," and that I found incredibly weird because the judge kept harping on about his location cannot be disclosed. And here, without my ID book, I was being allowed to go see him. Anyway, the bus dropped us off at medium security. We got out, we went in and next thing there's George on the other side of the glass.

'He got very, very emotional talking. The first thing he said to me is, "You've got to believe me, I didn't kill Lolly." I said to him, "I do believe you," I said to him. "But, George, the problem is, who did it?" He said, "That is coming, that is coming; that is all I've got left in this world and that is coming." And then Arthur said, "So you won't tell us, but you'll tell us you didn't kill him." And he slammed the window so hard that I thought that double-thick triple-thick glass was gonna come out of its bracket. He said to me, he said to Arthur and he looked him square in the eyes and he said, "My daughters think I'm a murderer; I left Cyprus with them now thinking I'm a murderer. I will not die with them thinking I'm a murderer. You can take it to the grave, that I will come out and I will tell everyone what the truth is, because I will not have my kids believe that I am a murderer. I am many things in this world; I'm a thief, I'm a crook, I'm everything, but I'm not a killer," and that was that. For me it was like the turning point.'

For a man who was meant to be under the tightest possible guard, whose life was in mortal danger and whom the cops needed to keep alive, security clearly wasn't a major concern. It's also a classic case of different arms of the police not working together.

'I asked Paul Schutte, the prosecutor, because there were stories,' says Van Heerden. 'After George was in hospital, we took him to Bara; they X-rayed him and the doctors said it could possibly be TB and sent him back with medication. The second time we took him his lungs were full of water. The lungs were drained, but then he had to be kept in hospital. We took him to Tembisa and while he was in Tembisa he told me he had made an affidavit already. I asked him to whom he made the affidavit and he said to Candice. I said to him, "Well, we haven't seen that – Owen hasn't given it to us."'

The affidavits leaked out in the media before Van Heerden even saw them. I wrote an article in the *City Press* about the fact that Louca was cooperating with other cops and coming clean, infuriating the investigating officer. Van Heerden says that once he finally read Louca's version as detailed in his statements, he thought there were inconsistencies with the forensic evidence.

'There were certain things in the affidavit that didn't gel with the physical evidence at the scene. According to George, Lolly came there and he gave him a beer and then this argument started and Krejcir shot him and kicked him. He was explaining that Lolly was shot in the chest, upfront. Lolly wasn't shot upfront in the chest, but from the side. So that didn't gel. When he was at Kgosi Mampuru I was doing the paperwork to take him to Pretoria West hospital for a check-up. I then put these inconsistencies to him about what he saw and what he couldn't see. He wouldn't have been able to see in detail what was happening. The bar was here and he was behind the bar. The shooting and where Lolly fell was behind the couch on the left-hand side of the bar. He would not have been able to see Krejcir doing certain things that he described in the affidavit and what he was also verbally stating after the affidavit came out. When Corrie [Maritz, another cop] put the inconsistencies to him, he changed his version to fit in, to, no, but he moved out from behind the bar and that is why he could see what happened.'

The version that Louca then gave in court in Palm Ridge also raised further inconsistencies.

'If you go and listen carefully to that version compared to the affidavit, you'll see he changed his version to fit in with … to make up for those inconsistencies, to make up for what was happening behind the couch. He had changed his version; the version he gave in court is different from the affidavit.'

In April 2015, Louca was wheeled into court and gave his dramatic Godfather-esque account of Lolly Jackson's murder, emotionally recounting the night and how he wanted to tell the truth for the sake of his children. He was dying and Blumberg had brought a section 49E application to have him released from prison because he was in such poor health. He wanted to return to Cyprus to die. He had stage-four lung cancer and the prognosis was poor. Judge Geraldine Borchers declined Louca's request to return home. Within a month, he was dead while incarcerated at the Kgosi Mampuru II prison in Pretoria.

Van Heerden was in Tzaneen when he got the call to authorise security to take Louca to hospital. 'Two or three days before George died, I tried to get him to plead, confess. He said he would think about it, but he died,' the cop says with disappointment.

Until the very end, Blumberg maintained that a grave injustice had been done. He was desperately upset about the hand Louca had been dealt. Ironically, Blumberg died from a sudden heart attack not long after. Blumberg was eccentric and fired up about the case, so I was never quite sure what to make of his claims that Louca had been poisoned and that his ill health was not because of cancer. Medical reports handed into court explicitly explain his cancer diagnosis. Van Heerden also doesn't buy this argument.

'I'm not a medical expert, but according to the doctor's report that was given to the Cypriots he had advanced lung cancer. I don't think poison can duplicate the symptoms of lung cancer.'

However, a police source with intimate knowledge of the case tells me there was a definite belief that Louca had been intentionally poisoned. The family was going to do a private post-mortem on the body in Cyprus, but changed their minds at the last minute.

'The information that we've got is that he was poisoned. One of the 205s that we had done on the phones that we got from Krejcir, there was a shit load of calls made to Cyprus from prison. The prison guard that Krejcir had made friends with in prison, he gave Louca whatever it was that they used. Krejcir said it over the phone. All these illegal interceptions make things so difficult because you can't use it. That's why they managed to keep one step ahead.'

Blumberg also believed the state might have deliberately wanted Louca dead. He once told me about an encounter he had with Van Heerden, which he believed had supported this notion, during which Van Heerden warned Louca that the only way he would return to Cyprus would be 'in a box'. The investigating officer shares with me what unfolded.

'That happened at Boksburg prison. We had taken George to Kempton Park court and it came out that George was phoning people outside the prison, stating where he was. That was also a problem – where I tried to have George "killed". We were taking him from prison – we also used to take him in a Nyala – but the guys at Boksburg prison, because they wanted to keep it low key, asked can't we just collect him in a car and take him to a spot just away from prison so that the warders don't see this whole thing and realise it's a high-profile guy. That's what we did. We picked him up and raced out to put him into a Nyala. I was accused of creating an opportunity for George to be killed by doing that. In the car I told him he was stupid. We were trying to keep him safe, but he's phoning all these people telling them where he was. He didn't know who they were talking to and when we got back to the prison, George became aggro. I told him if he carried on with that, the only way he'll get back to Cyprus was in a box. That's where that infamous "You'll go back to Cyprus in a box" comes from.'

Sean Newman also had conversations with Blumberg, over shots of Stroh Rum, about this. He shares his and the late lawyer's views on a potential poisoning.

'I saw from the guy I met that first time and how quickly he degenerated. If you want the honest truth, I think he was poisoned and I'm not the only one who is going to tell you that. Owen believed it as well. Owen went a little bit further, thinking it was an apartheid-era agent that had been developed to cause cancer and things like that. I dunno if I would go that far, but I believe that he was killed. I think dead men tell no secrets. I think George knew more than he was meant to know. I think it goes far deeper than just say Radovan doing the murder; it's who covered it up, who communicated with him. There were no steps taken to protect this witness and I said it at the time – I believe that George was an integral puzzle piece in not just Lolly's murder, but a lot of other things that could unravel a lot of questions and could lead to a lot for the bigger picture being exposed. I think we still only know about 2 per cent of what really has gone on.'

There is no doubt in the mind of Demetris Panayiotou, George Louca's brother, that Louca was poisoned. Panayiotou flew to South Africa and saw Louca shortly before his death.

'What I believe; actually, I'm sure, that George is being poisoned,' he told me on the phone from Cyprus. 'I don't know which way they used, but George is being poisoned because he knew so many things about everybody from Radovan, for some police with the high position and they wanted to close his mouth.'

He can't say for sure who was behind it, but Louca had his own suspicions and agreed that he had been poisoned. 'I don't know who poisoned George. If I knew it, I would tell you, but I don't know who. But I'm sure that people from underworld and some police cooperate together, and they want to get out George as soon as possible. He said to me that the last time I visited him in the prison and we had the conversation. He said to me, "My brother, I'm sure that they poisoned me. They found one way and they poisoned me. It's not possible," he said to me, "to get sick so quickly." And in a few months he was ready to go. I mean this is not possible. He was sure about this. He mentioned to me some people, I don't want to say the names, but I think slowly slowly, Krejcir is in the prison, I don't know if he will manage to get out. Everybody in South Africa, they know that somebody else pulled the trigger and it wasn't my brother. My brother had different cases, dirty cases. I'm not saying he's innocent, but I'm sure he's not a killer.'

Panayiotou doesn't have any hard evidence to back up his claims, but he does have the medical report showing Louca was healthy when he was first put on a plane back to South Africa.

'The only evidence I've got, before George has been extradited to South Africa, he's been examined everything to see his health how is it, and from the exam we get before he left to South Africa, everything was clear. How come from the time he left from Cyprus a few months he get the lung cancer stage four and he died? Let's say from the time we discovered that he was suffering from lung cancer after less than a month he passed away.'

He also clears up the rumours that he was phoned and threatened not to do a second autopsy when Louca's body arrived in Cyprus. He says there were no threats. 'No, no, no. When the body of my brother arrived to Cyprus, we took him to the hospital of the capital of Cyprus and there, there came some doctors. I explained to them I want to make a second autopsy to his body, and they explained to me that if they are going to do so it's really difficult to discover anything because from the time they took with some pipes all the blood out his body and they put some medicine just to travel from South Africa to Cyprus. This was the reason that I changed the mind. Nobody called me or threatened me or something.'

Panayiotou is emotional about how Louca was left to die in prison in a land far away from home. He has some poignant final thoughts about South Africa's justice system and how not everyone is equal before the law.

'We are very sad. We was expecting the South African authorities and the South African prosecutors, I had the meeting with them before George passed away and they promised to me that George would be released to his home to die. And also, I gave them a letter, evidence from Cyprus that he would be hospitalised, and also I provided them a ticket with Emirates as a sick passenger and everything. But from one minute to another minute they changed their minds. They knew it that George would pass away, he had only a few weeks life left.

'I used to live in South Africa. I think and I believe that if someone commit a crime, they have to face the law. I'm not against this. But I believe that in South Africa the corruption is so big, no human rights, no nothing. If you have money you can do whatever you want. If you don't, you die. Simple as that. Policemen, prosecutors, judges, everybody, they get involved with underworld. This I saw with my eyes, and I'm very disappointed. They let one guy die like a dog in a cell. They knew that George would pass away. They knew everything from the beginning. Just they give us problems and problems and problems. I think above is a God. Everybody we are going to see the God and we will let the God judge us.'

Stubbing out a Chesterfield at the News Café, PW van Heerden is adamant that he has not changed his mind about what happened in that house in Edleen in 2010, despite Louca's story.

'To this day, I believe George was the shooter. DNA on the firearm, the magazine of the firearm, George and Lolly – a mixture of their DNA on the magazine. On one of the spent cartridges found on the scene, George's DNA, so he handled that firearm at some stage. Cellphone records – he says Krejcir was there – don't show that Krejcir was there. I know he said to me and he also stated in the affidavit that Krejcir left his cellphone at the restaurant. If you look at the gap in the cellphone records between calls and you take the five or ten seconds that could be voicemail kind of stuff, there wasn't enough time at that time of the day for Krejcir unless he was doing low flying with a blue light to make it to the scene and back in that time. It would've left him with 20 minutes to move from the Harbour to Edleen and still become involved with an argument and do the shooting and threaten George to move the body; time didn't allow it. We tried our best to follow up.

'If I'd been able to speak to George earlier in Cyprus and hadn't been held back by various things, I might have had that version earlier and been able to follow up on it. By the time George got back and he provided his version – because we looked at the cellphone records from the beginning – we tried to get hold of Metrovich, who allegedly held the phones for Krejcir, but by then Metrovich was in prison in Ireland for assault. Also my dear friends at Interpol were requested to establish if we could go and speak to Metrovich and by the time they eventually woke up and replied to me – something like a year and a half later, sending them regular reminders – Metrovich had been released from custody in Ireland, hopped on a plane to Spain and disappeared into the European Union.

'Beeka was dead by that stage. All that we were left with out of those guys, except for Krejcir himself, were Arsiotis and Metrovich. Michael Arsiotis disappeared to Australia and was arrested there. We went to go see him – the Aussies arranged it. Arsiotis was willing to see us; as we got off the plane, they said to us that he is now refusing to speak to us. So we never met him. We hung around for a couple of days while they were trying to arrange with his lawyer. We went with to a police station, waiting for him to report. We sat in an office just slightly off from the entrance; they had a chat to him and we could hear him adamantly refusing to speak to us. We were on foreign soil so we couldn't abuse our hosts.'

Van Heerden isn't entirely clear about what Louca's motive was or if he was acting on someone else's behalf. It remains a mystery. 'I don't know, there are a lot of theories that I have. It is possible that George was set up by somebody to kill Lolly or it is a question of they had a meeting about the money flow and it got heated and it was a spur-of-the-moment thing. There are a lot of possibilities. I can't say that there was a specific motive.'

He downplays my suggestion that Krejcir could have paid off cops – himself included – to make the case wither away. 'It came to light that he did have cops on the payroll, on a lower level, that we could confirm. Higher up the evidence wasn't … there were stories …

'Joey Mabasa's version on that, I cannot dispute his version in the sense that he never received money. There is no evidence pointing to the fact that he did. That he was in an inappropriate relationship with Krejcir, ja. That's why I steer away from relationships.

'I cannot get into a cosy relationship with a criminal; it just goes against my grain. There is nothing pointing to Joey receiving money, but that the relationship was inappropriate, according to me. They saw a bit much of one another, but what results did it deliver?'

No one will be held accountable for Lolly Jackson's death. Either the man responsible is dead or the main witness against the accused is gone forever. His deathbed testimony in court will not be enough to convict Krejcir, particularly if there is no political will to bring him to justice for the crime. There will be a formal inquest, when Van Heerden gets round to scheduling it.

'It has to go for an inquest. I'm just tied up with this other thing, but if I can just get the time. I have to gather the outstanding couple of things and hand it back to DPP [the director of public prosecutions] and they refer it to the magistrate's court for an inquest. Whether it be an informal one or a formal one. At this stage I assume it will be an informal one.'

Van Heerden admits that there is an inkling in him, a belief that Krejcir could have played a role somehow.

'There was a guy from the Harbour. He stated that Ivan Savov had left the gun for George to collect and George collected the firearm from him.

Savov gave him this thing in a rag before the murder and George later came to collect it. This guy felt – it was a packet or a rag – something and he looked and realised he had touched the thing and, according to him, he then cleaned it with spirits. George then came and collected it and later he heard about the murder. This guy's timelines didn't fit in with George's movements. There are many possibilities. Krejcir could've been behind it; he could've put George up to do it. I still believe that somewhere Krejcir played a role.'

For now, it remains a mystery.

Casper Labuschagne pulled up at Eden Ministries in Kroonstad on his scooter and walked into the reception. The computer programmer and web designer had been living in the Free State town for a couple of years. He found it central, just a two-hour drive against traffic to Joburg. It's cheap and reasonably quiet. In his spare time, Labuschagne volunteered at the ministry, which took in destitute people but mostly cared for the elderly.

He was taken aback when a big, 'rough-looking guy', covered in tattoos, with short shaved hair, asked him about his scooter. 'Why the Cape Town registration?' the man wanted to know. It was the start of a fantastical conversation between the two men as Pierre Lodewyk Theron regaled his new friend with unbelievable stories as a brothel owner, a mob driver and a man on the run. Over four months in Kroonstad, Labuschagne listened as Theron spoke, in his Afrikaans-accented slang, but never using a swear word.

'He had a very flamboyant character,' Labuschagne recalls. 'He was in his fifties. He had served time in prison and he had all his prison tattoos and his prison gang rankings and everything else. A very rough-looking guy, but he had an outgoing personality. He was very intelligent. I don't think he went very far with school or whatever, but he was, you know, capable with anything he did or whatever.'

Theron shared his story about how he had owned a large brothel in Cape Town and then lost it all. He spoke with bravado.

'Pierre told me that at one stage he owned the biggest brothel in Cape Town and SARS cleaned out Pierre. He owned a house two blocks from the ocean at Bloubergstrand and it was because he never paid tax or VAT. He was cleaned out and he literally had his underpants left and then Mark Lifman bought his brothel.'

He then began to mention the names of Gemballa, Lolly Jackson and Radovan Krejcir. Labuschagne had a particular interest in the underworld and had read news reports about the murders closely. His attention was gripped when his new friend revealed that he used to be Krejcir's driver. Theron told stories about where he went, what he collected, who had visited. It was fascinating.

'Then he asked me, can I send an email and he said, well, he has to do it without me knowing,' says Labuschagne. He lent him his tablet, helped him with Gmail, attached a memory stick to the tablet and showed him how to send a pdf document. He then wiped the memory stick and deleted Theron's passwords. The email had gone to the cops.

A week later, Theron got a call from a prominent underworld character summoning him to Cape Town. He bought a bus ticket and was gone.

Labuschagne was worried about his friend. Out of concern, he cracked his password on his tablet and gained access to the pdf document. It was an affidavit that Theron had signed, an explosive disclosure of payments that he had authored in Kroonstad in 2014. Not knowing where to turn, Labuschagne sent me an email in late 2014 with the affidavit attached and a note of concern for his friend. What I read was incredible, but almost impossible to prove at that point.

What he had sent me was an early draft of an affidavit that Theron later gave to Colonel Gininda in 2015, describing various payments made on behalf of Krejcir. He names policemen, politicians, prosecutors, criminals and political parties as having received money from Krejcir. The affidavit lists payments from a bank deposit book allegedly belonging to Krejcir's Credit Suisse bank account in Liechtenstein.

It later emerged that Theron didn't vanish. He is expected to become a key state witness against Krejcir in the Sam Issa murder trial and other matters. He is not believed to be in witness protection. Paul O'Sullivan has been in contact with him but not recently. According to a report in the *Weekend Argus* in 2016, journalist Caryn Dolley (now at News24) had been in contact with Theron, who says he has no reason to hide. He is described as an information peddler, who has attempted to sell information about crimes to journalists for money. According to the report, Dolley met Theron in the office of Community Safety MEC Dan Plato as far back as 2012. Plato is accused of masterminding a smear campaign against top Cape Town policeman Jeremy Vearey. Plato admits to having dealings with Theron.

Also in 2016, Theron came forward claiming that he had not been paid for information he had provided to the police. He had met Plato several times and handed him information about top police officers and politicians. He told the *Cape Times* that he handed Plato a '3cm thick file' that contained information about the crime syndicate to which he belonged and its activities. In exchange, Plato promised 'a large amount of money'. According to Theron's affidavit, this money never materialised.

It is unclear how credible Theron's claims are. Some of them tie in with dates and events and other anecdotes, but much of it reads like fantastical fiction and the baseless allegations of a hitchhiker looking for a payout. A senior police source told me that Theron is 'a bullshitter', that 'everything he says is lies'. Ultimately, it will be for a court to test their veracity.

> *The following statement will highlight my position in the crime syndicate as well as my interaction with its members. I have made a number of notes and recorded some key events that took place over the past 14 years … As we speak I am still active as a driver for the mob and can be called upon at any time for any duty required of me.*

So begins Pierre Lodewyk Theron's affidavit about his life of crime. He explains that he has decided to author it because he has been diagnosed with leukaemia and he is HIV positive. He is owed a large sum of money by a number of 'Top Dogs' – whom he names – for jobs done, including the transportation of drugs, credit cards, diamonds and rhino horn, surveillance duties and pilot car driving. 'Finally, I would like to expose those involved in this crime syndicate for the injustice caused to innocent people and children. An example of this is the trading of drugs in which children are affected.'

Theron opened a brothel called Millionaires in Cape Town in 2000. Having spent 18 years in various prisons, he came into contact with various characters, including 'Bobby the White Monkey', 'Chinese George', Wally Hui, Cyril Beeka, Brett Kebble, Glenn Agliotti, Yuri 'The Russian' Ulianitski, Colin Stanfield and 'Geweld' Thomas. After selling the business, he started working as a driver for Beeka, Yuri and the Chinese 'sector' in Cape Town.

In 2007, while working for Beeka, he became aware of Krejcir. He says he met him for the first time that year, but reveals that Beeka may have actually met the Czech before his arrival in South Africa, in the Seychelles.

Theron goes into detail about the alleged business dealings between a prominent syndicate called 14K Chinese Mafia, Yuri the Russian, Cyril Beeka and Mark Lifman. He gives an account of Yuri's murder in Milnerton and who he believes was responsible for ordering the hit.

A subsequent version of the affidavit goes into further detail about how Theron maintained his relationship with Krejcir. 'During my association with Krejcir, we didn't immediately become close pals, but later on during 2010 and 2011, I drove several trips for him, shifting cars for him from Johannesburg to Cape Town and from Johannesburg to Durban,' said Theron. 'I always knew that there were illegal substances in the cars, but I never asked any questions, which resulted in him trusting me to the fullest.'

On 6 October 2013, Krejcir ostensibly made contact with Theron. He was looking for a guy to do a job. It was the week leading up to Sam Issa's murder. Theron hit the road and hitchhiked from Cape Town to Joburg. When he got to Grasmere, he says he phoned Krejcir and asked him to come get him. Krejcir sent Boris 'Mike the Bulgarian' Grigorov. He took him through to Money Point where he sat at the next-door restaurant, Izzo's, and ate lamb shank.

'Radovan then asked me how my trip was to Johannesburg and I answered him. Radovan asked me whether I am in possession of a gun. I told him that I have a gun with me. Radovan then asked me whether I would do a job for him and I told him that I would. This was the only and the last time that Radovan referred to a "job" or asking me about being in possession of a gun.'

During their conversation, Krejcir apparently spoke to Theron about the people who owed him money and his frustrations at what was going on at the time. 'The media says I killed Lolly, I killed Mark Andrews, I killed Ian Jordaan, I killed Cyril Beeka, I killed "Mr Cocaine" and all the others ... but the cunts owe me money, what must I do?'

The day after arriving in Joburg, Krejcir asked Theron to go to Midrand with Mike to pick up a car and bring it back. It was a white Ford Ranger double-cab bakkie. Before they left to fetch the vehicle, Krejcir received a call on his cellphone, which he answered in a foreign language. 'Radovan then ended the call and told me to take his black Mercedes and to go and fetch two blokes at the OR Tambo Airport. I then asked Radovan where I must pick them up at the airport and he responded saying that I must go to International Arrivals.' When Theron arrived at the airport, two 'white males of dark complexion' got in the car. They had just one small suitcase between them – they weren't going to be in town long, it seemed. The two were put up at the Mercure Hotel next to Money Point.

Theron recounts how he and Boris Grigorov then went off to fetch the Ford Ranger in Midrand. At Money Point, the vehicle was scrubbed clean, blue police lights were installed in the dashboard and then it was covered with a green canvas car cover.

On the Friday morning, the day before Issa was gunned down, Theron witnessed an altercation between Krejcir and Issa on the Money Point premises. He had met Issa twice before at the Harbour.

'As Sam Issa and Veselin Laganin mounted the steps, I overheard Mike the Bulgarian saying, "Here's the shit hitting the fan now." Johnny Chavot [Jan Charvat] was sitting on the couch and smiled whilst looking up at Sam Issa and Veselin Laganin entering the Money Point offices. After about two minutes, all hell broke loose inside the office. I heard both Radovan and Sam Issa shouting at each other, both doing so in foreign languages. The next moment Sam and Veselin came out, followed by Radovan. As Sam Issa and Veselin Laganin walked down the steps towards their vehicles, Radovan shouted in English: "I fuck you both."'

Half an hour later, Krejcir called Theron into his office. 'Things are going to get hectic this coming weekend,' he told him. Krejcir then sent him out of town, to sell a diamond in Springbok in the Northern Cape. At 9am the following morning, Theron phoned Grigorov, who told him 'Radovan snuffed Sam'. He knew this meant that Krejcir had killed Issa.

Theron watched the news reports from Cape Town as Krejcir was arrested in November. In December, he hitchhiked back to Joburg. At Park Station, he bumped into another Krejcir associate. He asked him to call Grigorov, who came to fetch him and took him to a flat in Bedfordview for the night. It was in this flat that Theron found a stash of bank books that allegedly revealed secrets of Krejcir's operations. The flat had no furniture, the bedroom doors were locked and there were boxes of documents and files stacked to the ceiling.

Grigorov had errands to run and asked Theron to repack the documents. 'I then started to sort out some of the boxes that were in reach. The second box that I started to sort out was one that contained bank deposit books. I started paging through some of the bank deposit books and took out one which contained certain prominent and well-known names of people and placed it aside.' Theron put the bank deposit book in his bag and took it with him as he boarded a bus to Nelspruit the following day.

Two months later, while hitchhiking back through Joburg, Theron was picked up by another Krejcir associate, 'Pauli'. Things took a turn when Pauli began to pepper him with questions about his previous visit to Joburg and the missing bank deposit book. Theron played it cool despite the book being in his bag all along. He asked Pauli to take him back to the Bedfordview apartment to look for the 'missing' book. After leaving him at the flat with a brand-new sleeping bag, Chesterfield cigarettes, a litre of Coke and a barrel of KFC, Pauli left.

'After Pauli left I moved a few boxes around to create an impression that I actually looked for the bank deposit book. I then spent the rest of the evening copying all the information which appeared to be details of trans-actions on a writing pad. The next morning at 4:30am, I showed him that all seven books were there. I could see that he was relieved and he said that he knew that someone was making a flop. He thanked me for my decent work and gave me R2000 for the road.'

So what did the book reveal? On the front of the book was inscribed: ZL-327/42806, Helvetia, Credit de Suisse, Zurich 2010–2013. On the inside of the back page in pen, it said 'Vaduz, Liechtenstein.' Names and amounts were written in the bank deposit book. The dates were all erased with black marker:

> Cyril Beeka
> R2.7 million
> Radovan Krejcir
> R62 million
> R17 million
> R29 million
> R34 million
> R91 million

And so it went on, a long list of names and amounts.

Under the name Glenn Agliotti, it showed amounts of R10 million, R11 million, R7.7 million and R5 million.

Agliotti denies that he had borrowed these sums of money from Krejcir.

According to the bank book, Cuban druglord Nelson Pablo Yester-Garrido and Krejcir were doing big business totalling almost R140 million. There is also an amount of R700 000 under the inscription 'Garrido court case'.

In a later draft of the affidavit, Theron elaborates on what this payment was for. He says that during one of his driving jobs for Krejcir, in February 2013, he was given a white BMW 320d to drive from Johannesburg to Port Elizabeth and a suitcase containing R700 000 in cash to deliver to the 'state team that was to prosecute Nelson Pablo Yester-Garrido for the 166 kilograms of cocaine, which was recovered in 2010'. A day after the delivery, the case against Yester-Garrido was 'withdrawn under sinister circumstances'.

Under Mark Lifman's name are the amounts of R1.9 million and R3.3 million, while there is R2.2 million for Jerome 'Donkie' Booysen. Lifman denies entering into any business deal with Krejcir.

For Lolly Jackson, there's an amount of R23.7 million, a likely reference to the international money-transfer scheme the two had operated together.

Then there are the cops on the payroll.

For F Steyn there's R409 000 – the loan made to East Rand Organised Crime cop François Steyn. There's R1.7 million for Joey Mabasa, R1.9 million for Richard Mdluli and R2 million for former Gauteng Commissioner Mzwandile Petros. A separate affidavit also makes claims against General Jeremy Vearey. According to the *Cape Argus*, the statement, bearing an unauthorised Provincial Community Safety Department and police ombudsman stamp, alleged that Vearey was working with a gang boss who had ordered the murder of a 28s gang leader in Strand in the Cape. Theron also claimed Vearey received R2 million from Krejcir. In a later affidavit, from October 2015, Theron claimed Krejcir had paid Vearey a total of R6 million without explaining the reasons for these payments.

Theron makes other claims about cops, both high-ranking and low-level. 'A lot of guys visited Money Point while I was there. Glenn Agliotti … and others like Shadrack Sibiya, Richard Mdluli. Both Richard Mdluli and Shadrack Sibiya were always making social visits,' he said. Theron also claimed that a marked police double-cab bakkie came to Money Point every day, and when it pulled in Krejcir would go out and give the passenger a thick roll of R200 notes and the bakkie would leave.

Suspended ANC Western Cape chairperson Marius Fransman allegedly got R800 000, while ex-State Security Minister Siyabonga Cwele's name shows R4.7 million and R2.2 million. While under 'ANC', Man 1, Man 2 and Man 3 apparently got R500 000 each.

A later variation of his affidavit also lists a payment of R27 million to Mexican druglord Joaquín 'El Chapo' Guzmán, who escaped from prison in Mexico through an underground tunnel and spent more than six months on the run. It is unclear what this payment might have been for.

As apparent proof of all these claims, Theron attached annexures to his affidavit. Most of these are pencil sketches, personal notes in his own handwriting and his own bank statements. Not exactly bombshell documents or evidence of payments. This makes it difficult to determine the veracity of his claims. It is a personal account of what he saw, experienced and wrote down from a bank statement book. Across the board, there have been widespread denials of his claims.

Pierre Theron may be mostly in the shadows for now, but if he does take the stand to testify and he can back up the claims made in his affidavit, many people in very high-ranking positions will have a lot of explaining to do.

WHEN RADOVAN KREJCIR AND HIS CO-ACCUSED – INCLUDING three Hawks members – were finally convicted by Judge Colin Lamont in the Bheki Lukhele case in August 2015, it was in spite of, not because of, the police investigators. Lamont laboured this point in his ruling. Krejcir was convicted of attempted murder, kidnapping and drug dealing, and sentenced to 35 years in prison.

In a judgment handed down in a trial within a trial, around whether or not co-accused Desai Luphondo's confession statement could be admitted as evidence, Lamont attacked the integrity of investigating officer Freddy Ramuhala. Ramuhala was torn to shreds as Lamont ruled that the statement could not be used.

Lamont harshly criticised Ramuhala's conduct both in court and during his investigation. The judge said Ramuhala, 'at various points in time, gave evidence before this court which was patently false'.

'It is a particularly saddening feature that a senior police officer of this calibre, who is involved with and attached to a senior unit in the police, can conduct himself in this manner in a court of law and also towards persons whom he arrests,' Lamont said.

Lamont also found that Krejcir's claims of torture were true. This was based on a medical report provided by a doctor and blood tests that showed Krejcir had been 'shocked and tasered repeatedly'. Ramuhala was rebuked for allowing this to happen and for denying it had.

In his final judgment in the main trial, Lamont again took a swipe at Ramuhala, reminding everyone about his earlier ruling: 'I found Ramuhala to be dishonest, devious and totally untrustworthy in a different judgment in this case. I stand by what I said there. He in addition to his dishonesty was reckless and uncaring about the accuracy of his evidence.'

In the end, the convictions were as a result of objective evidence and carefully weighed testimony from those players who had turned state witness.

'In my view the true result of the police's improper and inadequate investigation in this case is that it put the state case at risk. The state case was dependent upon an unlawfully obtained confession which was excluded in evidence and such witnesses as the state was able to marshal. By the nature of the events many of those witnesses fall into the category of accomplice. I am conscious of the fact that accomplice evidence can be and often is easily manipulated. An accomplice can easily substitute one person for another while maintaining the true set of facts. The accomplices in this case are accomplices in respect of different facets of the case which overlap to an extent. Some were hunters, some were drug dealers. There is sufficient objectively accurate evidence and factually corroborated evidence for their evidence to be accepted.'

Despite all this, Ramuhala, Bongani Gininda and their team were applauded by Riah Phiyega. In a statement released following the guilty verdicts, Phiyega welcomed the conviction and praised the cops, although she added that there was 'no doubt that there are more police officers involved in criminality linked to Krejcir'.

'Today's conviction should send a loud message to people from anywhere in the world that South Africa cannot be used as a backyard for criminal activities and for fugitives to run to. We believe that once his trials are over, Bedfordview and the circles he was moving in will be much safer places for law-abiding people to move, and that the horror stories so often mentioned in the same sentence with his name will be a thing of the past,' Phiyega continued.

'The SAPS has, through a dedicated task team of detectives, ably led by Captain Freddy Ramuhala, worked tirelessly to ensure that Krejcir's criminal activities are properly investigated and that those that he is in business with also get to experience the full might of the law.'

Both Ramuhala and Gininda received promotions for the work they did on this case.

A 9MM PISTOL AND SEVERAL ROUNDS OF AMMUNITION STASHED inside an exercise bike with double-sided tape. A taser. A pepper-spray gun. A knife. A screwdriver hidden inside the handlebar of an exercise machine. Hacksaw blades in the shower pipe. Ten cellphones, one hidden in the sole of a shoe. Several batteries stored inside the base of an electric frying pan. Multiple memory sticks. And an official Correctional Services uniform.

How porous must our prisons be if this is what was found concealed in Radovan Krejcir's prison cell in Zonderwater Correctional Facility during a raid.

Having found himself trapped, Krejcir was planning an audacious escape bid and he was going to use the hidden gun to shoot his way out. Police had been listening in on his phone conversations, and on the morning of his planned escape, they hit, turning his cell upside down. He had allegedly spent years corrupting police officers to buttress his criminal activities, and now he had turned to paying prison officials to get what he wanted. A number of them were apparently in on the plot.

'The threat is in prison. There are inmates and prison officials that are helping him,' said police spokesperson Solomon Makgale. 'There is absolutely no way prison warders would not have been involved.'

Amongst the other items discovered was a diary that held the names of witnesses and investigators involved in all of Krejcir's cases, as well as a detailed sketch of the prison building. Officials believed that the Czech's son Denis's girlfriend, Marlene Nezar, known as 'Molly', had smuggled some of the items to Krejcir in food and care parcels. Ex-model Marissa Christopher, Krejcir's former mistress and the mother of his young daughter, was also believed to have slipped him some of the contraband.

The escape plan was for Krejcir to be escorted out of the prison by a specific female police officer who would be taking him to see a doctor. He would overpower her and then flee. There were alternatives to how he would get out. The most outrageous suggestion was that a helicopter had been leased to whisk him away from Zonderwater. A chartered plane was also an option to get him out of the country. More realistically, a Mercedes-Benz was on standby to spirit him across the border. The idea was to go to Swaziland, spend a night at the Royal Swazi Sun in Ezulwini, hop across to Mozambique and then fly off to Argentina. According to *The Star*, R246 million had been made available for the prison break.

An official with inside knowledge of the search explains what was going to happen and alleges that former Cyril Beeka-lieutenant-turned-Cape-Town-crime-boss, Nafiz Modack, was assisting Krejcir.

'Krejcir likes to write things down and that was in his notepad that he had written down. And believe it or not, Nafiz Modack was going to arrange a helicopter. Nafiz Modack was going to arrange the vehicles and the papers to cross the border. Soccer field, helicopter, something to cut the wire with. You could see on the video of the searches that they recorded, there was a firearm, a gun that shoots bullets! Four or five tasers. He used Apple phones, he glues a magnet to the back here, shoves it underneath the steel stuff. The gun was in the bike. The treadmill had the phones, underneath there stuck with the magnets.'

Another report in the *Sunday World* suggested that flamboyant criminal William 'King of Bling' Mbatha had actually been the one to assist Krejcir with this madcap idea by sketching a plan of the surrounding environment of the prison. Mbatha had previously been associated with Krejcir when it came to light that he had allegedly assisted him with another one of his conspiracies to murder five people, including O'Sullivan. The newspaper also suggested that a prisoner who was supposed to escape along with Krejcir had leaked the plan to prison authorities because he believed the Czech was going to use other convicts as human shields.

Weeks later a Zonderwater warder, Marthinus Johannes Herbst, was taken into custody. Marissa Christopher was also arrested when she arrived at the prison with her child. It was believed that, in order to finance the escape bid, she had sold a Mercedes that Krejcir had bought for her, and had also helped to arrange a helicopter. The case is ongoing in the Kempton Park magistrate's court.

To his credit, Krejcir never gave up. There was not only one escape plot. There were many. There was talk of a bomb threat in a courtroom. The most alarming was a plan for a 'full-on war' against Zonderwater prison, which involved nearly a dozen men with assault rifles storming the prison to free him. A Correctional Services official who was in on the plan had allegedly briefed them on the weaknesses in the prison's security system, who was on duty and the number of officials at each post.

Krejcir's plan was to escape to a nearby Pick n Pay in Cullinan and then to a safe house in Mamelodi. An associate would distribute R5 million to the gunmen, who would then carry out 'strategic executions' of residents in the area so that police would be distracted by the killings and Krejcir could make a run for it. The plan was elaborate, ambitious and far-fetched. The problem for Krejcir was that undercover cops were posing as the hired guns. They made recordings of the discussions during which they planned the escape – and the game was up. The prison official was arrested. So too was another prisoner with a long history of violent crime who was apparently assisting Krejcir.

While in prison, Krejcir also allegedly cooked up numerous attempts to kill people. There were the conspiracies to take out O'Sullivan and Ximba, but after he was convicted, he also allegedly plotted to assassinate Judge Colin Lamont. Reports suggested that he had flown a European hit man in to do the job, but the plan was scuppered by the cops and they arrested the man when he tried to visit Krejcir in prison to receive his orders.

As a result of all of this, security around Krejcir was ramped up considerably. The number of officers protecting him when travelling to court or the doctor was increased exponentially. In a highly unusual move, it was also decided to move him to the highest-level security facility in the country, C-Max in Kokstad, before he had even been sentenced. During his regular court appearances for ongoing cases, it takes a small army to escort him into the Johannesburg central business district. With sirens blaring, it takes six vehicles – marked and unmarked – as well as eight metro police officers on motorbikes. I once counted a total of 40 officers in full combat gear lining the walls of the courtroom during an appearance. Considering that the Sam Issa trial has been postponed more than 30 times, it costs the state a small fortune but is a necessity to ensure there is no embarrassing escape.

There is another perspective to consider here: the view of Krejcir himself and that of his family. The argument is that Krejcir is the victim of a carefully constructed conspiracy to see him behind bars at any cost in order to claim a public relations victory. According to Krejcir, the witnesses who testified against him were a sham, the raid on his cell was designed to discover planted contraband and he is being held in inhumane conditions that are a violation of his human rights.

I have remained in regular contact with Krejcir's family in the Czech Republic. His wife Katerina and his son Denis are technically unable to return to South Africa. According to the Department of Home Affairs, Katerina's residence permit has been revoked and Denis is not permitted entry into the country. This means Krejcir has practically no contact with them or with his younger son, Damian.

In July 2017 Krejcir's family emailed me a tranche of correspondence they had sent to prison authorities and to the judicial inspectorate of prisons complaining about alleged inhuman conditions and the deprivation of medical care Krejcir has experienced in prison. The communication covered several months and detailed an apparent infestation of scorpions and rodents in his cell. They also claimed that he was enduring psychological torture, as he was being deprived of the opportunity to contact loved ones and was being kept in solitary confinement.

There were four separate complaints, relating to his being kept in solitary confinement, the psychological torture he was enduring, his right to be held with other sentenced adult prisoners as 'a group', and his inability to receive court documentation and prepare accordingly. He was adamant that he was being targeted and deprived of amenities as part of a conspiracy under the auspices of a security threat.

In a separate complaint titled 'Gininda and Ramuhala Conspiracy Unveiled', Krejcir and his family list how the police investigators have allegedly conspired against him. He argues that Colonel Gininda and Ramuhala from the Hawks special investigating team were duly appointed and handpicked by then Police Commissioner Riah Phiyega to personally persecute him at all costs and to ensure that he was charged.

I sent a media query to the Department of Correctional Services listing Krejcir's complaints and asked them to respond. This is what they had to say:

> The Department of Correctional Services (DCS) hereby confirms that it has received correspondence, via the Office of the Inspecting Judge, from offender Radovan Krejcir's family, and their concerns were addressed accordingly.
>
> According to the Area Commissioner of the relevant centre where the said inmate is held, the allegations are unfounded. The said offender has been placed in a single cell, in line with his security classification. When inmates are placed in single cells for security reasons, it is to ensure maximum safety and security through close monitoring. DCS is not aware of the inmate being victimized in any way. The inmate is treated according to his security classification. The claims that he is being victimized are unsubstantiated.
>
> The claims by the family are untrue. According to our records, the inmate has been allowed to contact his family. However, the contact is closely monitored for security reasons. The offender has access to a public phone to call his family and legal representatives, in line with his privileges as per his security classification. Furthermore, the inmate is allowed visits from family and legal representatives. The allegation that he is prevented from his right to a fair trial is baseless.

Krejcir has subsequently brought a court application in an attempt to have his prison conditions amended. He still has a considerable sentence to serve and, with a number of trials on the go, his sentence may well be extended if he is convicted.

In March 2018, 11 years after he arrived in the country, the Kempton Park magistrate's court finally ruled that Krejcir could be extradited to the Czech Republic. At the time of going to print, the justice minister was deciding whether or not this would happen. Krejcir remains an enormous financial burden on the justice system and his multiple ongoing trials are clogging the court roll – these factors may well influence the minister's decision.

There have also been suggestions that talks are ongoing for some kind of deal to be arranged that would see Krejcir being returned to the Czech Republic to serve his sentence there. Sources say Czech officials are negotiating with South Africans for a resolution to the situation, although there has been no official confirmation. I suspect that this would be a preferable outcome for Krejcir as the prospect of his family ever returning to South Africa is highly unlikely. However, he has always maintained that his life would be in imminent danger should he step back onto Czech soil. Too many people want him dead.

Equally, though, I also believe that a threat to his life exists in South Africa. If it is true that he has corrupted as many senior officials as claimed, there are a lot of people who might want him gone. It would come as no surprise to me if prison officials one day released a statement saying he has died. As Sean Newman said about George Louca, dead men tell no tales.

OVER THE PERIOD THAT KREJCIR WAS EXPANDING HIS EMPIRE, wreaking havoc and then self-destructing, the police's Crime Intelligence unit, which should have been collating intelligence on him and building a case, was dealing with its own internal crisis. Richard Mdluli remained on suspension despite fraud and corruption charges being withdrawn against him and murder charges being provisionally withdrawn. The massively controversial decision regarding the fraud and corruption charges was taken by Lawrence Mrwebi in December 2011, while the murder charge decision was taken by Andrew Chauke, the ranking prosecutor in Joburg, in February 2012. Chauke found that an inquest should be held instead.

An inquest was set up at the Boksburg magistrate's court in 2012. Witnesses were called and evidence was led and Magistrate Jurg Viviers found that there was no conclusive evidence linking Mdluli to Oupa Ramogibe's murder.

'What appeared to be a skeleton in the cupboard for Mdluli was, with respect, only a ghost,' said the magistrate. 'The only way of finding the answers would be with the assistance of the mythical Jacques Aymar and his divine rod,' he added, in reference to seventeenth-century French stonemason Aymar who claimed he could trace fugitives using a divining rod. The magistrate said it did not make sense that someone involved in a love triangle would run the risk of bringing five others into a plan to kill the third person in the triangle and be successful. Viviers found there was no evidence to implicate Mdluli and three others in the death of Oupa Ramogibe, and Mdluli's legal team described the decision as a 'vindication'.

Lobby group Freedom Under Law went to court seeking an order reviewing both the murder and fraud/corruption decisions by Mrwebi and

Chauke. As is so often the case with contentious decisions involving the law and the criminal justice system, civil society stepped into the breach in order to protect the Constitution and the rule of law. But in response to the court action, National Police Commissioner Riah Phiyega described the case as a 'fuss'.

On 23 September 2013, while the news attention was focused on the Westgate shopping centre terrorist attack unfolding in Nairobi, Judge John Murphy handed down a significant ruling in the Freedom Under Law application. The ruling was scathing, heavily critical of the National Prosecuting Authority and the police.

Murphy set aside the decisions taken by both Mrwebi and Chauke. He ordered the national director of public prosecutions to reinstate criminal charges and National Police Commissioner Riah Phiyega to restore disciplinary proceedings against Mdluli 'without delay'. The decision to reinstate Mdluli as head of Crime Intelligence was set aside.

'The prosecutors, the DPP and the IGI [inspector-general of intelligence] all opposed the withdrawal of those charges. [Glynnis] Breytenbach wrote a detailed memo to the NDPP [Nomgcobo Jiba] cogently motivating why the charges should not be withdrawn.'

Murphy found that Mrwebi 'saw no need to engage with the merits' of the case against Mdluli. 'He took the decision without regard to the merits of a prosecution in the interests of justice, and thus ignored mandatory relevant considerations,' said Murphy. 'The decision and instruction by Mrwebi to withdraw the fraud and corruption charges must be set aside. It was illegal, irrational, based on irrelevant considerations and material errors of law, and ultimately so unreasonable that no reasonable prosecutor could have taken it.'

Murphy also criticised Chauke's decision to refer the murder matter to an inquest rather than a criminal prosecution: '[An inquest] is not aimed at establishing anyone's guilt and could not competently do so. An inquest is no substitute for criminal prosecution because it cannot determine guilt. Chauke's motive for referring the matter to an inquest is therefore dubious. The identity of the deceased was known, as was the cause of his death. The only outstanding case was the culpability of Mdluli.'

348

Murphy found that there was indeed a prima facie case against Mdluli in the murder matter. 'There are affidavits from seven witnesses who personally witnessed Mdluli threatening to kill Ramogibe, or threatening and assaulting other people,' he said. 'This evidence presents a compelling prima facie case against Mdluli.'

Murphy also took Phiyega to task for her handling of the matter.

'She apparently sees no need to place any obstacles in the way of Mdluli's return to work, despite her constitutional duty to investigate allegations against him and the unfeasibility of his holding of a position of trust at the highest level in SAPS,' the judge said. 'For as long as there are serious unresolved questions concerning Mdluli's integrity, he cannot lawfully act as a member and senior officer of the SAPS, or exercise the powers and duties associated with high office in the SAPS.'

It was a resounding victory for Freedom Under Law and a devastating blow for the NPA, the SAPS and Mdluli. But, of course, the judgment went on appeal to the Supreme Court of Appeal (SCA) in Bloemfontein, which found that Murphy had gone too far in his ruling.

While the SCA confirmed the setting aside of Mrwebi's decision to withdraw fraud and corruption charges, it reversed the order setting aside Chauke's decision. It found that Chauke withdrew the murder charge pending the outcome of the inquest that he had requested in order to avoid a fragmented trial.

A year later, with Mdluli still on fully paid suspension, the NPA announced that it would reinstate some of the 18 charges against him in the Ramogibe matter, including kidnapping and assault. Crucially, though, he was not charged with murder. That trial is under way, with the state having called witnesses and led evidence. At the close of the state's case, Mdluli brought an application for a discharge, to have the case against him thrown out, but was unsuccessful.

Mdluli's lawyer has argued that the charges against his client were a conspiracy by high-ranking officers who wanted to oust him as national police commissioner. Mdluli has continuously maintained that there was an operation called Ulibambe Lingashoni (Don't let the sun set), which was a project engineered by those who conspired against him. The trial is ongoing.

Mdluli remains uncharged for corruption and fraud despite the High Court and SCA finding that he should be prosecuted. In July 2015, the Commercial Crimes Court in Pretoria struck his fraud and corruption charges off the roll due to incomplete police investigations. It is expected that the charges will be re-enrolled, but there is no time frame for when this will happen.

During his seven-year suspension Mdluli netted R8.3 million, including a basic salary of almost R5 million, a non-pensionable cash allowance of nearly R1.4 million, an employee pension contribution of almost R800 000 and a vehicle allowance of over R700 000. This also included a 'service bonus' of more than R400 000. It emerged in March 2018 that a further R4.2 million was paid to Mdluli upon his retirement, outside of his normal pension benefits. This means he earned in excess of R12 million during his seven-year suspension and subsequent retirement.

The police have given no indication as to why Mdluli's internal disciplinary hearing simply never happened. If previous patterns are anything to go by, it was conveniently dragged out until his retirement so that he could be sent out to pasture with a full pension. No questions asked.

IN THE CASE OF RADOVAN KREJCIR, SARS HAD SUCCEEDED WHERE other agencies had failed. Under the leadership of Johann van Loggerenberg, they had cut off Krejcir's supply chain and he was immobilised as a result. In May 2014, the taxman obtained a final preservation order against Krejcir and his companies. This was the death knell.

His mother, Nadezda Krejcirova, attempted to transfer money from the Czech Republic but SARS discovered the account and placed it under preservation. A trust set up by Krejcir's lawyers received the same treatment, as did a non-resident bank account. Krejcir was fighting battles on several fronts and running up massive legal bills in numerous trials. His ability to pay his lawyers was diminished and his resources depleted.

For many, the Krejcir case is a prime example of how successful Van Loggerenberg's unit was as a law enforcement functionary. It is to this case that Van Loggerenberg himself points in his book when justifying the effectiveness and necessity of the work done by the High-Risk Investigation Unit (HRIU):

> *I want to pause here to reflect on the impact that investigations, such as those SARS conducted into Krejcir, had on the HRIU and other units involved. The men and women who were part of these units dealt with organized crime and sophisticated criminals, who were generally dangerous people. At night, while most of us were asleep, or during the day when we were going about our normal business, they worked tirelessly to combat crime. All the while their lives were in danger. No case proves this better than this one.*

All of this changed in late 2014 and early 2015 when SARS was rocked by a massive headline-grabbing scandal that hit the front pages of the *Sunday Times*. There were allegations that the HRIU was a rogue unit, that members were running a brothel, that they were spying on Zuma and his associates, and had entered into illegal tax settlements. The narrative became entrenched in the public mind following a succession of sensational reports published in the *Sunday Times* in particular.

But it later became apparent that there was never any rogue unit. The newspaper was forced to apologise for its reporting on the matter. Auditing firm KPMG was left embarrassed after it admitted fault and retracted its report on the unit. But the damage was done. Van Loggerenberg and his team of investigators, who had a record of nailing tax criminals, were tarnished. They lost their reputations and their jobs.

In February 2015, Van Loggerenberg resigned from SARS after 16 years of service. What followed was an exodus of skill and capability as his staff followed him out of the organisation. It devastated the agency and hollowed out the entire capacity of the teams that had brought down Krejcir and so many others.

As a result, cases already on the books were mothballed. Some stalled, others were neglected, while even more were intentionally scrapped. The implications of this are difficult to fathom. By way of example, when Van Loggerenberg left SARS there were still many legs of the Krejcir investigation still to be pursued. This never happened and it meant criminals were let off the hook.

According to sources, SARS investigators picked up in Krejcir's bank accounts where money was paid to specific police officers. Most of these payments were made in cash or were off-book, but in some instances the money had gone into bank accounts. To back this up, there had also been testimony at the tax inquiry to confirm that payments were made to corrupt cops. And yet not one police officer has been prosecuted for taking money from Krejcir. Ever.

That would not have been the case if Van Loggerenberg and his team were still operational. It was always part of the plan, and part of Project K, that they would have gone after them. But it all came to a grinding halt.

One of the last remaining members of the so-called Rogue Unit, who stayed behind when most people moved on, agreed to give me an insider's perspective of how things had changed. The person has since resigned from the organisation.

'I felt like I was part of a team. Our morals and values matched and we were part of a team that had integrity, fighting for a greater good. We were chipping away at the bad guys, from illegal cigarettes to rhino-horn syndicates. It was all part of the bigger picture. That capacity is now gone, dissolved by [SARS commissioner] Tom Moyane. There's a team with some of the leftovers but the same capability doesn't exist.

'We were like lepers in the organisation, without any protection. We were questioned by the Hawks without any protection or support from SARS. What we did wasn't rubbish diving. Pravin [Gordhan] knew, Ivan [Pillay] knew, it was a full project signed off through the system. It wasn't clandestine. I felt dirty afterwards but we had done nothing wrong.'

The former 'Rogue' member says that with the current capability at SARS today, Krejcir and others like him will have a field day. 'He could do whatever he wanted. There would be no limits. There's still very good people at SARS but without proper support from the top, I don't know how much power they have. When I started, the energy was palpable. If you were even suspected of taking a bribe, you were shunned. There was integrity and pride and then a real switch when Tom Moyane started. People started to come in late, didn't want to put in the extra effort. You could feel the difference. It became pointless, like putting pieces in a black hole.'

IN MID-2017, I WENT TO SEE JOHANN VAN LOGGERENBERG TO TALK to him about the Krejcir case in particular and the state of the criminal justice system in general. We chatted in a boardroom at a forensic consultancy in Rivonia. There are still a lot of things he can't talk about as he is bound by law. He appeared more relaxed than he ever did during the height of the so-called Rogue Unit saga, but I could tell he was still burning about the whole debacle. Like many others to whom I've spoken who are now outside the state, there is an element of despondency about the current situation.

'I think the criminal justice system is broken,' he says matter-of-factly. 'It's worse now than then, but it was bad then already and the problem is that unless something sparks them into action, they do nothing, they just do nothing,' he says, referring to the Krejcir investigation. 'The cops are that weak now and they were that weak then. I remember how, I'm talking about hundreds and hundreds of people who would come to SARS to my office to meet with me and say we want you as SARS to investigate this because we've been to the police, we've been to the Hawks, we've been to the NPA, we've been to the AFU, nothing happens. You are the only guys who seem to be doing anything about criminals.'

Van Loggerenberg suggests that the problem with law enforcement is that it does not take a holistic approach. Cops go for big wins and easy victories. 'They didn't approach crime in the way we did. They didn't have the big picture; they were transactional. So, they would rather bust a truck of cigarettes than look at, well, where does this truck of cigarettes fit into an organised criminal enterprise and let's go for the head. They just don't operate that way; they never have, and I don't see any evidence of them doing it now.

'Probably the biggest challenge in respect of organised crime in this country is the fact that the criminal justice system and its different parts do not function, they are not organised and they do not work as a single system. You then have this institutional rivalry, and I think there's no better example of the undermining of one part of the system than looking at SARS and the criminal justice system. SARS was a small part of the criminal justice system; the SARS enforcement capacity at its highest level in the many years was less than 1500 people. That's tiny in comparison to the police or the NPA or the Hawks, but we were just so undermined.'

Van Loggerenberg believes that Krejcir was able to expand and position himself as a big mob boss because the criminal justice system was so fractured and so weak.

'He operated with absolute impunity, in open sight. It was not really necessary for him to bribe police officials. Those bribes that he paid wasn't to make cases go away or for protection or anything. It was for information. He needed to know if there was any possible future threat coming his way and he needed to know it in advance. So, it's not the kind of classic bribe where you've got me, now I'm gonna pay you to get off. It was him infiltrating the police and the law enforcement environment with a view to have early warning systems in place.'

Van Loggerenberg regrets having left the project in limbo, as he had plans for far greater things. 'It's a great pity that the initial project and the scope that I had in mind for it never saw itself to its logical conclusion in the end, because had that been the case it would not have ended with the sale of the Krejcir properties to liquidate against the debt and the cars. It would have included looking at the additional role players, and some of those additional role players would have been Mabasa and Steyn and Agliotti and all the lawyers and so on and so on. That would have been the logical conclusion of our project, but it seems the plug was just pulled on Krejcir's debt and that's the end of it – and that should never have been the case.'

With the current state of law enforcement in the country, I wonder what kind of position we would be in were 'another Krejcir' to arrive on our shores and attempt to take advantage of the situation. Van Loggerenberg's answer is enlightening in terms of the perspective it provides and, at the same time, alarming.

'There are many Krejcirs already, and there will be more – because they grow. They start as micro and small enterprises and, if left unchecked, they become bigger. I never considered Krejcir to be at the sort of apex level of organised crime. I consider him to be a medium, small-to-mediumish organised criminal enterprise and there are many of them in this country. Some operate on a localised level, so you would see that in the form of the gangs mostly operating in the Western Cape. At that level, they've got that kind of turnover. Those protection racket people in Cape Town, you know the bouncer gang outfits. You have the same in Joburg; you have the same but on a smaller scale in Durban, but the sort of localised crooks. I think the destruction, however, that Krejcir created in this country, in my view, had more to do with the display of the inability of the state to deal quickly with somebody who became so public so overnight.'

For many years, the Krejcir case eroded public confidence in the state's ability to fight a real organised crime threat.

'It's the most telling tell-tale sign for me of a sick criminal justice system, that somebody who's on an Interpol warrant, who had a particular history in another country, a developed country, of organised criminal enterprise. He's been convicted, that country wants him. He must go serve his sentence there. He then comes into this country and it takes so many years for our criminal justice system to bring him to book. That means there's something wrong – something wrong in our system.

'I don't believe you can attribute it to corruption. It's not corruption. He didn't bribe people to stay out of jail for all those years. It just took so many years for the system to wake up and realise, okay, we've got to do something about it. Now by then how many people had been murdered? How much money had been stolen? Look how much time it's taken to convict him and the energy and the resources. And, you know, it's valiant of those people who finally brought him to book, but we have to ask ourselves, if it takes so long to deal with somebody whose effective turnover as a criminal enterprise is around R110 million, you know that's a small government tender. Now we read about big fraud or allegations every Sunday. I mean, there's exposé after exposé by the media and again, you know, I don't see a responsive criminal justice system at all. It's a kind of apathy.'

IT WASN'T JUST SARS THAT WAS BEING HOLLOWED OUT. ALMOST EVERY other law enforcement agency and state institution with a capacity to fight crime was intentionally eviscerated for factional, political purposes. There is an entire book to be written on each of these institutions and much has been penned about them already, but, in crude summary, many good, dedicated, hard-working civil servants were forced out of their jobs, leaving behind organisations crippled, unable to perform their required functions. This specifically included the SAPS (Crime Intelligence and the Hawks), police watchdog IPID and the National Prosecuting Authority. And it all happened over a period of less than a year.

A month after Van Loggerenberg resigned, in March 2015, Robert McBride was first suspended as head of IPID for allegedly altering a report on former Hawks boss Anwa Dramat and Hawks Gauteng head Shadrack Sibiya. They were accused of illegally deporting a group of Zimbabweans wanted for murder.

McBride went to court and was ultimately able to reclaim his position. In April 2015, Dramat resigned as head of the Hawks after facing suspension in connection with the illegal renditions. In May 2015, Van Loggerenberg's superiors at SARS, Ivan Pillay and Peter Richter, resigned over the rogue unit allegations. Also in May 2015, then NPA head Mxolisi Nxasana took a golden handshake of R17 million to leave after effectively being pushed out by Nomgcobo Jiba and Jacob Zuma. In September 2015, Sibiya lost his job over the Zimbabwe renditions.

In most instances, the positions of these individuals were either left vacant or were filled on an acting basis, allowing the roles to decay. In others, blatantly unfit or more malleable candidates were installed. There was a remarkably similar pattern followed in all of these instances and Dramat,

McBride and Pillay later put out a joint statement stating that all these events at various state organisations were related.

'There appears to be a remarkable coincidence in the methods used to remove officials from these institutions, the players involved and their intersecting interests,' they said.

'In our view, attacks on individuals in these institutions are aimed at undermining the fight against corruption. A key part of all of our mandates was to investigate cases of corruption. In reviewing our individual experiences over recent weeks, we have discovered a convergence in the cases that we were working on. A common thread is that cases under investigation involved individuals or entities with questionable relationships to those in public office. Most of these cases involved state tenders of some kind that were awarded due to patronage with influential individuals in public office.'

They stated that the manner in which officials were removed followed a similar pattern: 'Internal documents or "allegations" from within institutions are leaked to select journalists. Working in tandem with "anonymous" sources, facts are distorted in the media … After the information is leaked, the institution in question then launches an "investigation" into the accused officials, using news reports as pretext. The results of these "investigations" are then leaked to the same journalists again.'

At the police, Riah Phiyega was officially suspended over her handling of the Marikana massacre. She was replaced on an acting basis by Kgomotso Phahlane. After a series of controversies around national commissioners, it would only get worse with Phahlane. In the short time he was in office he became mired in controversy and was the subject of a major corruption probe by IPID and Paul O'Sullivan.

The investigation centred round Phahlane's luxury home in the exclusive Sable Hills Waterfront Estate. On a policeman's salary, Phahlane bought a property for R8 million, some of which was allegedly paid to the contractor in cash, in plastic shopping bags out of the boot of a car. His relationship with the so-called interior decorator was questioned. She also happened to be the director of a company that had received a multimillion-rand tender from the police when Phahlane was the divisional commissioner for

359

Forensic Services. Phahlane bought an R80 000 sound system for his luxury home through this contractor. IPID also probed his wife's R4.3-million fleet of luxury cars and investigated the top cop for more than R1 million in 'gratuities' he had allegedly received from a Pretoria car dealer. He bought and sold a variety of cars to the dealer and, through the transactions, was accused of making more than R1 million.

IPID, under McBride, along with O'Sullivan, was pushing this investigation. The acting national commissioner retaliated and O'Sullivan and his associate, Sarah Jane Trent, were charged with fraud, extortion and conspiracy to contravene the IPID Act. They were accused of accessing confidential files containing information about Phahlane's house and of impersonating IPID officers. Two of the IPID investigators were also summoned to appear in court. A team of police investigators from the North West, under Major General Ntebo 'Jan' Mabula, was running the investigation.

An ugly turf war had erupted between the police and IPID as a result. The Irishman vowed to continue pursuing Phahlane and insisted he would bring him down, along with the North West cops. Finally, in February 2018, Phahlane and his wife Beauty, a brigadier in the police, handed themselves over and appeared in court on criminal charges of fraud and corruption. They were released on bail.

Phahlane, Berning Ntlemeza and Richard Mdluli were dubbed 'The Big Three' by O'Sullivan, who directed a great deal of time, energy and money at bringing them to book.

In September 2015, Ntlemeza took over as the head of the Hawks. He was the largely unknown general from Limpopo who had assisted Richard Mdluli in writing a report constructing a political conspiracy against him. Ntlemeza was overwhelmingly viewed as an Mdluli ally and was accused of being part of a conspiracy to remove Dramat and Sibiya and replace them. Not long after being appointed to the job, he undertook a major reshuffle, appointing new provincial heads across the board. An IPID investigator deposed to an affidavit in which he stated that Ntlemeza, Mdluli and their 'political principals' had hatched a plan to have Ntlemeza head up the Hawks and that the whole rendition implicating Dramat, Sibiya and McBride was all part of the plan. A court later found that Ntlemeza lacked integrity and honour and was dishonest and unfit for the job.

Pretoria High Court Judge Elias Matojane said in his judgment: 'In my view, the conduct of the third respondent [Ntlemeza] shows that he is biased and dishonest. To further show that third respondent is dishonest and lacks integrity and honour, he made false statements under oath.'

'Mal Bennie', as Ntlemeza was known, was eventually fired by then Police Minister Fikile Mbalula. That too was not without its drama – Ntlemeza defied a court order, pitched up for work, signed out a Hawks vehicle and phone and disappeared in Pretoria, setting up a very public standoff with the minister. The Ntlemeza debacle left the Hawks in disarray.

In Gauteng, Prince Mokotedi – former NPA Head of Integrity and one of the so-called cabal who went after Glynnis Breytenbach – was, surprisingly, appointed to replace Shadrack Sibiya as head of the Hawks after Sibiya was worked out. Mokotedi had resigned from the NPA ahead of a disciplinary inquiry. Between Phahlane, Mdluli, Ntlemeza and Mokotedi, the police, the Hawks and Crime Intelligence appeared to be well and truly captured.

At the NPA, Shaun Abrahams was promoted three rungs to become the national director of public prosecutions in place of Mxolisi Nxasana. Although he was vocal about being his own man and politically untainted, he was viewed from within the organisation as being a 'Jiba man'. He entrenched this perception when he made the controversial decision to withdraw fraud and perjury charges against Jiba in August 2015. The charges related to Jiba's handling of the case involving KZN Hawks boss Johan Booysen. A High Court found that Abrahams's reasoning for discontinuing the prosecution was wrong in law and that Abrahams was incorrect in his view that Jiba and Lawrence Mrwebi were doing their jobs well. In September 2016, Jiba and Mrwebi were struck from the roll of advocates for the role they played in protecting Mdluli.

In a scathing judgment, Francis Legodi found the pair unfit to practise as advocates. In reference to the Mdluli matter, he said: 'I cannot believe that two officers of the court who hold such high positions in the prosecuting authority will stoop so low for the protection and defence of one individual who had been implicated in serious offences.

'In fact, taking into account the kind of personality [referring to Mdluli]

Mrwebi and Jiba had to deal with, they should have stood firm and vigorous on the ground by persisting to prosecute Mdluli on fraud and corruption charges.

'By their conduct, they did not only bring the prosecuting authority and the legal profession into disrepute, but have also brought the good office of the President of the Republic of South Africa into disrepute by failing to prosecute Mdluli who inappropriately suggested that he was capable of assisting the president to win the party presidential election in Mangaung during 2011, should the charges be dropped against him.' Jiba and Mrwebi are appealing the judgment.

While all of this was playing out, the situation at Crime Intelligence was also becoming increasingly surreal. In the seven years he was suspended, Mdluli's position was filled by a dozen different acting candidates. And almost every one of these individuals left because of a controversy of their own. At one point there was an 'acting acting' head of Crime Intelligence because the acting commander was suspended. Chris Ngcobo was placed on special leave because of discrepancies with his qualifications. Pat Mokushane was fired for not having proper security clearance, having a criminal record and for allegedly running a side business from his office. Not to mention the alleged affair he had with a subordinate's wife. Most recently, former Zuma bodyguard King Ngcobo was embroiled in controversy when reports surfaced that he had submitted a fake matric certificate. Meanwhile, Mdluli clung onto the job while sitting at home in Boksburg. Those in the know in policing circles will tell you that, in reality, it was Mdluli who was still pulling the strings despite being on suspension. There were even suggestions that he was also moonlighting for state security while supposedly sitting at home.

The astonishing tale of a rogue cop with the nickname of 'Captain KGB' is perhaps the best illustration of just how defunct and debilitated Crime Intelligence was over this period and of the proximity of organised crime to the very police unit that was meant to investigate it and to those who wielded political power.

Morris Tshabalala is a criminal who worked for the cops. He is an armed robber who specialised in cash-in-transit heists. Tshabalala was first arrested in 1994 for a heist in Mamelodi in Pretoria and was convicted and sent to prison. But, instead of handing himself over to serve time in jail, he joined the police. He was on the lam and became a reservist in 1996. Tshabalala had intel on which the cops were able to act. He was registered as a Crime Intelligence agent in 2001, received Crime Intelligence training in 2003 and only got official security clearance in 2014. Police documents show that Tshabalala received a commendation from Commissioner Jackie Selebi in 2006 and was lauded for his role in helping to bring down top organised crime kingpins.

Tshabalala lurked in the shadows, straddling the cash-in-transit gangs and the police, sometimes operating undercover or, as his critics suggest, genuinely carrying out armed heists. In 2013, he was arrested again, this time in Sasolburg in Mpumalanga, in connection with a heist involving a Bidvest Protea Coin van. Three guards were wounded and R3 million was stolen in the incident. His co-accused was another CI officer, Willby Molefe. By this point, Tshabalala had earned a reputation as 'Captain KGB' and his arrest hit the headlines. His trial was covered in the media and he was ultimately convicted and sent to jail yet again, this time for 10 years.

According to Paul O'Sullivan, KGB had established links with the same criminal networks that Radovan Krejcir had utilised, and had executed heists with some of the same players. As an example of this, Phumlani Ncube, the debt collector whose bullet-riddled body was found near Heidelberg, was allegedly killed by Krejcir's hit men. Ncube, who was in the witness protection programme, was also believed to be a key witness against Captain KGB in the Sasolburg case. A second state witness against KGB, known only as Siphiwe, was also murdered. Both men were kidnapped and executed within days of each other.

We all assumed that Tshabalala had disappeared for a while, serving his jail term. The reality was very different. KGB served only two and a half years before being released on parole. But he walked out of prison and straight back into the police. He began receiving a state salary of between R20 000 and R30 000 per month, as well as the use of a state vehicle with a petrol allowance and a cellphone allowance. This was all despite the fact that he had a criminal record and had been convicted of a violent crime. It was also believed that Phahlane had played a key role in bringing KGB back into the SAPS and had personally signed him back on.

In 2017 I began to hear rumblings that KGB was back at Crime Intelligence. I sent an official query to Phahlane's office in February and again in March, asking if KGB was back at work. Twice, Phahlane's spokesperson explicitly denied this after making 'extensive queries'.

In February I received this response: 'It is evident that people are hard at work circulating rumours aimed at discrediting the acting national commissioner. The involvement of the person and the case referred to are foreign to the acting national commissioner.'

And then in March: 'I have been advised that the status quo of my previous response remains unchanged.'

I then began to hear that KGB had been involved in a heist at OR Tambo in March 2017. A gang posing as police and ACSA officials had made off with R200 million in foreign currency. KGB was supposedly part of the gang and had vanished after the heist. Again I went back to the cops. Nothing.

Then a senior general in the police, one with more than 25 years' experience, authored a report that was sent to IPID and to the Parliamentary Portfolio Committee on Police. In it, he made serious allegations of fraud, corruption and defeating the ends of justice and racketeering against Phahlane and other senior generals. Included in the report was the full extent of KGB's alleged criminal activity:

> The current information is that the robbery that took place at OR Tambo International Airport (ORTIA) recently where millions of rands (or dollars) were stolen, Tshabalala was among the robbers and at present nobody knows his whereabouts. There is circumstantial evidence that places him at the scene and he was part of the robbery and this is known to the investigating team as well as CI management and the acting national commissioner. Brigadier Botsotso Moukangwe has been appointed as the investigating officer to ensure that the evidence is diverted from

Tshabalala. General Phahlane instructed that this be done, as it is an embarrassment to the police. General Phahlane is more concerned with the police not being embarrassed, than apprehending Tshabalala.

The anonymous general also suggested that Crime Intelligence was trying to cover up KGB's involvement in the robbery by claiming that there was a section 252A application in place, which allows cops to go undercover and participate in intelligence operations.

KGB was in the wind. Only, he wasn't. In January 2018, he was arrested in Pretoria while checking in with his parole officer. He was charged with fraud, theft and corruption for allegedly defrauding the Crime Intelligence secret service account of more than half a million rand.

The charges related to blinds and curtains for safe houses in Pretoria – invoices were submitted by KGB and authorised by a major general. A sum of R563 005 was paid out in cash. It's alleged that the cost of the blinds and curtains was much less than claimed and that he pocketed the remainder of the money.

Included in the document authored by the anonymous general were the allegations around the blinds, as well as an invoice as proof. Acting Crime Intelligence financial boss, Obed Nemutanzhela, allegedly approved the requests from KGB – ironically, Nemutanzhela was put into the position to tighten controls around the slush fund following the Mdluli allegations.

During KGB's bail application, prosecutor Chris Smith revealed that KGB was also under investigation in connection with a R50 million budget allocated to a Crime Intelligence operation at the ANC's Mangaung elective conference. The money was not properly accounted for. The suggestion has long been that KGB was in charge of doling out bribes for votes at the conference. IPID also claimed that sources stated that KGB was well protected by politicians and police management.

'In 2012, he was appointed as the head of an operation named Rapid Deployment Intelligence. The operation was established to conduct intelligence work for Mangaung 53rd ANC conference which took place in

December 2012, claimed IPID national head of investigations, Matthews Sesoko, in an affidavit. 'He was provided with a budget of about R50 million. The budget was not properly accounted for and, as a result, IPID and the office of the inspector-general of intelligence will be conducting investigation in this regard.'

In his defence, KGB confirmed that he was a Crime Intelligence operative. He said he had resigned in 2016 and that he had signed on as an agent. He was paid monthly by his handler. He confirmed that he was indeed involved in a programme, but he could not divulge any of the details.

Morris Tshabalala was denied bail and was finally fired from the SAPS a few days later. The law eventually caught up with him but it took over a decade. For the record, Phahlane publicly denied that he played any role in bringing KGB back into the police, a denial that infuriated Paul O'Sullivan.

'Phahlane's lying. The lies are queuing up to jump off his tongue. [Tshabalala] was reinstated by Phahlane after coming out of prison and he's trying to deny it,' insisted O'Sullivan. 'KGB's role, as a lot of people in CI, is to look after himself and make money but to be free of criminal sanction, they have to perform tasks here and there for their masters. Some of the heists that are being carried out are being carried out by the cops.'

By all accounts, KGB was rogue, running his own criminal operation while also wielding the power and influence of being a Crime Intelligence cop and a go-to guy for politicians. A 'fixer', if you like.

In his book, *The President's Keepers*, Jacques Pauw made reference to the existence of rogue police units that were 'roaming the land' and that they were 'implicated in dirty tricks like break-ins at state institutions, illegal interceptions and intimidation' to ensure that sensitive dockets were stashed away. Pauw was told by his sources that two groups of rogue cops had been identified – one the remnants of Ntlemeza's men and known as the 'Eastern Cape group' operating from rooms in the Sheraton Hotel in Pretoria, the second a group made up of a mixture of Crime Intelligence and Hawks that has 'skulked for several months in the Court Classique Hotel in Arcadia'. The rogue cops apparently kill cases, threaten witnesses and fiddle with dockets in between booze binges and stripper parties.

Devastatingly, the result of all of this is a state that is unable and apparently unwilling to hold criminals accountable because the rule of law has been eroded to such an extent that it is almost invisible. The leadership that was at the helm of these institutions has been sidelined and replaced with individuals who are so distracted by personal vendettas and driving political agendas that the real work of fighting crime is being neglected. On the ground, the skill and experience required to tackle organised crime has also been eviscerated, which means that should the political will be there to turn around the institutions, the capacity has been lost. It will take years to rebuild and it will be an almost insurmountable challenge to reclaim that talent from the private sector. It is a dismal picture that should leave you very worried.

THE SERIES OF EVENTS IN THE UNDERWORLD AND THE OVERWORLD, in the criminal justice system and in law enforcement, ultimately brought about a meeting at Radovan Krejcir's Kloof Road mansion on 3 December 2016. Many of the characters who have featured in this narrative attended that meeting and it became the subject of an alleged plot of treason, assassination and espionage. If ever there was an incident in which the lines between good and evil were drawn in the country, it was this meeting. Here it was made clear who fell on which side, the accusers or the accused.

In December, the new head of the Hawks in Gauteng, Prince Mokotedi, opened a criminal case. The affidavit he used as the basis of the case was leaked to several journalists.

In it, Mokotedi says he was informed by a source that a meeting was held at Krejcir's house, which is 'now owned by Mr Paul O'Sullivan through intricate company shareholding'. The attendees included O'Sullivan, Robert McBride, who is the current head of IPID, Shadrack Sibiya, now the head of anti-corruption at the City of Joburg, 'some persons who were representatives of AfriForum, a minority rights interest group for Afrikaners', and members of the Democratic Alliance. They had a braai and discussed many things and 'they identified certain people as targets for vexatious criminal investigations and shaming in the media'. Apparently, 'the motive for targeting these individuals is that they are close to or are supporters of the president of the Republic of South Africa, President Jacob Zuma'.

According to Mokotedi, the people targeted included then acting Police Commissioner Kgomotso Phahlane, then head of Hawks Berning Ntlemeza, Mokotedi himself, NPA boss Shaun Abrahams and the Director of the State Security Agency Arthur Fraser. He claims that the attendees agreed that O'Sullivan should collect information and 'dig dirt' that would implicate these individuals in corruption and criminality and that cases must be finalised as soon as possible for prosecution.

Mokotedi goes on to allege that O'Sullivan was being assisted by Crime Intelligence cop Candice Coetzee, who at the time was on suspension for giving O'Sullivan information without authorisation. She was later cleared and allowed to return to work and was promoted. The group 'further agreed that Mr Robert McBride and Mr Shadrack Sibiya should use the resources at their disposal in their respective areas of employment to collect information on the targeted persons and put pressure on politicians to have these targeted individuals removed from office'.

Mokotedi then makes a claim in his affidavit about a potential revolution. He says they agreed that the activities they planned against the targeted group should be used to 'mobilise for an "Arab Spring" type of revolt in the country'. He alleges that O'Sullivan had been moving in and out of the country to mobilise support from abroad and to source funds. The 3 December meeting was meant to 'concretise and put in action a plan to destabilise the security forces of the country and to oust the president of the country through popular revolt'. This amounted to high treason and igniting a revolution.

He refers to another meeting that took place in April 2016, one that was attended by former Hawks members, agents from the Zimbabwean intelligence agency and Serbian nationals. The purpose of this meeting was to discuss how to deal with Ntlemeza and Mokotedi. It's claimed that those at the meeting resolved that both men should be assassinated. They would use foreign hit men, who would then be able to sneak out of the country.

'It is apparent that the group that met on 3 December 2016 at the house that belonged to Radovan Krejcir have the same intentions as the one that met at the hotel in Sandton and that there are those people who belong to both groups and or were present in both meetings.' Mokotedi wanted them all investigated for high treason, espionage, conspiracy to commit murder and corruption, amongst other crimes. The explosive affidavit and its charges were a clear escalation of the ongoing struggle for power within the country's law enforcement agencies.

When news of this affidavit broke, it was met with scepticism, particularly around some of the outlandish allegations. O'Sullivan reacted by labelling Mokotedi as a 'dishonest criminal with a badge'.

O'Sullivan described Mokotedi's founding affidavit as a work of fiction. There were attempts to get Mokotedi to take a polygraph test, but he pulled out at the last minute. McBride took the test and passed.

'This reduces the whole thing to nothing more than hearsay, if ever there was a source, which I believe is also a lie by Mokotedi. Without a sworn statement from Mokotedi's fictitious source, the document is not worth the paper it is written on. I notice that Mokotedi admits, publicly, that he and the others in his cabal are "close to or are supporters of … President Jacob Zuma". This is evidence that they have breached their oath of office.

'Now, when it is clear that Zuma's criminal empire is falling, which includes the likes of Mokotedi … this is their last-ditch attempt at avoiding the inevitable long road to prison,' O'Sullivan added.

As recently as January 2018, O'Sullivan told me that this docket was still alive and was being used by his foes in the SAPS as a vehicle to gather evidence against him. 'There's a whole team allocated to it; they're still out there. There's a colonel that's driving it and he's knocking on doors and using it to ask questions about me. Only about Paul O'Sullivan, not Sibiya and McBride. He's using the docket as a cover to carry on with false investigations about me.'

The allegations were a window into the war within law enforcement and an indicator of the battle lines drawn and where the players fell. The entire sector was beset by internal duels and the pursuit of personal, factional agendas.

As further evidence of this, in mid-2017, a dubious intelligence report began doing the rounds and was pushed onto a number of journalists who were sceptical about its authenticity and credibility. Operation Wonder was explosive in its contents but far-fetched. In short, it alleged that a band of rogue cops was part of a plot to assassinate Fikile Mbalula, or alternatively dig up a pile of dirt on him and bring him down. Ostensibly the 'Big Three' of Mdluli, Ntlemeza and Phahlane were the architects of this cunning plan and money to bankroll the project was sourced from the secret fund.

As Marianne Thamm wrote in the *Daily Maverick*, Operation Wonder is a badly written and dubious intelligence report:

> *The report was clearly planted and no one, not even the people whose lives were supposedly in danger, would go on record. As someone once said to us, 'it has too many holes in it and smells like a dead seal in a blocked drain'. This is what the 'Intelligence' of the country had resorted to, the levels they had sunk to.*

On the up side, there have been potentially positive developments within law enforcement.

In April 2017, Lieutenant General Yolisa Matakata was appointed acting head of the Hawks. A trained intelligence operative, her appointment was largely welcomed. In November 2017, Khehla Sitole, who had played a crucial role in driving the investigation against Krejcir, was appointed as the new national police commissioner.

In January 2018, Fikile Mbalula finally fired Richard Mdluli, paving the way for a permanent and present Crime Intelligence head to be appointed and for the organisation to get back to the business of collecting intelligence on criminals instead of being criminals themselves.

Mbalula had also taken a strong stance against corruption within the police ranks, vowing to clean up the SAPS and get the organisation back to the business of fighting crime. In February 2018, Mbalula was removed as police minister by newly elected President Cyril Ramaphosa. As his replacement, Ramaphosa named the former tough-talking, no-nonsense Police Commissioner Bheki Cele, despite the fact that he had been previously fired for the police headquarters scandal. Cele's appointment seemed to be a popular one and signals trouble ahead for criminals.

I SPENT TWO DAYS IN MID-2017 SITTING OUTSIDE MAJOR GENERAL Shadrack Sibiya's office in Braamfontein, waiting to interview him. His desk is full of papers and on the shelves there is a collection of books in which he features. Each time we start talking, his phone rings and the mayor's office is on the other end. Sibiya strides off on a mission to catch his next target. In his role as head of the City of Joburg's forensic department, he is corruption-buster-in-chief for the DA mayor, Herman Mashaba. We speak in snippets, interrupted by press walkabouts and arrests.

Sibiya is something of an enigma and I've often wondered where to place him. One day he's in a green safari suit, the next in a slick jacket and tie. His detractors often raise questions about his fancy Porsche Cayenne and use it to justify allegations of corruption. Others say he is definitely clean. Who knows any more?

Sibiya is a common denominator in the Krejcir and Mdluli cases. He was behind the first arrests of the Czech when the Hawks were still investigating him and he also oversaw the investigation into Mdluli and even testified in court against him. But Sibiya lost his job as head of the Hawks in Gauteng when he was implicated, with Anwa Dramat, in the Zimbabwean rendition saga. He blames this all on a political conspiracy against them to have them worked out of the system.

In March 2017, Sibiya told the South Gauteng High Court that his career was ended because of Mdluli. He explained that he ran into trouble after he began investigating the murder of Oupa Ramogibe. He said he had been the one to name the investigation Ulibambe Lingashoni, which Mdluli believes was a project created to incriminate him falsely.

Having investigated corruption – and having been accused of corruption himself – Sibiya treads a careful line on the topic, stating that there has to be firm evidence to prove an individual's guilt. In particular, he explains how difficult it was to show that Krejcir had corrupted senior police officers.

'You wouldn't know because you don't have evidence, hardcore evidence that, look, they are working with him. We would get information that says he's working with General Mdluli but anybody could come and say he was working with General Mdluli as much as they also said he was also working with me. Look how many times I arrested him, personally, aggressively so as well. Why would I work with him? And each time he wanted to call to meet with me I contacted his lawyer, Ian Small-Smith, and said, your client is wanting to have a meeting with me; I don't know what about. And Ian Small-Smith would advise me and say, "Please stay away from that meeting; nothing good will come of that meeting – don't," and I didn't. I've never met him outside the agreement or maybe where you find that his lawyer is not aware or is not present.'

Sibiya flatly denies any allegations of corruption and insists he never took money from Krejcir as some have claimed.

'I would have been arrested and then, remember, Radovan Krejcir is a very dangerous man – he's not a man that you would go and meet and come out alive. We all knew his character and that he was a sick person, in mind. Meeting Radovan Krejcir, I wouldn't come clean; there was no point where I would meet with him alone. I've never taken a cent from Radovan Krejcir.'

But, he points out, these allegations were a smear campaign fed by the ongoing fight between the Hawks and Crime Intelligence.

'Remember, at some point in our fight with Crime Intelligence during or after the arrest of Mdluli and this and that, they also tried everything in their power to try to discredit me. And putting my name – it was called disinformazia. Disinformazia, disinformation. Disinformazia is when they begin to spread rumours about you, talking about you to make you look bad, and leaking information to the media. You can research it and just check on Google, "disinformazia",' he explains.

'Are you saying that at no point did you have a corrupt relationship with Radovan Krejcir?' I ask explicitly.

'Not at all, and no one can even show that I ever received money and remember how urgent they wanted me in jail, how they tried to put me behind bars, but they haven't been able to get any closer to putting me, even to be able to take a statement from me, in relation to that.'

A few weeks before my interview with Sibiya, accomplice-turned-state-witness Bulgarian 'Mike' Grigorov testified in the ongoing Sam Issa murder trial in the South Gauteng High Court. He gave evidence about regular meetings between Krejcir and Sibiya at the Vaal and at a plot in Pretoria.

> GRIGOROV: *Accused number 4 and General Sibiya used to meet sometimes by the Vaal. General ... Accused number 4 we all know, the court knows that he had a holiday house, but General Sibiya also was having something. So by the Vaal also they use to meet sometimes.*
>
> DEFENCE ADVOCATE: *Were you ever present when these, were you ever present at any of these meetings between General Sibiya and accused number 4?*
>
> GRIGOROV: *I have been present, I have meet him with General Sibiya and accused number 4, yes.*

He expanded on this further while under cross-examination:

> DEFENCE ADVOCATE: *Was it only on one occasion that you were present when accused 4 met with General Sibiya or was there more than one occasion?*
>
> GRIGOROV: *M'Lord, on this occasion I was present. On another occasion I was supposed to be present, but I had to leave from the Vaal to Johannesburg. So, I was supposed to go for something like braai or so, but I did not go.*
>
> COURT: *Where was the braai?*
>
> GRIGOROV: *I was by the Vaal River by accused number 4 property. So we was supposed to go to the place where General Sibiya is making braai, but I did not go as I said. Also in the Vaal area, M'Lord.*

He testified about how Sibiya, along with Colonel François Steyn and other underworld sources, had confirmed to Krejcir that Issa was behind the Polo incident at Money Point, a move that might have precipitated the death of Issa.

Grigorov also testified about how Sibiya had allegedly told Krejcir and his men that Cell C was the most difficult cellphone network to track on the 'grabber' machine and, as a result, they only used Cell C sim cards in their throwaway burner phones to evade police scrutiny.

> DEFENCE ADVOCATE: *Tell us a bit when or were you present when General Sibiya told accused 4 this? Gave him this advice about the cellphones?*
>
> GRIGOROV: *M'Lord, when we were in Pretoria in the meeting, it was a conversation about the 'grabber machine'. The grabber machine is the machine that is used by police to trace cellphone number. It is called grabber. So they were discussing that. Discussing that the grabber machine is struggling with Cell C to trace down Cell C accurate. Not that he cannot. It can happen. But it is much more accurate with MTN and Vodacom. Accused number 4 later on when he was sending me for SIM cards. He told me that it is going to be only Cell C use for criminal activities, because also on advice of Sibiya and Sibiya is a general in Organised Crime and he is a person that deal with phone tracing on a daily basis. That is their job.*

These are damning claims, bordering on criminal. Sitting across from General Sibiya in his office, I put all of these allegations to him.

'I don't even know Grigor?' he looks at me quizzically.

'Grigorov.'

'Grigorov. I don't even think he knows me. I don't think he can point me out. I've never met him and I didn't even know about Sam Issa. When Sam Issa was murdered, I was in Bloemfontein. I received a call that says – remember, I was still head in Gauteng – I also got a call that Modise Maropeng, who's been arrested with Radovan Krejcir, was involved and I called him to find out where he was and he was also there; he came and I came here, we had a meeting. He said he was not involved in this thing,' says Sibiya, referring to his Hawks officer, 'Saddam' Maropeng. 'Grigorov, I don't even know him. I've never seen him; I've never met him. Even now I don't think he knows who he is talking about,' Sibiya repeats for emphasis.

In February 2018, an anonymous parody Twitter account with considerable influence, using the handle @AdvBarryRoux, dropped a series of tweets implicating Sibiya as part of Krejcir's criminal network.

#Shadrack Sibiya had a hand in the kidnapping of Bheki Lukhele and also he 'Sibiya' assisted in the murder of Phumlani Ncube who was murdered by Miya and his deputy assassins.

Shadrack Sibiya was again used as an escort after Miya, Mafunda & Baba kaJesu assassinated Sam Issa sometime late 2013. After they shot & killed him, they drove away while closely protected by Sibiya & his team until they were safe and sound.

On another occasion Shadrack Sibiya handed over a sports bag that had guns and Police Bulletproof Vests and Reflectors at a filling station at Eastgate mall a few metres away from the Money Point, the shop owned by Radovan Krejcir.

The account tweeted that evidence of these allegations would be led in court in the Sam Issa murder trial when witnesses who are overseas return to testify. This is yet to happen.

Sibiya told me in response to the tweets that he believes the account is being operated by someone closely aligned to the police, or possibly even someone within the faction of the SAPS that has been running a smear campaign against him. He flatly denies the accusations, insisting he played no role in assisting Krejcir or his network. Again, he points to the fact that he had arrested Krejcir three times.

A number of Hawks officers who served under Sibiya were arrested and convicted along with Krejcir. Surely this reflects badly on their leader, who should have known what they were up to?

'No, remember we've been involved in a situation where we arrested many police officials. I think the statistics are there to how many we've arrested, including, I think at some point, remember, I had to arrest 10 members of the Hawks and from the Vehicle Theft and Investigation Unit. It was detectives and Hawks, at the same time we arrested them. So I have been dealing with corruption and every now and then you do arrest one of your own and it happens. I can't say it makes me feel proud or bad. Remember, if you wake up one day and go and commit crime, I'm not with you and there's nothing I can do, other than to arrest you and, if we get to know about it, we arrest you; we deal with you accordingly and it has happened many times.'

I ask him what he believes, in his experience, made Krejcir so successful at corrupting cops.

'Money corrupts people,' he says simply. 'Unfortunately, we have a list of the people who were involved. I mean, if you talk about one of them was involved with his wife, and it's a general. He had a list of his own police officials that he worked with, but there are many police officials who would even be seen at his place and they would give an explanation as to why they were there: conducting an investigation or for whatever reasons, we wouldn't know. I don't think the minister or the national commissioner can account for a policeman who takes a bribe on the street and they would ask, as a minister, how do you feel? He will say, "I'm disappointed, but what can we do other than to deal with those people?" The same applies to me. I don't take personal responsibility for a policeman who acts contrary to his powers.'

And what about Mdluli? What made him so powerful and influential?

'He became powerful because, obviously, when you are the head of Intelligence of the country, you will become powerful because you will have a listening ear, starting from the president, the ministers; you play a very important role in the country, so what you say is whether you're misusing or abusing your powers, whether you're using the president's name or the minister's name or the authority; at the end of the day those that are below you won't know your powers … You operate at a higher level. So, that is what makes you powerful, and then too much power corrupts. The moment you find yourself with enormous power, you must know that some of the things will go wrong because you deciding and what you think, what you may think is right, you find that it is wrong, legally. Politically, [it] may be right, but legally you find out it is wrong and that is unfortunately the nature of the game.'

At this stage, in July 2017, Sibiya believes – like so many others I've spoken to – that Crime Intelligence and the Hawks are entirely ineffectual and that they have been broken by politics. All of this, he agrees, makes it easier for people like Krejcir to take advantage of the situation.

'You remember at some point Radovan Krejcir was being interviewed on TV and he said that's why I chose South Africa; I like South Africa because the Constitution at least protects everyone. Radovan Krejcir looked at the weaknesses within the system and the cracks within the system and the fact that he's got some of the police officials in his pocket; as a result, he survived and, unfortunately, due to the laws of the country and the Constitution, you could not just arrest him just because you feel like going to arrest him. The prosecution also got their own standard that you have to meet before going to be arrested or a warrant of arrest can be signed.'

Prince Mokotedi, current head of the Hawks in Gauteng, has accused Sibiya of colluding with Robert McBride and Paul O'Sullivan, amongst others, to launch a coup and to take out several senior cops and prosecutors who are part of an opposing 'faction' to them. Sibiya says he believes this is all politics.

'He hasn't even come to interview me or anybody up until now. This whole thing is hanging over our heads, like a cloud, but above all he's using this case to be able to have access into our different, let's say, our telephone conversations, Vodacom, MTN, the banks and movement control. He's using the case, he's abusing his powers to be able to get the powers from the judge, but if we can actually take him head-on and go to the court now, the judge will rule against him. He will say that this man lacks honour and integrity as well.'

Sibiya also dismisses claims that Paul O'Sullivan has been given too much freedom to run the police and IPID investigations.

'I also want you to know that Paul O'Sullivan, as much as many regard him as a nuisance, the bottom line is that if he comes to you to report a case, there's substance in that case and unfortunately many people, including the top police officials or police, whoever want to expose something, they tiptoe in the dark hours to go to Paul O'Sullivan and give him information with evidence.'

Although he's eagerly going about his job fighting corruption in the City of Joburg, Sibiya remains a cop. He harbours the resentment evident in so many others like him who were worked out of the system.

'My heart is bleeding every day of my life. I worked hard; in my life I've got many good cases that one can put on the table. I've run for this country; remember, I was the one who established the office of the Scorpions in Bloemfontein and in the Northern Cape. Remember, I was also running the joint anti-corruption task team of the president established by the former President Thabo Mbeki in the Eastern Cape, fighting corruption. I was in Gauteng; I've been to head office of the Scorpions. I fought a good fight. I was fighting crime in Gauteng and was doing well. Now, and remember I was the one fighting cash-in-transit up until zero! And all of a sudden, I was surprised unfortunately when the president – it is the president's prerogative to appoint people, but if you appoint someone like Ntlemeza, who knows nothing about organised crime from the detectives. He worked in a detective's space but at a higher level, and he also worked as a deputy provincial commissioner responsible for policing from uniform, into a complicated situation, a complex space like the Hawks; obviously he was bound to get poor service. Now Ntlemeza came in there, appointed his own people, played his own games there, did away with people who were operating there and who were making an impact, for his own personal reasons. Now I was pushed out and even now they cannot prove a case against me. They know very well that there is no case against me, but they are playing for time because as long as they're keeping me fighting outside the space in different court battles. I'm telling you now, even now, there's no case against me.

'I have to fight because the police is the only thing I know. I grew up in the South African Police Service; crime fighting is the only thing that I knew. So, unfortunately for me, had Dramat not opted to settle and leave, I think I would be back in the police. We were pushed badly, unfairly so, and we had no one, no politician wanted to enter into the whole affair and we tried our best and unfortunately only the court sympathised with us.'

As his phone rings again and he is summoned by the mayor's office to his next mission, General Sibiya assures me he is not bitter. But he still has unfinished business.

'I hope that one day I will get an opportunity again to serve my people in this country to fight crime, at a much bigger scale. We were doing that. Unfortunately, for political reasons, we found ourselves all out on the street again, but I hope that at some point things will be back to normal.'

WITH RADOVAN KREJCIR NEUTRALISED AND IMPOTENT, A VACUUM was created in the underworld. Who would take charge and capitalise on the situation? In Joburg, the scene was rather quiet as far as apparent mafia-related activity was concerned. It wasn't that there was no longer a so-called underworld of crime – there was still a strong foothold by various mafia groupings such as the Chinese triads, the Nigerians and the Congolese criminal networks – but they were all considerably more discreet than Krejcir. They didn't seek out the media spotlight or go in search of a reputation as a crime boss.

As Mark Shaw explains in *Hitmen for Hire*, the Nigerian and Chinese triads maintain high levels of internal integrity built on ethnicity, language and trust, whereas Krejcir was a less skilful operator, openly engaging in violent activities to establish himself in the underworld. It was a position that could not last. Shaw writes:

> Foreign criminals, like Radovan Krejcir, will appear periodically in the news. But although a high profile in the media may play to the criminal ego, it is not a sustainable strategy for long-term underworld survival. Sustainability requires the control and shaping of local supply and demand to suit global criminal markets. Alliances with local groups will be a prerequisite for stability, but so too will be a critical mass of foreign operators on the ground.

Two noteworthy incidents took place in Joburg after Krejcir was removed from the picture. The first was the shooting of Raymond 'Razor' Barras in Kensington. He was shot in his BMW in his driveway in February 2017 in what appeared to be a hit. Barras was a former debt collector working in the illegal cigarette trade. He had previously been in business with Faizal 'Kappie' Smith, one of the Kebble shooters, but the two had fallen out. Smith immediately distanced himself from the hit. It was widely believed that Razor's death was linked to the illicit tobacco industry. Players such as Smith and Mikey Schultz had moved into that game, working as muscle for some of the biggest producers in the country. It is a lucrative, largely unregulated activity driven by politically connected individuals.

The second incident was a shooting near Melrose Arch in northern Joburg in July 2017. Ralph Stanfield, alleged 28s gang boss, was travelling with a friend in a white Audi R8 when a gunman opened fire. Stanfield was wounded but managed to drive himself to Morningside Clinic. The incident appeared to be a spillover skirmish from a battle being waged in Cape Town.

The really interesting place to watch since the fall of Krejcir, and Beeka, has been Cape Town. The struggle for turf and power in the Mother City has been led by Nafiz Modack, who was affiliated to both Krejcir and Beeka. As a result, the violence from the underworld was overflowing into the 'upper' world throughout 2017 and into 2018.

Who is this Nafiz Modack who has suddenly risen to prominence, positioning himself as the new boss on the block?

'Modack is not a figure of significance,' a Cape Town policeman with a long memory of the gang game, General Jeremy Vearey, tells me. 'His father owned supermarkets. He's a boytjie from Heideveld, the richer part of it. The family moved to Joburg and he doesn't know the gang world. He has built himself in this environment through the residual background that comes with his father. When he settled here, he was also friends with Cyril up there in Joburg. He and Cyril were close. The people he's using in his network now, most of them are Cyril's old network from down here. He brought Jacques Cronjé back from KZN. It's Cyril's old network. Everyone, Grant Veroni, all these guys are from those days. These are the guys he's built himself around.'

After Beeka's death in 2011, Specialised Protection Services (SPS) – the company run by Mark Lifman and André Naudé – consolidated control of the nightclub security industry in Cape Town. However, after SPS was shut down, the hold was not quite as firm. Modack began to surround himself with a crew that included Beeka's former employee and heavy, Jacques Cronjé. He also formed an alliance with Colin, one of the Booysen brothers, from a well-known and prominent family with gang associations in Belhar in Cape Town.

In an attempt to seize control from the more established grouping of Lifman, Naudé and their ally, another Booysen brother, Jerome 'Donkie' Booysen, Modack began to make his move in early 2017. This meant that the two Booysens found themselves on opposite sides of what would become a war.

Beeka's links to the state are well known and he was working for intelligence agencies. It is believed that Modack inherited these associations. Sources say he is a police agent. It's also alleged that he led the takeover of the nightclub security industry in the city with the backing of the state. I have been told that he has the support of the agency and its leaders.

From late 2016 through 2017, the new crew in Cape Town began to make their presence known. They showed up at nightclubs, restaurants and businesses and allegedly threatened owners and managers. It was effectively an extortion racket remarkably reminiscent of the heyday of Elite in Johannesburg in the late 1990s and early 2000s. Businesses had to pay a fee and, if they did not, they suffered the consequences. Modack and his men 'barred' prominent members of the old guard from setting foot in the Cape Town central business district. There was significant collateral damage in the takeover and news reports were punctuated with violence, shootouts, murders and bust-ups in Cape Town and in Joburg.

On 7 November 2016, prominent attorney Noorudien Hassan was shot in his car outside his home in Lansdowne. He had represented some of the city's most notorious characters and had acted for some of those in the bouncer industry. He was also a suspect in what would emerge as the country's all-time biggest gun-smuggling investigation.

Less than a week later, two suspected gangsters shot dead the night manager of a hotel in Sea Point owned by Mark Lifman. Craig Mathieson was killed inside Hotel 303 and nothing was taken, suggesting that it was a hit and might have been a message to Lifman.

Simmering tensions escalated in March 2017. The catalyst was a property auction. A property belonging to Modack went up for sale in Richwood in the northern suburbs. Lifman attended the auction and, when Modack arrived, the volatile situation teetered on the brink.

Then a second Modack property went on auction in Parow. Again Lifman and his men were there. Tensions boiled over and ended in violence. There was a punch-up in the street, guns were drawn and knives pierced flesh. André Naudé left his flip-flops behind.

It was this street fight that triggered Modack and his crew to launch an onslaught on the city's nightclub security industry.

This is how News24's Caryn Dolley describes what happened next:

> Battles for power over aspects of the underworld have been playing out for years, leaving behind a trail of unsolved murders, shootings and arrests. On the night of March 29, 2017, after months of simmering tensions, a criminal coup was carried out in the Western Cape. A new faction emerged in South Africa's underworld and immediately started to grab control of nightclub security from a more established grouping. The apparent power tussle, which some say has been orchestrated by intelligence operatives, has ignited gang violence. The illicit drug, perlemoen and tobacco trade has been shaken up. It has exposed mysterious relationships between underworld figures and police officers. Rumoured links to politicians have been unearthed. This ongoing power struggle has resulted in several gun battles, murders and skirmishes on the streets of Cape Town. Violence has spilled into entertainment venues. Meanwhile bystanders remain at risk.

In April 2017, two men were wounded in a shooting at the popular upmarket Café Caprice in Camps Bay. In May, one person was wounded in a nightclub in Loop Street in a bouncer battle. In July, Ralph Stanfield was shot in the Melrose incident in Joburg. In August, Brian Wainstein – a man known as the 'Steroid King' for his involvement in illegal steroid activities

– was shot in his Constantia home while in bed with his wife and young child. In October, 30-year-old Nicole Muller, a mother of two, was killed alongside Donovan Jacobs at the Cubana nightclub in Stellenbosch in what appears to have been a gang-related shooting. In December, a Congolese bouncer was killed at a club on Somerset Road in Green Point after a fight broke out between Modack and his men and the venue's security. The bouncer was fatally stabbed, while a second person was injured.

Then, as Modack and his men attempted to encroach on turf in Gauteng, the struggle spilled over to Joburg in the latter half of 2017. They targeted several nightclubs in the city, but the showdown came in September when two groups of men with underworld links clashed in a brawl at Emperors Palace Casino.

The status quo in Joburg also began to teeter as things hotted up in a renewed struggle for power. On one side is an established faction with links to the old Elite crowd while on the other is East Rand bouncer boss, 'Tall' or 'Groot' Gerard Strydom.

In September, Strydom was shot several times in the KFC drive-through in Springs. His sister was sitting alongside him in his black Ford bakkie when two men opened fire. Strydom was hit five times in the chest but survived.

Then in December, Reigerpark gang boss Markie Groenewald was shot in Erica Street in the volatile suburb. Groenewald, also known as 'Terror' or 'Bin Laden', was a well-known gangster in Reigerpark and was the leader of the Dochs and Serpents gang. He had a criminal record as long as his arm. Several sources have told me that the more established faction in Joburg turns to Reigerpark gangsters to do its dirty work in much the same way that the Cape Town factions turn to the 28s and other Cape Flats gangsters. Groenewald was a gun for hire. His death was rumoured to be a revenge attack for Stanfield's Melrose shooting.

Throughout 2017 there were multiple attempts to take out Jerome 'Donkie' Booysen, with at least three separate attempts over a period of a few months. In May, he was wounded in a shooting in Elsie's River. In September, he was shot at while in his car in Bellville South, but he wasn't wounded. In October, the attempts escalated and the battle couldn't have been more public. Booysen was wounded in the domestic departures terminal at Cape Town International Airport. A second individual was wounded after being struck by a stray bullet. Booysen was rushed to hospital and put under heavy guard in ICU. But that didn't stop two men from trying to finish the job in the medical facility. The two, dressed up as women, came for him and also targeted one of his close allies but were unsuccessful. Photographs of the aftermath show a discarded brunette wig on the floor alongside blood smears and bullet markers.

The situation was becoming untenable. Police appeared to have no control at all. This might have been because of Modack's own connection to the cops and the possibility that he was, in fact, being backed by intelligence operatives.

In May 2017, reporter Caryn Dolley watched as Modack met with the Northern Cape provincial police commissioner, Risimati Shivuri, at an upmarket hotel near the V&A Waterfront. When she contacted Modack via email to enquire about the meeting, he responded by sending the journalist a photo of herself sitting in the lobby of the hotel with a message that read: 'WE HAVE EYES EVERY WHR HAVE A GREAT DAY FURTHER.'

Modack is believed to have met with the Western Cape detective head, Major General Patrick Mbotho, although the police officer has denied this. I have been provided with a photograph of Gauteng Hawks boss Prince Mokotedi meeting with Modack at a restaurant in Cape Town in mid-2017. Dolley has also published a photograph of him meeting with former President Jacob Zuma's son Duduzane Zuma and reported that 'Modack has repeatedly named the son of a leading politician as someone he had looked after when the man had been in Cape Town'. Sources say he is a police agent despite his criminal involvement, which is yet another example of how the SAPS, and Crime Intelligence specifically, use underworld figures as sources, rather than target them for prosecutions.

As Dolley has repeatedly reported, there are persistent rumours of police, Hawks and Crime Intelligence officers' involvement in the underworld, which shift as state agencies attempt to take down the main established players. Government has denied this. But Dolley has pointed to a civil trial in the Western Cape High Court in which Nelson Mandela's former bodyguard Major General André Lincoln was suing the SAPS for R15 million for wrongful prosecution.

Testimony in that civil matter showed that in the late 1990s Madiba 'tasked select police officers with infiltrating the underworld' in Operation Intrigue. Lincoln was appointed to head the Presidential Investigative Task Unit, which probed organised crime and links to police and politicians. Its mandate, according to evidence led at the court case, was 'a secret operation functioning in a covert manner gathering secretive or confidential information on its main targets through surveillance and infiltration of the criminal underworld operating around the nightlife of Cape Town, most of whom were connected to police officers operating on the ground'.

Lincoln was arrested. He believes this was done to quash investigations into high-ranking individuals. There has always been a flimsy, blurred line between the underworld and law enforcement, and this was as evident in the 1990s as it was in 2017 with Modack, the new boss on the block.

THE PIERCING, OVERWHELMING STENCH OF CLEANING DETERGENT catches in my throat as I walk into the historic red-brick building on Corporation Street on a busy midweek morning. The building, the SAPS Provincial Detective Service office, used to be the old Labour Building. The ceilings are high and the place is steeped in history. Through the open windows and beyond the black palisade fencing, you can hear the incessant hooting of taxis driving by. On this day in November 2017, the country's focus is just two blocks away, on parliament, where then Public Enterprises Minister Lynne Brown is facing a grilling over her relationship with the Gupta family and Eskom.

The large corner office in the building is occupied by Jeremy Vearey, now the Cape Town cluster commander. Vearey rushes in from a meeting with community policing forums, dressed in his government-grey suit, and has an hour before his next appointment. He is a busy man. If you want to know anything about the gang history and landscape in Cape Town, Vearey is a veritable encyclopaedia. He grew up in Elsie's River and knows this terrain better than just about anyone. He has relationships with the players and has insight into the dynamics and the politics.

Vearey's own story has been turbulent of late. He has recently found himself demoted, fighting a Labour Court battle and warding off allegations of corruption and a campaign aimed at tarnishing his reputation.

In June 2016, Vearey was shifted from his job as deputy provincial commissioner for detective services back to the position he had previously occupied as cluster commander. Similarly, his colleague Peter Jacobs was demoted from his role as the province's Crime Intelligence commander. They believed the decisions were a result of political factionalism, which was laid bare in the Labour Court hearing.

Vearey had been involved in recording a contentious statement by state capture whistleblower and former member of parliament Vytjie Mentor in which she made explosive claims about the Gupta family and President Jacob Zuma. Vearey argued that the subsequent political storm around the affidavit led to a belief that he was involving himself in factional politics. He had always been seen as a 'Phiyega man', allied to former National Police Commissioner Riah Phiyega. When her people were purged, he was also targeted.

Vearey and Jacobs had been leading a massive investigation into how illicit firearms were being smuggled by police to gangsters for use in murders, and the duo had managed to crack down on those responsible for selling stolen police guns to criminals. The case centred on an ex-police colonel, Chris Prinsloo, and Vereeniging arms dealer Alan Raves, who had sold over 2000 guns to Rondebosch businessman Irshaad 'Hunter' Laher. The guns were supposed to be destroyed but instead were sold on to gangsters who used them to flood the ganglands and to commit crimes.

Vearey and Jacobs argued that when they were transferred, the entire firearms investigation was allowed to grind to a halt. The implications of this were massive. Think about that: stolen police guns, handed over by cops to gangsters, used to kill.

Vearey has also been extremely vocal about what he believes is a smear campaign against him, orchestrated by Western Cape Community Safety MEC Dan Plato. The MEC allegedly leaked information peddler Pierre Theron's affidavits to the media, which contained claims that Vearey had received bribes from Krejcir.

Vearey has claimed that senior police officers in the province were trying to frame him for setting up the notorious underworld killing of Nathaniel 'Nigger' Moses, the suspected head of a group of hit men. There were also allegations that he was working with gang bosses. The claims exposed deep rifts within the Western Cape police structures. Some cops and prosecutors I speak to don't trust Vearey. Others say he's the best there is.

It is against this backdrop that I sit down with Vearey at the large polished wooden table in his office on Corporation Street and settle in for a history lesson. Cape Town Gang Dynamics 101. There are some things he can't speak about on the record because investigations are ongoing and what he says might compromise himself, the investigators and the cases. It's a delicate dance.

'Let me explain about gangs and organised crime from the perspective of how long it has been institutionalised, and understand the symbiotic relationship with police and then from a totally different point of view,' he begins.

'What people misunderstand is that we had a history of corruption with all the gangs that goes back to the late 1800s. You can go to the numbers gangs that started in the 1800s, and they functioned with corruption with police. It's an institutionalised form of relationship between gangs and police – it's always been part of South African policing. There are records at Scotland Yard. The names might change, the areas might change, but you are talking about the practice that becomes institutionalised in a particular way.

'Let me explain the simple logic of it ... The police intervene in society. We go there for a short while to intervene or disrupt an activity for whatever purpose. We are the only force that gangs ever have to contend with. We are the state in those areas so we become the logical point for recruitment. It's not a tendency that is only here; it's all over the world. It's a point that people miss because they think of this thing as individual cops with brown paper envelopes; it's not that. It's something where as soon as you set up an organised criminal group or syndicate – highway robbers, like they used to be in the 1800s – you're functioning as an organised group, you traverse certain territory, you have to be highly mobile and you're moving big goods. In order to do that the only force you contend with is the police – wherever you are. It's natural to target them and to think that way, as the leader of a gang, that this is my turf area and I need cops on my payroll.'

The main problem with the current scenario, he says, is that there is a history of not policing gangs in the country. In the SAPS prior to the 1990s, there was zero control over the gangs. 'Let me tell you, literally, there wasn't. But you had a high amount of gang leaders on the payroll of units like Murder and Robbery. None of the gangs was ever addressed. Let me use an example:

the Hard Livings gang was formed in the early eighties. It was allowed to grow unfettered to the threat it is now. Any gang … the Americans gang in the Western Cape was started in 1982, allowed to grow unfettered. It was never tackled as an organised crime entity. The 28s, 27s, 26s come from the late 1800s and were never tackled as an organised crime entity. But certain key people were recruited because they inform on lesser crime.'

What I'm especially intrigued by is the fine line that is walked by police in using criminals as sources and witnesses. How do the cops decide who to go after and who they will use as their agents and, if the bad guys are agents, are they being protected rather than prosecuted?

'This is not unique to the South African Police,' Vearey emphasises. He points out the prevalence of this in all major RICO (Racketeer Influenced and Corrupt Organisations Act) investigations in New York, such as the case against the Gambino mafia family. South Africa's equivalent is POCA, the Prevention of Organised Crime Act, which creates the framework for the super-charge of racketeering, used against gangsters, mafia networks and organised crime.

Before the legislation was introduced in 1998, there was no capacity to deal with these threats as they grew into what Vearey calls 'organised banditry'. The ability to penetrate structures and gather information was also poor. 'The intelligence capabilities in this country before the nineties while these gangs were growing from the seventies and eighties did not focus on that. All intelligence was focused on political threats. That wasn't applied to gangs, so if you want to understand why we have it at the scale at which we have it now, it's a combination of that – no capacity focusing on it in a structured way. And the second thing that didn't exist is the legislation to deal with it. We are as current as the US.'

On the face of it, there appears to be a distinct difference between the perceived 'underworld bosses', such as Krejcir, Beeka and Lifman, and the gangsters from the Cape Flats or Reigerpark. Vearey quickly disabuses me of this notion.

'That is the myth that makes it difficult to understand for people,' he interrupts me. 'Organised crime is organised crime. It's a group conspiracy; it's a grouping in a pattern of perpetrating crimes. Whether the crime is dealing with stolen goods, committing heists, drug smuggling, extortion of businesses, it's the same. It's a group – whether the one group prefers to tattoo itself or the other group decides to sit in suits and ties and have a meeting at the One&Only Hotel, it's the same thing. They're just in different geographical environments. They just peddle in a different product. It's the same phenomenon.'

To understand the current state of affairs, the players and the politics, Vearey takes me on a journey through the last three decades, a highlights package if you like, of how the extortion rackets in the city evolved into what they are today.

'Up until the 1990s the gangs like the Sexy Boys, Hard Livings, the Americans, they had structures that bordered – in terms of turf structures – on Cape Town. They had Woodstock, they were running the sex industry on Woodstock's streets, they had businesses that bordered on Claremont, so they were right next to the city. We dealt with them and their extortion,' he says.

In these early days, Cyril Beeka was still a bit player. 'If you're talking about the big players back then, you're talking about a group called the Paragon Foundation; they were bouncer guys who started this practice. They sold cocaine. Later it evolved into Red Security and Pro Security and that. Beeka was still a junior boy; he was just a muscle. Jacques Cronjé was junior muscle. They started this business of that but they made a mistake. While they were busy with extortion they were fine. When they moved into the drug world they started stepping on the Americans' toes. These guys were involved in supplying product to rich clients here. That white crowd here, these guys started attacking them for selling the product. This was in the nineties. They said, "Who the hell are you guys? Oh, you have your own pipeline in with flights from Brazil, we're taking over. You're either part of us and we take over your distribution or you're dead." And they literally destroyed all of them. To the extent that the only person who survived was Beeka and Jacques Cronjé because they became the henchmen for these groupings who were now moving into town.

'Back then the first area they targeted was Sea Point. The Americans gang had the top part and the 28s had the bottom part and had Green

Point. The Hard Livings were also in Sea Point – literally and physically taking over clubs and all of those things. These guys were then brought into the fold: the Pros, the Reds and them.'

Then came the 'big war'.

'The Americans were chased out of Sea Point. Then we prosecuted and got Staggie out of Sea Point also,' says Vearey, referring to notorious gangster Rashied Staggie. 'The 28s, some of them we got out of the Green Point area. They then started using and building Cyril, in particular the Sexy Boys, as their person to work the drugs in Long Street. They needed a respectable and different face. Cyril and them became the convenient front for the gangs.'

Beeka's stature grew until he was seen as the boss of the city. He formed an alliance with Yuri 'The Russian' Ulianitski, who was actually from the Ukraine, and Hoosain 'Moroccan' Ait Taleb, a member of the Moroccans gang. Ulianitski's schoolboy friend Igor 'The New Russian' Russol flew out to join them. They targeted clubs in Cape Town where drugs were being peddled. Beeka's company, Pro Security, grew in prominence, its main rival being PPS, Professional Protection Services, André Naudé's outfit.

Beeka went on to have a major fallout with Ulianitski and the two ended up despising one another. Beeka's reign didn't last. Greed got the better of him, as is so often the case. He was growing Red and Pro Security into a formidable force and the Sexy Boys were beginning to warn him. In around 1998/99, he was run out of town.

Beeka moved to Joburg, while his right-hand man, Jacques Cronjé, fled to Durban. They were personae non gratae in Cape Town.

In his place, Ulianitski took over as the gang favourite, until 'The Russian' was taken out in May 2007.

Meanwhile Mark Lifman, a clean-cut boy from Sea Point, was beginning to rise to prominence. He forged an unlikely association with the gangs through Jerome 'Donkie' Booysen. As a property mogul, he was buying industrial property out in the northern suburbs, such as Delft and Belhar, and he met Booysen at an auction.

Police say Booysen was buying these properties to use as drug outlets but when the cops started looking at seizing these houses, the Sexy Boys changed their operation. The belief is that Lifman was a front for securing industrial property to be used in the abalone trade and large-scale drug production on behalf of the gang. If true, this would mean that Lifman's wealth was made off the gang, leaving him indebted to them. There is also the suggestion that the Sexy Boys helped Lifman with the sexual abuse case he faced in the 2000s and on which he was subsequently acquitted, twice.

Lifman pleaded not guilty to charges of indecently assaulting seven boys, the attempted murder of a man who allegedly procured the boys, and defeating the ends of justice after his arrest. Because of poor and contradictory evidence, Lifman was granted a discharge on four of the charges. He was acquitted after one of the state's key witnesses against him turned hostile and recanted his evidence. I've been told that the Sexy Boys helped change the witness's mind about testifying but Lifman strongly denies this.

In 2010, Cyril Beeka did something he was not supposed to do. He tried to return to Cape Town and retake what he believed was rightfully his. Only, he hadn't realised how much the ground had shifted. Vearey believes he knows who killed Beeka and why, but this is one of the things he can't talk about.

Two years after Beeka's murder, a Sexy Boys gang member, Leon 'Lyons' Davids, was gunned down at a party in Belhar. He had turned state witness in the Beeka case but he had left the witness protection programme and got a job running a nightclub in Loop Street. Reports suggested that he had been taken out by his own gang for snitching.

I still can't quite comprehend how no one has been charged for shooting Beeka or Lyons when so many people I speak to seem to know exactly who was responsible. One Cape Town cop I spoke to told me that the Hawks were carrying the docket and were given solid information but that 'they literally fucked up the matter.' It's unclear if this is because of corruption or plain incompetence.

I wonder about all the stories that suggest that Krejcir could have been involved in Beeka's murder. They had had a fallout and a punch-up in the run-up to the shooting and there have always been suggestions that he had had a hand in it. Vearey doesn't believe this to be true. 'No. For one simple reason: they were very good friends,' he says.

While in Vearey's office, I noticed a framed photograph hanging on the wall above his desk. It's a faded snapshot showing a motley crew of young men standing against the backdrop of a harbour. The image was taken decades ago in Portsmouth harbour when Vearey, then an ANC operative, was sent to train with the SIS under Thatcher.

One of the other men in the photograph is Russel Christopher, a former MK soldier and intelligence operative who once headed security for parliament. All the pieces of the puzzle in my head fall into place at once. Vearey and Christopher trained together when they were both in the ANC's intelligence structures. The full extent of their relationship later came to light in Nafiz Modack's bail application, when it emerged that Christopher and Vearey had met with Modack in May 2017 and discussed Modack's proximity to other senior police officers. I ask Vearey about Christopher and his history in this world.

When Christopher was at the National Intelligence Agency, he worked on a project investigating Cyril Beeka. But then Beeka started working for the state. Christopher and Beeka became close, so close in fact that Christopher's daughter, Marissa, referred to him as 'Uncle Cyril'. It was Beeka who introduced Marissa to his friend Radovan Krejcir.

Marissa Christopher is the former *Playboy* model who was Krejcir's mistress, who had a child with him and who was arrested for allegedly attempting to assist him in breaking out of prison. In 2012, Russel Christopher told *City Press* that Marissa is 'past family and I have nothing to do with them whatsoever'. While he had heard rumours of Krejcir's relationship with Marissa, Christopher did not have contact with his ex-wife or his daughter.

If ever there was a story that shows the proximity of organised crime to law enforcement and the blurred line between the two, this is it. It explains why Beeka always enjoyed the protection of the state and why he was never prosecuted – because he had a protective relationship with the intelligence forces, despite being a rogue. It also illustrates the degree of intimacy that comes with intelligence practices and the relationships between handlers and sources. Only in this case, it's a classic example of what can go wrong.

After Beeka's murder, his company, Pro Security, merged with the opposition PPS to form SPS, Specialised Protection Services, headed by

Naudé and Lifman. Its directors included both Booysen brothers, Colin and Jerome. The situation in Cape Town's nightclub industry was relatively stable for a while – until Nafiz Modack rocked the boat.

I ask Vearey about the relationship between Beeka and the new boss, Modack, and whether there is a turf war, a battle for power, or how he would define what is currently going on. Evidently, he finds it a far more nuanced situation than media reports are suggesting.

'People are misapplying these concepts. It's the wrong way. Gangs have moved beyond these things. It's about a space that becomes a market area that you monopolise. Everything that happens within this space, from drug sales to extortion to prostitution to whatever happens there, is the monopoly of the gang that is there. It's not about posturing on street corners any more. That's the junior guys. The big thing, it's a business zone for you. When the Sexy Boys and these guys started looking at Sea Point, Green Point and Long Street, they were looking at these areas in terms of clubs known to generate profit. They didn't need to own the whole of Sea Point Main Road; they went for the one club and this restaurant and that thing, get the extortion and also use the doors to get the drugs. That's how the relationship with the door guards and these things started. It's a different concept; they don't need to posture on street corners like they do in the Cape Flats environment.

'Using the same metaphor from the Cape Flats to explain what is happening here in town is a bit misconstrued. Here the extortion requires me just threatening you and you being scared of my face, me being Colin Booysen standing in front of you. Nafiz doesn't threaten anybody – they'll beat him up on the street. If Colin walks into your fancy five-star restaurant, and just sits there and opens his mouth and speaks in a certain way, your clientele is not going to come back. He doesn't need to threaten you. What Nafiz needs to do is to collect and say, "I'll bring this guy around again."'

He says Modack and Colin Booysen have apparently been going to a number of businesses around Cape Town doing exactly this. I've also spoken to a number of business owners who have experienced the sharp end of this alleged extortion.

'They went to a lot,' Vearey confirms. They operate behind the front of different security companies, the main being TSG, 'The Security Group'.

'Modack brought the business acumen of setting up a company through which you can do this instead of wandering around like gangsters and doing something. You get forced to go into a security contract. The pattern here is that wherever TSG is the security at an event or attached to a place, that place that they are at gets the events licence easier. If it's a place, you get your liquor licence easier because of the corrupt network these guys have. The worst thing here is the corruption that makes this happen. That, to me, is the story; the story is not how many dead bodies are lying around, because that is few and far between. Modack gets the money to finance so that local faces can buy the security companies. A lot of things they do are they buy dormant companies just to get guns. There was a dormant company called Eagle Security; they bought it because it was dormant but it still had guns on its books so they bought it to get the accreditation.'

What, then, is the current state of play in Cape Town? It's November 2017 when I'm in Vearey's office and Modack and his crew are yet to be arrested. It looks as though they have free rein of the Mother City and people are worried about the escalating violence, but perhaps not nearly as much as they are worried about their taps running dry because of an ongoing drought.

'I don't believe in speculation because I'm a detective. I'm telling you that the people involved here have a history of violence; they do not have a history of negotiations. They have a way of getting access to events and things through corrupt practices and they have the network to do it in the city. They are not – bodies piling up – I don't like that,' he says.

As I'm still attempting to grasp the interfamily dynamics and the lie of the land, Vearey jumps up and starts rushing around his office, closing blinds and switching off lights. He's off to his next meeting. I follow him, badgering him with questions. Why haven't they arrested Modack? Are the cops close? I shadow him down the passage, through the security doors and out onto the street. A police car swerves and pulls up next to the kerb and, with a final flurry of answers, General Jeremy Vearey jumps into the passenger seat and disappears, off to fight his next criminal.

I'm left standing on the pavement, dazed, staring at Table Mountain, trying to digest what he has told me.

PERCHED AT THE PEAK OF THE AVENUES IN FRESNAYE, ON THE slopes of Signal Hill and overlooking the Atlantic seaboard and the twinkling ocean, is a sleek, angular, modern home. It's the very last house on one of the shorter, steep roads that bear French names, giving the suburb an air of exclusivity and panache. It is here where Mark Lifman, the de facto 'Mayor of Sea Point' who has earned a reputation as the 'businessman gangster', lives. The walls are white, the gallery of modern art features mostly portraits of women and the décor is minimalist. On the day I visit, workmen are upgrading security around the building, installing more electric fencing. An armoured vehicle is parked in the garage.

I have not previously met Mark Lifman but I have heard the stories. I'm not quite sure what to expect. He has been polite and cordial in arranging the interview. To my knowledge, he is not media-friendly and has never given a proper sit-down profile interview. It's part persecution complex, part a deep distrust of journalists, the legacy of decades of news reports about him. My request comes a few weeks after Jacques Pauw's *The President's Keepers* is released and Lifman got a bad rap in the book, particularly around his dealings with SARS. He's been looking for an opportunity to respond and my timing is fortuitous. Also, the atmosphere in Cape Town is tense because of Modack's and Lifman's apparent rivalry.

Lifman is busy with his travel agent when I walk in. He's courteous and welcoming, dressed in a pair of sweatpants and a T-shirt and trainers. His square jaw is clean-shaven and his hair flops to the side. There's none of the big show with fancy suits and big, burly bodyguards I've witnessed with other high-profile individuals before. There is a pile of paper folders on the tables (for each of the properties he's trying to sell) and there's a pristine copy of Pauw's book next to him. He tells me he's yet to read it. There are two young men milling about. One is his personal driver and the other is doing his 'apprenticeship'. One occasionally munches cereal out of the box in the kitchen while we speak.

Lifman has asked his long-time attorney, the well-known William Booth, to sit in on the interview. We speak for so long into the evening that Booth eventually has to leave us. For three hours, Lifman talks. He tells me the story about how he made his money, how he lost it and how he made it again. He regales me with anecdotes about how he came to know the key players in the Cape Town 'underworld' landscape and his explanations for the allegations he has faced both in the courtroom and outside it.

Lifman begins with why he has decided to speak. He is put out that for years journalists have 'written sources or opinions or guilty by association', not reports that are 'true and verified'. According to Lifman, Jacques Pauw falls into this category, it seems.

In *The President's Keepers*, Pauw meticulously unpacks Lifman's tax woes, his R388-million tax bill and how, instead of being taken down like Krejcir and Agliotti were, Lifman has used political influence and the 'rogue unit defence' to wriggle out of paying the taxman.

According to Pauw, the Lifman investigation, led by Johann van Loggerenberg and SARS's National Projects Unit, was massive and expensive: a tax inquiry was held, over 90 witnesses testified and Lifman was presented with his tax bill. According to an affidavit from SARS acting Commissioner Ivan Pillay, quoted by Pauw, investigators probing Lifman received several death threats and one official's home was burgled.

SARS penalised Lifman for a host of infringements, including tax evasion, failing to submit his tax returns, making false disclosures and instructing his tax advisers to miscalculate his tax. Lifman litigated and, while the matter was tied up in court, the so-called Rogue Unit scandal struck and Van Loggerenberg and his team were out. Pauw writes that it should have been a straightforward, done deal to collect from Lifman. He was ready to be taken down and his taxes collected.

Pauw suggests this did not happen because of Lifman's political connections. In 2014, he was photographed by the *Sunday Times* at President Jacob Zuma's birthday rally in Athlone, alongside ANC provincial chairperson

Marius Fransman, his bulging muscles covered in a bright yellow ANC T-shirt bearing Zuma's face. In 2015, *City Press* reported that Tom Moyane was 'approached to go easy on Lifman as the businessman is an important man because of his money and influence and his proximity to powerful people'.

Pauw also laments the fact that an interdepartmental task team – established in October 2012 to bring down Lifman – has to date not been successful and Pauw cannot fathom why this unit never cooperated with SARS and why Lifman was not prosecuted on any of his tax matters.

In a February 2015 letter from the director general of the State Security Agency, Sonto Kudjoe, to SARS boss, Tom Moyane, Kudjoe says the interdepartmental task team has confirmed that Lifman is involved in criminal activities including corruption, dealing in foreign currency, illicit cigarette and drug smuggling and paedophilia, amongst other crimes. The SSA urged SARS not to negotiate a settlement with Lifman because of the impact such a deal could have on 'turf wars' in the Western Cape. 'If the individual settles with the revenue service it is of concern to the SSA that the individual and his syndicate will continue with their illicit activities.'

In late 2016, Lifman launched an application in the High Court to have his tax audit reviewed, using what has now become known as the 'rogue unit defence', that he was unfairly targeted and victimised.

Van Loggerenberg is irate about this as he insists that the so-called Rogue Unit never investigated Lifman. 'It was at the time when the project against Lifman commenced, which was in late 2013. The unit was known as the HRIU. It was not assigned at all to Project All Out. It was, in fact, a National Projects Unit that was assigned to conduct that investigation. I had put this to Lifman repeatedly in February 2016, when he sought to meet with me on the issue,' Van Loggerenberg told me.

Pauw concluded that while Lifman might have been the first alleged organised criminal or big-time tax evader to benefit from the void left by the disbandment of SARS's investigation unit, he will not be the last.

But Lifman insists he is not a tax dodger.

'I had an accountant. He was 80-odd years old. But he's past his sell-by date. He didn't do my taxes properly and then I moved to another guy; he pulled the wool over my eyes and took my money. We were doing taxes, but he was behind. We haven't done VAT for one of my companies. I can't do tax returns and I told SARS that. I can only give it to a professional to do it on my behalf. When we submitted everything at the end of the day and it came to that 11-odd million, that was my correct tax bill.'

Lifman genuinely believes that Johann van Loggerenberg wanted to bring him down at all costs. He eagerly shows me messages he has exchanged with Van Loggerenberg since the book came out.

'You read in the book, they wanted to destroy me; they wanted to use SARS to take me down. This rogue unit. I didn't know how I was involved with that because I was never involved in the cigarette industry, but obviously the fact that I even ventured into cigarettes and I had this so-called big name of being in the underworld, which is so untrue, they became frightened and they thought that I was going to take over the whole of the Western Cape. I remember they were protecting BAT, Philip Morris, all the so-called legitimate tobacco operators. All I know, if there's a mafia, those are them, because that's a bad business and, on my mother's life, I have never sold a packet of cigarettes. I'm against smoking and I was in the very beginning stages of negotiations with Adriano [Mazzotti] to sell his cheap cigarettes into the Western Cape markets – the informal market. We haven't even got a price from Adriano; he gave me some samples and that was as far as it went. That is when I received a letter from SARS from Van Loggerenberg and it was about the tobacco industry and this whole thing. I owe SARS R11.6 million, by the way, and I'm happy to pay them.'

I ask him if he pulled strings to sort out his problems with SARS.

'I told you, I owe SARS the money and I'm still fighting with them. They've got a caveat over all my properties and the properties that I've been selling. I'm getting the money to pay SARS. I know what I owe them, from what we've submitted and their review, but I've been told that the review was what I've submitted originally. But now they're saying I must pay them 11.6 plus penalties and interest.'

I quiz him about suggestions that he is politically connected. If he isn't, then what was he doing in an ANC T-shirt at a political rally?

'Politically, I've never registered to vote in my life. I've never supported one political party. I want this to be very clear.'

He explains in detail how he was invited to the rally at Vygieskraal Stadium by a woman whose charity in Gugulethu he was supporting at the time. It was called Ilitha Labantu, run by Mandisa Monakali.

'Mandisa phones me the one day and says it's the president's birthday at Vygieskraal Stadium and she wanted me to come with as a guest of hers for the charity and she wanted to introduce me to the president and tell him that I've been supporting her charity for all of these years. It was a Saturday afternoon and it was about 40 degrees outside. I arrived there and Mandisa took me in; she told me to put the ANC T-shirt on and I was sitting and chatting to an Indian guy whose family was involved in the struggle and he's involved in some youth league. I never met the president. I met a lot of other people and I bumped into Marius Fransman, whom I knew from the escort agency. Marius Fransman was a customer at the escort agencies. One of the girls that used to work with me ended up being his secretary. There's the story of how I came to be there. I know Marius Fransman from his associations with certain ladies and I found him to be quite pleasant.'

Fransman was approached for comment. He undertook to get back to me and never did.

'The DA's Dan Plato, there was certain allegations made and I met with him at Jerome's house one evening and we discussed certain issues about me. I told him they were barking up the wrong tree.'

Lifman believes journalists are quick to associate him with stories because of his bad-boy reputation. 'That, to me, is an issue. Out there everyone is painting this picture that I am a criminal, gangster, drug dealer and all the rest of those things. You've asked me what my story is and we're here to discuss my story.'

I have asked him to tell me his version of his truth and so he does.

Mark Roy Lifman was born in Cape Town, grew up in Rondebosch until he was 12, and then he and his family moved around the mountain to Sea Point. His mother was a schoolteacher. Lifman attended Temple Israel, had his bar mitzvah and grew up in the Jewish faith. He matriculated from Sea Point Boys' High School in 1984, at the age of 17, before enrolling for his national service in Pretoria.

'I was a normal kid. I played sport. I was pretty naughty and didn't like studying, like most kids. I breezed through school. I didn't take it seriously. I matriculated with, I think, a D or an E result. I was a very opinionated young child. I reckon I had my mother's character; I said what I believed and if I believed something I stood by it. I matriculated in 1984, played rugby, tennis, cricket, water polo, table tennis; represented the first team in most of them, nothing irregular.' He talks fast and with little intonation.

What did he aspire to be when he was older?

'I was a great salesman,' he says, unsurprisingly. 'I was a Boy Scout and we had to sell flower bulbs and I went to the haunted house in Rondebosch and sold them. I had no fear – I was confident. I was a go-getter and wanted my first car to be a Mercedes-Benz. I had ambitions.' He wasn't necessarily after material wealth, he says.

'I didn't know what material wealth was, but I wanted to be self-sufficient and successful. With that independence, obviously financial aspirations are there too. I had to make money because I believed that would give me security. When you're young you are impressionable and you want to create an impression. I was an entrepreneur.'

After finishing the army, Lifman's parents pressured him to study. He lasted three weeks at a technical college before he pulled out. His dad then got him a job with an old Jewish man called Yaldor. Mark Lifman built his business career on the foundation of chocolate mice and marshmallows, aged 19.

Like any successful start-up entrepreneur, he set about establishing a business from his home. 'I wasn't comfortable working for a boss so I withdrew from working with Mr Yaldor and started making peanut clusters and coconut clusters from my mother's kitchen.' He moved from the sweet business into property when a family member invited him to join him in a development selling houses in Blue Downs.

'I used to rent minivans to bring in the factory workers because they were all first-time home buyers. I used to sell 30 houses per month in those years,' he says proudly. When he noticed there was a transport issue in the area, he bought three minivans and started Liffy's Transport. 'At the height of it I had 30 of these minivans running staff for hotels, as well as commuters to Sea Point and Cape Town. I was 20 years old. It was a tough business and I was a tough guy; I was in good shape and used to stand up to these guys. I would drive the vehicles myself if a driver never turned up for a contract. Liffy's Transport ended up transporting millions of people up and down the streets of Cape Town.'

But then, in 1989, there was a collapse in the first-time home buyers' housing market and Lifman stopped selling 30 houses a month. Then there was a taxi war between the Western Cape Black Taxi Association and Lagunya – Langa, Gugulethu and Nyanga – Taxi Association. His vehicles were destroyed and he was wiped out.

He looked around for another business opportunity and found it selling dried fruit and spices, of all things. He made a fortune – and then lost it.

Having dabbled in sweets, property, transport and spices, Lifman was on the hunt for the next industry. He found it in pastries. He opened a King Pie at Cape Town station and ended up with several more pie franchises.

One of these franchises he sold to André Naudé, a bouncer and an electrician in the Air Force. Lifman forged a friendship with him that would last for years. The two would end up going into business together in nightclub security.

It was at that stage of his life that he started going to auctions to buy equipment for his pie shops. 'At one of the auctions I met a guy called Rael Levitt,' he says, referring to the disgraced former Auction Alliance boss. He went into business with Levitt, but then that also ended. 'My relationship with Levitt came to an end when I was arrested in 1999 on child-molesting charges. Obviously, they couldn't associate themselves with me so they got rid of me.'

Lifman delves into the scandal himself, without me taking him there. He speaks about it openly, mostly because he maintains his innocence. 'I got arrested and spent 12 days in jail.'

Lifman got out of jail and went straight back into auctioneering. His strategy was to buy and hold, to play the long game instead of swinging the assets.

'I then went and started buying houses in Eerste River, Kuils River, Brackenfell. It would cost you about R20 000 and from there you'd need to pay repairs to the property.'

It was through this venture that Lifman's path crossed that of Jerome 'Donkie' Booysen. In 2001, Lifman bought three properties in Delft for R10 each. While renovating one, the evicted owner arrived with a mob of gangsters who tried to attack Lifman and took back ownership of the house. Lifman turned to his friend, the bouncer André Naudé, for help.

'I said to André, this guy tried to kill me and we must go and sort him out. He said, no, he knows someone who might be able to sort this out for me and he introduced me to Jerome. I met Jerome once and I gave him the details. He went off and phoned me a couple of hours later and told me that the guy is gone and I can go and take the house back – he had sorted it out. Jerome said he had no money – he just came out of a massive court case with the police. He said he was working for the council and he wasn't earning much, but he can help me deal with any issues in those areas where I had problems with the properties.'

At the time, Booysen was working as a building inspector for the City of Cape Town. He had been a star rugby player in his youth and was well known in Belhar and surrounding neighbourhoods. Along with his brothers, Colin and Michael, the Booysens had emerged as the leaders of the Sexy Boys, one of the most prominent gangs on the Cape Flats.

Lifman says he had no knowledge of his new friend's gang affiliations.

'I had no idea. He was working at the council as a building inspector. He was a rugby player – he's in the hall of fame.

'Listen to me,' Lifman says earnestly. 'If Jerome came and sat at the table with you now, you wouldn't ever associate him with gangsterism or anything like that. He's the most unbelievable guy. Him and I have grown unbelievably close; we're business partners in some ventures of property together and we've had this relationship for the last 17 years, since 2001.'

So it was that Booysen began helping Lifman deal with problematic tenants who refused to move out of his properties.

'I couldn't deal with people. I wanted to go in there and moer people and carry on like I used to do in my taxi days. This man had a way with people

– he would talk them into going peacefully and I never had any issues.

'We started buying houses together and we were also doing maintenance on blocks of flats where I bought flats. I just went to the auction, bought the house and phoned Jerome to get the team in and fix the place up, and then sold it. We built an unbelievable portfolio.'

One of Lifman's most high-profile purchases was a landmark Sea Point hotel, the El Rio, which he renovated in 2005. At the time Sea Point was seething with drug dens and prostitutes and the El Rio was the heart of the drug trade. Lifman credits the turnaround of this building as the catalyst to turning around all of Sea Point.

'If people ask me where I made my real money from, it was out of property. I always had this thing about building stuff up – I always wanted to make things better. Whatever I touched, I wanted to fix it; I don't want to be a slumlord. The building was overrun with foreigners and it was terrible; drugs, prostitution, the whole story. Everyone thought I was going to turn it into a brothel and a drug den because I was buying all these funny houses and because I was connected with Jerome. I did a lot of good things. El Rio was the one that I really made a mark on Sea Point with. Once that building was cleared, the whole value of Sea Point swung.'

Lifman acknowledges that his bad reputation came from his associations with people like Jerome, as well as his business partnership with Yuri Ulianitski.

'I met Yuri at the Poker Club in Sea Point,' recalls Lifman, who is a keen player. 'Yuri was running a casino, a brothel; he was involved in odd businesses. He was actually involved in the Fairmont [apartments] with me. He was a partner. Yuri was a character. I tried to get him on the straight and narrow to get him into good business, which we did. We did some properties together and we had some good projects going, but he gambled. He gambled away everything that he had.'

Lifman was with Ulianitski at his birthday dinner the night 'The Russian' and his daughter were shot. There have been rumours that Lifman might have tipped off the shooters when Ulianitski left, but he vehemently denies this.

'I was with him at dinner; I left early. He finished the meal and his daughter was playing with that clay that they brought her. I was tired,' he says about that night. To this day, he maintains he has no clue why Ulianitski was killed.

'There are a lot of rumours, but I have no idea. I think some things had gone wrong for him. I know they were coming for him for a lot of cases, for stupid stuff that he'd been involved with. The guy that was working for him was a police informer – who I'd actually told him was a police informer. Yuri was happy-go-lucky; he didn't really care about anything. There were a lot of people who weren't very happy with him. As a matter of fact, I was kind of dissociating myself from him as well; we'd had some arguments about him being involved in the wrong stuff. He wasn't paying his gambling debts. I had to pay them for him. He would come sit at a table, play with the guys and lose R100 000 and I would have to pay it for him because I was the owner of the club. When Yuri died he owed me R606 000.'

Together, they had owned a brothel called the Castle in Milnerton, which then moved to town. 'Doing business with Yuri wasn't simple; it was his way and only his way. I'd been involved in the casino with him for about three months and then we got arrested for the Jockey Club matter. Yuri had his own style and I wasn't making any money out of him. That was a one-way relationship.'

The 'Jockey Club matter' Lifman refers to is his banning for life from the sport of horseracing for two alleged incidents of corruption in which jockeys claimed they had been intimidated and bribed to throw races. He subsequently challenged his banning.

While Lifman did business with most of the prominent Cape Town players, he says he never had any direct dealings with Cyril Beeka, except the time Beeka came to beat him up.

'I was acquainted with him; I never really had any business with him. Yuri and Beeka had history. That was when they had the bouncing business together – I didn't know either of them at the time. I knew Cyril because they were at the clubs. They had a big fallout and they hated each other. I believe that my 1999 story came because of Cyril Beeka – the thing with the child-molesting charges,' Lifman reveals.

'I was acquitted, but they charged me twice. They charged me once for child molestation and the second time they said that the pimp charged me with defeating the ends of justice and he brought people. The police tried to bribe the witnesses. The big acquittal was that the one who had to give the evidence came forward and said that they gave him R500 to make a statement against me.' Lifman is sure that Cyril Beeka was behind the prosecution.

'Cyril, who hated Yuri, saw me as a person who was making Yuri stronger, I assume. I refused to let Cyril's security do any of my venues because I didn't want to be involved in any of the criminality. I mean, these people are just thugs.'

In around 2009, before Beeka was killed, Lifman reached out to Radovan Krejcir. He had heard about the new player in town and was hoping to get some funding for a property venture.

'I heard about this billionaire that had come to South Africa. Because of all the stories about me, when I went to the banks for finance, I wasn't an ordinary client going to the banks; I mean, Mark Lifman was a paedophile, Mark Lifman is connected to this. You know, it's complicated,' he says tongue-in-cheek. 'I was always looking for funding. I heard that a property agent had been showing this very wealthy Czech properties in Top Road, Head Road and Arcadia Road [in Upper Fresnaye]. I phoned the agent and asked for the guy's number because I wanted to meet him. I phoned Radovan and said I believed that he was a wealthy businessman and that he was interested in the property business. I got on with him like a house on fire. I went up to Joburg and met with him. We were going to do property together. I said to him I heard that he was a billionaire and he said is that all that I've heard. I said something about that I heard he had a lot of money and money was nothing to him.'

Lifman had his eye on the Galleria Centre in Milnerton and he hoped Krejcir would be his backer. He didn't get a cent out of him.

'I don't think he had money, to be honest with you. I think it was all smoke and mirrors with him. He was a complete bullshit artist. Then I started to hear stories and then he started talking about schemes and started telling me about somebody in Absa and if I gave him the account number that if he puts money into that account we must buy gold and take the gold. I said, first of all, that's a paper trail and I'm not prepared to be involved in anything that leads to a paper trail where there's crime involved. He and I never actually got into any business together. He started coming to Cape Town and he wanted to be in the clubs and, because of my reputation at the time and because of what I was involved with, I could get people access to the clubs and I was like a VIP host. People would phone me asking for tickets for here or there.'

Lifman kept his distance from Krejcir, but there was one incident that infuriated him. It involved his friend Chico Lopez, a McLaren and a classic Krejcir scam.

'There was this guy called Chico Lopez who I was friendly with at Shimmy Beach Club. He was a helluva nice guy; he actually does Bitcoin now. Chico had a McLaren and a friend of mine, Justin Divaris, had given me a McLaren to drive as well. Justin and I were in school together,' he tells me about the man who was also once Oscar Pistorius's best friend and one of the first people on the scene of Reeva Steenkamp's murder.

Chico 'sold' his car to Krejcir, but it was a sham deal. The money was deposited into his account and then reversed. 'I knew Radovan was going to buy the car with Absa money and take the car, steal it, and Chico would be left with this reverse payment out of his bank account. What happens? Exactly what I said. Six weeks later I get a message from Chico saying he'd sold the car and he got paid. I said well done. Two days later all hell breaks loose. Chico's money got withdrawn and the account got suspended. They wanted to charge Chico for corruption and fraud. Chico's minus the car and the R3 million he sold it for. As it happened, we got the car back in the end, after a year and a half. Radovan hated me for that and we had a screaming match.'

The showdown occurred at the lawyer Ian Small-Smith's offices at BDK Attorneys in Joburg. Both Lifman and Krejcir happened to be there at the same time, but for different reasons.

'He asked me to chat – we went into the back room and he started telling me about my meetings with Sibiya, because I told Sibiya about the car and what had happened. I wanted to help Chico, so I said I knew a guy in Joburg who could take his case and I know the case won't be corrupted – I thought,' he says sarcastically.

Lifman says he felt betrayed by what had happened because he was simply trying, in good faith, to help a friend. Krejcir confronted him with what he had heard. 'I stood up and said, "Listen, you piece of shit, you knew I was friendly with that guy and you still stole from him. What kind of relationship do you want to have with me when you're stealing from my friends?" I wanted to moer him, but the reality was it was just a screaming match – they could hear us in reception. He asked me who I think I am and I asked him who did he think he was and it ended in that sort of shouting match.'

So now Lifman had not only fallen out with Beeka, but with Krejcir too. He believes they were both extortionists extraordinaire. Of course, Lifman has his own theories about why Beeka was taken out.

'Cyril was involved in a lot of extortion and racketeering. I know a lot of people were getting knocked by him. There were people telling me stories. It is hearsay; they would buy drugs and the drug dealer would come to deliver the drugs and they would just beat him up and take the drugs. This used to go on a lot, I believe, and that was the type of personality.'

After Beeka was shot dead in 2011, his right-hand man, Jacques Cronjé, frantically turned to Lifman for help. This set in motion the amalgamation of Beeka's company and André Naudé's to form SPS.

Lifman is insistent that he has never been involved in any bouncer extortion rackets and that he has always wanted to run a clean business, ensuring the safety of patrons at night spots.

'I wanted to do this thing without any thuggery – if a bouncer stepped out of line, he was dealt with according to the code of conduct. One of the most frightening things for a kid going out to a nightclub is being beaten up by the bouncers and by thugs, and I wanted that to have controls. We wrote a code of conduct, a constitution document and a service-level agreement. All of that cost me close to R100 000. It was a proper business that would receive management fees from the nightclubs – reasonable amounts of money at the same levels that they were receiving before and we were giving a proper service. No extortion at all. Basically, the same model that was in place before without the heavies. Without these guys going around and beating people up and all that crap. The best part of it all is for the first seven years we never had any violence in the clubs; we never had any incidents. After the Hawks came and shut down SPS we still continued the business, we just did it in other people's names because I still wanted there to be control and I used to have management meetings and meet with the club owners and things were run properly. If you go out there and ask people – they want that back; people are frightened out of their wits at the moment.'

As far as Lifman is concerned, what Modack and Colin Booysen have been doing in Cape Town over the past few months is the exact opposite of what he set out to do.

'There's an extortion racket going on with Modack and Colin Booysen. Modack was involved with Cyril originally. He was like a lackey for Cyril. Once Cyril was dead, he hooked up with Radovan and they used to steal cars together. Modack was a small-time criminal who is now trying to become a big-time criminal and an extortionist of note.'

I ask him to explain the dynamic between his friend Jerome and his brother Colin. How did it come to be that two brothers found themselves on opposite sides?

'They used to be together and Colin was involved in The Embassy, the escort agency, with me. Colin was involved in some of the houses that we did, but he had his own business. He also got involved in the bouncing business with André and then he just stole the business from André. They had like a coup. Colin basically teamed up with Modack and a bunch of other criminals and overthrew the bouncing business and threatened the guys that if they didn't come to their side they'd do stuff to them.'

Lifman gives his version of what happened at the infamous auction that triggered the takeover in the industry, the showdown that was the catalyst.

'When everything went pear-shaped with Colin Booysen going rogue, he pulled this coup d'état. Modack's properties were being sold; he was being sequestrated in his personal capacity and these were two properties being sold by the executor. The guy who was handling this had given the auction to auctioneers and asked me to arrange security. I'd asked André's guys to go and do security there. They arrived there with three minibus taxis and about four cars; Modack and all his goons and Colin came with his skollies. They just started attacking people. I managed to get the auctioneer, Mr James – who is about 74 years old – his daughter and the assistant, [and] I put them in the

Range Rover and I managed to get them out and I took them to my house. Modack had been threatening weeks before the auction not to do the auction as it was his properties. They cancelled the first auction because Modack intimidated the buyers and chased them away. The second auction I was there. The first property was sold and the second property they were in the process of selling it when Colin and his boys arrived and disrupted the whole auction.

'What that guy has done – and, listen, we are no angels, none of us are angels, Jerome has a past and I have a past,' he tells me. It's a line I have heard many times before.

'But it's simple, Jerome has done a hell of a lot of good, not only in his community, but in the whole of Cape Town. He is a good guy and I will stick by that guy. I won't ever desert him and I know he is never going to desert me. You know there's that old saying "blood is thicker than water" – Jerome chose me over his brother because he knew what his brother was doing was wrong. He knows that his brother is going to be punished for that, that he will face the law that is coming his way.'

During the interview, Lifman phones Jerome Booysen and puts him on speaker phone to talk to me and vouch for all that he has said. The call is brief, but Booysen seems to confirm their close relationship.

Lifman has made it his business to keep an eye on what Modack and Colin Booysen have been up to in the city. He has mounting evidence against them, he says. 'They're going to prominent business people in the town and basically threatening them. Those business people are getting phone calls from unknown numbers telling them that their kids are going to be in danger if they don't conform – it's disgusting. I spoke to a friend of mine today who has been a victim of them. He's been paying them R20 000 a month for extortion. Some of them have made statements. I think the authorities are dealing with this problem, but people are scared. I'm not scared. They've brought all the cockroaches back into play: Modack, Jacques Cronjé, Colin Booysen.'

I ask whether Modack has the protection of the police and the state, considering all the rumours that he is being backed by the government or that he's a police source.

'Modack is a registered police informer, but he's a criminal, so the police are entertaining criminals and that's a problem. And, for me, if they're entertaining someone like him, they are one of him and they are criminals too. I don't know who those people are. I don't know who Modack's contacts are, but all I know is that whoever his contacts are they need to be very, very careful because what this guy is up to, he is going to drop all of them.'

Is he dangerous?

'Individually, he's a rabbit; he's like a girl,' Lifman says. 'But with all his 30 to 40 people that he walks with, he thinks that he is God, something out of a magazine. I think he's been watching too many movies. I've never been arrested for extortion or intimidation. I mean, I've collected money from people – debt collection – but if someone brings me a debt collection and I see that it's false, I won't handle it.'

How do you see all of this playing out?

'I believe they are all going to jail. I do. I believe the authorities are working hard to deal with these criminals and put them away for a long time.'

Surely he should be worried that the cops are also working on him, building a case and collecting evidence to see Mark Lifman behind bars too? He doesn't think so. He's been dealing with the authorities for over 21 years and has not been convicted – and does not expect to be in the future.

'I want to see a better Cape Town; I'm not the drug dealer or the criminal they're trying to make me out in the press. If I was a criminal, why have they never convicted me of drug dealing, extortion, racketeering? People ask how I've made so much money; my money has been made in property. I submitted my tax returns,' he says.

For Lifman, the future from his angular perch in Fresnaye was looking bright. 'I've got fantastic friends all over the world. This year I've done 10 trips overseas. I've had a fantastic year. I don't let things get me down. I'm very angry about things because I believe people like this should've been dealt with long ago. There might be people out there who believe that I should've been dealt with long ago.'

A few months later, in February 2018, as Lifman returned from one of his overseas jaunts, he was taken into custody at Cape Town International Airport on what his lawyer described as an 'illegal warrant' on a case opened by Nafiz Modack.

IN DECEMBER 2017, THE NET FINALLY CAME DOWN, ENSNARING Nafiz Modack and his men. With it, the viscera of the underworld takeover, the bits that are usually kept hidden by an agreed omertà, came tumbling out in the public domain, like the entrails of a gutted fish.

First, Grant Veroni, the director of the Bellville-based security company trading as The Security Group (TSG), was arrested on two charges relating to the alleged possession of an unlicensed firearm and ammunition. He also faced a fraud charge in a separate case in which it was alleged that he hired fake security guards in order to obtain firearm licences for them.

During Veroni's bail application, Sergeant Edward Edwardes told the court about how Veroni, along with Modack and Colin Booysen, was intent on taking over nightclub security in order to take control of the drug trade. He testified about how security industry regulators from the umbrella body, PSiRA, feared for their lives if they took on certain security companies. Edwardes revealed that Veroni had been linked to a number of the nightclub shootings, but had not been charged in two decades because 'people out there are too afraid to lay complaints against these people' and 'they fear for their lives'.

Another of TSG's directors, Hussain 'The Moroccan' Ait Taleb, a martial arts expert, was also arrested and faced a charge of conspiracy to commit murder for allegedly contracting two men to kill a club owner who refused to pay a protection fee.

Then, in December 2017, came the big breakthrough: Nafiz Modack, Colin Booysen, Jacques Cronjé, James de Jager, Ashley Fields, Mathys Visser and Carl Lakay were all arrested on extortion charges. The arrests were part of a large-scale investigation into underworld activities in Cape Town and came on the back of a letter the group had sent to club owners, wishing them a happy 'fest of' season and informing them they would be charged double for their services in 2018. General Jeremy Vearey was instrumental in overseeing their arrests.

During the bail application of the seven, details of gross police corruption were revealed as it emerged that senior cops were allegedly protecting Modack and working with him and his crew.

After a statement was first made in November to investigating officer Colonel Charl Kinnear, he registered an inquest docket to ensure the investigation was concealed. Had he registered a criminal case, any police officers with access to the criminal record system would have been able to see its existence. Kinnear explained that his move was 'because of senior police involved with the group'.

Kinnear testified about the existence of a recording of Modack in a meeting with Vearey and Russel Christopher, the former State Security Agency official and father of Marissa Christopher, which took place in May 2017.

'Nafiz Modack states he was dealing with high-ranking police officials and, should there ever be a problem, Tiyo and Mbotho can sort it out,' said Kinnear. The investigating officer was making reference to Major General Mzwandile Tiyo, the Western Cape's head of Crime Intelligence, and Major General Patrick Mbotho, the provincial head of detectives. Curiously, Tiyo and Mbotho were the two who replaced Vearey and his colleague Jacobs when they were dubiously demoted by police bosses.

Kinnear also pointed to the meeting between Modack and the Northern Cape Police Commissioner Risimati Shivuri, as evidence of the influence Modack wields in the police. He also testified that Modack claimed to have political clout, a reference to his relationship with Duduzane Zuma.

Kinnear told the court about more recorded conversations between Modack and a 'Serbian', believed to be George Darmanovich, in which he makes explosive claims about Vearey. Kinnear testified: 'Modack said Vearey was working for the 26s gang under Jerome Booysen, for the 27s gang under the leader known only as "Red", and for the 28s gang under Ralph Stanfield. He also claims Vearey arranged the hit on lawyer Noorudien Hassan with Jerome Booysen and Mark Lifman. In his recorded conversation with the Serbian, Modack said Vearey, Lifman and Jerome Booysen were framing him for incidents taking place in the underworld.'

Writing on Facebook, Vearey's response was this: 'Let me get this straight. The 26s gang say I work for the 28s and the 28s gang claim I work for the 26s. Now a Frans [a person not affiliated with gangs] says I work for the 27s gang and assassinated Hassan? What next? At this rate I probably killed [President] Kennedy too and organised the drought in the province.'

The extent of Modack's relationship with Krejcir also showed itself during the bail application. Kinnear testified that Modack was in partnership with Krejcir and claimed he was in possession of a recording of Krejcir asking Modack to do a job for him. He wanted Modack to collect a R12-million debt from Demi Jackson, Lolly's widow. The money would be shared 50-50.

Kinnear told the court about how Modack and Booysen had extorted over R420 000 from the Grand Africa Café & Beach near the Waterfront, amongst other venues. Police had also established that Modack had been busy with extortion activities in Johannesburg. A statement had been provided, implicating him in such practices at Andrew Phillips's The Grand, an upmarket strip club in Rivonia.

It was also suggested that the men might face charges in connection with the death of a bouncer at Cubana in Green Point in December 2017, the fatal stabbing of a bouncer at Beerhouse in Long Street in 2015 and the murder of the Hotel 303 manager. Kinnear testified that during the height of the underworld takeover, Modack wanted both Lifman and Donkie Booysen to be taken out. He also planned on killing Colin Booysen, so that he could run the industry himself, and had recruited Igor Russol, the Ukrainian who had taken over from Yuri 'The Russian', to help him. Unfortunately for him, Russol turned state witness against him and provided police with insight into Modack's operations.

Kinnear testified: 'Modack said he wanted to take over all the clubs in town and needed Russol to do it. He was going to first make peace with Jerome Booysen and Mark Lifman, let the dust settle and then have them both killed. Then, after he owned everything with his partner Colin Booysen, he would kill Colin as well. Russol said Modack had offered him work and lodgings and asked him to arrange a meeting with Lifman and

Jerome Booysen to broker a peace deal. Russol was told to kill both men after the peace pact was set up. However, he told Modack he could not go around killing people; it was not the jungle,' said Kinnear. 'These men are a danger, as was evident when, during an incident at the Cubana in Green Point in early December, a bouncer was allegedly stabbed to death and another injured in an ongoing turf war, because Modack and his crew had refused to accept a table outside.'

Russol allegedly told investigators that he acted as 'muscle' while Modack used his experience under Cyril Beeka to extort money from successful Cape Town business people of Jewish heritage. Top defence lawyer Pete Mihalik was also named as being something of a middleman for Modack. André Naudé accused Mihalik of selling a gun that was taken from one of Naudé's bodyguards at the Parow auction. Naudé claimed that Mihalik had contacted him and told him that he wanted R20 000 for the firearm. Naudé says he sent 'Steroid King' Brian Wainstein to Mihalik's chambers to pay the money and collect the firearm.

Kinnear went on to tell the court, 'It is my opinion and experience that these men will return to instil fear in the business owners and return to extorting and threatening them and their patrons.'

Another statement read out in court, and authored by Lieutenant Colonel Peter Janse Viljoen from the Hawks, went into detail about the 'turf war'. 'My role in this task team is one of handling informers close to the groups involved in this turf war as well as analysing information and confirming it,' he said.

Viljoen claimed that in April 2017 he received information that a group of 63 men aligned to the numbers gangs and to Mark Lifman was preparing to attack clubs where Modack and his men were providing security. Police intervened and intercepted the men on their way to carry out this attack.

He also claimed that Modack's faction was in possession of a hand grenade that it planned to use.

'On 28 April 2017, information was received that the Modack group is in possession of a M26 hand grenade, which they plan to use against the Lifman group. This hand grenade has not been found yet and information is that it is being kept at one of the clubs under the security of the Modack group,' he said.

Then there were other explosive allegations of planned hits. It was claimed that Crime Intelligence had tipped off the investigating officer that Modack was plotting to have him, his colleagues Major General Jeremy Vearey and Captain Sharon Jaftha, and the prosecutor Esna Erasmus murdered.

There was a mountain of allegations against Modack and his co-accused. But as commonly occurs in criminal cases, the pendulum swung with force as the defence was allowed to lead its case and discredit all of these claims. Much of the state's case fizzled out under this scrutiny.

Kinnear, the investigating officer, was repeatedly quizzed about how Lifman was really driving the police investigation into Modack. He was questioned about how many times he had been to the businessman's Fresnaye house.

'This matter is nothing more than officers of the law being corrupt and being in cahoots with people,' pointed out defence attorney Bruce Hendricks.

The allegations against prominent attorney Pete Mihalik were also pedalled back significantly. The prosecutor stood up in court and stated that the detail about him should never have been led. 'It has no substance and was uncalled for,' said Erasmus. She went as far as suggesting that certain individuals had used the bail application 'to hurl accusations, which are irrelevant to the case, at others'.

Modack's advocate then claimed that Lifman had put out a R20-million hit on Modack and there was a conspiracy to kill him while he was being held at Pollsmoor prison. Lifman laughed this off, saying he would rather do the job himself than spend that kind of money on Modack.

Towards the end of February 2018, Magistrate Joe Magele handed down his decision in the Cape Town magistrate's court. He found that the state had failed to fully explain elements of its case, and information that the investigating officer had testified about was false. He made findings on audio recordings and video footage that had been presented to the court as evidence of apparent extortion. In reference to the audio clips Modack's legal team had presented to the court, which featured Modack speaking to a complainant in the matter, Magele said, 'To my mind this recording seems to create the impression there were no threats.' Then, in reference to a video of Modack and a group of men walking into The Grand in Cape Town, Magele said, 'I saw a couple of men walking briskly through some yard.'

At the end of a two-month bail application full of fireworks, Modack and his co-accused were allowed out on bail. The case is ongoing.

As the cops saw that the Cape Town case was crumbling, they charged Modack and Jacques Cronjé with a case in Joburg. This was the incident in which the duo had allegedly attempted to extort Andrew Phillips of The Grand in Rivonia. The state alleged that Cronjé visited several nightclubs around Joburg and had attempted to strong-arm owners into security contracts.

'When the owner or manager refuses their services, they were then threatened by Nafiz Modack and Jacques Cronjé,' testified the investigating officer on the case. Phillips said no to them and opened a criminal case.

Prosecutor Yakes Chondree said that Cronjé then tried to extort half of Phillips's business, worth R20 million, by threatening to expose that Phillips was allegedly linked to the murder of Lolly Jackson. This information had allegedly come from Krejcir.

Modack and Cronjé allegedly sent threatening messages, saying they would burn down The Grand.

Modack had called the manager and shouted: 'Phillips, you must get your fucking boere ready with their guns, we are on our way and there is going to be fireworks.'

A message had also been sent from Modack's phone: 'Phillips you motherfucker I will get all ur cops arrested watch me u fucking with the wrong person ur fucker.'

But, again, the state could not back up its case in court. The prosecutor admitted that information could not yet be corroborated or confirmed and further investigation was needed.

Modack's lawyer in this matter, Johan Eksteen, jumped at the opportunity to capitalise on this. 'When the state realised the wheels are falling off the cart in Cape Town, they ran to Johannesburg,' he argued.

The Wynberg magistrate's court granted both men bail, stating that 'an extremely poor case' was presented by the prosecution.

Magistrate Syta Prinsloo slammed the investigating officer, and described the case as 'nonsensical'.

Modack believes that the case against him is being driven by Lifman, who he says is controlling the cops who arrested him. In February 2018, when Lifman was taken into custody at Cape Town airport, his lawyer argued that this was done by cops controlled by Modack. The policemen had been to see Modack in prison and taken a statement from him about an incident that had happened nearly a year previously. Lifman was arrested for allegedly pointing a firearm at the Parow auction standoff in March 2017.

Yet again the police are in the middle, used by both factions to drive personal vendettas and agendas.

Ｉ COUNT AT LEAST SIX MEN SITTING AND SMOKING ON THE BALCONY of Hassen-Harmse Attorneys on the seventh floor of the Mandela Rhodes building in the vibrating Cape Town city centre. The motley crew is there as protection for Nafiz Modack, who has just been released from custody after being granted bail. There has been so much chatter about murder plots and hits that he moves with a pack. For him, there's safety in numbers and the men surround him as he makes his way in and out of the busy building. The juxtaposition of these men with the fancy lawyers' offices makes for a memorable sight.

Modack leaves most of his posse outside as he sits with me in a boardroom, bringing only the security industry veteran and his current right-hand man, Jacques Cronjé, with him. The lawyers also sit in on the interview while we talk. The man who has earned himself a reputation as the new boss in town isn't quite as intimidating when he's on his own, although he definitely has a presence about him. He's in a leather jacket, jeans, sneakers and sunglasses, and has his ubiquitous black leather man-bag with him. He spins his three thick silver rings as he leans back in the chair and speaks confidently. He has three cellphones on the boardroom table that hum regularly.

'I grew up on the Cape Flats. I was into the supermarket business, properties, vehicles, all my life,' he starts. His family owned a franchise of grocery stores called Modack Supermarkets. 'They were bigger than Pick n Pay. I think it's four brothers who had supermarkets across the whole of the Western Cape and Johannesburg. I had a showroom in Parow, a car dealership for exotic cars. I was the only one in Cape Town with exotic cars and our floor plan was over R50 million. Everything was paid up.

'My father had a heart attack in 2011 and then the bank called up all his sureties. I signed surety for a few places. One building in Bellville, I signed surety there, it was R32 million, and for Standard Bank I signed surety for R50 million just for overdrafts. When they called up the facilities, the money wasn't available immediately so we gave them properties as insurance for the sureties. For that reason we and the bank agreed I would do voluntary sequestration.'

He explains that he was also involved in corporate security at the time, 'doing banks and, like, armed response for big companies like diamonds and jewellers'.

Modack had a history in the underworld before launching an ambitious industry takeover in 2017. He had been friends with Cyril Beeka and had business dealings with Krejcir.

'I met Cyril through a friend many years ago at Cubana in Green Point. After our meeting, we just took off and he used to come visit at my house all the time. He's the only guy who would drive everywhere with me. If we go party, I must take him home. Nobody else. He would sleep at my home without a firearm, that's how he trusted me.'

Modack says he became very close to Beeka and his family, but there was no business relationship; it was strictly friendship. Cronjé, who has been around the block many times and describes himself as 'old school', also worked closely with Beeka over the years. Cronjé is gruffer than Modack as he recalls the halcyon days when he and Beeka were in charge of the city.

'Basically, it all started in the early nineties. Towards '97/'98 myself and Cyril Beeka joined the Lions and basically he ran the security in town with the Dogs, keeping a safe haven for the people to go to the clubs and that. Then we took it a step further, getting clubs to sign on and that. We had a good record; 10 years of providing service to the night life. Not one murder took place. We had a good understanding and a good relationship with the club owners. We had one thing in common; we were anti-drugs, we didn't sell drugs at the clubs. We tried to keep it quite tidy. We did, but maybe we did it in the old-school way and differently to how the people are doing it today. In that time I knew Nafiz, and he knew Cyril very well; they were friends. There were other businesses that Nafiz and Cyril did and, with time, Nafiz got on board with Cyril Beeka.'

It was Beeka who introduced Modack to his friend Krejcir.

'Ja, he introduced me to Krejcir. That's the time me and Krejcir had a fight in the club,' says Modack. I've heard so many versions of what happened in that incident in Casa Blanca on Krejcir's birthday, but the one that Modack tells is by far the most compelling and animated. After all, he was directly involved.

'He smacked a friend of mine. I walked up to him and asked why did you do it. He pushed me and I said if you do it again, I'm going to fuck you up. He pushed me again and it was a physical fight. I hit him over a glass table and his bodyguards jumped up – I think, like, 10 – and Cyril's bodyguards jumped up – like, 20 – and everyone was pushing everyone and eventually the fight stopped. What happened then was he came back to me and gave me his hand, like apologising. I gave him my hand and, as I gave him my hand, he punched me with his left hand and that's the time I punched him back. Cyril jumped up and then him and Cyril was in a fight. Cyril hit him only two shots – he's a dojo black belt – one in his nose and one in his mouth and immediately there's cutting here – 15 stitches, I think, and above his eye another 12 or 13 stitches. That is how I met Radovan Krejcir.'

After that exciting introduction, the two men undertook a few business ventures together around supercars. This includes the infamous incident involving Chico Lopez's McLaren, which saw Mark Lifman and Krejcir almost come to blows in Ian Small-Smith's office in Joburg. When Modack tells the story, it's a convoluted tale with explanations of money collected from Congolese nationals staying in his buildings, accounts being frozen and tens of millions of rand stolen from SBV cash and transferred to car dealers. All in all, Modack downplays his relationship with Krejcir. 'I met him a few times, he was a friend of mine, but no other business besides the car sales.'

But the relationship between the two did continue. After Krejcir was put behind bars, there were suggestions from Crime Intelligence sources that Modack was going to procure a helicopter to break the Czech out of prison. I ask him about this and he looks very surprised.

'No ... They don't know who they're talking about ... No comment on that.'

There was also the claim in court that Krejcir had asked Modack to collect a debt from Demi Jackson. Modack confirms this.

'Ja. That was legal; it was a normal contract because I do deal with debt-collection companies and attorneys. What happened in that case is that his attorneys had to give our attorneys we work with for debt collections, they had to give them the documentation; proof of funds, proof of payments, the dates, who the money was paid to and all that. The only reason why it was on hold was because the attorneys needed to forward the documents to our attorneys. Because of fees outstanding, they said that is why they're not giving the documentation.'

Modack praises Krejcir and agrees that he's in jail because of a conspiracy.

'He's a very intelligent guy and he knows what he should and shouldn't do. I think his only mistake was getting involved with kidnapping that guy. But obviously he's also politically motivated. People from Cape Town who are involved in the underworld and in drugs are obviously paying people in certain places to keep him inside. But if I was the government I would extradite him to his own country and not waste the money of innocent people.'

When Cyril Beeka was killed in March 2011, Modack immediately had his suspicions about who was behind the hit.

'Cyril said to me that Radovan and Donkie have a hit on him, and the day when Cyril was shot Donkie called me first from his cellphone at five past five to say Cyril was shot. Cyril said to me he was going to meet him that particular day.'

Modack has said that when Beeka was gunned down, his life changed after he got an ominous message threatening him: 'You next.' Modack and Cronjé exchange a glance when I ask them if they know who killed Cyril. They nod and agree to tell me. In their opinion, it was Lifman and Donkie Booysen. Obviously, Lifman and Booysen deny this.

Modack pushes his view that Lifman and the cops are in cahoots and that's why the businessman is evading the law. He alleges that the same investigating officer always gets appointed to Lifman's cases and those cases never go anywhere. 'I mean, the investigating officer in the murders – someone else of National Intelligence is reopening all those cases. I actually had a meeting with them this morning. Obviously, it can show you a pattern that there is corruption in the police. The cases run and go to court, but then it says no evidence. Obviously, the police knows what evidence to use and what evidence not to use.'

Modack waited six years after Beeka was killed before rising to take over his mantle. The catalyst, he agrees, was the notorious auction in Parow where he and Lifman came head to head. Modack was being sequestrated and his properties were on the block. Modack's version of events is a complete contradiction of the one given by Lifman. It sounds like a scene out of a movie.

'I went to the auction not knowing Lifman was there. I went with one bodyguard, pulled up at the auction and asked him what he was doing there. He told me I must fuck off, so I told him he must fuck off, but he was standing with, like, 20 guys. The auctioneer then didn't want me to bid, but I said I was bidding for somebody else. He opened the auction at R200 000 – the property was worth about R2 million. I said he won't get the place for 200, then he said to me he's Mark Lifman and I don't know who he is ... I met him once with Cyril, I think in 2006/7. Just like "Hi, this is him," but I didn't have his phone number or nothing. He said at the auction – they actually sold it at 200 000 – I said to the auctioneer, Michael James, that he's not going to give the house to him for R200 000 and he said I don't know who he is blah blah. I told him, "Fuck you."

'There was the next auction, this auction was at 11am and the next one was at 1pm. He said to me I can tell Colin [Booysen] this and that about him and he can do whatever he wants, but not to disrupt the auction – we must get the fuck out of the auction. We went to the next auction. I stopped the auctioneer and said I want to register because he's not selling the house to Lifman. One guy who was with Cyril – his name was Sampie – him and Colin Booysen had an argument, and after that argument Sampie pushed him and Colin smacked him, or something like that. Everyone was fighting, Lifman pointed a gun at me, André pointed a gun at me, a private investigator pointed a gun from behind. When they pointed the gun I said, "Shoot," and none of them wanted to shoot. The other people who were standing behind – Colin's people and my people – had a physical fight in the road. That's when everyone ran away and left. After the auction I spoke to the auctioneer Michael James's daughter; her name is Samantha. I asked her what he's doing at the auction and she said they've asked him to do the security for the auction because there was going to be problems. So I asked her how do they phone an underworld guy to do the security for them against me. I actually have a recording of it where she tells me that Lifman said shit was going to happen. He jumped into her car and drove away with her. He left all his bodyguards there.'

That was the start of everything. Modack then took a decision to move.

'That was how it went. Knowing that I know they are selling drugs in Cape Town and knowing people are getting raped in the clubs. Bad things happen in the clubs. That night I went to tell them they must put somebody else in charge who was going to be clean and fair. We went to a few clubs and everyone said, "Yes, it's fine," but they didn't sign it over to me, they signed it over to a company called TSG. But every person agreed that they were happy that Lifman was not going to be in town; they were happy that drugs were not going to be sold in the clubs.'

'So did you decide to do it because you wanted to get back at Lifman or because you felt there needed to be a change?' I ask.

'There needed to be a change. There were very few people who were going to take him on and he knows I'm not afraid of him. So I took him on and there are a lot of people who want to do it but they can't speak for themselves.'

'Why do you think nobody has taken him on?'

'He has money and I think he has a lot of contacts with police – that's why people don't take him on. But all those cases will be reopened again.'

Modack's two main allies in this 'new' grouping are two old hands, Cronjé and Colin Booysen. Cronjé says he met Modack through Beeka and they remained friends.

'We always stayed in contact with each other while I was in Durban. Basically, I took the opportunity to come back and it was a door opening for me. I will stand right by him; he is standing for the right cause, you know. Especially for one reason: he's against drugs; he doesn't sell drugs, and the other group's main reason to be involved in the clubs is to control the drugs. That's the truth.'

Modack insists he is not actually part of the TSG company and he hasn't been part of an extortion racket.

'TSG is a security company themselves. They offer security services to anybody. Anybody who needs security, they can provide them with the service. TSG was opened in 2012 and I only met [TSG boss Grant Veroni] in late 2017.'

There's no doubt in Modack's mind that Lifman is running the cops against him.

'He is using cops. Look, there is a lot of clean cops, but there are a lot of dirty cops as well. But everyone in this case, you can see that Lifman is working with the police. For example, in late January where Grant Veroni, the owner of TSG, was rearrested for some charge and then he made an affidavit before he was arrested, stating that Mark Lifman phoned him two weeks prior to his arrest to say that he was going to be arrested for this charge, this is how much the bail is going to be, this is what the conditions are going to be. He should sign all the clubs back to Lifman and Naudé then they will let him go. He said no. He put it on record. Surely people inside the courtroom were involved in it, people inside the DPP were involved in signing the warrant of arrest and knew about it. How else would Lifman get the information that that guy was going to be arrested on a particular day and that he was going to be released on R3000 bail, unless he's a fortune teller?' says Modack sarcastically.

I ask about the allegations that Modack took out hits on the cops and the prosecutor while he was behind bars.

'That's bullshit. They came up there to add some spice because they could see there was no proof of evidence in the case and the case was falling apart. That's exactly what happened and they came up with the allegations.'

There are several allegations that arose out of the bail application that he would specifically like to refute. Key amongst these is the claim that advocate Pete Mihalik sold a stolen firearm on his behalf and allegations made by Igor Russol in an affidavit presented to the court.

'This never happened. Not only was there no statement in the docket but no evidence as such existed. This was false allegations as Colonel Kinnear and General Vearey knew advocate Mihalik is the best criminal defence advocate in Cape Town and probably the country. It was fake allegations to remove him from our legal team. Lifman paid Igor to give a statement against me and Colin and Pete Mihalik. Igor contacted me for a job, his family was gonna be killed in Ukraine. I have all the messages from him. He said if I don't help him out his family will suffer, he will let his wife become a dancer at a strip club and his daughter a dancer at Mavericks, so I felt sorry for him and gave him cash to bring his family to Cape Town. He worked by me for one month and was a liability, then I got rid of him. And Igor can't even harm a fly. Why would I tell him I wanna arrange a hit on Lifman and Donkie? He got paid 10k to give the cops that statement but I guarantee he will never come testify as whatever he said was bullshit. They came up with many allegations – I have hand grenades and whatever.'

'Do you have a hand grenade?'

'I don't even know how to use one! That's all allegations to add spice to it so that the judge would say no bail. Then the agreement also was let out under oath from the investigating officer in Johannesburg that he's going to arrest me and Jacques for intimidation and extortion on the day we get bail in Cape Town. He read it out under oath to the judge. Two or three weeks before we actually went to Johannesburg.

'We appeared in Joburg three times. The judge actually asked on record what accused number one was doing there; he didn't see that I did anything wrong; he didn't see any intimidation or extortion.'

What about the messages sent to Andrew Phillips?

'Jacques phoned him to offer him security because Jacques was the partner of Cyril Beeka and then he said no. This was in October last year. We found out that Andrew Phillips and Lifman, they are friends, they play poker together. I also found out that Jacques has the recording of Cyril Beeka and Radovan Krejcir where Andrew Phillips gave them the order to execute Lolly Jackson, and for that reason they were both going to get 50 per cent shares in Teazers and The Grand.'

Neither of them will produce the recording or say whether they will hand it over to the cops as requested.

'There was a story behind the one message that I sent him. He gave a message to someone to threaten me. I replied via the message. It wasn't picked up in court because it wasn't necessary. It's all bullshit; it's from numbers not linked to me. This investigator was only supposed to arrest us on 28 February; he arrested us three weeks before that because they saw that there was no evidence in this case so they wanted us to go to Johannesburg and they tried to centralise both cases, but the judge didn't agree to it.'

Modack also denies that he took out a hit on Lifman. In fact, he says the reverse is true. There has been a hit taken out on him.

'Ja, there was a few times, that's why I'm walking around with security.'

'Are you worried for your safety?'

'Not at all. Whatever happens, happens. Obviously, I'm not going to look for it.' He shrugs his shoulders and appears nonchalant.

There has been a lot of speculation about who Modack is actually working for and about the fact that he's been photographed with so many senior cops. I've been told on the record that he's a registered police source. I've also been told that he's on the payroll of the SSA.

Modack has always been vague about his involvement with the state. When asked about this in a previous interview with News24, he denied buying information from Crime Intelligence officers, or selling information. He would not comment on how he had got hold of the 'classified documents' about police generals that he claimed police had illegally removed from his Plattekloof home. He said he worked with several wealthy international clients, 'foreigners and big investors', and provided security to 'people right from the top down'. Including politicians. He's been photographed with Duduzane Zuma and I've been told the two men are close.

When I ask Modack if he is a registered police agent, his response is emphatic: 'No, I'm not. [Gauteng Hawks boss Prince Mokotedi] wanted me to register, but I didn't register. I said I'll give him the information for free to make everything safer in Cape Town. I mean, if I was a registered informer, the moment these people locked me up I could pick up the phone and ask him to get me out immediately.'

He says he is cooperating with the police to clean up the city.

'Look, if they want information I can give them information to make Cape Town safer and to make the clubs safer. That's my duty as a South African citizen and that is what I've done. There are no corrupt allegations against me to say I've phoned this guy to help me or that guy. It's crap.'

Modack insists that the meetings with the cops are 'just to make Cape Town safer' and denies the claim that he's a registered source.

When I follow up with a specific question as to whether he is working for the State Security Agency and if they are backing his takeover, his response is 'No comment'.

Officially, the State Security Agency says it can't comment on this. 'Operational information as to how sources are recruited and the identity thereof is strictly prohibited from disclosure. At all material times, the SSA must follow the law and all regulatory prescripts in the conduct of its work,' says spokesperson Brian Dube.

Modack says it is Lifman who is the registered source. 'They got that information from Mark Lifman. Lifman is a registered informer. When the incident happened at the auction, [a cop] took Lifman to Parow police station to open a case and lay a charge there.'

Following Lifman's arrest, he claimed he was targeted by a group of cops acting at Modack's command. Again, Modack insists that this is not true.

'I go to the police station. I don't phone someone and ask them to do me a favour. Normal procedure was followed. Anyone who is not locked up is allowed to open a case – it's law.'

He's also questioned General Jeremy Vearey's motives and says the senior policeman is pursuing this matter because it's 'personal'.

'I got information that Vearey is linked to Jerome Booysen. All the evidence came out in court and they still say the allegations are not there. Other police are doing the investigation so we will have to wait and see what the outcome is. He's the one who had links with the gangs all over the years, not myself. Even Colin said to me that Vearey is his brother.'

Aside from his proximity to the police, questions have also been raised about Modack's close association with politicians. What is the story with Duduzane Zuma then? I ask.

'There's no story. I just walked into him at the One&Only. Whatever cop was surveilling us took a photo. There is no relation; they just blew it out of proportion when they got the picture.'

As was the case with Krejcir, I get the sense that Modack may be a built-up myth in much the same way the Czech was. He's being touted as the new 'Don' in town. I ask him if this is true.

'Not at all.'

'Have you taken over from Cyril?'

'Not at all.'

Modack doesn't know whether he will be arrested again, but for now he's just carrying on with his business. 'Anybody can be arrested for anything. I don't know, we'll see what happens. Carry on. Selling motor vehicles and properties.'

He's not quite sure how this standoff between the two factions is going to resolve itself. I venture that there may be more violence, more bloodshed.

'I have no idea; it will just play out in its own time. When TSG took over the security, there were only two shootings in the clubs, one at Caprice and one by Coco. That were the gangs and we gave that information to [police investigator] Paul Hendrickse and he arrested them, that's why there's no more shooting at the clubs. The way they're putting it is, we shot at the clubs; the time the shootings happened, TSG already had the security – they didn't have to go there and fight to get the contract. The public thinks we were there to take over the club and people got shot innocently. Those people went there particularly to cause ructions in Cape Town.'

Modack wants the residents of Cape Town to know that he and his men are not violent. They are there to bring peace and stability to the nightclub scene and to remove drugs from the clubs. He wants to assure everyone that the clubs are safe.

'We didn't bring the violence; the violence was there, but the police kept it subtle. Every day people got raped in the clubs, but the police covered it up. Their police was covering up everything, that's why no one knew what was happening in the clubs. Now if someone walks on the street and slip on the banana peel, they will phone the police and say Modack was there,' he says, echoing a phrase we have heard many times before from Krejcir.

'We've cleaned up town so all the gangs are out of Cape Town. People who go there to enjoy themselves can be sure that they're not going to get hurt or shot. It's safe to go there. The media are saying we are causing havoc; it's not like that. Cape Town is safe now.'

'I APPRECIATE THE REQUEST PRIMARILY BECAUSE THIS IS THE FIRST time that anyone who has ever written on me asked for my view or response,' reads the email in my inbox from head of the Hawks in Gauteng, Major General Prince Mokotedi.

It's March 2018 and I'm putting the final touches to this book. As he had left the NPA under a cloud and played a central role in the rift in the SAPS, I want to hear what Mokotedi has to say. We meet on a Saturday afternoon at the Wits Business School where he's studying for a second master's degree.

Prince Mokotedi has never been a media darling. During Jackie Selebi's corruption trial, he testified for Selebi against his own employer, the NPA. He was seen as being part of the pro-Zuma camp in the NPA and instrumental in removing Glynnis Breytenbach. He then left the NPA before he could face a disciplinary hearing for allegedly leaking information to the media. When he was named head of the Hawks in Gauteng in 2016, replacing Shadrack Sibiya, the reaction was largely negative. When he opened the bizarre case of treason and espionage after the Krejcir mansion meeting, it seemed that suspicions about his political agenda were confirmed.

Mokotedi has some things he would like to get off his chest upfront: he is more than qualified to be in charge of the Hawks in the province, he has a history of policing, his motive is not political and he was never part of a 'cabal' with Nomgcobo Jiba and Lawrence Mrwebi at the NPA to protect Richard Mdluli.

'Before I joined the NPA I was with the Ministry of Police. I was there since the mid-1990s. People thought I was born in the NPA, but I was not born in the NPA. I started my career in the police. Throughout my career I got a BA in Governance from Franklin & Marshall College in the eighties.

I did a postgraduate diploma in Social Science Research at Stellenbosch. I did a Master's of Social Science Research at Stellenbosch. I have a BA in Police Science (from UNISA). I have an LLB (also from UNISA) and I'm doing another master's now (at Wits). The master's I did in Stellenbosch was on policing – police cynicism. I can tell a police officer from a mile away because I studied police behaviour,' he points out over cooldrinks in the canteen. There is no security detail and he looks like a student in jeans and a casual shirt.

Mokotedi lists his achievements during his time at the NPA, and how he set up the enforcement unit from scratch. He is at pains to distance himself from the narrative that the prosecuting authority was deeply divided and that he was partially responsible for that.

'I think I met Mdluli three times in my life. There was zero communication between me and Mdluli. As for Jiba and Mrwebi, I never sat with them like this on more than three occasions. The first time I sat with Jiba and Mrwebi together was when they were suspended. The first time that they were suspended. They asked me to do an affidavit in their support, to explain my role in this whole thing, and I did that. That was really the first time that I sat with them together. We never planned to or orchestrated to remove or target anyone. I am pretty close with them separately.

'I think we all exaggerated the split in the NPA. The tension for me at the NPA was much more at the top levels, was much more around your deputies who were there at the time. As for your nine directors of public prosecution, they were not involved. In my interview with Redi Tlhabi on 702, I said that if I am with the Zuma clique, then there has to be a Zille clique because you can't have only one faction. I respect Zuma, I think he was one president who was able to carry and properly articulate the principles of the National Democratic Revolution. I think he is one president who was able to properly do that. I think he was one president who said let's look east and not west and, having grown up in the socialist movement, I find it very attractive. The personality and how he is characterised in the media, that is something else. But he decided that we as a country will make friends with BRICS and I find that very attractive. I share his political views and respect him. I'm not a political person. At the intellectual level, at the policy level I found his ideas attractive. I support that South Africa should move out of the International [Criminal] Court.'

Mokotedi also wants to set the record straight about why he left the NPA before clearing his name in a disciplinary hearing.

'I was sure that Mxolisi [former NDPP Mxolisi Nxasana] was going to fire me. And I was sure that Karen [van Rensburg, former NPA head] was going to fire me. I think they had taken the position that I was a nuisance to them. I wasn't taking abuse. Mxolisi was very abusive; he's an emotional wreck – he would bang the tables in meetings. I don't think he's the brightest – I mean, I've worked with all four of the previous NDPPs, and I don't want to say he's the dumbest, but he's not the brightest. I still think that he's not fit and proper. The charge sheet I was given had nothing to do with leaking information, by the way; the charges were quite frivolous.'

After leaving the NPA, Mokotedi disappeared for a while and then came in from the cold and was appointed by Berning Ntlemeza at a time when the SAPS was deeply politicised, raising questions about the politics of Mokotedi's appointment.

'I think I was ready. Remember that when I left the NPA I was a chief director, in police language I was a major general. When I left the police I was a director. I qualified in that sense. I have a degree in policing, I have a degree in law, I have a master's in policing. I've always been ready. I could've taken the position five years earlier even. I've never doubted my capacity or ability to take over the Hawks in Gauteng.

'You know the political thing in the police does not exist. In the NPA you can argue because Jiba, Mrwebi and I were there and we were wrongly seen to be linked to Zuma and so on, but in the police – I'd be very frank with you, you can much rather talk about your relations with criminal gangs. The political thing in the police does not exist. Actually, if you come in there with political clout you'll be very isolated. I sit with the generals; sometimes I think they are deliberately oblivious to the whole political thing that is happening.'

To my surprise, Mokotedi even suggests that Mdluli was 'isolated' within the SAPS because of his political alignment to former President Zuma.

'It's my own interpretation of how I see things. This animal called police spews you out. That is why you find Mdluli has been spewed out. That is why you find our previous national commissioner was spewed out – Phiyega. That's why I say in the police you can talk criminal things but not political things. If there would be a capture, it would not be political, it would be criminal.'

But what about the astonishing claims he made about treasonous plots and assassination attempts? That certainly stinks of politics, and both O'Sullivan and Sibiya have told me they believe Mokotedi is still pushing an agenda against them.

'Remember, there were intelligence reports that said within some circles they say Mokotedi is a straight guy. They were worried when I said I'm going to unbundle these things and so on and so forth. There was really an effort to get me out. If it means shooting me down … I always carry my gun with me because I'm not afraid to investigate if there's a basis for investigation. The day that I opened that case a police colonel came to me and said, "Prince, this is what I heard from a very close source." Now this man is a police colonel, he's not a source. When a senior police official comes to you and says that is going to happen – if it was about me only, I would be fine because I had bodyguards – it was not only about me, it was Ntlemeza and all of those guys, so it was important for me. It wasn't just about reporting; it was to say that there must be an investigation on this thing. If a colonel who has a source that is inside, you cannot ignore it; if I ignore it, the next thing Ntlemeza gets shot, then they'll say Prince did nothing. A number of people came forward and said they were hired to kill us. We have a guy in witness protection who said he was hired and that Paul O'Sullivan paid him to kill us guys.'

For the record, O'Sullivan completely denies this.

'That investigation is ongoing, and if there's one docket that worries Paul O'Sullivan, it's that one. Paul O'Sullivan is like a psychopath. Once he puts his mind to something he doesn't easily change, and when he gets a distraction he cracks. If there's one person who understands Paul O'Sullivan, it's me. I can easily provoke him and I can easily get him to sit down and talk to me. There is no direct investigation on [Sibiya]. This was purely on Paul – the assassination stuff. Sibiya's things were around Arab Spring kind of a thing. There's no docket against Sibiya in my office.'

The essence of Mokotedi's message is that there are no politics at play in the police structures, but what he is very worried about is the capture of the SAPS by criminal syndicates. He is extremely concerned about this 'criminal capture' of individuals.

'I think that for you to look at it at the top you're going to miss it. What police do; they don't hunt in packs. But you'll find General So-and-so with Warrant Officer So-and-so. There's no racketeering or clique at the top. I've studied that because of my line of work. You'd find one or two guys with a lot of support – junior staff pushing for X-Y-Z. Take Sibiya, for instance; he had his own clique – an extensive one – pushing for Indian business people; he had a hand in the Israeli gangsters; he had a little bit in the Chinese gangsters.'

For the record again, Sibiya denies this too.

Mokotedi tells me a story about a trip to police provincial headquarters several years ago when he visited two different high-ranking cops in the same building. Behind closed doors, both officers warned him about the other being on the payroll of syndicates.

'Here am I, you have two senior police officials – this one is saying that one is in the pocket of the Bulgarians, and that one is saying the other one is in the pockets of the Chinese. I'm saying this to you to say that the capture is not in the political sense.'

Krejcir is a prime example of this. However, I have always had the impression that once Krejcir was removed, the network around him collapsed and effectively disappeared. Mokotedi tells me this is not the case. Investigations are ongoing.

'Remember, the Krejcir thing is not finalised; there's still a lot of things that are being investigated. I must say it properly; the investigators are looking at a number of things – it would be appropriate to restart a bigger project to look into his other operations and people he was working with. Remember what happened here: you had a clique yet again, the boss is just removed. I think the way that they dealt with the Krejcir matter was unwise because you simply remove the boss. There is still a network that is operational. You just removed the boss.

'You can't have a successful criminal operation without a police network supporting you. It's impossible. You remove Krejcir and a few guys and that's it. I interviewed Krejcir for about six hours in prison,' Mokotedi reveals. 'I went there with Intelligence guys and clearly there's a bigger issue. You can't sit with Krejcir and he doesn't mention Sibiya. Every third sentence will be Sibiya or a general in the context that they were supporting him.

'It's murder, corruption … We strongly think that Krejcir had something to do with the murder of Cyril Beeka. There's a payment that's been made in the name of Cyril Beeka. And there were other police officials involved there, so that's what we're trying to figure out.'

This brings us to the so-called new Don on the block – Nafiz Modack. I've been given a photograph of Mokotedi meeting with Modack at a restaurant in Cape Town in July 2017. Why is the head of the Hawks in Gauteng personally meeting in public with a suspected criminal kingpin? Is he a state agent, as I've been told?

'He's able to help us establish where and how the exchange of the money took place and the actual killers, you know, those boys who were on motor-bikes …' says Mokotedi, referring to the Beeka hit.

'Is Modack a registered source?'

'I believe so. At least up until last year July.'

'Why was there a change after July?'

'I think it is because he is not observing protocol – he is doing things that are unlawful – and then hides behind some relations with a general. Saying he was with a general.'

Mokotedi also confirms that Modack is helping the Hawks with another investigation. They're convinced that there is a 'grabber', a device used to listen to phone calls, in the criminal underworld. It's being rented out to different syndicates and even to politicians to use.

'We pretty much suspect who might have the grabber and what they're using it for. We pretty much have an idea of where that grabber might be. We know that they are probably somewhere at the Michelangelo [Hotel in Sandton]. Modack was helping us to find it, because he was also using it. It's rented out to criminals. They say you pay about R5000 for them to listen to someone else.'

A phone-signal 'grabber', or IMSI catcher, is a powerful device that is able to intercept calls and messages or clone a phone. Its potential in the hands of criminals is terrifying. It could be used to listen to journalists, to police investigators, to politicians or to rival criminals. Another police general has corroborated Mokotedi's claim, and both men have given me the name of the well-known local businessman who controls this rogue grabber.

When I interviewed Modack, I did ask whether all this was true.

'Yes. No comment on this. But if they found the grabber, South Africa would be much safer,' said Modack.

'So it's true that there's a grabber?'

'Yes. I know there is one in circulation. A grabber works if you take that person's cell number, you can listen to that person's conversation, which is illegal. The state is doing it, but they're not supposed to do it – they need to get a 205. They were also listening to my calls illegally. They couldn't use it in court.'

I also asked Modack if the grabber is being used by the wrong people for the wrong reasons.

'Obviously for the wrong reasons, but I don't know who the person is who has the grabber, but there is one. They say it's in Gauteng somewhere. It belonged to the government before; one in Johannesburg and one in Cape Town, but the Cape Town one disappeared,' he told me.

Mokotedi downplays the photograph of his meeting with Modack, explaining that it is virtually insignificant in comparison to the true extent of their interactions.

'There is nothing untoward – he would come to our offices and I'd say, Modack, what do you have? We would task him even. That photo is small compared to communications between me and him. I would say I gave you So-and-so to talk to and he would send things to me.'

Again, a fine line is being trod between investigating suspected criminals and law enforcement agencies using them as sources and agents.

'It is inevitable and especially because currently most of your senior officials have put their hands in their pockets – they don't want to be involved. They wouldn't go to a crime scene so we're sitting with a problem where our guys on the ground have no leadership. Nobody wants to touch anything. Nobody wants to be involved in anything else. For me, as a senior police official, it's disturbing because you find yourself alone, working on quite complex matters where nobody else wants to be involved. Nobody wants to touch organised crime.'

Mokotedi paints a picture of terrifying inaction, of a police leadership that has been so rocked by scandal after scandal that no one in management is willing to take on organised crime because they are so fearful of the repercussions for their own careers. I wonder what the implication of all this is, in real terms.

'It means that we are in trouble as a country. There's no appetite to tackle organised crime head-on. There are a number of reasons; one is that senior police officials don't want to get involved. They say that if they go talk to this one, they're in trouble or in the media. We can close our doors to them, to people like Modack, but then it means we've closed our intelligence-gathering capacity to them. Remember, our agents are not well trained to infiltrate your organised crime groupings. Our structure of intelligence is not adapting to the sophistication of organised crime in our country. They still want to give an agent R200. We call it "pap geld". I mean, come on, if I want an agent to infiltrate I must give him an X5, I must give him a Mercedes-Benz because he needs to be able to play the part. If you bring me a police constable, he will never be able to play that part. We must draw our agents from the police service – that's the big problem. Nobody wants to deal with this thing.

'We had a meeting with our African counterparts on the issue of drugs and they give you their targets who are hiding in South Africa and 90 per cent of them are not on our radar. I met with the Israeli police attaché and they were saying they were reluctant to see me. But after speaking to other people they decided to come see me because they have a serious problem. I asked why they were reluctant and they said with my predecessor they realised that they were going to be compromised and they explained why. They would say there are four fugitives from Israel who are in our country who have committed serious crimes in Israel and Europe and nothing is being done. They gave a whole list of the Israeli mafia in the country. The scary thing is that none of those people are on our radar. One of them reports here at Bedfordview every day because he's on bail for some other thing.

'What I'm saying to you is that this thing is much more complex. We're in much more trouble than what the ordinary person thinks. We haven't touched the Israeli, Chinese or Greek mafia. We haven't touched anything. They're saying we're stupid.'

Mokotedi tells me that in each criminal investigation his members are doing, there would be at least six or seven cops who are part of the criminal syndicate. Since he took over at the Hawks in 2016, at least 120 police officials have been arrested for corruption, and the numbers are increasing.

'It would need a serious revamp of the DPCI [Hawks] if we were to get anywhere. I think the DPCI needs a fresh revamp, even if it means all of us move out, because the guys are not trained to investigate proper organised crime. So we really need to sit down and reconfigure the DPCI. The bigger challenge we have are people removing money from this country illegally. I want to give you this picture that says we are in much bigger trouble. I can give you whatever. Tons and tons of examples relating to that. Almost all of Sandton is owned by the mafia, the apartments. It's mafias there from all walks of life. Everyone from the mafia can settle in this country because they feel comfortable because we're not doing much. I'm just saying it's a much bigger problem than we think. We are doing our utmost best under the circumstances.'

I N RESEARCHING THIS BOOK, AS I SAT ACROSS FROM GANGSTERS, generals, prosecutors and relatives of those who had been slain, I felt deeply concerned about the state's inability to combat organised crime and the implications of that for all citizens.

The criminal justice system has been intentionally broken for politically motivated reasons and organised crime is capitalising on it. The players can spot the weaknesses and they prise them open with money, power, influence and corruption. The police's and the NPA's capacity to fight organised crime has been vastly compromised and time after time we have seen how the kingpins, the Dons, are either on the payroll of the police because they are agents or sources or, alternatively, they have top police officers on their own payrolls to protect them from investigation and prosecution. In some instances, both scenarios apply.

Politics, the police and organised crime are frighteningly intertwined. Richard Mdluli and Radovan Krejcir, two protagonists in parallel stories, are prime examples of this. Mdluli acted with the hubris engendered by political protection to advance his own cause and plunder the Crime Intelligence funds while abusing the capabilities of his agency to pursue the narrow political interests of his principals. Krejcir was able to identify the weaknesses in the system wrought by police officers such as Mdluli and Joey Mabasa, to build a criminal empire on the foundations of various strata of corruption, from street-level patrol cops to the very top commanders.

That same dynamic is replicated in different spheres of the underworld throughout the country, from the illegal cigarette trade to rhino poaching to abalone smuggling to the taxi industry to Cape Town's extortion rackets. The worlds of crime and policing are inextricably linked. Granted, it is not a situation unique to South Africa – it occurs around the world. But this is the South African version of the story, which I've come to refer to as the Ministry of Crime.

There are three elements to the Ministry of Crime. The first is political interest protected through the abuse of the criminal justice system. This is done by means of selective prosecutions or by keeping people in positions they are not necessarily fit to hold. This is why the capture of the NPA is crucial in ensuring that the politically powerful are not prosecuted. The second is the protection afforded to these individuals by those at the police and the Hawks. These are the Mdlulis and the Ntlemezas, and this element explains the evisceration of all the agencies in the country that have law enforcement capabilities. The third element is the transactional relationship between the police, particularly in Crime Intelligence, and the organised criminals through the informant system.

Many of the experts I spoke to have shared their insights and reflections on the nexus between these three worlds and the patterns that repeat themselves as politics, policing and organised crime collide.

'In a way, your Ministry of Crime is the intersection between the political, the transactional and the secret world,' explains Professor Mark Shaw. 'Mdluli and his appointment and protection by Zuma is not disconnected from the transactional. Like tapping somebody's phone and putting somebody's phone illegally on the list that the judge approves. There are transactional requirements. Just getting money to send your children to school, money to protect yourself from the system. The connection here is that some of these things are overlooked if you're playing the game. Mdluli is such a classic example. A person like Mdluli cycles through all three of these worlds. That's why he is a key figure and that's why he has protection. More complex, in a way, is the use of the underworld and information brokering. It's not disconnected. These three things intersect with each other and out of that come the actions of the Ministry of Crime.'

Shaw explains further using the practical example of Radovan Krejcir.

'Remember, Krejcir is not from here, so he is an outsider parachuted in. His language is money. And he found willing people, so someone like Mdluli, in my view, takes that cash and he feeds his own internal police network, but he relies on political protection and in order to do that he acts in particular ways. I think that's the complex interface that is occurring.'

Former Police General Solomon Makgale explained to me what these dynamics would look like in practice. 'The higher echelons of the criminal justice system are in a mess. Most leaders are associated with certain politicians, while some have skeletons in their closets. In exchange for money and favours, such as promotions and political protection, they are prepared to look the other way when there is crime committed. There is no gangster, drug lord, high-level criminals in rhino horn, abalone, cash-in-transit kingpins, etcetera, that is not known to the police. For example, they know that you owe the taxman R10 million and that you've committed such-and-such a criminal offence at some point. So, they'll come to you and tell you that they'll sort you out with the taxman or whatever legal problems, so you've got to pay them. It is about politicians who want certain investigations to disappear – their children, girlfriends, wives, business partners, family members – and investigations against political opponents to be intensified. Business people also do the same. They can pay cops to do dirty work for them, including commercial espionage. So it is the nexus of bent cops, corrupt politicians and shady business people that compromises police investigations into organised crime. Some junior officers see the mess at the top and decide that they should also cash in. Consequently, there is no political will to sort out the mess that SAPS Crime Intelligence and the Hawks have become.'

Policing expert Gareth Newham has followed the events in the SAPS for decades. He explains the politicisation of the police and other law enforcement agencies and how this Ministry of Crime has evolved. The politicisation of policing and prosecuting is rooted in the fact that the president, solely, appoints the national director of public prosecutions and other significant role players in the sector, at his own discretion. This system is fundamentally flawed.

A broken criminal justice system is also conducive to the flourishing of organised crime. A captured system is even better, which is why criminals are so intent on getting Crime Intelligence officers in particular into their networks and complicit in their criminality, as Newham explains.

'Crime Intelligence officers are the least accountable and have access to the most information. Crime Intelligence almost operates like a police agency, a completely separate division within SAPS. It's almost like the old Security Branch; you could almost say it's undercover. They have access to all the surveillance technology. They're the guys who are supposed to, in an ideal model of policing in South Africa, identify who's doing what and then give the information where the detectives can find the evidence. So in other words, they don't do arrests, they don't raid buildings, they just tell the units that do, that's where they're going to find contraband, what time, who's involved and what to look for. That's what they're supposed to do.'

It is because of the opaque nature of the Crime Intelligence environment that Mdluli was able to get away with whatever he was up to.

'It's the most powerful component of policing because you can get information that no one else can get, you can get world-class surveillance technology at your fingertips, you can locate people, you can listen in on their phone calls, you can read emails, you can get their WhatsApps, you can listen to them having chats in houses. You can find everything about them, their bank statements, what they own; you know, it's like nothing's off limits. If you want to do it legally you have to get a judge to authorise it, but the vast majority of these things don't work that way. If they have an idea that someone may be involved in a crime, they survey them; when they get the evidence, then they go to the judge. So it becomes an incredibly powerful tool of the police. Then you put people there who are not your most ethically sound people; they might be connected to politicians and they know a lot of stuff that's going on.'

Paul O'Sullivan agrees that the shady secrecy around Crime Intelligence allows criminal elements to use it to their advantage.

'My view is that Crime Intelligence has since the days of Selebi been a tool of the underworld. Nothing has changed. They use so-called secrecy to conceal their criminal conduct, whilst looting funds that are supposed to be used to pay undercover agents to get intelligence on criminal syndicates. Worse still, these thugs actually provide intelligence for the targets of underworld hit men. Put simply, if Crime Intelligence was shut down, crime would reduce, because we would be disempowering a lot of criminals. For Crime Intelligence to work, it needs to have a proper internal affairs division, which polices their activities. The inspector-general for intelligence is a waste of taxpayer funds and they have no teeth or investigative capacity. The auditor general is not allowed to audit the Crime Intelligence slush funds. This must change and they must be held accountable for abuse of taxpayer funds.'

Because of this environment and culture, there need to be very clear guidelines around where the line is drawn between the police and their agents or sources. As Joey Mabasa told me, if you want to find intelligence in organised crime, you have to get your hands dirty. So where do you draw the line?

'You have to have very clear protocols for doing that in your agency, which I don't think we have. You're going to have to train people for that. So, you don't say, "Okay, this is what we do in South Africa, you're Crime Intelligence, go find information, go make friends with corrupt criminals,"' explains Newham, highlighting what is currently happening. 'I mean, you'll be told if you're a Crime Intelligence guy, "Go, go and make contacts, go get informers." I mean, you've got to go and go hang out with criminals and be willing to pay them for information. Claim their claims, pay them and then demonstrate that that information gives you something. So that's being embedded, being undercover is a perennial policing problem internationally. So the FBI and places like that have whole academies that train you.'

The police end up losing cops to the dark side, led astray by the lure of money and the good life. 'You're hanging out with bad guys all the time and when you're in the police it's rules and regulations and you're doing everything wrong. You're being crapped on all the time for not doing enough and you're late and you haven't filled in this form and blah, blah, blah and there's a ton of paperwork. Then you go and do your job as an undercover agent and it's parties and it's drugs and it's girls, it's living the high life, driving fancy cars. Now do that for a number of years and stop thinking you want to go back to the police, especially when you also realise, doing that, how most of the guys that do this never get arrested and prosecuted and that the chances of you actually going to jail are minimal,' Newham laughs. 'I mean, there were four convictions under the Prevention of Organised Crime Act [POCA] last year!'

Newham says the statistics paint a picture of the state's depleted capacity to fight organised crime. The powerful legislation put in place to prosecute racketeering and gang-linked crimes, the POCA Act, saw only four convictions in the whole country over the 2016/2017 period.

So where are we, in reality, in the fight against organised crime?

'We're nowhere!' Newham exclaims. 'I would say, we haven't even really got out of the starting blocks. I mean, we've got Krejcir. Who else do we have? It was because he was so blatant, because the media were all over it, because he was linked to 10 murders, because the politicians were saying here's a guy who is making us look like a bunch of idiots.'

It's safe to say that Crime Intelligence has been captured for political gain. 'There's 9000 people in Crime Intelligence, in the police. But you just need to capture the top. The others can carry on doing their work. Just look at the statistics. You'll just see deterioration, some indicators drop in three years by 50 per cent.' He too has heard about how very little, if any, actual Crime Intelligence work is being done.

'They all say the same thing. They potter about and they're not doing anything because the people who are high enough to, the people on top who should be doing the strategy and making sure that Crime Intelligence is happening in the country, are appointed to do Crime Intelligence on Zuma's enemies and allies so that they know who's voting what way, and so they can't do that and run or give guidance and dedicated instructions and monitor what the rest of Crime Intelligence is doing.'

Former Deputy National Commissioner General Godfrey Lebeya was probably one of the country's most qualified police officers. He wrote a textbook on organised crime and has a doctorate on the topic, but was removed during Phiyega's purge. He says the work being done to combat organised crime has deteriorated.

'When you compare them with others, they can do much more. They can

447

do much better than what we are doing as of now. I can say this because if I compare the product today with what we have been able to do in 2011, they are doing very little now. I am seeing portfolio committee or parliament researchers doing comparisons between the successes that we were able to achieve in 2011 and 2016 and they can't match close to that time. Organised crime has to be identified by Crime Intelligence, and the current Crime Intelligence is not that effective. Crime Intelligence has for a long time not been having a head of the division and then those who are sitting there are in acting capacity. So, what management is supposed to be doing is to finalise the issues with the head so that the division can operate effectively. I will put an acting divisional commissioner, who is not supposed to take instruction from a suspended person. We still have got competent people who from time to time will be seeing the successes, but it is weakened compared to where it is supposed to be today because we are supposed to be improving, not going down.'

Western Cape police ombudsman and former NPA head Vusi Pikoli has spent a great deal of his career looking at the relationship between organised crime and the police. He says it's a historical relationship that goes back decades. He uses the example of Italian mafioso and fugitive Vito Palazzolo, who came to South Africa in the 1980s and established deep political connections.

'Let's take Palazzolo … South Africa failed to extradite Palazzolo despite everything that was seen as goodwill to extradite him. I undertook a trip to Italy to try to facilitate the extradition of Palazzolo, but I failed. Rumour has it that Palazzolo had watched people, for instance National Intelligence Agency, within the police. People who were supposed to be surveilling him, he buys them off and then nothing happens. We gave up – we had all the intelligence, we went to Italy. There was no will to have the guy extradited.'

Pikoli, who initiated the prosecution of Jackie Selebi, says police officers need to be ethical when dealing with criminals.

'The network between the police and criminals is highly problematic. People who are supposed to be enforcing the law are getting involved with organised crime syndicates. That is the reality. You will always have rotten cops in the system. It's a question of personal integrity, what else can I say.'

Measures also need to be taken to ensure that agencies are not captured for political motives. Again, it comes down to who appoints the people in charge of those institutions, says Pikoli.

'Is the leadership of these institutions not the particular issue? The type of people who get appointed in these institutions. Also, the powers that the president exercises, I think, should be somehow capped. The president appoints the chief of the Defence Force, there is no laid-down procedure as to how to do that. He appoints the national commissioner of police, he appoints the national director of public prosecutions, he appoints the statistician general. If you've got an evil president who is deep into criminality, he will obviously appoint heads who are a part of the game. For instance, it's important for civil society to make sure that what we're saying, we are not taking the power from you as president; there has to be a laid-down procedure to encourage transparency and openness. So at least once a person gets appointed, the public will have some confidence because, as the public, we participated in the appointment.'

Ultimately, it comes down to the political will to make the required changes. Significantly, the momentum of that political will received a considerable boost at the ANC's Nasrec conference in December 2017, with the election of Cyril Ramaphosa as the president of the ANC. He provided the impetus for Police Minister Fikile Mbalula, the self-styled 'Minister Fear Fokkol', to execute a clean sweep. In just one week in January, three separate events took place. Morris 'Captain KGB' Tshabalala was arrested on charges of fraud, theft and corruption while reporting to his parole officer. Richard Mdluli was finally retired off on pension by 'mutual agreement', which meant he left the SAPS, but he did so with R12 million in his pocket. He was due to go on pension a few months later anyway, so that deadline was simply moved forward. Then, Mbalula also announced that a new process was under way to appoint permanent heads of both the Hawks and of Crime Intelligence.

In February 2018, Bheki Cele was appointed minister of police in place of Mbalula, and who he appoints to head the Hawks and Crime Intelligence will be absolutely crucial because they will have to restore credibility and integrity to their roles and rehabilitate public confidence. They have to be individuals who are apolitical and who are in the business of policing.

Even Joey Mabasa, who left the organisation under a cloud of shame, agrees that the police cannot afford to be politicised in the way that it has been.

'I think, as a way forward, we need to get the right people in the strategic posts, irrespective of whether it is a comrade or not. The police have lost a lot of good people. The people who are remaining … oh my gosh, it's terrible. We cannot continue as "comrade, comrade" when the country is going down; this is what is killing the police. To deploy someone because he is a comrade, but he doesn't know anything. I hope they will realise that they will have to put the right people in the strategic posts. The police have lost a lot of good people.'

After years of senior police officers being vulnerable to corruption and bringing shame upon the service, the venality can no longer continue. If it does, it will allow all the other 'little Krejcirs' out there to expand and grow their networks and empires into dangerous, criminal mafias that undermine the country's justice system and put every one of us at risk. We are watching as the cycle is repeating itself again with Modack as the chief protagonist.

I'll leave the last word to an anonymous senior police officer who has spent decades treading the fine line of fighting organised crime in the underworld while trying to remain a good, clean cop:

> You're going to have to get rid of the rot from the top and work down. It's definitely not going to be easy. It is very damaged. It can be fixed, but it is going to take a long time and it's not going to be in my lifetime. If you don't, you won't have a police service that you on the street can depend on – they're supposed to be there when you are a victim and they're not. They're too busy enriching themselves somewhere else.

AUTHOR'S NOTE

I AM SITTING IN ONE OF MY REGULAR COFFEE SHOPS, LAPTOP OPEN in front of me, when my phone rings. It's not a number I recognise, but the voice on the other end is very familiar.

'Mandy, it's Radovan.'

Radovan Krejcir is a sentenced, convicted prisoner and he's phoning me in the middle of the day from jail. Through his family and legal team, I had managed to get a message to him that I am writing a book and want to interview him. He agrees. He is keen to get his version out there. We come up with an elaborate plan as to how I will draft questions and send them via his lawyers, he will prepare his answers and then we will arrange phone calls at specific times.

Only, it's not that simple. He is moved to the highest security prison in the country, in Kokstad, and then moved again. He's allowed little to no contact with the outside world and it's practically impossible to speak to him. So I put in an official request to interview him with the Department of Correctional Services.

Every couple of weeks, I check in with the spokesperson, who is very apologetic. Finally, months later, as this book is about to go to print, I get a formal reply. It's a no:

Kindly be informed that, after due consideration and consultation, your request for an interview with inmate Radovan Krejcir has been disapproved by the Acting National Commissioner of the Department of Correctional Services, Mr JM Mkabela.

Of course I'm not surprised, but I do think it important for the record, considering Krejcir is one of the key protagonists of this story.

Similarly, I thought it important to approach Richard Mdluli for an interview. In February 2018, I wait in the corridors of the South Gauteng High Court as the just-retired head of Crime Intelligence is due to make an appearance in the Oupa Ramogibe trial.

Ironically, two floors up, Krejcir is appearing in the prolonged Sam Issa murder matter. There is such heavy security around Krejcir that I can't get anywhere near him. In contrast, I am able to walk right up to Mdluli at the elevators and greet him face to face. He's dressed in a sharply cut suit with a fine tie pin and pocket square. For a man who has become a 'bogeyman', who is thought to wield such power and influence, he's easy to talk to. I explain the book to him and we chat briefly about how he has been represented in the media thus far. He agrees that the time is right for him to speak and he assures me he will give me an interview the following week. I should arrange it through his lawyer Ike Motloung.

I speak to the lawyer. I send emails, messages, make calls. I am met with cold silence. It's such a great pity that we don't get to hear from such an enigmatic character so that we can better understand the events of the past decade from his perspective. I would have relished peeling back the layers and listening to him speak.

My approach to journalism is that it is not for me to pass judgement, although I am under no illusions that it is possible to be truly objective. However, I hold the view that I have a responsibility to be the conduit for different versions of the truth. I have endeavoured to get as many voices as possible onto these pages and readers have encountered various people telling their own truths.

It is up to you, as the reader, to draw your own conclusions.

ACKNOWLEDGEMENTS

A BOOK LIKE THIS WOULD NOT BE POSSIBLE WERE IT NOT FOR TWO particular sets of people: those who write the stories and those who have the courage to speak out about them.

To my colleagues in the media who have shared court benches with me and, more importantly, information, thank you for allowing me to draw on your work in this book. I have made every effort to acknowledge and credit specific journalists in the text wherever possible.

To all those police officers, prosecutors, investigators, agents and sources whose names for obvious reasons I have not been able to mention, thank you for being brave enough to speak to me and for trusting me with your stories.

Thank you also to those who cleared time in their diaries to give me extensive on-the-record interviews. I hope I have done your truths justice.

To the lawyers who have provided knowledge and insights over the years, I am grateful.

Katy Katopodis and the team at EWN, thank you for indulging my obsession with Bedfordview and the 'underworld'.

Sean N, thanks for sharing my enthusiasm for this story since that rainy night in Edleen. Solomon, thanks for always having faith in me and for taking me along for the ride.

Thank you to Karel Weber for all your assistance with transcribing, and to Jess Littlewood for helping with research, transcriptions and interviews.

Publishing is very much a team sport and I am forever indebted to my team at Pan Macmillan, led by Andrea Nattrass and Terry Morris. Your attention to detail and professionalism are unrivalled. My thanks also to Kevin Shenton of Triple M, Russell Martin, Karen Lilje at Fire and Lion, Sandile Nkosi, Veronica Napier, Eileen Bezemer, and other members of the

Pan Macmillan team who have helped along the way.

Sean Fraser, the massage voucher is in the post. You pored over the text with such meticulous care. Thank you. Also thanks to Natasha Joseph for lending me your editing brain and sharing your thoughts. And to Christa Eybers, for your assistance with photographs and constructing the organogram.

This book was written in coffee shops and restaurants around the country. To all who supplied caffeine and wifi, please know that I would not have made it through without you (especially you, Laylas).

To Margi and Marcelle, thank you for taking the pressure off me so I could focus on this.

I have incredible friends who always show such interest, concern and care for me and for my work. Your support is invaluable and I love you very much.

To my family: you make me laugh and cry and scream and love and laugh some more every day. You are everything to me. Sean, thank you for being my partner on this wild ride.

And, finally, to all of you who stop me on the street and in shopping centres and who tweet me and email me to give me tip-offs, and who sell and buy my books, thank you, too.